FURBEARING ANIMALS OF NORTH AMERICA

OTHER BOOKS BY LEONARD LEE RUE III

Animals in Motion

Tracks & Tracking

The World of the White-Tailed Deer

The World of the Beaver

The World of the Raccoon

New Jersey Out-of-Doors

Cottontail

Pictorial Guide to Mammals

Sportsman's Guide to Game Animals

The World of the Red Fox

Pictorial Guide to Birds

The World of the Ruffed Grouse

Game Birds of North America

The Deer of North America

FURBEARING ANIMALS OF NORTH AMERICA

LEONARD LEE RUE III

A HERBERT MICHELMAN BOOK
CROWN PUBLISHERS, INC.   NEW YORK

*This book is dedicated to very
special friends of mine—
three generations of Spaces:
Ralph, Fred and Eric
Danita and Glenn Wampler
Gary Knepp*

All photos by the author except where noted.
Range maps by Irene Vandermolen.
Copyright © 1981 by Leonard Lee Rue III
Inquiries should be addressed to Crown Publishers, Inc.,
One Park Avenue, New York, New York 10016
Printed in the United States of America
Published simultaneously in Canada by General Publishing
Company Limited
Library of Congress Cataloging in Publication Data
Rue, Leonard Lee.
Furbearing animals of North America.
"A Herbert Michelman book."
Bibliography: p.
Includes index.
1. Fur-bearing animals—North America.
2. Mammals—North America. I. Title.
QL715.R79   1981   599.097   80-24618
ISBN: 0-517-53942X
Book design by Camilla Filancia
10 9 8 7 6 5 4 3 2 1
First Edition

CONTENTS*

Acknowledgments *vi*
Preface *vii*

I ORDER: MARSUPIALIA *1*
  FAMILY: DIDELPHIDAE *1*
    1. OPOSSUM, *Didelphis marsupialis* *1*

II ORDER: RODENTIA *13*
  FAMILY: CASTORIDAE *13*
    2. BEAVER, *Castor canadensis* *14*
  FAMILY: CRICETIDAE *13*
    3. MUSKRAT, *Ondatra zibethica* *31*
  FAMILY: MYOCASTOR *13*
    4. NUTRIA, *Myocastor coypus* *44*

III ORDER: CARNIVORA *53*
  FAMILY: CANIDAE *53*
    5. COYOTE, *Canis latrans* *53*
    6. GRAY WOLF, *Canis lupus* *64*
       RED WOLF, *Canis niger* *64*
    7. ARCTIC FOX, *Alopex lagopus* *74*
    8. RED FOX, *Vulpes vulpes* *81*
    9. GRAY FOX, *Urocyon cinereoargenteus* *93*

IV ORDER: CARNIVORA *102*
  FAMILY: URSIDAE *102*
    10. GRIZZLY/BROWN BEARS, *Ursus arctos* *102*
    11. BLACK BEAR, *Ursus americanus* *119*
    12. POLAR BEAR, *Ursus maritimus* *132*

V ORDER: CARNIVORA *143*
  FAMILY: PROCYONIDAE *143*
    13. RINGTAIL, *Bassariscus astutus* *143*
    14. RACCOON, *Procyon lotor* *152*

VI ORDER: CARNIVORA *165*
  FAMILY: MUSTELIDAE *165*
    15. MARTEN, *Martes americana* *165*
    16. FISHER, *Martes pennanti* *177*
    17. SHORT–TAILED WEASEL, *Mustela erminea* *187*
       LONG–TAILED WEASEL, *Mustela frenata* *187*
    18. MINK, *Mustela vison* *204*
    19. WOLVERINE, *Gulo gulo* *216*
    20. BADGER, *Taxidea taxus* *227*
    21. STRIPED SKUNK, *Mephitis mephitis* *237*
       SPOTTED SKUNK, *Spilogale putorius and Spilogale gracilis* *237*
    22. RIVER OTTER, *Lutra canadensis* *254*
    23. SEA OTTER, *Enhydra lutris* *267*

VII ORDER: CARNIVORA *279*
  FAMILY: FELIDAE *279*
    24. MOUNTAIN LION, *Felis concolor* *279*
    25. LYNX, *Lynx canadensis* *292*
    26. BOBCAT, *Lynx rufus* *301*

VIII ORDER: PINNIPEDIA *312*
  FAMILY: OTARIIDAE *312*
    27. NORTHERN FUR SEAL, *Callorhinus ursinus* *312*

Glossary *329*
Bibliography *330*
Index *335*

* N.B. The sequence in which the orders, families and species appear in this book are as outlined in *The Principles of Classification and a Classification of the Mammals* by G. G. Simpson, American Museum of Natural History, 1945.

ACKNOWLEDGMENTS

Writing a reference book is a fantastic way to increase one's own knowledge, but I never intend to create the impression that I "know it all," because I don't. None of us does. Although I write the books, when friends of mine, such as Joe Taylor, the Spaces and the Wamplers, talk about wildlife, I sit and listen. These are people, like myself, who have spent their lives working and living with all kinds of wildlife. Their knowledge is included here and I thank them for sharing it with me.

I belong to the American Society of Mammalogists and to the Wildlife Society because their journals, written by wildlife professionals, contain data on most of the latest research being done on wildlife. I get the magazines published by most of the state fish and wildlife departments to keep up on their research on the local level. Before I started to write this book, I contacted every state, asking for copies of their latest research data and most of them responded to my appeal. And I buy wildlife books. My personal library now contains over 8,000 volumes. My bibliography contains some of the titles of the hundreds of books and articles that I read before I attempted to write this book. They were written by people that I have met, would like to meet or I wish I could have met. My thanks to each and every one of them.

This book on furbearers is much larger than originally planned. When I started to assemble the material, there was more data available than I had anticipated. The tremendous interest by the general public for more knowledge about all of the wild creatures that share this planet with us has fostered an ever-increasing amount of research.

My thanks to my editor, the late Herbert Michelman, at Crown Publishers, for allowing me to expand the book to accommodate the additional data and to add two additional species that I felt would make the book more complete and for encouraging me while I did so.

Thanks, too, to Gene Deems, Jr., of the Maryland Department of Natural Resources, who helped me with special data from the International Association of Fish and Wildlife Agencies.

Some of the species in this book were also discussed in *Game Animals of North America,* but that was 12 years ago. Since I wrote that book, I have traveled hundreds of thousands of miles, have taken hundreds of thousands of wildlife photographs and had hundreds of thousands of new, personal experiences. I thank God that I was able to do that.

Special thanks go to my sons, Leonard Lee Rue IV, who now goes under the professional name of Len Rue, Jr., Tim Lewis Rue and James Keith Rue. They have all been on trips with me, helped me and shared wildlife experiences with me. A number of Len's photos appear in this book.

Special thanks go to my sister, Evelyn Rue Guthrie, who has just given birth, simultaneously, to a lovely baby daughter, Kristin Lee Guthrie, and to this book. Neither would have seen the light of day without her. Evelyn does my typing and no one else can read my handwriting.

And last, but definitely not least, my special thanks to Irene Vandermolen. Irene shares my love, my life and my work. She gives a purpose to my life. Many of her photographs appear in this book.

Again, my heartfelt thanks to everyone who has helped me in any way with this book. I could not have done it alone. God be with all of them and with you, my readers.

LEONARD LEE RUE III

Blairstown, New Jersey
December 1980

PREFACE

Back in 1968 I wrote *Game Animals of North America*. It was a very successful book with more than 700,000 copies sold. It was successful, I believe, because no other book offered so many facts so conveniently organized. Ever since that time I have wanted to write a book in the same style and format on the furbearing animals of North America. Today, I have just finished writing such a book.

The furbearing animals, for the most part, are not as well known by the general public as are the game animals. The furbearers are not seen as often as the game animals because most of them are nocturnal and many are true wilderness creatures. Perhaps it is because they are so rarely seen that the sight of one in the wild provides such a tremendous thrill.

I will never forget seeing my first wolf up on the Alaskan tundra in broad daylight. In my 17 years of guiding wilderness canoe trips in Quebec, I had seen thousands of wolf tracks. Many nights we were serenaded by the wolves howling out in the darkness beyond our campfires. Were they protesting our invasion of their realm or were they as curious about us as we were about them? I saw their tracks, I heard them howl, but I never got a really good look at a wild wolf until that unforgettable day in Alaska.

The sighting of a wolverine is worth a thousand sightings of moose, yet even today seeing a moose is still a thrill for me. People consider it a real wilderness experience to be able to see some of the furbearers. It is—but then I get a thrill out of seeing any wild creature.

Not only are most of the furbearers seldom seen but most people know almost nothing about them. Even the knowledge of many of our more common animals, such as the opossum, skunk and raccoon, is based on half-truths, myths and superstitions. Raccoons do not have to wash their food before they eat it. Opossums do not sleep hanging by their tails. Skunks do not use their musk unless provoked.

What I have tried to do is to present all the latest facts about these fascinating wild creatures in an informative, enjoyable style. After reading this book you may not see more of these animals, but they will no longer be unknown to you. Actually, reading this book should enable you to see more of these animals because you will know where they live, what they eat, what they do, how, when, where and why. To paraphrase Mrs. Grossinger, these animals will no longer be strangers, they will only be friends you haven't met. May this book introduce you to them if you don't know them and expand your knowledge of them if you do.

MARSUPIALIA

FAMILY:

DIDELPHIDAE

The opossum is the only marsupial found in the United States, with the young being born prematurely and brought to term in the mother's pouch. The opossum has numerous relatives throughout Central and South America, but Australia has the largest number and the greatest variety of these ancient mammals.

The North American opossum is also unique in that it is the only mammal on our continent with a prehensile tail that can be used for grasping like a hand. It is the only mammal in North America that has 4 fingers and an opposable thumb on each of its hind feet.

The opossum is omnivorous, feeding upon almost anything that it can find or catch. It is this willingness to eat anything, its adaptability to various environments and its high reproductive rate that have allowed the opossum to dramatically increase both its population and its range.

OPOSSUM, *Didelphis marsupialis*

INTRODUCTION

David's Psalm 37, verse 11, says: "But the meek shall inherit the earth." The opossum is doing its best to fulfill that prophecy. In the past it has suffered setbacks, but the opossum is used to surviving—it's been doing it for over 70 million years, making it one of our oldest living mammals. It has truly walked with giants, inhabiting the earth at the same time as the dinosaurs. The lumbering brontosaurus is gone, the ferocious saber-toothed tiger evolved and is gone, the fast eohippus is gone, but the opossum, along with time, marches on.

DESCRIPTION

The opossum is a cat-sized mammal that resembles a silver rat, with its naked ears, long, scaly tail and silver-tipped fur. An adult male opossum may measure up to 36 inches in length, of which the tail measures 12–15 inches. Weights average 6 to 7 pounds for the male and 4 to 5 pounds for the female. Dr. William J. Hamilton, former professor of mammalogy at Cornell University, recorded the heaviest male; he weighed 11 pounds 2 ounces and the heaviest female, 7 pounds 4 ounces. The greatest weight I can find for a wild opossum is 14 pounds. A tame opossum owned by Dr. Johns of Clauton, Alabama, weighed 35 pounds. The northern opossums are slightly heavier than their southern counterparts in November. After this period the southern opossums will weigh more as they are more active and continue to feed, while those in the north are forced to den up. The males are stockier than the females.

The face of the opossum is almost pure white, the nose is pink and the eyes are like black shoe buttons. The ears have a soft leathery feel, are hairless, colored black with the top quarter white. There are 4 rows of vibrissae (whiskers) that are about 3 inches in length.

The guard hairs on the opossum's back are 2¼ inches long, pure white. The underfur is 1¼ inches long, kinky and white with a black tip. The white guard hairs sticking up through the dark underfur give the opossum its silver-grizzled coloration. There is a darker streak down the middle of the back. On the opossum's belly the guard hairs are almost completely absent; those that are there are short; the undercoat is about one-half inch in length, sparse and almost white. The fur on the opossum's legs is black. Albinism is quite common in the opossum, melanism (a large amount of pigmentation) occurs and some ani-

Large female opossum. Opossums have little value as fur because their hair is coarse and their skin is very thin.

Large male opossum. Note large naked ears, feet used for grasping and almost naked prehensile tail.

mals appear to be reddish-brown. The male opossum has a large gland beneath its chin whose secretion stains its chest yellow. There is no apparent molting of the opossum's winter coat as in many other animals; the hairs are shed individually.

The opossum's tail is prehensile, making it the only animal in North America that can use its tail for grasping. The scales of the tail are an off-white color. There are some stiff, short bristles on all surfaces of the tail except the bottom.

The opossum has 5 toes on each of its feet and is plantigrade, registering all the toes and foot pads in its tracks. The 5 toes on the front feet are narrow and when widely spread cover about 165 degrees. The inside toe, corresponding to the thumb, can be spread slightly wider than the others and can function as a thumb. The hind foot of the opossum is of tremendous interest because there are 4 fingers and a definite thumb. Closely resembling the human hand if the thumb is held as far from the fingers as possible, it is an opposable thumb and is a great aid to the opossum when it climbs on thin branches or picks up an object. There are nonretractable nails on all of the toes except for the thumb and I don't know why.

The opossum does a lot of "grinning," displaying all its teeth and it really has a mouthful to display with 50 teeth, more than any other North American mammal. It has 18 incisors, 4 canines, 12 premolars and 16 molars. The canines are long, sharp and curve slightly to the rear. The molars have many sharp points.

I have always claimed that the opossum has to be the stupidest animal on earth. It will step into a bare trap that almost every other animal will avoid. But the opossum doesn't need to worry about my concern for its intellectual capacity, for it has been roaming this earth for eons and will continue to do so for a long time to come.

Vernon Bailey, formerly chief field naturalist of the U.S. Biological Survey, was interested in the opossum's brain case. The larger the brain case, in relation to the total body size, the more intelligence a creature has. He found that the opossum's brain case held 25 dried beans while a raccoon's brain case held 150 dried beans. William Hamilton did the same thing, but he used the skull of a house cat because it is closer to the opossum in size and weight. The house cat's brain case held 125 beans to the opossum's 25. There are no convolutions in the opossum's brain (biologists claim the more convolutions in the brain, the higher the intelligence). However, the opossum has been here a lot longer than either the raccoon or the house cat.

DISTRIBUTION

Primarily a southern animal until late 1890s; then started north. Now found from Mexico to southern Ontario and from plains states to Atlantic. Introduced in California, 1910, has since spread north along coast to British Columbia. Rare in some western states. Absent from Nevada, Utah, Idaho, Montana. Found in New Jersey Palisades, 1895; upper Hudson Valley, 1900; Connecticut, 1927; New Hampshire, 1915; northern New York, 1953; Canada shortly thereafter.

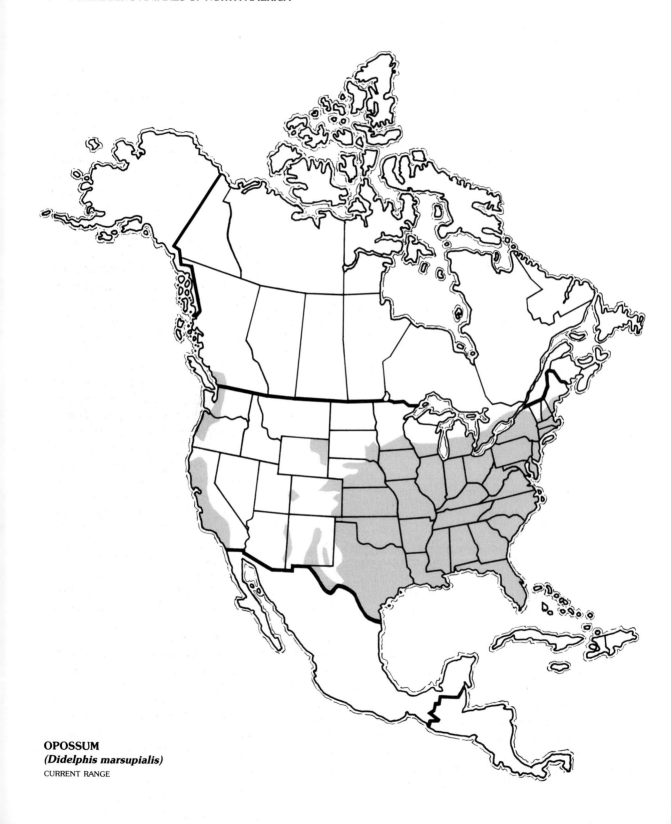

OPOSSUM
(Didelphis marsupialis)
CURRENT RANGE

TRAVEL

The opossum is an inveterate traveler, although it does its traveling over a comparatively small area. With the exception of the winter den, and the female's use of a den while she has her young, the opossum seems to arrive at a different location in the range each morning.

Livetrapping has shown that the opossum's home range is about 50 acres. Opossums are not territorial, as a number of opossums may overlap their home ranges. On good habitat it has been figured that there are about 20 opossums to the square mile. Livetrapping and tagging of opossums show that 7 miles is the greatest distance traveled by an opossum from its original point of release.

Another deterrent to the opossum's constant traveling is a dependable food source. When grapes or persimmons are ripe, an opossum will stay in the area until the food is depleted. I have had opossums visit my bird-feeding station consistently, night after night, to eat the grain or the food scraps that I put out for them. They were very punctual, arriving each night within a few minutes of a given time.

LOCOMOTION

Opossums usually walk very deliberately, carefully searching the ground for anything edible. They are constantly snuffling under the leaves for insects, nuts and fruit, under rotted pieces of wood for grubs. They meander; they usually don't follow footpaths, trails and roads but cross and recross the terrain. If disturbed, the opossum runs off at what can only be called a very fast walk. As it waddles off at its fastest speed, its tail goes around in circles to help it keep its balance. Because the opposum is built so low to the ground, it can go under bushes, brush or any type of vegetation that becomes an obstacle to its pursuer. It is amazing how such a slow animal can get away so often. The opossum will seek refuge in the first hole in the ground or crevasse in the rocks it comes to. It can climb well but seems to do so only as a last resort.

The tree it climbs may be just a sapling, which will get the opossum out of the reach of a dog but from which it can be plucked by a man. The opossum is a good swimmer and can escape by taking to the water. Recent research has shown that the opossum, although primarily a forest animal, is seldom found more than 750 yards from water of some sort. It has now been learned that the opossum also frequents water to search for food.

FOOD

Diet is varied, a trait that keeps population high. Insects the most important food, being numerous during the warm months, easy to catch when nights are cool, and a rich source of protein. Fruits of all kinds are secondary, the opossum taking them either from the ground or off the tree or vine. Next are crayfish, snails and earthworms, followed by rabbits and mice—principally only the young, although it will attack adults if the chance arises. Opossums also scavenge fish on riverbanks after spawning season and eat frogs, salamanders and small snakes. Grain is not a major food but an important incidental. Ground-nesting birds and their eggs and some tree-nesting birds and eggs make up a small part of the diet—in the northeast the rise of opossum population led to a downswing in ruffed grouse population. During hunting season wounded game that escapes from hunters becomes a food source. Opossums killed on highways often have been lured there by animal carcasses. Cannibalism is common when one opossum finds the carcass of another. Opossums often scavenge in garbage cans or dumps.

BEHAVIOR

Everyone knows that the opossum is famous for "playing possum." This bit of misinformation is often all most people know about the opossum. It does happen but not often. From personal experience with thousands of opossums I would say it happens no more than 10 percent of the time and almost never after dark.

An opossum "playing possum." This happens infrequently, with only about 10 percent of all opossums doing it.

When playing possum, the animal falls over on its side, its mouth gapes open, copious amounts of saliva drool out of the mouth, a greenish glandular mucus and feces are voided, the front feet are clutched into balls and the body becomes limp. In this state the opossum can be picked up, poked, prodded, shaken or bitten by a dog, without giving any sign of life. A breath rate is difficult to discern, as is a pulse rate. Some scientists claim that this is an involuntary condition, like fainting, known as "catatonic shock." It is caused by a short-circuiting of the opossum's electrical response system. I cannot disprove this theory, but I do know that the same shock will have less effect on the same opossum the next time and after three or four trials, the shock will not affect the opossum at all. I also know that even the opossums that go through all of the stages seem to recover from the supposedly involuntary shock at will. If the opossum is left alone and thinks the danger has departed, it soon arises, looks around and takes off as fast as it can. Opossums have a tremendous tenacity for life.

The chances of seeing an opossum playing possum are almost nil at night. It is usually seen when the opossum is caught out in the open or forced out during the daylight hours. Under the cover of darkness, when the opossum is in its element, it is usually able to make good its escape or, if cornered, it is more apt to put up a fight. The opossum is no coward, but bear in mind it is an animal that weighs only 4 to 8 pounds.

When the opossum stands its ground, it rises up as high as it can get on all 4 legs, holds its tail straight up over its back and, with widely gaping jaws, faces its enemy. I have seen opossums bluff much larger raccoons away from food at the feeder. The opossum is not a born fighter, but at times it is more than willing to stand its ground.

Opossums are very clean animals and spend a great amount of time grooming themselves. Even while feeding, they will stop and spend as much as 20 minutes washing their forepaws with their tongues, then they'll wet their forepaws and thoroughly scrub their faces. They often sit upright and groom their bodies.

We have watched the opossums at our feeder eating fatty meat scraps. They eat, then stop and wash themselves, eat, then wash themselves again. We have always wondered why they didn't wait until they had finished eating, but they don't and we still don't have the answer.

People also "know" that an opossum hangs by its tail. Not true. Pictures are often drawn of an opossum sleeping or hanging by its tail. It is true that the opossum uses its tail as a fifth hand when it climbs, uses it as a brake when it descends a tree headfirst and holds on with its tail when it climbs from one branch to another. A young opossum can support its body weight with its tail for a considerable period of time, but an adult cannot. The tail soon loses its grip and the opossum is on its way down.

The tail is used by the opossum to carry things. When it moves into a den or is refurbishing the one it is using, it will carry lots of leaves and trash into the den with its tail. The opossum gathers the leaves together with its front feet, passes them back to its hind feet that then push them back to where they are looped up by the tail rolling down and forward. With its load secure, the opossum takes its bedding home.

Underground dens are preferred by the opossums, but where these are scarce it will utilize a hollow tree. If both of these are lacking, the opossum has been known to take over a squirrel's leafy tree nest, adding lots more leaves to the original nest.

Opossums are among the most adaptable of wild

creatures. If they do not find a situation that is customary, they adapt to whatever is available. Thus opossums are quick to find dens in urban areas, denning under porches, in garages, in storm tiles, sewers or any other shelter.

Opossums are almost strictly nocturnal during the warmer periods of the year. During the winter, when they are hungry, they are frequently out during the daytime, particularly if the weather moderates. The opossums usually come to my feeders about 8:30 P.M., never while it is light.

Different animals cope with the cold of winter in different ways. Some migrate, some hibernate, some have adapted and some just cope. The opossum has always been a southern animal, its northward range expansion having been fostered as mentioned earlier, by a generally moderating climate. The opossum does not migrate, it does not hibernate, it cannot even spend extended periods of time in its den as do the raccoon, skunk and bear.

The bottom of the opossum's feet is bare, its ears are naked, its tail sports only a few bristly hairs. Opossums gorge themselves in autumn, becoming very fat before the onset of winter. I have seen fat layers of an inch in depth, beneath the skin, surrounding their bodies. One large male opossum that was livetrapped in early December was found to have lost almost 50 percent of his body weight when retrapped the following spring.

During the most bitter weather the opossum stays in its den for as long a period as is possible, its body temperature dropping no more than three or four degrees during this lethargic period. It has been found that the females stay in their dens for longer periods of time than the males but neither can stay in their sanctuaries long enough. If the cold is protracted, two weeks or longer, the opossums have to come out to seek food. Their tail tips and their ear tips invariably freeze off. Both appendages may lose additional portions on succeeding jaunts. The opossum does not seem to be handicapped by this loss. No infection takes place because of the freezing. Occasionally there is self-mutilation of tail tips by opossums in captivity.

If the winter is a long one, many of the opossums die of starvation. Our recent hard winters have been a tremendous setback to the opossums in the northeast. The January thaw, occurring around the 24th to the 26th, and the thaws of February 12th and 20th, see tremendous increases in opossum activity as they scramble about searching for food.

SENSES

Sense of smell highly developed and most important. Night vision is very good, but vision poor at long distances. Sense of taste probably not well developed.

COMMUNICATION

Opossums are amazingly quiet animals. The most commonly heard sound is their loud hissing. I have also heard them growl. Their wide, gaping mouths and sharp teeth make a tremendous visual statement. Opossums at my feeder gape and charge at one another, but usually the gape alone is enough to make a lesser opossum defer to the larger.

Opossums will void their feces at the base of large trees in their areas. I do not know if this is merely their toilet area or constitutes claiming that particular parcel of turf.

BREEDING

Opossums are solitary animals except for their brief time of mating and when the mother is carrying her young. Carl Hartman in *Possums* claimed that the opossums in south Texas occasionally had 3 litters per year, but there is very little evidence of that occurring and over most of their range there are 2 annual litters. In the opossum's most northern range it may have only a single yearly litter.

The breeding season extends from January in the south to February in the north, through to August, with two peak periods, one in mid-February, the second in June. The female comes into estrus and remains in heat for about 28–32 hours. If not bred she will recycle every 28 days until she does conceive.

The males are polygamous, breeding with every available female. Young opossums do not breed in the same year they are born but are capable of breeding in the first estrous period when they are 6 to 8 months of age.

The male opossum has a double-headed penis to fit the female's double womb. Linnaeus gave the opossum its Greek name *Didelphis,* which means double womb, because of this unusual feature. Folklore depicted the male breeding the female through her nostrils and then the female blowing the young into her pouch. Opossums copulate in the normal animal fashion, although they often lie on their sides.

BIRTH AND YOUNG

The opossum is a marsupial—the only pouched animal in North America. It is related to the marsupials in South America and those in Australia, such as the wallaby, the kangaroo and the Tasmanian devil.

Marsupials have a short gestation period and the young finish their development in the pouch on the mother's abdomen. Baby opossums are born just 13 days after conception. One scientist described the fetuses as living abortions.

When the female is about to give birth she sits upright with her hind feet sticking out to the sides, her head bent forward. Naturalist Henry Sheak gives an eyewitness report of the event. He writes: "The young appear at the genital opening and after being licked free of liquid and embryonic envelope by the mother, they climb 'hand over hand' into the pouch. Because of the position of the mother during parturition, the young must climb upward to reach the pouch."

Baby opossums at birth weigh 0.16 of a gram; it takes 23 young to equal the weight of a penny. The fetus body is smaller than that of a honeybee. It has no ears, the eyes are dark spots seen through the skin, the hind feet are little clubs, the tail a stub, the body hairless and pink. The front feet, however, are fully developed, the toes have nails and can be used for

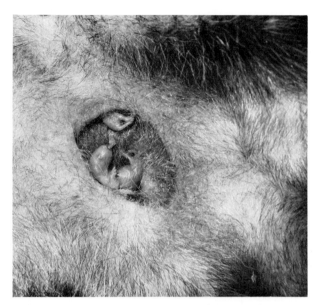

Baby opossums in mother's abdominal pouch. Note how the newborn fetus is fastened to a nipple.

grasping. The tiny fetuses, after being cleaned by the mother, crawl upward rapidly to the pouch, a distance of 3 or 4 inches. They have been timed at making the trip in less than a minute.

The mother's pouch has a rim that is controlled by muscles that allow it to be relaxed and open or tightened and shut. The pouch stretches greatly as the young grow. Inside the pouch, the female usually has 12 nipples arranged in an inverted U shape with a 13th nipple in the center. Opossums have been found with as few as 9 nipples and as many as 17, but 13 is the norm.

As each fetus enters the pouch it seeks out a nipple and swallows it. The nipple then expands to fill the fetus's mouth and throat, effectively fastening it in place in the pouch. Once secured, the fetus does not let go of the nipple for 6 to 7 weeks and can be removed only with great effort. If there are more young born than there are nipples to accommodate them, they die and are ejected from the pouch. The young nurse—the milk is not pumped by the mother as was once believed.

Opossum litters are larger in the North than in the South. Research in the various states shows 6.8 young per litter in Texas, 7.4 in Kansas, 8.9 in Missouri, 9 in Iowa and I have found 9–11 normal in northwestern New Jersey. William Hamilton removed 25 embryos from a New York opossum. This is most unusual and the record for one litter.

There is a tremendous variation within the same litter in the same pouch, so much so that biologists despair of establishing a norm for size and age. The length of time that it takes various stages of development to occur has been determined by investigation of captive animals.

The opossum's pouch is an efficient incubator. The little ones are nursed, warmed and protected. The female cleans out voided material, but the pouch becomes stained. The sex of the fetuses can be distinguished at 2 weeks of age. Shortly thereafter the hair covering begins to push through the skin. The young are able to open their mouths and release the mother's teat between the 55th and 68th days. Their eyes open between the 58th and 72nd days. The young stay in the pouch until between the 80th and 87th days.

Several years ago I raised three families of opossums and learned many fascinating things. During the time the young opossums were older than 60 days, they would often come out of the mother's pouch although they remained fastened to her nipples. If the day was quiet, the mother would lie on her side, relax the muscles of the pouch and all the little ones would hang out of the pouch backward, still fastened. If she was disturbed, they would all scramble back inside. Because of their large size the babies had trouble fitting. Sometimes the mother would climb into her nest box dragging some of the young behind her. I never did see one come loose.

After the 80th day, the young released their hold on their mother's nipples and began to venture out of the pouch. Drawings and paintings frequently show the mother opossum going about with her tail bent up over her back with all of her babies hanging by their tails wrapped around her tail. It just doesn't happen;

Opossums do not sleep hanging by their tails. They do use their tails as well as their feet in climbing, as demonstrated by this opossum, about 7 weeks old.

Baby opossums stay in their mother's pouch until they are about 6½ weeks old. They then ride around hanging on to her fur.

the opossum's tail cannot be bent forward as depicted. The baby opossums ride around hanging on their mother's back, their tiny paws clutching her hair. Sometimes the mother leaves some of her babies back at the natal den while she forages, because their combined weight is a tremendous handicap to her. The young are weaned between the 95th and 100th days. Now when the mother opossum goes out and a baby falls off, it doesn't matter. At this age the little ones are big enough to go off on their own. And about this time the female comes into estrus again and is bred for her second litter. Most of the young are gone by the middle to end of May and the next litter is born in mid-June.

With many species lactation prevents the occurrence of estrus, but this is not true of the opossum. Another interesting fact is that as soon as the female is bred, her nipples, which have been stretched to as much as 1½ inches in length and perhaps one-quarter inch in width, shrink drastically so that they will be small enough for her next litter to get in their mouths.

The young disperse an average of about 400 yards from the natal den.

LIFE SPAN

Potential: 5–7 years. Oldest on record: 8 years.

An opossum's right hind foot. Note the close resemblance to the human hand with the 4 fingers and the opposable thumb.

SIGN

Bodies along highway the most common sign—hundreds of thousands killed by automobiles each year. Tracks are distinctive, the only track that shows a thumbprint. Tracks seen most often in mud at edges of ponds and streams. Wandering tracks seen in snow, with tracks darkest where animal leaves den. Feces seldom seen.

ENEMIES

Worst enemy the automobile, followed by men and dogs. Opossum has few natural enemies because few animals will eat one. Red foxes reportedly will eat opossums, as will vultures, though not in my experience. Vultures do not eat opossums in my New Jersey area but do in the South. Dogs will kill but usually do not eat opossums. Great horned owls kill and eat opossums but prefer skunks.

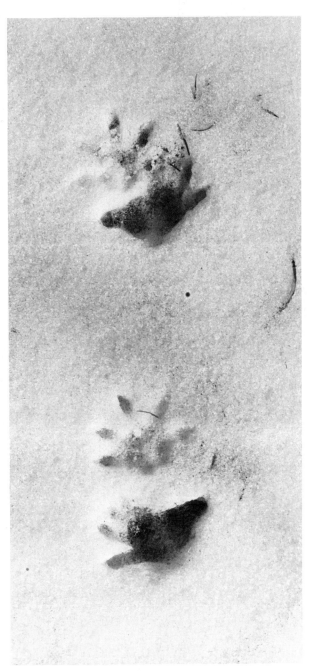

Opossum tracks in snow. The track of the forefoot appears as a star; the thumb of the hind foot shows clearly.

Solitary nature of opossum leaves it relatively free of ectoparasites. Dens do not become infected because opossum uses different den each day. Opossums subject to chiggers and ticks and occasionally fleas.

Intestinal parasites such as roundworms, flatworms and tapeworms afflict opossum. Sometimes tapeworms so numerous they fill the stomach cavity.

HUMAN RELATIONS

Most people are turned off by the opossum's similarity in appearance to a big rat. Actually, I think it is a most attractive, clean and interesting animal. It sure is different! When obtained young, some opossums become very tame, although I have never had any that I could consider a pet.

For many years the fur of the opossum was so low in value that it hardly paid to skin them. When I was trapping for fox, the opossums were a nuisance. There were at least a dozen opossums for each fox in any given area and your chance of catching an opossum before the fox was 12 times greater. It was not until the opossums had been caught that you could begin to catch a fox, making for a lot of extra work and frustrations.

COMMERCIAL VALUE

IAFWA* statistics: 1,064,725 pelts sold in U.S., 1976–77, $2.50 average price, $2,661,813 total (statistics lacking for many states). Huge pelt sold in 1979 for $10.

Today there is an organization called the Possum Growers and Breeders Association of America, Inc., whose president, Frank B. Clark, of Clauton, Alabama, is promoting the use of opossums as food. Their slogan is "Eat More Possum."

*International Association of Fish and Wildlife Agencies.

RODENTIA

The rodents are the most numerous mammals on earth. Most of them have short life spans, but a very high reproductive rate. All rodents are characterized by having 2 upper and 2 lower opposable incisor teeth that continue growing throughout the animal's life.

Some of the rodents, such as squirrels, provide food for man. Some of the mice and rats are beneficial because of the number of noxious weed seeds that they eat. Many of the mice and rats are particularly destructive, eating and spoiling grain and damaging buildings. Medical research depends heavily upon mice and rats for experimentation. The diseases carried by some mice and rats have killed more people than all of man's wars combined. The beaver, muskrat and nutria are among the most valuable furbearers due to the huge numbers of their pelts that are taken each year.

Some members of this order spend the winter in true hibernation.

FAMILY:

CASTORIDAE

The family name *Castoridae* that is given to the beaver is in reference to its castor glands. Beavers are found in both North America and Europe and until recently were considered to be two distinct species. Today, the two species are being challenged by the taxonomists who feel that the two species are identical and should be classified as one.

FAMILY:

MYOCASTOR

The nutria is the only member of the *Myocastor* family. The nutria does not belong in North America; it is a native of South America. Since its introduction into the United States, it has become a nuisance in some areas, in others it is considered a very valuable furbearer.

FAMILY:

CRICETIDAE

The muskrat's family name is *Cricetidae*. This is a very large family group and contains the New World rats and mice, true hamsters, mole rats, Malagasy rats, maned rats, voles, lemmings and gerbils. The muskrat is actually a really big mouse. It is one of the most important furbearers in North America.

BEAVER, *Castor canadensis*

INTRODUCTION

With the exception of man, no other mammal has the ability to so alter its environment to suit its needs as the beaver. The beaver is famous for its dam-building abilities with the resulting ponds going through the evolutionary steps of open water, swamp, marsh, meadow and back to forest again.

Everyone finds the beaver interesting, although it is not universally loved. It is fascinating, constructive, destructive, a boon or an abomination—all according to whose trees are being cut down, whose land is being flooded or whose river dammed up.

When beavers build on wilderness land owned by the state or federal government, they create an outdoor laboratory second to none. The entire area becomes a Mecca for wildlife of all sorts and for people interested in wildlife.

When beavers flood pastures needed for grazing, destroy crops, fell valuable timber, destroy trout streams, block culverts, flood roads and create havoc in general, an anguished outcry is justifiably heard from those being hurt financially. The beaver is no respecter of anybody's property. When a beaver locates conditions that are to its liking or can be made to its liking, it starts to work with a vengeance. Once a beaver has claimed any piece of territory as its own, it cannot be forced to leave except by livetrapping and removing it or by death.

DESCRIPTION

The beaver is the largest rodent in North America, second only to capybara of South America. It is directly descended from the prehistoric Castoroides that roamed the earth a million years ago. The prehistoric

Although large beavers like this one average between 55 and 75 pounds in weight, they are not fighters and are very vulnerable on land.

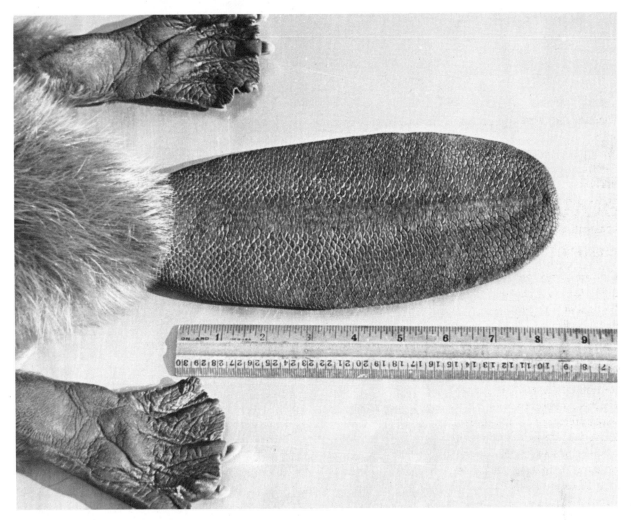

The scaled tail and the webbed hind feet of a 55-pound beaver.

beaver was gigantic, weighing between 700 and 800 pounds. Entire skeletons of Castoroides have been found in Indiana. The beaver is unique among mammals because it does not stop growing with age.

The tail of the beaver is also unique. The platypus's tail has the same general shape but is fur covered. The beaver's tail is a flattened appendage of cartilage and bone that is covered with scales and a few sparse, stiff hairs. It looks like a shoe sole. On a large specimen the tail is 9 to 11 inches in length and 3½ to 4½ inches in width, or more, and is one-half an inch in thickness. If identified on an animal it is positive proof that you are looking at a beaver.

Adult beavers average between 40 and 60 pounds and measure about 48 inches in length. The beaver stands about 8 to 9 inches high at the shoulder, but the back is humped as high as 12 inches or more. A 90-pound beaver caught by Henry Mullins in Otterville, Missouri, in December 1960, was 60 inches in total length.

For years the world-record beaver was one taken by Vernon Bailey in 1921 on the Iron River in Wisconsin. This giant beaver weighed 110 pounds. That record was broken by John Webster of Tie Siding in the Laramie Mountains of Wyoming. On December 2, 1938, Webster caught a beaver that weighed 115 pounds liveweight. After being skinned, the beaver weighed 109 pounds. These weights were confirmed by the district forest ranger and the Wyoming Game Commission. I can find no record of a greater weight for our present-day beaver.

The beaver is classified as a rodent because it has

4 incisor teeth in the front of its mouth, 2 on the top and 2 on the bottom. As with all rodents, these 4 teeth grow throughout the entire life of the animal. All rodents are constantly chewing on things because they must keep their teeth worn down. Occasionally a rodent will suffer from malocclusion, where the teeth do not oppose each other and are not worn down properly. The teeth then continue to grow in an arc, eventually growing back and piercing the animal's skull. Or, the teeth may prevent the animal from opening and closing its mouth so that it starves.

The forepart of the 4 incisor teeth is bright orange in color and is composed of a very hard enamel. The rear section of incisors is composed of a softer material known as dentine, which wears faster than the enamel, giving the ends of these teeth their chisel shape.

The beaver also has 16 hypsodont rear molars that are comparatively flat-topped with many ridges to grind the vegetation that is the beaver's food.

The beaver is a semiaquatic mammal, spending a lot of its time in the water and depending upon the water for protection against its enemies. Its large, compact body works on the principle that for its mass it has a relatively small surface area, which is very efficient for conserving body heat.

The beaver has long been famous for its fur. The long guard hairs on the beaver's pelt are about 2 inches in length overlaying a very soft, dense undercoat whose hairs are a little less than one inch in length. The guard hairs are usually plucked or cut before the fur is used to make fur coats.

Beaver fur ranges in color from a light blond to jet black. The black pelts have the greatest value and come from the northern areas while the blonds come from the south. Most beavers appear to be dark brown with reddish guard hairs. Occasionally pure albinos occur.

Mark L. Weaver, of Weaver's Beaver Associates, based in St. Anthony, Idaho, has been able to genetically breed beavers that are white, blue, jet black and golden. These strains have been stabilized so that they now breed true, reproducing the desired colors.

Beaver's incisor teeth. The 4 large incisor teeth are the identifying, universal characteristic of all the rodents.

Birds have only one body orifice, known as the cloaca, which serves as the genital tract as well as for the excretion of body waste materials, and so does the beaver. The beaver's cloaca contains the urogenital system, the rectum and 2 sets of glands embedded in the walls. On both sides of the cloaca, within the body, are 2 large (3- to 5-inch) castors or scent glands. Although not seen, these glands can be felt and are often confused with the testicles. These glands give off a thick, yellow, sweet-smelling oil that is used for communication. To the rear of the castors are 2 smaller oil glands that are used for waterproofing the fur. The oil from these glands is rubbed on the beaver's guard hairs which helps to trap air in among the fine undercoat. A healthy beaver, properly groomed, does not get its body wet when it dives beneath the surface of the water.

Beneath the beaver's skin are a very tough layer of tissue and a layer of fat that also provide excellent insulation. These 2 layers make the beaver one of the most difficult of all mammals to skin.

In keeping with its aquatic life, the beaver has a transparent eyelid, known as a nictitating membrane that covers the eye when the beaver submerges. These waterproof goggles allow the beaver to see underwater without getting any irritating substance in its eyes.

BEAVER
(Castor canadensis)
CURRENT RANGE

The ears and nose of the beaver are valvular and close tightly when the beaver dives.

The beaver is able to exchange more of its lungs' oxygen capacity than are we humans. The cardiovascular restriction shuts off the submerged beaver's blood flow to its extremities, forcing more blood to the brain. The beaver's exceptionally large liver also stores oxygen. Although beavers usually stay underwater for only 3 to 5 minutes, they can stay under for as long as 15 minutes and can swim almost a half-mile without coming up for air.

There are 5 toes on each of the beaver's feet. Each of the toes is equipped with a stout nail. The 2 inside toenails on each of the beaver's back feet are split and are known as the "combing claws." The second nail is more highly developed and these nails are used by the beaver in grooming its coat.

The front foot, from the end of the palm pad to the end of the longest nail, is 2 1/2 to 3 inches in length. There are no web or stiff hairs between these toes, but they are very flexible. The hind foot of the beaver is about 7 inches in length and can be spread 6 to 7 inches in width. There is a thin web of skin between each of the toes, which greatly increases the propulsion surface when the beaver swims.

DISTRIBUTION

Originally found throughout North America, about 60 million on the continent around 1600. Fur trade nearly extirpated beaver by late 1800s. Today, through conservation, beavers are found over almost all their former range, wherever food and water exists to support them, though range cannot be as extensive due to takeover of habitat by humans.

TRAVEL

Beavers are regular stay-at-homes. There is a dispersal each spring of young beavers approaching their third year. These 22-month-old beavers leave the colony to go off on their own before the adult female gives birth to her young for that year.

Research has shown that when the young beavers leave their natal area, they are just as apt to go downstream as to go up. This is contrary to the general belief that the young beavers usually work their way upstream. It has also been found that most of the young travel between one and 5 miles before establishing a colony of their own. One tagged beaver in New York State traveled 17 miles from the point of its release to where it was recaptured. This is the longest accurately recorded distance of a beaver's travels.

LOCOMOTION

Beavers seem to do everything very deliberately; they are cautious animals. On land they usually walk, and walk slowly, constantly stopping to sniff the air for potential danger. When alarmed, they gallop, their fastest speed but a gait that allows them to be outrun very easily by a man.

Beavers had long been reported to swim at 2 miles per hour. Tests that I made showed that beavers usually swim at 3 to 3 1/2 miles per hour under ordinary conditions but much faster when they want to. About 6 miles per hour is the beaver's top speed on the surface of the water.

When swimming, the beaver uses only its hind feet, with its front feet curled into little balls and carried high against the chest. When the beaver swims through brush, the forepaws are used to facilitate its passage by pushing the obstructions aside. When swimming underwater, the forepaws are usually fully extended just before the beaver breaks through the surface.

When the beaver swims in leisurely fashion, it uses both its hind feet in unison. As the feet are brought forward, the toes are closed and curled to prevent drag. Then the toes and the webs are widely extended as the feet propel the body forward. One huge beaver's hind feet extended to 9 inches, although 6 to 7 inches is about normal.

The beaver's tail is used primarily for steering. By canting the tail away from its ordinary horizontal position, it becomes a very effective rudder. When the

Beaver feeding on aspen. The beaver eats the bark, leaves and twigs. (Photo: Irene Vandermolen)

beaver is towing a branch in the water, it compensates for the directional drag of the branch with a countertwist of its tail. When the beaver is swimming at its top speed underwater, the tail is undulated up and down, which produces a sculling effect and increases the animal's speed.

FOOD

Main food the leaves, twigs and inner bark of trees it fells. Generally the sticks used in the dam have first been used as food and are barkless. Beavers eat 1 1/2–2 pounds of food per day, or all the bark, leaves and twigs on a 1 1/2-inch diameter aspen. In spring beavers busily feed on skunk cabbage sprouts and roots, grasses, sedges, ferns and water plants. Later in season diet includes twigs, leaves, fungi, berries, flags, spatterdock, water lilies, and duckweed. Algae forming in warm water an important midsummer food, high in protein. If near farms beavers eat wheat, oats and especially corn—where wood is scarce, I have seen dams built of cornstalks—carrots, apples, potatoes, turnips, alfalfa, clover and nuts. In September work increases furious-

ly and the animal lays in its winter store of tree branches and saplings, felled by the hundreds and dragged beneath the water and anchored in the mud. One to 2 tons necessary to survive the winter. Wood stored for winter is felled after sap has returned to roots, minimizing chance of spoilage. During winter these branches are retrieved for food and eaten in the lodge. Bark is eaten by rotating branch in forepaws, leaving spiral teethmarks. Although very rare, there are reports of beavers eating fish.

BEHAVIOR

Beavers appear to be stodgy, dull creatures because they do almost everything with slow deliberation. They study everything before they act upon it.

No one has ever accused beavers of being playful, yet young beavers do stand on their hind feet and "wrestle" with each other. Occasionally beavers will slap the water with their tails, apparently just for the fun of it.

In areas where the beavers have complete protection, or at least are seldom molested, they will carry on

A large beaver carrying an aspen branch to the water.

much of their activities during the daylight hours. They will be most active in the late afternoon and the early morning, sleeping through the midday. Where disturbed, beavers carry on almost all of their activities under cover of darkness. Beavers are very punctual. In the course of having spent thousands of hours observing and photographing them, I found that the beavers in a particular colony left the lodge to feed at about the same time each day.

Ordinarily, the large male is the first to leave the lodge. It is his job to scout the territory thoroughly before the younger beavers go ashore to feed. The male usually swims in circles around the edge of the pond, testing the air for telltale signs of danger. Occasionally, a young beaver will become impatient and hurry up

on the bank to feed. When this occurs, the large male will charge at the young one and perhaps even butt into it with his head. It is only after the adult male decides that all is safe that the family goes about its evening activities.

When a beaver cuts down a tree, it has no control over the direction in which the tree will fall. The beaver prefers to drop the tree into the water and most trees growing near water do just that because they get more sunlight on the side facing the water and the heavier limbs there cause the tree to fall in that direction.

Paintings and drawings usually show a beaver cutting a tree with its head held upright. It would be impossible for a beaver to cut a tree in this fashion. The beaver will stand up against the tree, turn its head parallel to the ground and bite into the tree. Then, moving its head higher, but held in the same position, the beaver makes the top cut. The distance between the top and bottom cut is determined by the diameter of the tree. After making the two cuts the beaver then grasps the wood with its incisors and wrenches the chip loose. Then the entire procedure is repeated. Naturally as the beaver cuts into the center of the tree, the chips become smaller.

If the ground is level, the beaver may move around the tree as the cuts are made so that the cuts are

A large beaver diving underwater with a branch that it will anchor in the mud. The branch will provide food during the winter when the water is covered with ice. (Photo: Irene Vandermolen)

equally deep all the way around. This makes the cut look like a poorly sharpened pencil stub. If the tree is on the side of a hill, the beaver will make most of the cut from the uphill side. The beaver continues to cut till it hears or feels the last remaining fibers start to tear apart as the tree starts to fall. Then the beaver makes a dash for the safety of the pond. On rare occasions, the tree may fall on the beaver, killing it and proving that the beaver did not control the direction of the tree's fall.

When the tree is down, the beaver usually eats some of the leaves and twigs first and then the branches are cut off and hauled to the water. The trunk of the tree, if it is 6 inches in diameter or less, may also be cut into pieces and then dragged, rolled or pushed into the water. The beaver may push the log with its forehead or lie against it sideways and push with its shoulder. Beavers are exceedingly strong and can move logs weighing much more than they do.

When the beavers are cutting trees in a dense stand,

Large ash tree felled by beaver.

A beaver cutting down an aspen tree by biting chunks out of the wood.

where the diameter of the tree is large, the beaver had no intention of felling the tree; it merely ate the bark. In other instances, the beaver may have started the cut and then been frightened away by potential danger. The beaver may or may not come back later to finish the cut. Sometimes a tree will have many uncompleted cuts at different heights. The high cuts were made by a beaver standing on top of the snow. A record number of 11 cuts were seen on one tree before it was finally felled. The stump looked like a string of gigantic beads.

Most trees felled by beavers are from one-half to 8 inches in diameter. They can cut off the one-half-inch sapling with a single bite, while they can fell a six-inch aspen in 10–20 minutes. There are a number of records of trees between 50 and 60 inches in diameter being felled by beavers.

The brilliance of the beaver's dam-building abilities is always being extolled. The beaver does a fine job but I think its perseverance should get far more credit than it does. Once a beaver decides where it is going to build its dam, that is where the dam is going to be built, come hell or high water. Many, many times the beaver could have done the same job with just a fraction of the work if it had only chosen a slightly different location. Before we go any further, though, we should explain why the beaver builds a dam.

Although the beaver is a large animal, it is not a fighter. It needs deep water in order to escape from its enemies. There is always more food growing along a small stream in relation to the water and the landmass than there is along a large lake edge. So the beaver prefers to build a dam on the small stream in the midst of plenty. Whereas the beaver would be vulnerable along a small stream, the erection of just a 2-foot dam added to the stream depth will usually give it ample protection. A pair of beavers can build a 2-foot dam 10–12 feet across in a couple of nights. Never satisfied, the beaver will enlarge the dam as time goes on but for the present the small dam will suffice.

Most dam building is done in the spring when the 22-month-old beavers leave the parental colony and establish a new colony of their own. Even in well-

where they all grow straight and have no leafy branches, they will lose one out of every 5 trees that they cut. Under conditions like this, the trees often fall into and lodge in the surrounding trees and do not come down. The beaver may make additional cuts in the initial tree in an effort to get the tree to fall to earth. This may or may not be successful. The beaver almost never cuts the supporting tree to make both trees fall.

Whenever you visit an area where the beavers have been felling trees, you will quickly note how many cuts have been started and then abandoned. In some cases,

A beaver lodge built as part of the wall of its dam. This is unusual.

established colonies, more work is done on the dam in the spring. It has been discovered that a beaver will respond by building dams when it hears running water. The spring rains and melting snow cause a lot of runoff and at this time the adult beavers work the hardest on their dams. This results in providing the deepest water, ensuring maximum protection just about the time the female gives birth to her young.

During a flood, the beavers will open a spillway in the dam to lessen the pressure on it. When the waters have receded and the dam is no longer threatened, the beavers simply plug the gap up again.

During the summertime, the dam often falls into disrepair as the beavers do very little work on it. In autumn both the dam and the lodge are again put in tip-top shape for winter.

When the beavers build a dam, they drag the branches to the site and wedge the branches into place on the stream bottom, usually with the butt end upstream. The branches are weighted down with mud and rocks. Layer after layer is added.

At first the dam is porous, which is as it should be so that the water pressure does not wash the branches away before enough mass and weight have been accumulated to hold it in place. When this has been accomplished, then the beaver begins to pack the face of the dam with mud, leaves and debris from the stream bottom. Little by little, the water level is raised and the weight of the water helps to pack the material used in the face of the dam. The dams are always much wider at the base than they are at the top. On a narrow stream the dam may be straight. Where there is a swift current, the dam is usually bowed on the upstream side, which greatly strengthens it.

An average beaver dam will be 5 to 7 feet high and perhaps 75 feet long. Many dams will be 1,000 feet long and a couple have been over 2,000 feet in length. The highest dam I have personally seen was 10 feet high, packed into a deep gorge.

After a colony has become established, the beavers frequently build auxiliary dams both above and below their main dams. The auxiliary dams, serving two purposes, reinforce the main dam and prevent undue pressure upon it and also facilitate bringing in food more easily from a greater distance. It is much easier for a piece of wood to be floated and towed than to be dragged over dry land.

When all available food within easy reach of the ponds has been used, the beavers then dig canals back into the forest, if the land is fairly level. Some of the canals may be 100 feet or more in length. These canals not only facilitate food gathering but also allow the beavers to escape from any enemy that surprises them back in the woods.

Beavers are air-breathing mammals and must have the chambers of their dens or lodges above water lev-

Beavers build dams to ensure water deep enough for safety. This beaver is forcing another stick into its dam. (Photo: Len Rue, Jr.)

el. Bank burrows are usually dug at the same time the main dam is first constructed. These are just temporary shelters and will be used later as auxiliary shelters. Or the beavers may pile up wood on top of the earth over the top of the burrows and then dig up into the stick mass to form a bank lodge.

The ultimate in beaver construction is the "castle" type lodge that is completely surrounded by water. To construct a lodge of this type, the beaver piles up logs, sticks, mud and rocks in a mass on the bottom of the pond. As the mass rises above the water, mud and rocks are no longer used. The future lodge is a solid mass of material and is usually raised up 5–6 feet above water level and is perhaps 12–14 feet in diameter. I have seen lodges that were 8–9 feet above water level and 25 feet in diameter.

After the major initial construction is completed, the beavers dive underwater and cut their way into the center of the mass. When they are above the water level, they cut out a chamber that will be 3–4 feet across and perhaps 18–24 inches high. Additional plunge holes or tunnels will also be cut in. Each lodge has at

Beaver pond and lodge. The lodge has a good coating of mud.

In the winter the mud on a beaver's lodge freezes as hard as concrete, affording excellent protection.

least 2 entrance ways, most often more.

The chamber will have 2 levels. The first and main level will be 3–5 inches above the water level and will be the feeding and draining platform. After the beaver has drained most of the water from its fur, it then moves up to the bed area which is 8–10 inches higher. The bedding is made of wood fibers shredded like excelsior.

The outside of the lodge is then coated with liquid mud, except for the peak. The uncoated center section acts as an air duct. In subzero weather, the beavers' warm breath can be seen emerging from the lodge like smoke. The mud-coated section of the lodge makes the lodge waterproof and weather-tight. It freezes to the hardness of concrete in the winter, preventing the beavers' enemies from digging through

once they can reach the lodge over the ice.

If the beaver colony remains fairly constant in size, with the yearlings moving out when they are 22 months old, the food supply may not be overtaxed. Many times the stumps of the trees felled by the beaver will grow a profusion of sprouts, all ideal beaver food. A colony of beavers consumes about 1,000 trees a year.

When the time comes that all available food within easy reach has been consumed, the beavers will be forced to abandon their colony. They usually move no more than perhaps a half-mile; they will move no farther than they have to.

There is a great deal of controversy about beavers versus trout. For the first year or two after the beaver has built its dam, it may improve the quality of the conditions for trout. The newly enlarged areas create cold-water trout pools where there had only been a stream before. The flooding of new land and the impoundment of water creates almost unlimited food for the trout and provides deeper holes in which they can survive droughts.

However, within a couple of years, all of these advantages are nullified. As the trees are cut down along the new pond, the sunshine heats up the water, lessening its oxygen content, and trout need lots of cold water and oxygen. The silt accumulating behind the dam covers the gravel beds that the trout need for spawning. The dam itself often prevents the movement of trout up or down the stream. After 2 or 3 years, a beaver dam is a detriment to trout, although a boon to fish that can live in the warmer water.

SENSES

Sense of smell primary, used to pintpoint food, danger and other beavers. Hearing is acute but secondary in importance—cutting and chewing of branches is so noisy nothing else can be heard. Vision is generally poor, although the animal can readily detect motion and the nictitating membrane allows it to see relatively well underwater. Taste buds well developed—beavers display taste preferences and will not eat soured branches.

COMMUNICATION

Beavers are extremely vocal. They talk to one another almost constantly. It is very easy to hear baby beavers whimper and whine inside the lodge. When the younger beavers accompany the parents to feed outside the lodge, there is an incessant murmuring among all members of the family. They make a prolonged OOOOOOOOOOH sound. A more strident note is a YAAANK, which sounds very much like the call of a white-breasted nuthatch. An angry beaver hisses.

The best-known sound of the beaver is its alarm signal made by forcefully slapping its tail on the surface of the water. This sharp crack, given on a quiet night, can be heard for a mile or more. It is a signal that is usually responded to, by most beavers, most of the time. Occasionally, I have seen beavers that heard the splash but did not run to the water or dive underwater if they were swimming. They were alerted by the loud splash but were determined to check out the danger for themselves before responding.

The beaver's scent post or pad is another means of communication. I have found that solitary beavers make and use these scent posts much more frequently than do beavers in an established colony. Because of this, I feel that the scent posts are used more for advertising the presence of an unmated beaver than a declaration of territory by an established colony.

The scent posts are piles of mud and grass and sometimes a few small twigs that are perhaps 8 to 10 inches high and 10 to 12 inches in diameter. The mud on these pads is usually fresh. The beaver deposits castoreum, from its huge castor glands, on the top of this pad. This sweet-smelling oil is attractive not only to the beaver but to all animals, including humans. It is even used as a base for some perfumes. I have been able to smell this castoreum for long distances and have often worked my way upwind until I located the scent post. I wonder how far the beaver can smell castoreum. I would also imagine that a few drops of castoreum placed in water would travel many miles downstream and still be detected by a beaver searching for a mate.

BREEDING

Most beavers are monogamous, although there are a few records of one male breeding with several females. Most beavers are sexually mature by the time they leave the parental colony at 22 months and this may also be a reason for their being forced out. It could be an effort by the established beavers to maintain the status quo or to cut down on the sexual competition. In the far north some of the young beavers do not breed till their third year.

Most breeding is done during late January or February. Actual copulation takes place in the water. Although the beavers have no difficulty in telling the sex of another beaver, it is exceedingly difficult for a human to do so without a physical examination. If the female is nursing, her nipples will show, but at any other time there are no external sex organs. The male's penis is retracted within the cloaca and can be felt only if a finger is inserted in the urogenital tract.

BIRTH AND YOUNG

The gestation period for the beaver is 107 days. Prior to the female's giving birth, the dam is repaired and perhaps heightened. The male beaver and the yearlings usually leave the main lodge to set up temporary quarters in an auxiliary lodge or in a bank den. In May or June the young beavers are born.

Four baby beavers is a normal litter, although 3 to 5 are common. A study done in Michigan showed one female with 6 young, one with 7 and one with 8. One captive beaver in Salem, Oregon, had 9 young. And there is one record of 10 embryos found in a dead female. There is a definite correlation between the number of young in the litter and size and weight of the mother, the largest females having the largest litters. Unlike most mammals, the female beaver is as large and sometimes larger than the male.

Overly large litters produce lots of friction between the young because the female has only 4 nipples located on her chest. The 2 lower nipples produce more milk than the top 2.

Several birthings of beavers in captivity have been witnessed and it is a process that may take several days. During this time the female sits upright with her tail protruding in front of her body.

The baby beavers are fully furred when born, their eyes are open, their incisor teeth have irrupted through the gums, they are 12–15 inches in total length and weigh 13–16 ounces. Within an hour the babies are nursing. Baby beavers have been seen swimming when they were only 13 hours old. They readily take to the water without the urging that many semiaquatic mammals must exert on their young.

When the baby beavers are 2 weeks old, they weigh about 1 1/2 to 2 pounds. By this time they will come out of the lodge to follow after the parents and to feed upon whatever vegetation the parents are eating. At this stage, I have seen the mother beaver carry her young, horizontally, in her mouth when she wants them to be in a definite spot that perhaps they don't want to go to.

The young are weaned at about 6 to 8 weeks of age. The female usually stops lactating about 90 days after giving birth.

At one year of age a beaver weighs about 18 pounds.

The average beaver family now consists of the 2 adults, 3 kits, or baby beavers, and 3 yearlings. Males slightly outnumber the females in the sexual ratio at birth and in the yearling stage. From that time on there will be more females than males in the adult age group, perhaps because the males are more venturesome and this would make them subject to greater predation.

LIFE SPAN

Beavers difficult to age after 3 years. Average life span: 10 years. Oldest on record: 21 years, a beaver caught in the wild in West Virginia.

SIGN

Bright, white peeled sticks in or near ponds and streams, and dead trees standing in water. Smell of castor pads, sight of tracks and fibrous fecal droppings at bottom of still ponds and lakes.

ENEMIES

Man the greatest enemy, as hunter and trapper but more as competitor for habitat. Wolf the principal enemy in north country. At a disadvantage on land, beavers also prey to coyotes, wolverines, bears, bobcats, lynxes and mountain lions. Otters, fishers and owls kill baby beavers. Otters probably not a match for large beavers. Beavers subject to lice and mites, and on land flies and mosquitoes. Flying insects can be avoided by returning to lodge. Internal worms also plague beaver. Tularemia a virulent disease among beavers, at times wiping out majority of an area's population. Tularemia killed thousands of beavers in Ontario in 1949–51, and in Minnesota in 1951–52. Beavers living in running water less susceptible to the disease because the microorganisms that cause it are flushed away by the water. Animals in still water suffer more.

HUMAN RELATIONS

The first Indian that the Pilgrims met when they stepped ashore in what became Plymouth Colony, was named Samoset. He wore a beaver robe. By sign language, the Pilgrims indicated to Samoset that they wanted him to bring them more beaver robes for trade.

The Indians revered the beaver. All the northern tribes had legends about the "beaver people" and looked upon them as kin. The Indians did hunt and trap the beaver for food and for fur but the small numbers that they took did not make even a dent in the beaver's total population.

The white men changed all that. Not only did the Europeans trade with the Indians for beaver fur, they organized trapping groups of their own. Fortunes were made, wars were fought and the continent was explored with the skins of the beaver being the driving force. The beavers were trapped and hunted at all times of the year and wherever they were found.

The beavers were used at first with the fur left on the skin as regular fur. In the late 1700s, beaver hats became popular. These were not made from the skins. A special comb was used so that the soft underfur could be pulled out, leaving the guard hairs attached to the hide. It had been discovered that the beaver's underfur had microscopic barbs which allowed this fur to be pounded into a superior felt. This is what the beaver hats were made of and some of the best felt hats today are still made of this underfur. The beaver's skin was known as "parchment beaver" and was made into leather or glue.

Beaver hats remained fashionable until about 1870. In 1832 a process to make hats of silk was perfected and the beaver hats began to go out of style. By this time, however, it was almost too late; most of the beavers in the world had been eliminated.

But not all of them. The beavers are back now, and, with the superior protection they have been given, they should be with us as long as they continue to have suitable habitat. In many areas, beavers have increased to the point where they are considered a nuisance. Some of the states have removed the beaver from the protected list in an effort to control their numbers and their damage.

Three beavers turned loose in Itasca State Park in Minnesota in 1901 increased to 250 beavers there by 1913. In Arkansas alligators have been reintroduced into areas plagued by beavers to control their numbers.

COMMERCIAL VALUE

Price of pelts very low but large catches still possible—two Georgia trappers caught 630 in a recent season. IAFWA statistics: 232,710 taken in U.S. in 1976–77, average price, $16 per pelt, total $3,723,360. In Canada: 404,625 beavers at $24.31 average price, $9,836,998 total.

MUSKRAT, *Ondatra zibethica*

INTRODUCTION

Furriers used to call the skins of this mammal Hudson seal, Red River seal, water mink, plucked beaver, velvet coney, Bisam mink, and so forth. The Algonquin Indians called it musquash and the Hurons called it ondatra. Captain John Smith wrote in 1612: "Mussascus is a beast of the forme, and native of our water rats but many of them smell exceedingly of muske." Father Le Jeune, a Jesuit missionary, in 1635, called it le Rat Musque, which has long since been Anglicized to muskrat. With the passage of the Fur Products Labeling Act, all of the fancy furrier names have been dropped so that today, "a muskrat is a muskrat is a muskrat."

The Huron Indian name, *ondatra,* has been consolidated into the muskrat's scientific name. The *zibethica* is Latin, adapted from "zibet" or the civet cat because of its musky odor.

DESCRIPTION

It is unfortunate that the muskrat is called that because it is not a rat, although, by being a rodent, it is related to the rats but also the squirrels, chipmunks, woodchucks, and so on.

The muskrat is a rodent because of its 4 incisor teeth in the front of its mouth. The incisors are a dark yellow in color and grow continuously throughout the life of the animal. The teeth are chisel-sharp, self-sharpening and protrude forward. They are used for food gathering and fighting. Occasionally the muskrats suffer from malocclusion and the incisors do not wear down but continue to grow, eventually causing the death of the muskrat. Folds of skin, the mouth flaps, close behind the incisor teeth of the muskrat

and the beaver and allow these animals to cut and dig for food underwater, with no water entering their mouths. There are 3 molars on each side of each jaw that are flat-topped and ridged for the grinding of vegetation which is the muskrat's main food.

The muskrat is a compact, semiaquatic mammal looking very much like an oversized meadow mouse. The compactness is emphasized by the apparent lack of a neck.

Muskrats differ in size and weight according to the locale in which they are found and the food available to them. An average large male muskrat for my area of northwestern New Jersey will weigh 3 pounds 4 ounces and be 22 inches in total length with the tail being 10 inches of that total. The tail is flattened vertically about one inch in height, is covered with scales over 9 inches of its 10-inch length and has a few sparse, stiff hairs.

The muskrats of Louisiana and Texas average between 1 pound 8 ounces and 2 pounds 3 ounces. They are about 22 inches in total length. These muskrats are also more wary and nervous than their northern counterparts.

The largest muskrats that I can find records on are those of the Montezuma Migratory Bird Refuge at the upper end of Cayuga Lake in New York State. The adult females averaged 3 pounds 5 ounces with the heaviest being 5 pounds. The adult males averaged 3 pounds 10 ounces with many of them going over 4 pounds and the heaviest being 5 pounds 4 ounces. On these large rats there was an average of 8 ounces of fat. The largest bodied male, although not the heaviest, was 25 inches in total length, of which 14 1/2 inches were body length and 10 1/2 were tail length. The tail was 1 3/16 inches in height.

An adult muskrat stands about 4 1/2 inches high at

An adult muskrat showing large hind feet and the vertically flattened tail.

the shoulder but, as with most rodents, it sits with its back humped up so that its back is much higher. I have measured a number of muskrats that had a heart girth of 11 inches and one that had 12 inches.

The muskrat's fur is sleek and waterproof. The guard hairs are glossy and about 1¼ inches in length. The underfur is three-quarters of an inch in length, dense and kinky. Most muskrats are dark brown to black on their backs, shading to a light gray on their bellies. Many very black rats are found although they are not truly melanistic because the belly is lighter in color than the back. Albinism is not uncommon. I have several very light, pastel-colored muskrat skins in my collection. Floyd Phillips, of Oswego, New York, reports on one colony that has produced 30 muskrats that are spotted brown and white.

There are 5 rows of vibrissae with the longest whiskers being a little over 3 inches in length. The muskrat has dark beady eyes. Its ears are about three-quarters of an inch in length and are almost hidden in the fur.

There are 5 toes on each foot; 4 major toes and a tiny thumb on each forefoot. The forefoot, from nail tip to heel pad, is about 1¾ inches in length; the hind foot, from nail tip to heel pad, is about 3¼ inches long. There are stiff curving hairs on both sides of each toe on the hind foot that measure about one-quarter of an inch in length on the inside of the foot and about one-eighth of an inch on the outside and between the toes. The hind foot can be spread about 2¼ inches in width, giving the muskrat a good propulsion surface.

The 2 musk glands are about 1¼ inches in length, have nipples, and are located on both sides of the walls of the anus. They give off a rich, yellow, sweet-smelling musk that is similar to a beaver's castoreum. It is an odor that pervades all muskrats and one that is attractive to most mammals.

DISTRIBUTION

Found in every state except Florida. Reason for absence there unknown—possibly predation by alligators, yet muskrats and alligators coexist in Louisiana and Texas. Absent also from parts of Georgia and South Carolina coasts and desert Southwest. Introduced in California in 1900s, where now well established.

TRAVEL

The home range of a muskrat averages about 200 feet in diameter. Its actual defended territory is much smaller than that and the size is determined by many factors. There are times when a dozen muskrats, a family group, may share the one winter lodge. At other times, at other seasons and for other reasons, the adults will drive out the young or kill them and each other.

The largest dispersal of muskrats from the natal den, and perhaps even from the entire area, is in the early spring before the onset of the mating season. Most of the young move no more than 200 feet if the marsh is not overpopulated. Although both sexes may

MUSKRAT
(Ondatra zibethica)
CURRENT RANGE

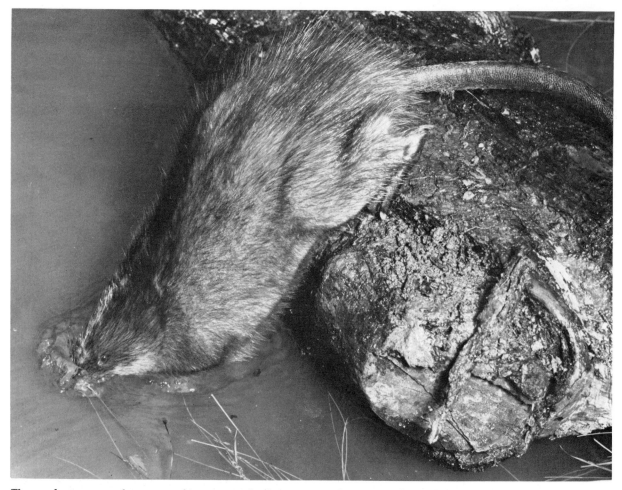

The muskrat escapes from most of its enemies by diving into and swimming beneath the water.

move and at times adults as well as young do move, if there is a longer exodus it is usually the males who move the farthest.

At times of food shortages, where the muskrats have suffered an eat-out (when overpopulation obliterates the food supply), or when drought has dried up the water in the ponds in the summer or allowed them to freeze down to the bottom in the winter (a freeze-out), there may be a general egress with all the muskrats moving out. There have also been unexplained mass exoduses of muskrats when all the conditions in the pond were ideal. No one can explain the reason for the latter occurrences. During these vacating moves from their natural haunts, muskrats show up miles from where they had been and end up in places they shouldn't be. Most of these muskrats are annihilated by predators or accidents in mild weather and by predators and freezing in the winter.

The longest recorded distance of travel for a tagged muskrat was 20 miles. Many nuisance muskrats are livetrapped, moved and released elsewhere. To see how far muskrats had to be moved to overcome their homing instincts, distances were recorded with tagged muskrats. One male muskrat was released at longer distances each time and returned five times. The muskrat made its last trip back, a distance of 4,800 feet, in 24 hours. One female muskrat returned after being released 5,400 feet from its lodge. The tests also showed that muskrats removed beyond 1 1/2 miles do not come back home.

LOCOMOTION

Muskrats walk and gallop or bound. Perhaps bounce would be a better word for it because when they hurry they just bounce along.

When they swim, their front feet are held up in front of their chests with the toes folded down. I have never seen a muskrat use its front feet for propulsion, although I have seen the front feet used for turning.

The hind feet, with their hair webs, are the major source of propulsion. The feet can be turned out at the ankle so that at times the feet almost stick out sideways from the body like those of a duck. This is seen most often when the muskrat is swimming underwater.

The tail is used primarily for steering, although most of the time it is also moved from side to side, producing a sculling effect that helps with propulsion. This sculling action is the best way to identify what creature is swimming when seen at a distance; nothing else has this action or produces a similar wake.

Muskrats usually stay underwater for about 5 minutes but can stay under much longer. The cardiovascular restrictions that take effect when the animal dives shunts the blood from the extremities to the brain. A muskrat in laboratory tests was forced to stay underwater for 12 minutes with no ill effects. However, a free-swimming muskrat was seen to stay underwater, of its own volition, for 17 minutes, surface, dive, and stay under for another 10 minutes before resurfacing. Then it would not dive, even when threatened. I have seen this same reaction with beavers and ducks. After two or three forced dives, they refuse to dive again, perhaps because of the carbon dioxide build-up in their blood.

FOOD

Primarily a vegetarian, eating variety of available wild and cultivated vegetation. Favored foods: cattails, pickerelweed, bulrush, smartweed, white water lily, sedges, spatterdock, black willow, duck potato, wild rice, water milfoil, coontail, duckweed, corn, carrots, apples, turnips, parsnips, bark of small tree sprouts and so on. Most muskrats do not store food for winter—the few that do probably learned the trait directly from others. Storing more common prior to hard winters and successive mild winters may cause trait to be

A muskrat feeding on cattail roots on the feeding shelf on the side of its house.

A muskrat feeding on material it has brought up on the ice. It will make a mound of this vegetation, called a "push-up."

forgotten. Most common stored foods are ear corn and duck potatoes, a bushel or more being laid by. Muskrats eat more meat than do other rodents, some eating more meat than vegetation when available.

Diet includes freshwater mussels, clams, crayfish, frogs, salamanders and fish. Fish are either scavenged or caught, those being the slower, rough fish. When fish are concentrated by drought or freeze-out, muskrats prey upon them more. Also eaten occasionally are turtles, dead ducks, other muskrats, and even their own tails. They eat 3 1/2 ounces of food a day. With food in abundance muskrats are picky eaters and waste more than they consume. They build feeding beds in marshes and will favor specific feeding spots where residue of food is scattered.

BEHAVIOR

Muskrats are often referred to as being the beaver's little brothers. They do many of the same things except for building dams.

Muskrats living on streams and rivers, where there is water current to contend with, build bank tunnels and dens. The entrances to their dens are underwater, although they may be exposed in times of drought.

Where possible, the muskrats prefer to dig in under tree roots or rocks so that predators cannot enlarge the entrance.

The tunnels are usually one to 2 feet under the water level and slope upward so that the living chamber is above the water level. Muskrats prefer to dig into high banks because of the protection the additional earth provides to both the tunnels and the chambers. In low banks, the tunnels may be close to the surface. Many times I have broken through the roofs of tunnels I did not know were there. Cattle and horses frequently cave in the tunnels and chambers of muskrats that have been constructed in pastures. In areas where the pond is a shallow depression, the muskrat tunnel may be several hundred feet long before enough elevation can be gained to get above the water level. Such tunnels frequently cave in.

Muskrats build houses in lakes and ponds where there is little or no water current. Although they may be forced to build in water as shallow as 6 inches, they prefer depths of one to 3 feet. Muskrats do not use sticks and mud in building their houses but construct them out of whatever marsh grasses are most common in the area. The entire mass is usually built up from the floor of the pond, although occasionally it

A pile of mussel shells opened and the meat eaten as food by a muskrat.

will be built on a log or even on masses of floating vegetation. The material is piled up solid like a miniature haystack with most of the houses measuring 3 to 4 feet in diameter and rising above the water 3 to 4 feet. When construction of the outside is about completed, the muskrat dives underwater and cuts and digs its way up into the center of the house, where it creates its living chamber above the water level. The material that is removed from the interior of the house is added to the lodge's exterior. Most of the material that is used in the house is wadded up to about the size of a softball. Some of the larger houses will have several chambers inside. There are usually at least two or more underwater entrances to each house.

The houses may be built any time they are needed but most of them are built in the spring after the dispersal or in the fall when the lesser dispersal takes place. Muskrats have their main dispersal in the spring (usually of adults) and a lesser one in the fall, of juveniles.

The material placed on the house is wet and will freeze. Many times in subzero weather, the insides of the thinner-walled houses also accumulate a layer of ice from condensation and splashing from the muskrat's fur. Despite this freezing of the walls, a muskrat's house does not provide the protection that a beaver's lodge does; it is much more easily dug into by predators.

In times of scarcity, the muskrats often eat the insides of their houses since they are constructed from the same material as the food they eat.

A muskrat house in the Delaware River at Pahaquarry, New Jersey. This is most unusual because most muskrats do not build houses in areas where they can be washed away by flooding.

When muskrats build their houses, they create openings in otherwise dense stands of cattails and reeds. These openings greatly enhance the marshes for ducks and increase the marsh's duck-carrying capacity. Five muskrat houses to the acre indicates excellent conditions for them; more houses are the result of overpopulation with the chance of a devastating eat-out.

The muskrats also construct feeding houses. These structures are usually no more than 2 feet high by 2 feet in diameter. In the summer most muskrats eat on feeding shelves or platforms; level spots above water on the side of their houses. With the coming of cold weather, they build the little feeding houses in the marshes close to their food supply.

One fall some muskrats living on Poxono Island, in the Delaware River, made a feeding house on a log caught on a sandbar about 250 feet from their den. There was a good bed of elodea just off the sandbar that the muskrats were feeding on. The feeding house gave them protection from hawks and owls as they fed in the safety of their shelter.

After the ponds freeze up, the muskrats will chew up through the ice, or open up cracks in the ice, so that they can get above water. To keep these holes open, the muskrats plug them with vegetation which freezes but is more easily opened than solid ice. As the muskrat continues to use the hole, more and more vegetation is pushed up through the hole, creating a feed house on top of the ice. The plugs of material and the resulting houses are called "push-ups." These push-ups not only prevent the muskrat from being seen, they also keep it from being exposed to the wind and cold. One winter I saw 17 muskrats on the ice of one small lake busy feeding and creating push-ups along the cracks in the 16-inch ice.

Shallow ponds are a threat to muskrats if they freeze to the bottom. The muskrats need at least 3 inches of water beneath the ice to move around in, although they sometimes can tunnel through the mud beneath a freeze-out. If a muskrat has been feeding on submerged vegetation, it may lose this source of food when it is encased in ice. An occasional complete freeze-out may trigger a mass migration of muskrats in the middle of winter where most of the animals die in snow from the cold.

In summertime, as the water level drops, the muskrats will dig canals from their houses to their feeding areas. A prolonged drought may dry up a marsh completely, exposing the muskrats to predation of all types.

Dr. Paul Errington ("Mr. Muskrat"), former professor of zoology at Iowa State University, has come up with definite proof that muskrat populations have cycles that are synchronous with the cycle of the hares and grouse of the north country. He had no idea why this should be so nor what extramundane factors linked the cycles, but several decades of close observation and meticulous records proved his conclusions. The actual numbers of muskrats may not agree with the cycle because of localized conditions of drought or other natural factors, but the temperaments and actions of the muskrats were linked to a ten-year cycle.

For example, he found that when the population cycle is high, the muskrats would or could stay in a bone-dry marsh three times longer than they would under the same condition when the cycle was low.

The muskrat is a fighter. A beaver cornered on dry land may attempt to escape or just sit there to see what is going to happen next. A muskrat, cornered any place, rises up on its hind feet and is ready to fight. Many times the muskrat will attack by trying to climb up your leg, biting all the way.

When a muskrat marsh becomes overcrowded, the adults fight, often killing each other. Mothers drive their weaned young ones out of the area and they may even kill and eat their own nestlings. Errington found that when the cycle is high, the muskrats are much more tolerant of each other and less fighting occurs. He found the cyclic highs to be in the years 1941–43 and 1951–53. During these high cycles he found as many as 10 muskrat pairs and their families per acre. He also found that the muskrats tolerated three times as many muskrats in an area during the high cycle as they would during the low.

During periods of the low cycle, when overpopulation occurred, the muskrats generally withdrew from the congestion by emigration. Savage fights between adults were common as were attacks upon helpless young.

Muskrats may be active at any time of the day or night. I do a cursory study of muskrats every day as I look up from writing this to watch the muskrats swimming and feeding in my pond just 200 feet away. They are most active, though, from early evening through the night to early morning.

Muskrats are very adaptable. They can live in mountain streams or big city parks. They can live in crystal-clear lakes and ponds or highly polluted waters. They are found in sloughs, potholes, streams, rivers, irrigational canals, and so on. They do not do well where water levels fluctuate more than 3 feet per day or in areas that are scoured frequently by heavy flooding. They ride out occasional floods by sitting in bushes, on floating vegetation or debris.

They can live in coastal marshes if there is enough of an influx of fresh water to offset the salt water, making it brackish. The higher the salinity, the less favorable it is to muskrats. They cannot live in coastal areas subject to high tides. Louisiana's 4-million-acre coastal areas are ideal because the average mean tide there is 18 inches and is influenced more by the wind than by the moon.

SENSES

Smell and hearing of about equal importance. Vision good only at detecting movement—danger recognized only when it moves or can be smelled or heard. Sense of touch valuable when seeking food in roiled water, and taste well developed, although taste preferences not evident during starvation periods, proving their adaptability.

COMMUNICATION

Charlie Smith, an old Algonquin Indian, was my mentor in many woodcraft tricks. During the 17 summers that I guided canoe trips into Quebec's wilderness areas, I worked with Charlie and it was he who taught me how to call muskrats. His call was made from a thin strip of birch bark held within a split twig. When blown upon softly, it made a high-pitched squeak similar to the sound made by the muskrat itself. He could call the muskrats right over to his canoe where he could then kill them for food.

Muskrats squeak, squeal, hiss and, when angry, chatter their teeth. The sounds they make are similar to those made by the brown rat.

Although the muskrat does not make castor pads like the beaver, it does deposit drops of its scent on rocks, logs and vegetation for the same purpose of advertising its presence. Muskrat droppings look like date pits and are about the same size. Three or 4 droppings per voiding is common. These droppings are also conspicuously displayed on rocks, logs and vegetation and deposited for the same purpose as the scent. The droppings are usually very dark when fresh and lighten with exposure to sunlight. Knowing this can be a guide to when the droppings were deposited. A hard rain will frequently wash the droppings away, wiping the slate clean so that you have a new timetable to work with.

BREEDING

Late winter or early spring is a time of great restlessness among the muskrats. Those in the north have been hampered by the ice and by the time the ice breaks up the rats are eager to move. I am firmly convinced that they respond to the urge to move as much as to the pressures that force them to move.

Early March is the onset of the breeding season in my area of northwestern New Jersey. Ice is breaking up on the ponds and dead muskrats suddenly are found by the dozens on the highways.

This is the period of the greatest dispersal and although some adults of both sexes may also move, most of the travelers are the younger muskrats, with the preponderance of those being males. Sixty to 70 percent of the muskrat population does not move at this time.

Muskrats are more monogamous than not. Live-trapping produced only paired muskrats from each house. This has been verified by my personal observations over many years. Although both the male and the female muskrats build the house and maintain it, he usually lives in it with her only up to the time that the young are about to be born. Then he leaves or is driven out of the house by the female who becomes very aggressive over the house and the immediate territory just prior to giving birth. The gestation period for the muskrat is 28–29 days.

I have witnessed the copulation of muskrats on several occasions. Let me give you a record from my journal, dated April 5, 1968; 1:08 P.M.

It's an overcast day, blustery but mild. On the little island opposite the house in the front pond I watched two large muskrats breeding. There is a shelf of land all around the island so that the muskrats were in about 2 inches of water. The male was a little darker in color but the female was equal in size.

The female made squeaking noises. The male would swim around her, smell of her genitals and then mount her. Copulation was short, only 5 seconds or so. Then the female would move off, a few times even swimming away a few feet, then returning. The male mounted her 5 times. One time while copulating they both lost their footing and fell over on their sides in deep water, which caused them to part.

Young muskrats just about large enough to leave their mother and go off on their own.

This activity took about 8 minutes of time. Between copulations the muskrats would groom and scratch themselves with their hind feet.

In Louisiana most of the muskrats breed between November and March, with the least amount being done in July and August. There may be 7 or 8 litters per year, although the litters average only 5 to 7 young per litter.

In the northern sections of the country some breeding may take place as early as January but most of it occurs in early March. Most of the northern muskrats have 3 litters per year, with the first litter being born in April, the second in late June or early July and the third in August or September. Occasionally there may be as many as 5 litters per year in the North. The litters in the North have 6 to 8 young per litter. Errington found a number of litters that had 11 young each. A report from Germany records 14 young muskrats born to a female at one time. In good years an average muskrat female will raise 15 young, many will raise 20 and there is one record of a female producing 46 young in one year. Female muskrats are considered aged if they live through their third year.

Less than 5 percent of the young females born in the earliest litters will breed in their first year and then only if conditions are ideal.

In view of the muskrat's fecundity, it becomes obvious that control of the population is needed and, if not provided by man, the job will be done by nature. Research in New Jersey has shown that one million muskrats can easily explode their population to 7 million in two years and their food supply cannot stand such pressure.

When the muskrats experience a very successful early breeding season so that the habitat is quickly filled to capacity, the resultant pressure will cause the female to stop at 2 or 3 litters. If the early litters of young are not successfully raised, or if the habitat is underpopulated, then the muskrats will continue to reproduce by having the third, fourth and even fifth litters.

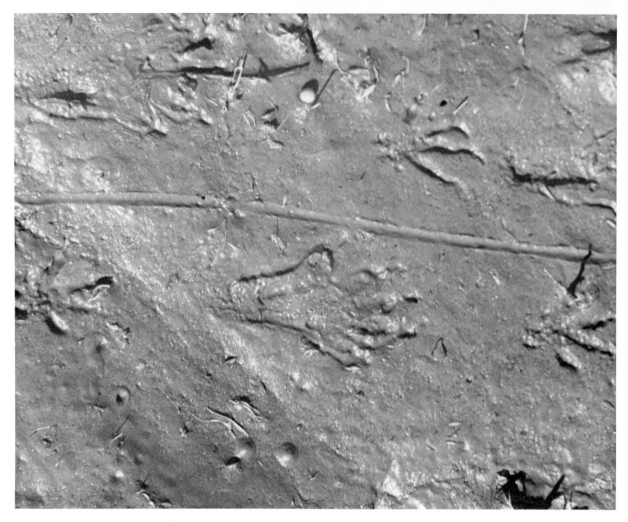

Muskrat tracks on a mud flat; note the mark where its tail dragged.

BIRTH AND YOUNG

The young muskrats are born naked, blind and helpless. They average about 4 inches in total length and weigh about one ounce. Most of the babies are born in snug houses, some in earthen bank burrows and in some of the coastal marshes, in open nests.

The young have strong suction while nursing and if the female is disturbed at this time, she may dash away with the little ones still fastened to her nipples.

The young muskrats grow very rapidly. By their seventh day they are 6 inches long and are furred; at 14 days, they are 7 1/2 inches in total length and their eyes will have just opened. At 21 days they will be 9 inches in length; they are weaned at about their 24th day and

by the time they are one month old they will be 12 inches long and out on their own. If conditions for food are favorable and the cycle right, the female will breed again at this time.

LIFE SPAN

The muskrat has a potential life span of 4 years, although few if any ever reach this advanced age. I can find no records of muskrats that have lived to be 5 years old.

SIGN

Houses in marshes and ponds, or tunnels in stream- and riverbanks, with earth tailings deposited in front of entrances. Droppings prominent on rocks or logs projecting above water. Tracks conspicuous in soft ground with tail mark in middle; in snow tracks are muddy. Ice plugs on frozen ponds and feeding houses on ice often seen. Passage beneath ice leaves trail of air bubbles. Piles of mussel shells show feeding.

ENEMIES

Mink the main enemy of the muskrat, sharing the same habitat. In 70 percent of the cases mink predation upon muskrats is possible only because the muskrat is dying or handicapped. Adult muskrats can usually defend themselves against minks. Raccoons are the second enemy, mostly in attacking the young in the nest. In some marshes, 50 percent of muskrat houses have been found torn apart by raccoons. Drought makes muskrats vulnerable to red foxes, coyotes, badgers, dogs and pigs. Muskrats also eaten by owls, hawks, eagles, cottonmouth moccasins, alligators, bullfrogs, garfish, black bass, snapping turtles and pike.

Muskrats have fleas, lice and other external and internal parasites. The hemorrhagic epizootic, known as Errington's disease, is the most serious cause of death, striking in late fall or winter when the animals are most concentrated. The virus grows in the mud and infects muskrats by contact. "Hot spots" of virus occur and trigger epidemics even after they have been uninhabited for 5 years. Such hot spots generally arise in ideal muskrat habitat that had attracted high concentrations of animals. Symptoms are bleeding from body openings, white spots on the liver and intestines filled with bloody fluid. Pneumonic type of the disease cannot be resisted by antibodies. A devastating disease, killing thousands—in Canada 18 muskrats were found dead in a single house.

HUMAN RELATIONS

Up to the late 1800s, the muskrat had little commercial value. It was trapped for its fur and food and was more important as food than fur. Today, the muskrat is still a major source of protein for many people in many parts of the country, especially in the southeastern states. The muskrat is a clean animal, it eats clean food and the meat is good. I have eaten many of them over the years. The meat is very dark as is true with all animals that swim underwater.

After World War I the price of muskrat furs skyrocketed from 10–15 cents up to $4–$5. The fur has a 50 percent durability of the river otter (which is considered 100 percent and all other furs gauged against it), is luxurious and can be dyed to any color desired. The muskrat soon became the number-one furbearing animal in North America with catches some years totaling 19 million. During the Depression, trapping muskrats was one of the very few ways of making money for a farm boy.

The trapping of muskrats is a necessity. As I have already shown, the muskrat is extremely prolific and destructive of its habitat. At least 75 percent of the muskrats of any given area should be removed annually to curtail the disease and destruction of habitat that occurs because of their overpopulation. In many areas of the country trapping muskrats is big business. It is the major source of income for many people in the coastal areas of New Jersey, Maryland and Louisiana.

Ted Abbot, of Crapo, Maryland, became the world champion muskrat skinner when he skinned 5 muskrats in 1 minute 2 seconds. He is a professional trapper and needs all the speed he has, having taken as many as 1,848 muskrats in one season.

In northern Canada and Alaska the muskrats are also trapped but the majority are taken by shooting during the time of the annual spring ice-out. Some of the Athabascan Indians shoot as many as 2,000 muskrats in a month during the period of high water.

Muskrats are usually censused in the fall by counting the number of houses in a marsh and multiplying by five.

By digging their burrows into dikes, dams and levees, muskrats can be very destructive in some areas of this country. They cause havoc in irrigation ditches, farm ponds and in areas of controlled agricultural water impoundments. To prevent damage to my pond I encased wire into the face of the dam when it was built. I just like to have muskrats swimming around.

The muskrat was introduced into Czechoslovakia in 1905 by Prince Colloredo-Mansfield, who took three pairs back with him from Alaska. The prince put the muskrats in two ponds southwest of Prague and from there they spread throughout most of Europe, following the extensive system of canals. Today Germany, Belgium and Holland have forces of professional trappers to combat the destructiveness of the muskrat. Holland, depending for its very life upon its dikes and canals, is particularly hard hit. Holland is a muskrat heaven. To assist the professionals in ridding Holland of the rodents, the Dutch have also offered a bounty of 5 guilders so that private trappers find it profitable too. Despite these measures, the Dutch may be losing the war. In 1976 a total of 62,322 muskrats was taken and in 1977 the catch was up to 75,327. I'm not sure if that increase in the catch means an increase in the total number of muskrats or an increase in trapping activities. Only in Siberia and Finland is the muskrat welcome in Europe. There it is doing no damage.

COMMERCIAL VALUE

IAFWA statistics: 7,148,370 muskrats in 1976–77 season; $4.75 average price; $33,954,758 total. Top 6 producers: Louisiana, 965,889; Wisconsin, 761,059; New York, 669,174; Ohio, 596,840; New Jersey, 486,017; Maryland, 417,400. In Canada: 2,554,879 at average price of $4.20. Total: $10,719,316.

4

NUTRIA, *Myocastor coypus*

INTRODUCTION

The nutria is a native of South America. Nutria is a Spanish name meaning "fish otter" because the early Spaniards mistakenly thought it was related to the otter of Europe. Its scientific name, *Myocastor,* is a combination of two Greek words, *mys* for "mouse" and *kastor* for "beaver," properly linking this animal with the rodents. *Coypus* is the Latinized version of the Araucania Indian word *coypu.* These Indians, some of whom I met in the mountains of Argentina and Chile, have long used this animal for fur and for food. In Europe the word *coypu* is more frequently used; in North America the name nutria has found favor. It is the only species of the family *Myocastoridae.*

DESCRIPTION

At first glance, the nutria could be mistaken for a beaver. It is smaller than an average adult beaver and much larger than a muskrat. The beaver's tail is flattened horizontally, the muskrat's is compressed vertically and the nutria's tail is round.

An adult nutria will measure from 22 to 25 inches from its nose to its tail base, with the tail being from 12 to 17 inches, giving it a total average length of between 34 and 42 inches overall. There is little difference in size and weight between the sexes. The average weight is 15–18 pounds with many of the largest ones weighing 25 pounds or a little more. The highest recorded weight is 37 1/2 pounds.

The nutria's tail is its most conspicuous identifying feature. Twelve to 17 inches in length, it is almost perfectly round, tapering to the tip. It is covered with scales except for the basal end which is covered with fur for a length of a little more than an inch. A few scattered, stiff, bristly hairs protrude between the scales. The nutria is not a creature adapted for extend-

An adult nutria; note its round tail.

ed periods of extremely cold weather. Nutrias in the northern states and Canada frequently lose parts of the tails, sometimes as much as half of the distal end, through freezing. This loss does not handicap the nutrias.

The nutria actually has 3 different sets of hair. The primary guard hairs are about 3 inches in length and are usually a solid dark brown in color. The secondary guard hairs are more numerous and from 2 to 2¼ inches in length and have alternating color bands of dark brown and a very light, reddish-brown ending in reddish-brown tips. These hairs give the nutria its basic coloration. The hairs are longest down the center of the animal's back and the darkest in coloration. The underfur is a very soft, kinky wool that is about five-eighths of an inch in length. Although this wool appears very dense, it is far less so than the underfur of either the beaver or the muskrat. Both albinism and melanism occur in wild nutrias and in captivity both white and yellow-colored strains have been developed because these colors are easier to dye.

Most fur animals in the United States become prime, meaning they acquire their full winter coats, in November, when the weather is getting cold and the animals need protection against it.

Nutrias become prime much later than our native animals. About 20 percent of the nutrias become prime in November, about 60 percent are prime in December and almost all of them are prime in January. This late priming is because the nutria is an animal from South America, below the equator, where the seasons are reversed. Our November corresponds to their May. The nutrias in the United States are not completely synchronous with those in South America because they do prime up earlier than their southern counterparts.

A unique feature of the nutria is the location of the female's mammary glands and teats. Whereas most mammals have their teats on either their breast or their belly, the nutrias' teats are located high on their sides. On a nutria having a heart girth of 12 inches, the teats are located down 2 inches from the spine or 4 inches up from the center of the belly. The number of nipples varies from 8 to 12. This placement allows the nutria's babies to nurse while they cling to her back as she swims.

With most mammals the skin of the belly is usually of the poorest quality because of the thinness of the skin, the shortness of the fur and the scar tissue in the skin because of the nipples. With the nutria, however, the best fur comes from the belly, the guard hairs are shortest, the undercoat softest and there are no nipples to mar the skin. This is the only fur animal that I know of that is occasionally skinned by cutting the skin down the back.

When a nutria is skinned, the pelt is cut off square in front of the eyes, and again, I know of no other animal pelt that is handled in this fashion. The pelt is then measured from that cut to the base of the tail and only those skins that measure over 23 inches are classified as number-one skins.

A nutria is a regular "whisker-puss." Its vibrissae are very numerous, almost pure white and about 4 inches in length. It has more whiskers than any other small mammal that I know. They are down-curving and droop like the whiskers of a walrus and are their equal in length.

The 4 large reddish-orange incisors protrude from the front of its mouth. A flap of fur, fitted behind these incisors, effectively closes the animal's mouth when it

Note the large incisors and long whiskers of this adult nutria.

is swimming or is underwater. As with other rodents, the incisors grow throughout the nutria's life and must be constantly worn down to prevent overgrowth. As the nutria ages, its incisors grow darker in color. The nutria has 4 premolars and 12 flat-topped molars used to grind the very coarse vegetation that it feeds upon, giving the animal a total of 20 teeth.

On both sides of the nutria's mouth, in the corners, are sebaceous fat glands that produce an oil that the nutria uses in waterproofing its fur. The nutria, like the muskrat and the beaver, spends lots of time grooming itself. It sits upright and combs its hair and fur with its front feet. Then it rubs its paws against the corners of its mouth and puts the oil over its fur to make it more waterproof.

The nutria's eyes are dark brown and will shine red in reflected light. Its ears are about one inch long and are buried in the fur of the animal's head so that only the tips protrude.

There are 5 toes on each of the nutria's feet. The front foot has 4 well-developed toes and a small thumblike toe on the inside. The toes are very dextrous and are used by the animal to hold its food while it is feeding. The forefoot of an adult nutria, from heel pad to nail tip, is about 1 1/2 inches in length.

The hind foot of the nutria is unique in that although there are 5 toes, only the 4 inside toes are joined by a thin, skin web. The fifth toe, the pollex, corresponding to our little toe, is long and fully developed but free of the web, a peculiar characteristic leading to the questions, Which way is the nutria evolving? Is it progressing more as a water- or land-dwelling mammal? The hind foot from heel pad to nail tip is about 3 3/4 inches in length.

DISTRIBUTION

Originally in South America from Brazil to Tierra del Fuego. Important fur animal in Brazil, Bolivia, Uruguay, Paraguay, Chile and Argentina.

The nutria, like the beaver and the muskrat, spends a lot of time grooming and oiling its fur to prevent it from matting, and to keep it waterproof.

NUTRIA
(Myocastor coypus)
CURRENT RANGE

An adult nutria; note that the outside toe is not joined with a web as are the other toes.

Imported into Europe before brought to U.S., nutrias grown on farms in France, Germany and Switzerland as South American nutrias declined. By late 1700s nutria was a very popular fur animal, like beaver. By late 1800s nutria extirpated from most of South America.

First nutrias imported to U.S. 1899 to California for commercial growing but venture unsuccessful. After another failure by a Washington State rancher in 1932, Tabasco sauce heir E. A. McIllhenny brought nutrias to Avery Island, Louisiana, in 1937. Began with 6 adult pairs and 8 baby nutrias. In 1939 several escaped ranch compound and lived in wild. Ranch population flourished abundantly and in 1940 Mississippi flood swept compound away, releasing nutrias. Price for pelts fell from 1920s peak of $13.50 but ranching continued. Today found in Louisiana, Texas, Mississippi, Alabama, Florida, Arkansas, California, Oregon, Washington, Idaho, Utah, Ohio, Kentucky,

Virginia, North Carolina, Maryland, Pennsylvania, New Jersey. Some states such as New Jersey lack genuine resident populations but have strays from other states.

TRAVEL

The nutria ordinarily does not travel far. Where the population is exploding, the range naturally is expanding and an egress of individuals does occur. The nutria is a much more sociable creature than the muskrat and more tolerant of others of its own kind. Research shows that 4 colonies to the mile of dikes or levees indicates a high population, with 6 to the mile being exceptional. Based on this, it would indicate that the individual family group's territory would be about 1,000 feet in diameter. On exceptionally good habitat, the territories of family groups overlap, resulting in higher densities.

LOCOMOTION

The nutria, although awkward on land, is frequently found some distance from water when it is seeking a favored food, particularly domesticated crops. The nutria walks and, when disturbed, it has a bounding, bouncing gallop.

It is a semiaquatic mammal and spends a large portion of its time in the water. It swims at a faster rate than the muskrat because it has a much larger surface area on its hind feet. The nutria travels at a normal speed of 2 to 3 miles per hour in the water. It can, of course, swim faster when threatened. The tail is carried on the surface of the water and is used for steering.

The nutria usually lives in bank burrows like many of the muskrats. The entrances to these burrows are about 9 inches in diameter and from one to 2 feet beneath the surface of the water. The tunnel is usually unbranched and extends at least 5 feet into the bank ending in a chamber that is above the water level and 18–24 inches in diameter. The chamber will be lined with grasses brought in for use as bedding. To reach these chambers the nutria must swim underwater.

In South America, some of the nutrias live so far south that the water surface there occasionally freezes over and the nutrias must swim beneath it. Nutrias do not do well where ice covers the water surface for extended periods of time.

Nutrias have remained submerged for periods of up to 5 minutes, but they cannot remain underwater as long as the beaver or the muskrat. An indication of this appears in the flesh of the nutria, which is pink in color. Mammals that are designed by nature to spend long periods underwater have more and larger blood vessels running throughout their muscles, making the flesh darker. The larger blood supply provides a greater storage supply of oxygen, allowing the animal to remain submerged for longer periods of time. It is this extra blood supply that makes the meat of muskrats, beaver and seals appear almost black.

FOOD

A vegetarian with a voracious appetite, occasionally competes with muskrat for food, and for living space if in same area together. Nutria more tolerant of space competition than muskrat and where both feed on same food nutria will force muskrat out although nutria not a serious threat to muskrat. Adult nutrias eat 2 1/2–3 1/2 pounds of food per day. Nutria larger than muskrat, with larger teeth and with bacteria in caecum (a pouch opening onto the intestines) to break down cellulose in coarse food it prefers. Muskrat favors brackish, coastal areas; nutria the freshwater ponds, lakes, impoundments, streams. Muskrat dives for roots and tubers; nutria a surface feeder.

Nutrias imported to Texas, New Mexico, and elsewhere to rid waterways of water hyacinth, alligator weed, coontail and bladderwort, which prevent boat traffic and rob fish of oxygen. Program was ineffective because nutrias would not eat the nuisance plants. They preferred rushes, reeds, grasses, pickerelweed, cattails, bull's tongue, arrowhead, square-stem spike rush, saw grass, cut grass, bulrush, maidencane, etc. Also feed on crops: alfalfa, clover, sugarcane, rice, tur-

Nutrias are good swimmers and take to the water at the first indication of danger. Because nutrias have a limited home area, a blind facilitates in taking photographs of them.

nips, cabbage, corn. Although many U.S. researchers say nutrias feed on all root crops except white potato, one researcher claims captive nutrias in Europe are fed primarily on white potato. Facts unresolved.

High populations of nutria can cause eat-out when all favored foods consumed, and frequently vegetation of an area changes completely when competition of favored foods disappears and less-favored foods take over.

BEHAVIOR

When the nutria is feeding on water plants it prefers to cut the vegetation loose and carry it to a floating feeding platform. Constructed of dried vegetation, it has a diameter of about 24 inches. The platforms are used most heavily in the winter because, to the nutria's hairless feet, they are warmer to sit on than the cold or frozen earth.

In large marsh areas, where the nutrias do not make their preferred burrows in the dikes and levees, they will build expanded floating platforms in the emergent vegetation that will be their den. They make no attempt to roof over these platforms, although they are protected from the wind by the tall reeds. The surrounding vegetation also acts as a shield that offers a measure of protection against the nutria's being seen by predators. In winter the nutria family huddles together to share body heat.

Nutrias prefer to live in burrows when the opportunity presents itself and any resultant cave-in can ruin the dikes and levees, causing them to leak or collapse. Where cattle graze on the dikes and levees, their weight frequently causes the burrows to collapse. This will force the nutrias to abandon the burrow and probably leave the area. It has been found that two-thirds of the nutrias will leave the levee and dike areas when cattle graze there.

Nutrias are really creatures of the more moderate temperate zones and are handicapped by extremely cold weather. People are often surprised that the fur from nutrias and muskrats from Louisiana is as good as the fur from more northern regions, even though Louisiana is generally much warmer than our northern states. The reason is that, although Louisiana does not have as cold an air temperature as the northern areas, the water temperature is nearly the same in both sections. After all, fresh water can only get down to 32° F. and then it becomes ice, regardless of the air temperature. So the semiaquatic mammals that have to contend with water that is nearly the same temperature grow equally dense coats of fur.

The nutria is crepuscular and is active from before sunset, throughout the night, till just after dawn. It is usually very shy and retiring. I am not sure if this is an inherited trait or a response to almost constant persecution both in South America and now here in the United States.

Nutrias prefer still water rather than that which has a fast-flowing current.

SENSES

Hearing and smell of equal importance to animal's safety. Nutria shy and always alert for danger. In my experience stationary objects not regarded as dangerous unless recognized as such by hearing or smell. Taste well developed because food preferences are marked.

COMMUNICATION

Young nutrias make a whimpering, whining sound when they are disturbed or hungry. The older animals make a bleating sound and occasionally a grunting sound like a small pig. Angry nutrias hiss and sometimes chatter their teeth.

BREEDING

Nutrias breed throughout the year and, although they have a peak period in South America, in September or October, they do not have one in North America. Occasionally the male nutria will be monogamous but most of the time each male will have 2 or 3 females. When the male has more than one mate they all share the same burrow and each family group becomes the nucleus of a small colony. It is reported that there is some fighting between rival males in securing females.

Young females develop very rapidly. They are capable of breeding when they reach the age of about 5 1/2 months or a length of 26–29 inches overall. This seems like a strange criteria, yet research has shown that no female was found to be bred that was less than 25 inches in total length. Of course, by the time the young nutria is 5 1/2 months old, she is usually over that length limit so that it gives researchers an accurate key to the nutria's age by measurement. If food is scarce and the female is not up to par, she will usually be 8 months old before breeding.

The female comes into her estrous period and remains in heat for 2 to 4 days. If she does not conceive during that period, she will recycle again in 24–26 days and this pattern will repeat itself until she is bred.

Ordinarily nutrias have 2 litters per year, sometimes 3. As the female becomes older and heavier, the general size of her offspring increases but the actual number of young follows a definite pattern. The first litter will usually be a small one, with perhaps 2 to 4 young being born. This is to be expected because the mother is a juvenile when first bred and her own body lays prior claim on the nutrients ingested.

Most females breed again in what is known as post-parturition heat period, which occurs within 48 hours after she gives birth. If the female does not breed at this time, she goes back to her regular cycle.

The second litter is generally larger with perhaps 4 to 6 young being born. This is again to be expected as the female herself is now larger and heavier.

The third litter will be smaller than the second, with the number of young dropping to 3 or 5. The fourth litter will again increase in size with 5 to 7 young being born. The fifth litter, following this larger-smaller pattern, will be smaller than her fourth. And so it goes, although no one knows just why. This variability also occurs among different species of mice.

The average number of young nutrias per litter is 6, with 11 being the largest number ever recorded. Any female that has produced 6 litters has about used up her breeding potential. Those that produce 7 are extremely rare.

BIRTH AND YOUNG

The gestation period for the nutria, between 128 and 131 days, is extremely long for an animal of that size. When they are born the young are very precocious. They are fully furred, their eyes are wide-open and their incisor teeth have irrupted through their gums. The young ones can crawl about within a matter of a few hours and they are capable of swimming within 24 hours. When the young are born they weigh about 8 ounces. They have a total length of about 12 inches, of which 7 inches is body length and the tail is 5 inches. The parent nutrias often bring in various types of vegetation for the little ones to eat. Two young nutrias, at the known age of one week, were seen feeding upon vegetation about 60 feet from the natal den. Their mother was not in the area and after the young had fed, they returned to the den by themselves. The young nutrias that are born in the floating nests usually move about earlier than those born in burrows.

When the young nutrias are one to 2 weeks old the mother often takes them on excursions outside the den. The little ones cling to her back, their feet enmeshed in her fur. As her nipples are usually close to the waterline, the little ones can nurse as the female swims about.

LIFE SPAN

Four years is old; record is 5 years 11 months for animal in London zoo.

SIGN

The most conspicuous signs of the nutrias are the entrances to their burrows in dikes, levees, and pond and lake banks. Their feeding platforms are also very conspicuous, although their nest platforms are usually more carefully hidden. Trails where the nutrias come out of the water to go overland are visible. Their tracks can be seen wherever there is mud for them to walk through. There can be no mistaking the hind foot of the nutria because there is no other animal I know of that has 4 toes encased in a web, with the fifth toe being free. Uneaten parts of its food plants litter the area.

ENEMIES

Many natural enemies, although big males able to put up a good fight—2 large nutrias have stood off an attack by 5 beagles. Young of course preyed upon more than adults. Enemies are alligators, snapping turtles, garfish, cottonmouth moccasins, hawks, owls, eagles. Few external parasites beyond fleas and lice. Mosquitoes in nutrias' still-water habitat prey upon them. Internal parasites are flatworms and roundworms. "Nutria itch" in man due to skin coming in contact with roundworm larvae in water, which penetrate skin. Severe inflammation results—may require medical treatment. Nutrias also plagued by seeds of smooth beggarstick, common plant in typical habitat, seeds of which have two barbed awns that entangle in fur and may puncture skin, producing sores and lesions that can be infected with bacteria and fungis. Heavily infected animal becomes listless, stops eating, and may die. Pelts of such animals nearly valueless due to holes or thin scar tissue.

HUMAN RELATIONS

Muskrats had very little value until the early 1900s. They gradually became North America's most important fur animal, a position they still retain for sheer numbers, although deferring to the raccoon now in total value. Nutrias were imported because nutria fur, in other countries, had a substantial value. When the first pen-raised nutria pelts were sold on the market, they were of much poorer quality than the wild imported nutria skins. Many fur ranchers went broke, many released their captive animals, others lost them through floods or other disasters.

When the feral nutrias established themselves, they had such little value that the trappers considered them a nuisance, merely killing them and throwing them away. There was no real nutria market in this country as most of the furs were sold in Europe. Local fur buyers had no outlet and so refused to buy them.

In 1959 I made my first trip to South America and was amazed to see the high prices nutria fur coats were bringing, especially since nutria had very little value in the United States.

The trappers found that the nutria was very difficult to skin. It took as long to skin one nutria as it did 2 or more muskrats and then no one would buy the skin anyway.

COMMERCIAL VALUE

Nutria has assumed position as fur animal once occupied by muskrat: 8,337,411 muskrats taken in Louisi-ana 1945–46; today yearly take less than 1 million. In 1943–44, nutria harvest in Louisiana 436, skyrocketing to 1.5 million in 1964–65 and to 1,890,853 in 1976–77. As late as 1962 price per pelt only 57¢ but prices increased substantially since. In 1976–77, the take according to IAFWA, 2,018,815; average price $5.25, $10,598,779 total. Louisiana Fish and Game Department has unsuccessfully promoted nutria meat for human consumption. In 1963–64, over 8 million pounds of nutria meat sold as mink food at 10¢ per pound. When mink pelt price dropped and ranching declined, meat sold to U.S. Government for use in screwworm project. Meat has value as animal food or as fertilizer when dried.

Total nutria population peaked in 1959 with about 20 million in the U.S., most in Louisiana. Population lower today and stabilized.

Nutria raising has been promoted as a get-rich-quick scheme for years, promoters getting up to $1,800 for a male and 2 females. Riches from nutria never materialized, and today price for pelts too low to make ranching profitable.

CARNIVORA

The carnivores are flesh-eating mammals that range in size from the diminutive least weasel up to the huge polar bear. Although all of these mammals prefer to eat meat, many of them feed upon many other types of food and are considered to be omnivores.

The 4 long, sharp canine teeth that are designed for grasping prey is a characteristic of all of the carnivores. A penis bone is also present in all of the males of this order.

FAMILY:

CANIDAE

All dogs, dingoes, jackals, wolves, coyotes and foxes belong to this family. They are among the most intelligent of all mammals. They do not chew their food but use their carnassial teeth to shear off chunks small enough to be swallowed. Most of them have long legs, are able to run fast, have good endurance and are efficient predators. A great deal of controversy is generated by this group of mammals and people's feelings directly reflect their relationship with them. Some of the canids are very efficient killers of mice. Some are a control factor on the rabbit and hare populations, a definite plus unless you are a hunter who resents the competition. Some of the canids kill deer and the larger hooved mammals. This may or may not be objectionable. It is one of the main reasons why the wild, hooved mammals that are alive today evolved into the fast, strong, graceful creatures they are. The great affinity we have for this family group undoubtedly stems from the close association we have had for thousands and thousands of years with the domesticated dog. The wolves have a highly developed social order. The wolves and coyotes may hunt in packs.

COYOTE, *Canis latrans*

INTRODUCTION

The name coyote is derived from the Aztec Indian word for this animal, *coyotl.* It was changed to *coyote* by the Spaniards, although occasionally it was spelled in different ways: *ciote, cuyota* and *cajeute.* The coyote's Latin name was given to it by naturalist Thomas Say in 1823. The Latin name is apropos because *canis* means "dog," while *latrans* means "barking" and the coyote does a lot of vocalizing. The

A large, heavy-bodied male coyote in winter. (Photo: Len Rue, Jr.)

coyote's barking and howling is one of the few tangible connections that still link today to yesterday's romantic Old West.

DESCRIPTION

An adult male coyote looks like a slightly built German shepherd dog. The coyote is often confused with the timber wolf in areas where their ranges overlap. The major difference between the two species is size. Wolves average about twice the weight of the coyote and are much larger. The coyote has much longer, more pointed ears; a specimen I measured had 5½-inch ears from the inside notch to the ear tip. The muzzle of the coyote is narrower, although the wolf's is longer, being 7¾ inches long compared with a coyote's 6 inches. The wolf has a much larger nose pad than the coyote. Both of these canids have bushy tails but the coyote usually runs with its tail down while the wolf runs with its tail carried straight out or even higher.

There is a wide variety of shadings in the color of the coyote going from a very light, sandy-red to a very dark, grizzled-gray.

An adult male western coyote stands 23–26 inches high at the shoulder, measures 44–54 inches in total length, of which 12–16 inches will be tail, and averages about 30 pounds in weight. A recent Minnesota research project weighed 1,200 western coyotes taken in that state and the adult males averaged 30 pounds in weight; the females averaged 25 pounds. The heaviest male coyote in the survey weighed 42 pounds.

The new eastern coyote, *Canis latrans var.,* is a crossbreed between the small northeastern timber wolf and the western coyote. It has now been recognized as a true-breeding subspecies. This is a much larger animal than its western counterpart with the males averaging 50 percent heavier and the females 70 percent heavier. Weights of over 60 pounds have been recorded for a number of eastern coyotes.

In 1972 and 1973 I personally weighed two female eastern coyotes caught by my good friend Joe Taylor in the mountains behind our home at 34½ pounds

Female coyotes like the one shown here are more slightly built than the big males.

and 38 pounds respectively. Both coyotes were in good shape, even though the heavier coyote did have some porcupine quills in its nose.

The coyote has 5 toes on each of its forefeet and 4 toes on each of the hind feet. Only 4 toes show in any of the tracks because the fifth toe on the forefoot is high on the inside of the foot and does not register in the tracks. A coyote's foot is much narrower than that of a comparably sized dog with the 2 outside toes slightly behind the center 2 toes.

The 42 teeth of a coyote are apportioned as follows: 12 incisors, 4 exceptionally long, thin canines, 16 premolars and 10 molars. Coyotes do not really chew their food. They swallow small prey or food items whole and scissor off small pieces of meat from larger prey with their carnassial teeth.

The coyote's large yellow eyes have black pupils. The fact that the pupil is round instead of vertical shows that the coyote was primarily a diurnal animal. That it now carries on most of its activities under the

cover of darkness is the result of the unrelenting pressure put on the coyote by man.

The guard hairs on the coyote's pelt are about 3 inches long on the back with the undercoat about 1 1/2 inches in length. The hair on the belly is about one inch shorter in each category. Starting on the coyote's neck is a mane or ridge of erectile hairs known as the hackles, that widens behind the shoulders and is 5 inches in length and usually much darker than the rest of the coyote's pelt. This hair then continues as a ridge down the coyote's back to the tail. I can find no record of a sebaceous skin gland being located in this tuft behind the shoulders but all indications are that there should be one. The darker back streak continues down the top of the tail, terminating in a dark tip.

DISTRIBUTION

Coyote adaptable to modern conditions and has vastly expanded range. Now found from Arctic slopes of

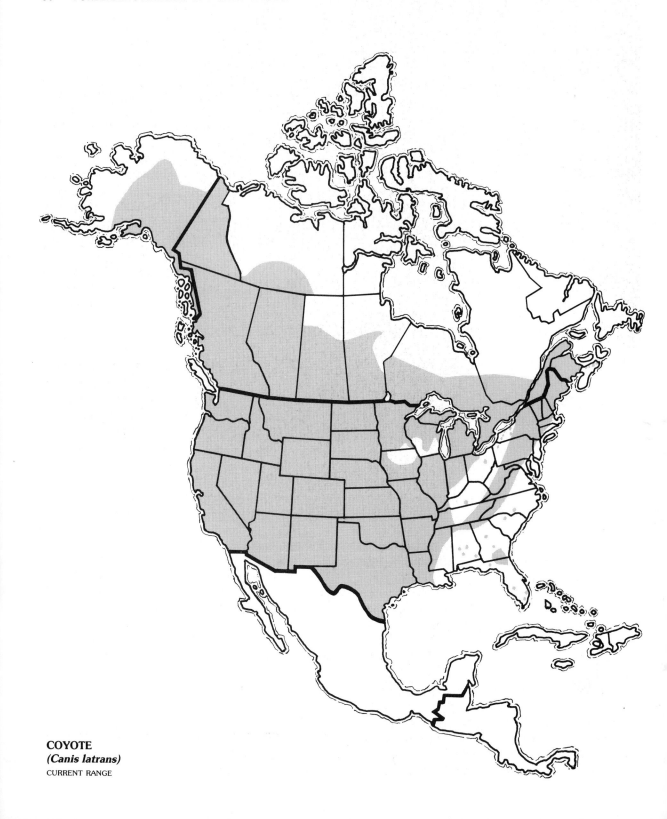

COYOTE
(Canis latrans)
CURRENT RANGE

Right front foot of a coyote. The dewclaw or fifth toe is not shown.

Alaska through Canada and U.S. to Costa Rica. Unknown east of Mississippi before 1950, since has become established throughout eastern U.S. as subspecies; many having been brought from West by hunting clubs to run with hounds, others as pets, which escaped and lived wild to be absorbed into population of larger eastern coyote. Hybrids occur: I photographed a coyote-dog cross in 1958 in New Jersey, an animal later found to be 7/8 coyote. Full-blooded coyote killed in New Jersey same year.

In the East coyote protected where scarce, hunted where numerous due to livestock predation.

TRAVEL

Coyotes do not migrate, although in dispersal time, when the young leave the natal area, they do emigrate to new territories. They have rapidly colonized new areas in the East and most of this would be caused by dispersal of the young. Records of tagged coyotes show that the females usually travel no more than 10–30 miles from the natal den, whereas the males average 40 miles or more. Some of the coyotes have traveled more than 100 miles during dispersal. One tagged coyote traveled 125 miles in two weeks.

When food is plentiful a coyote travels no more than 5 miles per day and the home territory for a female may be 6 square miles. A male coyote's territory is much larger, with some males covering as much as 36 square miles. While the female's territory does not usually overlap that of another female, the male's territory may encompass that of several females and overlap that of other males. During periods of food scarcity, the coyotes will concentrate wherever food is available and territories will be temporarily abolished, although dominance is not.

LOCOMOTION

The coyote walks, trots and gallops. Its walk is about a 3- to 4-mile-per-hour gait. However, the coyote usually trots, like a dog, whenever it is going any place. A leisurely trot is 6 miles per hour; a fast trot, 7 to 8 miles per hour. This ground-eating gait can be maintained hour after hour and with it the coyote can cover tremendous distances.

When surprised or scared, the coyote runs with its body flat. There is no motion lost in high bounds. The ears are laid back and the coyote seems to flow. When a coyote walks, its steps are about 13 inches apart; when it trots, the stride lengthens to about 22 inches; when it gallops, it covers about 10 feet with each leap. There are many records of a coyote running at 35 miles per hour with the top recorded speed of 43 miles per hour clocked by an automobile speedometer. Unless pursued by greyhounds or whippets, the coyote seldom has to run that fast. As its favorite habitat is brushy areas, the coyote usually needs just enough speed to get into cover.

FOOD

A carnivore, teeth designed for meat-eating only, but will eat anything—variety of diet a key to survival. Ear-

Coyote hunting.

ly studies misleading due to restricted number of animals studied. Like bear, coyote supplements meat diet with vegetation when necessary. Two to 3 pounds of food needed per day. When available foremost prey are jackrabbits, snowshoe hares, cottontail rabbits, prairie dogs, mice and rats. In Oregon coyote observed killing 12 field mice in 27 minutes. Skilled coyote can kill porcupine, circling to tire it, flipping it onto its back and attacking unprotected throat or belly. Game birds not an important food but game animals, mostly pronghorn antelope and deer, are killed. Coyote probably kills more deer than any other wild predator, because coyote population is so high. In some years at the Texas Wilder Wildlife Refuge, 70 percent of whitetail deer fawns die in their first month, with coyote predation accounting for half the deaths, killing fawns by biting through head, neck or spine. Larger eastern coyote able to kill prime deer in winter say reports from New York, Vermont and Maine. Hunt singly, in pairs or family groups, usually of 5–7

animals. Prey also on pronghorn, mostly fawns but occasionally adults, using a relay system to run animal to exhaustion. Records show pronghorn does chasing coyotes away from areas where newborn fawns were hidden. One report in 1949 blamed coyote predation on antelope population's inability to spread to upper and lower plains. Some coyotes kill sheep, lambs being most vulnerable but adults also killed. One government-funded study at ranch in Montana in 1974 showed loss of 330 lambs and 33 ewes from March 15 to September 30, 17.8 percent of all sheep on ranch. Next year, 394 lambs, 50 ewes lost, although percentage was smaller. In these years coyotes went uncontrolled. In late 1975, 46 coyotes removed from ranch and losses declined to 214 lambs, 13 ewes. Study made clear case for sheep rancher's argument to control coyote population.

Carrion a major food in winter when deep snow prevents hunting of mice and rabbits. Coyote suffers in light winters when elk, deer and bison thrive, but feasts when they die in hard winters. Coyotes provide natural sanitation, cleaning up disease-spreading carcasses, a function checked by poisoning efforts using contaminated carrion. Coyotes learned to neglect carrion and feed on fresh meat only, leading to higher sheep predation. Coyotes gradually returned to eating carrion after 1972 law forbade use of poison in most areas.

BEHAVIOR

I had always claimed that the wolf is the most intelligent animal in North America. However, the wolf is not adaptable. When man moves into an area, the wolf moves out. The coyote not only adapts to man, it thrives because of man. It is estimated that thousands of coyotes live within the 640 square miles that make up the Los Angeles city limits. The eastern

Winter is a time of hardship for most animals, although this large male coyote is in good shape.

coyote has filled the void left by the extirpation of the wolf and the mountain lion and lives in close proximity to tremendously large populations of people. Today I say that the coyote, particularly the eastern coyote, is the smartest wild mammal in North America.

Where coyotes are not molested, they are active in the early morning and late in the afternoon. Their songs and howling can be heard each evening. Where the coyotes are under moderate pressure, their howling is heard after dark and they are not seen except when one crosses the road in front of a car. Where coyotes are under extreme pressure, they will not even howl and the only sign they leave is their tracks in the snow or sand.

Except during the birthing period, coyotes do not den up. They will seek out shade in the summer and some shelter from a downpour of rain but their dense coats provide excellent insulation against cold and they will sleep out in the snow.

Coyotes can live in extensive forest tracts but they prefer the clearings in the forest or open, brushy areas. They are found, however, in almost every type of habitat from swamp to desert.

Coyotes have a social order, although not as large or as complex as that of the wolves. Nor does the coyote family stay together as a group as long as the wolf family.

Within the family group there is a social hierarchy and each member knows its place within the group. Circumstances often alter the situation and individual members may be able to move up or be forced down the social structure. When strange coyotes meet, they take each other's measure and dominance is established by bluff or fight.

My son Len Rue, Jr., and I sat up on a hill in Yellowstone's Lamar Valley one winter. Below us three young coyotes were on a collision course with one very large coyote. When the coyotes met, two of the younger ones, which I took to be females, ran up to the big coyote and crouched in front of him like puppies playing and then licked him under the chin. Meanwhile, the third young coyote, a male, rolled over on its back exposing its throat. The large coyote ignored the two females and went to the prostrated male and put a front foot on the young male's chest. Dominance being established, all four coyotes milled around for a while and then they split up and continued on their separate ways.

Coyotes do a lot of gaping—stretching their mouths wide open. They can open their mouths wider than either a dog or a wolf. One body sign confusing to me is that a coyote will often gape its mouth at an opponent, hunch its back, and tuck its tail between its legs. This sign seems to mean both aggression and submissiveness. Evidently I am missing part of the signal being sent between the individuals.

Coyotes are quick to take advantage of any opportunity that produces food. They have been known to frequent areas where haying is being done because the machinery flushes wildlife from the high grass. Coyotes have often been seen following a badger. When the badger attempts to dig out a ground squirrel, the squirrel escapes by dashing out the other end of its burrow and the coyote is there to interrupt its flight. The badger gets nothing from this operation except the exercise because the coyote does not share.

Early writers often referred to the coyote as cowardly or "slinking" or used other derogatory terms. The coyote always knew what guerrilla handbooks now preach, that it is better to strike and run away and live to strike another day. Pound for pound, a coyote can give a good fight to any dog but most dogs have too much of a weight advantage. In an era when most hands are turned against it, the coyote survivors are furtive but they will be here tomorrow.

SENSES

Smell most important but hearing very acute, able to hear mice beneath a foot of snow, can hear mouse squeak at several hundred yards and human footsteps at great distances. Eyesight excellent and can recognize man immediately by sight. Large ears and good eyesight the attributes of an animal in the coyote's original open range. Taste not well developed.

COMMUNICATION

As already mentioned, the coyote is famed for its vocalizing. Its howls are more frequent than those of wolves. One of my favorite listening spots is Mammoth Campground in Yellowstone National Park. There, each evening, as if on cue, the tourists are treated to a coyote concert. One coyote will start with a barking howl. An answer comes from up the canyon. A third answers from a nearby hilltop and soon the entire area reverberates with the music of the coyotes, which seem to try to outdo one another with song.

Coyotes are easily triggered into howling. Almost any high-pitched sound will start them off; a siren, a person singing, and I've even got them to howl by playing my mouth organ in the highest register.

Coyotes howl to keep in touch with one another, to hunt together and, what seems most obvious, just for the sheer pleasure of it. Coyotes also growl, hiss, whine and squall.

BREEDING

There is enough evidence recorded on known coyotes to prove that the adults remain mated for life if circumstances allow them to do so. They are monogamous and devoted to each other and to their pups. Some young coyotes are sexually mature enough to be able to breed when they are 9 or 10 months old and some of the females do. Most of the coyotes do not breed until they are 21–22 months old.

Coyotes give vent to their emotions by howling very frequently and the late January and February nights become a cacophony of song. Estrus usually occurs in late February or March, depending upon the latitude, with the coyotes in the South breeding before those in the North. In the coyote's world, as in most other similar situations, it is the female who makes the choice of the mate. Fighting among the males may occur but the female chooses the one she will mate with and will launch a slashing attack on any male that she does not favor.

Neither the male nor the female coyote is capable

Coyote listening for the movement of mice beneath the snow. (Photo: Len Rue, Jr.)

of breeding throughout the entire year. The male produces viable sperm for a period of 3 or 4 months while the female usually has a single heat period that lasts for about 20–21 days. Although the coyotes may copulate a number of times during this period, the peak of the breeding activity takes place between the first and second week of estrus. Like dogs, breeding coyotes frequently get "tied-up," remaining fastened for 20–30 minutes. After the peak of the estrous period has passed, the female will turn on her mate and force him to leave her alone.

As soon as the bond-pairing has been formed or reformed, the coyotes make preparations for their forthcoming litter by seeking out a den or by constructing one. Unless molested, an older pair of coyotes will utilize the same den year after year. If a new den must be dug, the coyotes prefer the sandy soil of streamside banks. Usually the coyotes will take over an abandoned coyote or badger den and renovate it to their liking. The coyotes usually have several den sites in mind and if the adults feel that the pups are threatened, they will not hesitate to move them from the natal den. One pair of coyotes moved their 5 pups a distance of 5 miles in one night. That was a busy night.

BIRTH AND YOUNG

The average coyote litter consists of from 5 to 7 pups. The largest litter on record consisted of 19 pups. A very interesting fact was brought to light by extensive coyote research done in California. It was found that where the coyotes were unmolested, 4 or 5 pups was the average litter size. Where the coyotes were subject to heavy control, the litter sizes increased to 8 to 9 pups. Man, inadvertently, may be responsible for the large coyote litters. Man has upset the natural controls under which a stable coyote population operates. By limiting the number of coyotes in a given area, more food is left available to the survivors and larger, healthier litters are the result.

The pups are born after a gestation period of about 63 days, with most litters being born the latter part of April. The newborn pups have short, brown fur but are blind and helpless. From the time of the pups' birth till their eyes open 10–12 days later, the female seldom leaves the den. She is fed at this time by the male, who usually catches more food than is needed.

It is this lack of help from the male domestic dog, with which female coyotes will breed, that dooms most coy-dog litters. Another factor is that for some unknown reason, female coy-dogs usually come in estrus in November which means that the pups will be born in January or February, a time when food is at its lowest supply. These two factors are the major reasons why most of the dog blood has been bred out of the eastern coyote.

The pups are usually strong enough to begin to crawl out of the den when they are 3 to 4 weeks old. The pups engage in rough-and-tumble play, fighting and stalking each other and everything small that moves within their area. Pieces of bone, hide and feathers are treasures to be contested for almost continuously. By 8 to 9 weeks of age the pups begin to follow after their parents and to learn to hunt for themselves. Insects, frogs, toads and mice are their first prey but with practice comes the skill that is needed to survive. It is at this time that the pups are weaned and the den abandoned. At 5 to 6 months of age the pups are just smaller, lighter editions of their parents and some of them may drift off to make their way alone. Some of the pups may remain with the parents or they may drift apart, only to regroup and drift apart again. By November or December the family is usually split up permanently. Where the coyotes are heavily hunted, there is little dispersal because there is usually some territory that is vacant. It is where the coyotes are unmolested that the greatest dispersal takes place and this is particularly true in those eastern states where the coyotes have complete protection. The protection guarantees that colonization of the new areas will be achieved in the shortest possible time.

LIFE SPAN

Studies show 57 percent of coyote pups die or are killed by 7 months of age, most within the first 2 weeks. Potential life span like dog's, about 12–15 years. One in wild in New Mexico found 9 years after being tagged as a pup. Record: 18 1/2 years, a coyote in National Zoological Park, Washington, D.C.

SIGN

Tracks often seen in snow, dust, sand, and mud, with track of front foot 2 1/2 inches long by 2 inches wide, hind foot 2 1/4 inches by 1 3/4 inches. Track is narrow and outside toes more in line behind inside toes than with dog or wolf. Scent stations also seen, identified by urine stains in snow near grass clump or protruding rock. Both male and female use scent posts and both may urinate with leg lifted, though male with leg pointed backward and female with leg forward. No attempt made to cover scat, which is frequently seen near roads and trails. Scat more common when coyote has fed on vegetation. Den sites kept hidden particularly when coyote hunted or trapped. Dens located along dry washes, stream beds, canyon sides, etc. Coyote one of the largest animals to make or utilize an earthen den. Den can be identified by prey remnants around entrance and nearby vegetation flattened by pups.

ENEMIES

Formerly the wolf was the chief enemy when the two species coexisted often. Today the dog is the major enemy, most of which chase coyotes but only racing dogs have the speed to catch one. In far north in deep snow, lynx can kill weakened coyote. Bears and mountain lions kill coyote pups but seldom get chance at adults. Golden eagles kill pups and attack adults occasionally. More coyotes killed by disease than predation: mange, distemper, heartworm, rabies. Coyotes frequent scratchers, plagued by ticks, lice, mites, mosquitoes, fleas; also internal parasites.

HUMAN RELATIONS

Man's relationship with the coyote changed with the introduction of sheep into the coyote's habitat. The early explorers and the early settlers had no quarrel with the coyote. To many of the Indian tribes the coyote was a friend, a relative, an ancestor or a deity. The Navajo Indians, who are sheep and goat herders, have always had a reverent respect for the coyote. Their losses to the coyote have always been minimal because they herd their flocks. The introduction of large flocks of sheep into the coyote's habitat by the white ranchers changed the status of the coyote for all time.

I was raised on a farm and can understand the enmity that some of the ranchers felt toward the coyotes threatening their livelihood. I am also a naturalist and cannot understand some of the ranchers' avowed determination to exterminate all coyotes, at any cost and by any means. I can go along with the control of individual destruction of animals or even widespread control in areas of heavy depredations; I just cannot go along with the extirpation of any species.

Bounties have been placed on the coyote for more than 100 years and have never been practical. Bounties are usually a political ploy and are too subject to abuse. Today very few states pay bounties.

The widespread use of poisons has been discontinued, although the poison sodium cyanide is being used in the M44 "coyote getter" type of device, which shoots poison into the coyote's mouth when the baited trigger is pulled.

Aerial hunting by the general public has been discontinued, although it is still used by government agencies in emergencies.

Steel traps are still one of the most widely used methods of reducing coyote numbers locally and, when skillfully set, this method can be selective. As the animals caught are not killed, nongame species can be released. Catching coyotes in live traps is impossible.

Much experimentation is being done with such antifertility drugs as diethylstilbestrol. This drug is placed inside chunks of tallow which are then spread over a wide area during the coyote's breeding season. To date, the results have not been good.

Tests are being continued where lithium chloride is placed in collars around the necks of the lambs and adult sheep. When the coyotes attack the sheep and break the collar, the taste of the chemical makes the coyotes sick and they develop an aversion to sheep.

Experiments using tabasco and other superhot concoctions are also being put on sheep in order to discourage the coyotes from killing them. Only moderate success has been achieved with these methods. Much more research should be done along these lines because they are methods that are acceptable to almost everyone. And we do need sheep, not only for food but because wool, a natural fiber, becomes more important as oil-based synthetics become scarce.

That the all-out control methods used by the United States Government in the past against the coyote have failed can be seen by the following:

In 1946 an estimated 294,000 coyotes were killed in the 17 western sheep-producing states by federal control agents. After 28 years of continual and concentrated efforts to trap, shoot, poison and otherwise destroy coyotes, the federal control agents reported a kill of 295,400 coyotes in the same 17 states in 1974. This is why it is mandatory that all new, effective means of coyote control be explored.

COMMERCIAL VALUE

Reports from 30 of 48 contiguous states: 1976–77, 320,323 coyotes, compiled by IAFWA. Take from other states would add about 50,000–75,000 to total. Average price per pelt 1976–77, $45, total $14,414,535. Today pelts bring $100 each.

GRAY WOLF, *Canis lupus* · RED WOLF, *Canis niger*

INTRODUCTION

There has always been, and will probably always be, a tremendous amount of controversy about the wolf. The discussion of no other species of wildlife causes as much admiration, animosity, conjecture, confusion and personal bias. More research has and is being done on the wolf than on any other species, with the exception of the white-tailed deer. Excellent, factual books are coming out on the wolf at the rate of two or three a year. The titles of some are listed in my bibliography. Adolph Murie started the in-depth studies with his work on the wolves of Mount McKinley in the early 1940s. All of this information is needed if we are to ensure that the management programs being devised are of the greatest benefit to man, to the wolf and to the wolf's world.

DESCRIPTION

There is disagreement among even the taxonomists over how many subspecies of wolves are currently found in North America. There are thought to be 18–20 subspecies and this number will probably shrink with reclassification.

The wolf looks like a very husky German shepherd with shaggy hair and shorter ears. The guard hairs on a wolf's winter coat are about 4 inches long. The dense, woolly undercoat is about 2 to 2½ inches in length. The hair of the mane or hackles down the neck and the center of the back is about 5 inches long with an enlarged tuft behind the shoulders. This tuft is not as conspicuous on the wolf as it is on the coyote. This may be the location of a sebaceous gland. The wolf, as do all canids, has scent glands in its anus, on the top of its tail and in the pads of its feet.

The Mexican wolf is the smallest subspecies with those in Alaska probably the largest. The eastern wolf averages about 60 pounds while there are many records of Alaskan wolves that have weighed 175 pounds. The Detroit *Free Press,* around 1960, had an article on what was claimed to be the heaviest wolf ever. The giant wolf weighed 210 pounds and was caught in a snare near the Porcupine Airport at Timmins in eastern Ontario. This wolf had a reputation as a cattle killer. It had a total length of 76 inches and measured 55 inches at the heart girth.

Male wolves vary in length from 5 to 6½ feet, fe-

The lobo, or buffalo wolf, was the largest subspecies of the wolf in North America. The last of the wild adult lobos were exterminated by the U.S. Biological Survey of 1932. This captive specimen is one of the offspring of the pups that were raised by a Dr. McCleery of Kane, Pennsylvania, when the last of the wild adult lobos were killed.

The timber, or gray, wolf, which has a much broader head and stockier body than the coyote.

males are 4½ to 6 feet. Of this length, the tail will be from 13 to 20 inches long. Adult wolves stand 26–32 inches high at the shoulder, although there are records of a few that were 36 inches. I have seen wolf skins over 8 feet in length and wish I had been able to measure the animal.

In coloration the wolves vary from pure white to coal black and there are tremendous variations even among litter mates. The Arctic wolves are white with black edging to some of the hairs. The most common color for the wolf is a grizzled-gray with darker markings on the back. The more southern wolves tend to be more rusty or sandy colored.

The red wolf's Latin name *niger* means "black" because naturalist William Bartram, who gave this wolf its scientific name back in 1789, did so from the black phase of this animal. The red or sandy-red coloration is much more common. It is believed that the red wolf is actually a hybrid between the small eastern wolf and

the coyote. If this is so, it should be very close in form to a similar hybrid, the eastern coyote. One of the great fears of biologists today is that the red wolf will be absorbed into the coyote population and disappear as a true breeding form and there is good basis for this fear. The red wolf may actually be bred out of existence.

The red wolf is much smaller than the gray wolf, an average adult male weighing about 55 pounds and a really large one weighing 75 pounds. They are leaner and more rangy-looking in appearance, a fact emphasized by their shorter hair and lighter weight on a frame that is almost as large as that of the gray wolf.

Wolves are cursorial animals, designed for running. They have the narrow chest that allows both feet on the same side of the body to be placed in line. The long legs are not only an advantage in running but they enable the wolf to travel in deeper, soft snow than most animals.

There are 5 toes on the front feet and 4 on the hind feet. As with all canids, the fifth toe, or dewclaw, is not a functional toe and does not register in the tracks.

The wolf has 42 teeth—12 incisors, 4 canines, 16

Note the patch of long shoulder mane hair common to both the wolf and the coyote.

Wolves are now found only in the northernmost areas of North America. I photographed this wolf using a 400-mm telephoto lens.

premolars and 10 molars. The jawbone is about 7½ inches long and the muscles of the jaws are very powerful. Wolves can splinter large bones to get at the marrow.

The large canine teeth are used primarily for grasping, although the wolf also uses them for slashing. The last premolar and the first molar in both jaws are known as carnassial teeth and are used for shearing meat into pieces that are small enough to be swallowed. The expression to "wolf" your food is apt because no wolf or other canid actually chews its food. Any piece of food that can be, is swallowed whole, and the stomach and the digestive tract do the work of breaking it down.

The wolf has large yellow eyes with black pupils. In areas where they are unmolested, the wolves carry on a good part of their activities during the daytime. Where they are active only at night, this is primarily because of the pressure put on them by man.

DISTRIBUTION

Gray wolf originally found from Mexico to Arctic and from Atlantic to Pacific coasts, although not in true deserts due to lack of food.

Earliest wildlife laws placed bounty on wolves, not for their danger to man (only case of attack on humans was by rabid wolf), but their heavy predation on livestock. Today wolves extirpated from most of contiguous 48 states. A few are in Wisconsin and upper peninsula of Michigan; largest population in Minnesota with about 1,200–1,500. Minnesota wolf no longer classified as endangered but as threatened, meaning some control can be used against wolves in 2 of 5 protection areas. Increase in wolf population (along with attacks on livestock and pets) brought reclassification.

Wolves also found in Glacier National Park (Montana), and Yellowstone (Wyoming), where 6 were sighted about 1976 after absence of years. Wolf killed by car in 1968 near Adirondack Park in New York although officially no wolves there. Wolves being taken in Quebec south of St. Lawrence River and in time will move across border to northern U.S. Adirondacks would be ideal for wolf although no plans to introduce it there.

Red wolf originally found in forest and swampland throughout southeastern U.S. from Atlantic coast to east Texas. Loss of habitat restrict it now to southwest Louisiana and southeast Texas. Two mated pairs recently released on Bull's Island, near Charleston, South Carolina, in attempt to maintain species (one pair swam back to mainland).

TRAVEL

Wolves are territorial and usually have well-defined boundaries that they and other wolves honor. The amount of territory occupied and the amount of traveling done within that territory are determined by the availability of food. Extreme hunger may cause the wolves to invade the territory of another pack. Pack territories may range from 100 square miles to 600 square miles and during the winter the wolves may be forced to migrate to areas where they can find their prey animals, returning to their own territories in the spring. It is not uncommon for wolves to travel 40–60

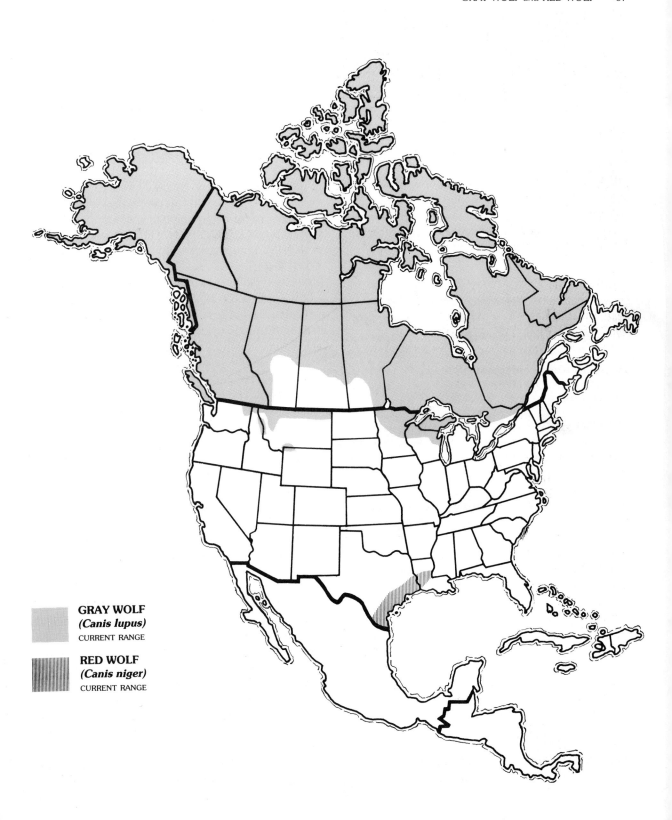

GRAY WOLF
(Canis lupus)
CURRENT RANGE

RED WOLF
(Canis niger)
CURRENT RANGE

miles per day, although they do not do this unless forced to.

In 1966 while I was studying foxes in McKinley National Park, my good friend Charlie Travers and his wife, Ruth, were studying wolves that were hunting caribou in the park. After fruitless weeks of searching for the wolves' den, they came to the conclusion that the den must have been outside the park boundary. This meant that the wolves would have to be traveling at least 50–60 miles round trip to feed their pups.

LOCOMOTION

Wolves walk, trot and lope. They are most famous for their trot which they use in traveling from place to place, a gait they can keep up for 20–24 hours. It has now been well established that the wolves' average speed while trotting is about 5 miles per hour. There are many records of wolves traveling as many as 40–60 miles at a time and one record of 124 miles in one day.

When wolves catch wind of their prey they usually continue in their follow-the-leader, single-file manner. When the prey is sighted, they spread out and, with barking and excitement, charge. This charge is to test the prey and also to surround it if possible. If the prey runs, the wolves then lope at speeds of up to 40 miles per hour. This speed has been verified several times and once for a distance of 4 miles.

Wolves swim more than any other North American canids. The areas they inhabit in the north are laced with streams and rivers. When prey escapes from a wolf by swimming out in a lake or crossing a river, it is not that the wolf can't swim at that time, but that it prefers not to.

FOOD

Wolves will eat 6–8 pounds of food per day if fed on daily basis. In wild they more commonly gorge 18–20 pounds at one time, sleep for 15–20 hours, and may not hunt again for 2–4 days or until hungry. If prey very large, such as moose or caribou, carcass is revisited until all is eaten except skin, hair and contents of stomach. All but largest bones and antlers taken away to be cracked and marrow extracted. Skin consumed in times of scarcity.

Groups of large prey are tested to determine weakest of group by repeated charges. Wolves kill big game about 10 percent of the time they attack. Determined stand by cow or bull moose can face wolves down. I observed 2 young caribou bulls tease a wolf by provoking it to chase them and running a quick circuit to provoke it again. A lone wolf can almost never catch a lone caribou when both are healthy, but wolf pack can catch almost anything if it is determined, even the healthiest bull caribou in its prime. Wild sheep taken only when crossing valleys between winter and summer ranges, not in more advantageous home range where they can escape along cliffs.

Wolves at one time important to control of deer population in U.S. Pattern has been for deer to expand as settlements cut forest and forced wolf out. Study shows pack of 8 wolves successful in 46 percent of 36 chases of deer, 29 killed in 63 days—1 deer for 8 wolves every 2.2 days. Most deer killed by "hamstringing," bringing deer down by cutting tendons of hind leg. Study showed 10 percent of deer herd removed, although wolves not responsible for entire figure because study took place in winter and some deer would have died of starvation.

I inferred decline in wolf population in McKinley National Park due to large beaver population. Overlarge colony had removed food from immediate area and far searches for food made beaver vulnerable to predation. When wolves returned beavers were wiped out, victims more of their own population explosion than of wolf predation.

In spring and summer wolf feeds on readily available small animals: grouse, ptarmigans, varying hares, marmots, ducks, geese, small birds and their eggs, mice and voles. One wolf seen eating 22 mice. Salmon caught in shallows during salmon runs, and wolf eats dead and dying salmon floating on surface after spawning. Eats less vegetation than any other North

A gray, or timber, wolf, trotting: its most common gait. The wolf is tireless and has been known to travel 60 miles or more in a single day.

American canid, but will eat some abundant berries and occasionally grasses.

BEHAVIOR

Wolves are highly intelligent animals. They have the ability to learn and to develop responses to conditions that are different from the responses that would be made by instinct. They also have the ability to remember what they have learned.

Wolves that live where they are unmolested have a stable and complex social order which governs all of their activities. When the wolf family is fragmented, their social order, like that of humans, breaks down completely.

Each wolf family, or pack, has its own well-defined territory that is guarded against the incursion of other packs. There is usually a buffer zone that amounts to a no-man's land between the rivals' territories. Researchers have just discovered that in these buffer zones, prey animals thrive because they are not hunted. The surplus prey animals then spill over into one wolf territory or the other, where they are hunted, but the core area remains inviolate.

Wolf packs are usually family groups consisting of the adult parents, the yearling pups and the pups of the year. Other adults that may or may not be related may also be members. Pack sizes or groupings may change according to circumstances. The average pack consists of 7 or 8 members. In the winter, two or more packs may join together, only to split and regroup almost continuously. A pack of 15 may split to 8 and 7 animals one day and be 12 and 3 the next.

Pack size appears to be determined by the number of wolves that can be fed from a prey animal and a minimization of the amount of conflict that would occur in maintaining dominance among the members of a really large group.

One thing that researchers have not been able to figure out is why one adult strange wolf will be accepted into a pack while another strange wolf will be driven off or even killed.

At the top of the pack's hierarchy is the alpha or dominant male and his mate. The beta wolf is the number-two male wolf and is the assistant to the leader. These three wolves dominate all the other wolves and their activities. A strange wolf may be adopted into the pack but has a low standing in the hierarchy until by age or strength it can work its way up. However, strange wolves do join organized packs and this eventual infusion of new genes prevents excessive inbreeding which is usually detrimental to a species.

Occasionally, in winter two packs may merge but split up again when food is more available. In the recent study by Durwood Allen and David Mech of the wolves on Isle Royale, Michigan, 17 wolves were recorded as regularly hunting together.

In wilderness areas the wolves may hunt at any time

of the day or night, although they most frequently spend the warmer parts of the day sleeping. In the far north it is either daylight or dark, depending upon the season, but most activity takes place in the late afternoon and evening.

Cold weather does not bother the wolves. They curl up in the snow, cover their faces and paws with their bushy tails and go to sleep. They are often buried by drifting snow which really helps them to conserve energy as it acts as a blanket of insulation. It has been found that during periods of food shortages the wolves spend far more time sleeping than is usual, conserving their energy.

Deep, powdery snow is a handicap to the wolves because they can only move through it by exhaustive bounding. At such times the wolves take to traveling on windswept rivers and lakes or high ridges.

Where wolves have been hunted from the air they learn to shun the open areas and to seek shelter as soon as they hear a plane's engine. Where researchers have accustomed the wolves to planes, the wolves go about their activities with no fear of even low-flying, circling aircraft.

Wolves are friendly animals, as befits the precursors of the domestic dog. They spend a lot of time playing, even the adults engaging in activities that can only be described as play and for only the benefits that can be derived from play. Although wolves do fight among themselves, such fighting is kept to the barest minimum. The recognition of the individual's place in the social hierarchy reduces the need for fighting. The adherence to this system is more analogous to the caste system of the India of yesterday, where everyone knew his station in life, than the more upward mobility found in the systems of most Western nations.

Their responses to man, if the pups are taken at an early age, are the same as they would be to other wolves. They become very affectionate.

Even full-grown wolves that have been caught in traps often wag their tails and go through the submissive gestures when the trapper approaches. My good friend Charlie Smith, an Algonquin Indian, told me that his nephew had on several occasions removed full-grown wolves from his traps, tied their legs together and carried them home alive without the wolf attempting to bite.

SENSES

Sense of smell most important. Like dogs, wolves have wet noses to help them capture scents, which are gases and must be mixed with moisture to be detected. Wolf's long muzzle houses chamber of nostrils that is lined by epithelium containing mucous membranes and nerve endings, which carry molecules of scent to olfactory bulbs, from which electrical impulses are generated, go to brain stem and scent is identified. Wolves observed detecting prey at 300 yards when downwind, missing prey completely when upwind. Under ideal conditions wolf found cow moose and two calves 1 1/2 miles away.

Hearing is excellent, beyond human's in high frequencies. Wolves have been known to respond to howling 4 miles distant.

Vision good at detecting movement at great distances. Although wolves are color-blind this may not be handicap as most prey not colorful. Easily identifies stationary man.

Taste probably plays small role.

COMMUNICATION

Wolves have a very elaborate communication system. With the exception of the chimpanzees and dolphins, probably more studies have been done on their methods of transmitting information than on any other mammals. They use a wide and comprehensive set of visual, auditory and olfactory signals.

Wolves define their territorial boundaries by urinating on the perimeter, much as other canids have scent stations. A major difference being that the wolves' marking spots are as effective as a fence. The odor of the wolf's anal gland is particularly individual and is a personal identification.

Wolf body postures and facial expressions have kept scores of researchers busy for the last several decades. The higher the wolf's tail is held, the more domi-nant its status. Each level, from the tail being held almost straight up to being curled between the legs, runs the gamut of emotions from self-confidence, to threat, to being depressed, to defense, to submission.

The ears and the curling of the lip, exposing the ca-nines, are the important features of the wolf's facial expressions. The normal position is for the ears to be up and forward and the lips held together. An anxious wolf holds his ears back but high. Wolves threaten by keeping their ears up and wrinkling their upper lips so the canines are fully exposed. An attacking animal has the same lip expression but the jaws are held wide open and the ears go back. Most of us have seen the same expressions on dogs and the latter is especially terrifying used by a German shepherd or Doberman pinscher.

A sign of affection and of submissiveness is "muz-zling." This is done by lesser wolves appearing to kiss or actually licking a dominant wolf under the chin. Puppies do this to get the parents to regurgitate food for them. This is very similar to the action done by young gulls, gannets, and others to get their parents to regurgitate food.

A wolf that has been beaten in a fight will, like a dog pup, roll over on its back, exposing its throat and often urinating. This is clearly the "I give up" sign and it usually, although not always, is honored.

Everyone who has ever had anything to do with any member of the dog family knows all too well the pen-chant they all have for rolling in the most odorous substances they can find. They love to rub such ma-terial in their ruff or hackles till they also reek. And as yet we don't know why.

Wolves howl, whimper, growl, bark and whine. Of these, the wolf is most famous for its howling. It is tru-ly one of the most thrilling sounds to be heard in the world. I rate it with hearing an angry elephant trum-pet.

When a wolf howls, the angle at which it holds its head above the ground has a bearing on the sound. Most wolves start off low and raise the notes and their muzzles as they continue. The howl lasts anywhere

from one to 11 seconds. Wolves do not howl in uni-son. If they are howling in concert, when two wolves reach the same note, one wolf immediately changes pitch. Wolves may howl at any hour of the day. They do very little howling during the time the pups are in the den so as not to betray its location.

One of the main objectives of howling is to assem-ble the family members or the pack, either before the hunt, to hunt or, afterward, to reassemble the group.

Wolves can easily be triggered into howling either by imitation of their howls or by high-pitched mechan-ical means such as sirens or whistles. In many areas, particularly Algonquin Park in Ontario, people go out in groups to call and listen to the howling of the wolves.

BREEDING

The wolf leads an exemplary family life. The parents are devoted to each other and to their pups. To call a human male who chases after all the girls a "wolf" is a disservice to the animal. Wolves remain mated for life.

Young wolves are capable of breeding at 22 months of age. One of the most important pieces of information coming out of the latest wolf research is that these young wolves are prevented from breeding by the older wolves. This enforced birth control limits the size of the pack so that the pack's territory and food supply balance. The dominant wolf pair is usu-ally the only pair that breeds in each pack. An unmo-lested pack has a tendency to maintain a stable population. Where the wolves are heavily hunted and the pack is fragmented, the young wolves then breed and the increased numbers of breeding pairs in an area actually raise the wolf numbers to offset the hunt-ing losses. This enforced breeding control within the pack also leads to dispersal within the pack which also helps to maintain the pack's size.

The amount of howling that wolves do increases in January and February as the breeding season nears. The wolves have a long courtship period in which a great deal of affection and body contact is displayed.

The female has a single estrous period that lasts for 4 to 5 weeks. There are 2 weeks of intense courtship and about 2 weeks in which the female will accept the male sexually. During the latter 2 weeks the pair will copulate numerous times and may become tied-up several times. This fastening is caused by the male's penis becoming so enlarged that it cannot be withdrawn from the female. The purpose served by this extreme swelling is not known and in the wild it does put the animals, so fastened, at a physical disadvantage.

Often the wolves, if they have previously mated, have their den sites picked out. If not, as soon as copulation has been completed, the search for a den is made. If the wolves have to dig a den of their own, they prefer to do so in soft soil, on south-facing riverbanks or eskers. Usually more than one den site is selected or dug so that if the pups have to be moved everything is prepared ahead of time. Wolves frequently utilize dens that other animals, such as foxes, have made. They have also been known to use abandoned beaver houses. They prefer the dens to be in an elevated area for good drainage but close to water when possible.

BIRTH AND YOUNG

Sixty-three days after breeding, the female wolf brings forth an average litter of 6 pups. The newborn pups have a short, woolly, dark brown coat. The pups are blind at birth with their eyes opening about 12–15 days later. The pups' eyes are blue at first, gradually changing to yellow in about 2 months. The pups weigh about one pound at birth.

The mother stays with her pups almost continuously for the first week, nursing the pups and giving them the warmth they crave. She is fed by her mate or one of the other adult wolves.

The pups can walk quite well at 2 weeks of age and by 3 weeks are venturing out of the den. About this time the pups also begin to fight with one another to achieve dominance.

The feeding and care of the pups is done not only by the parents but also by the yearlings and other adult members of the pack. These wolves often baby-sit while the mother goes off hunting. Weaning takes place between 6 and 8 weeks, although it may be later with indulgent mothers.

At 3 months the pups are really no longer pups but are young wolves. Their play is more of a learning process and they begin to follow after the parents.

LIFE SPAN

Potential like large dog's, 10–12 years. Some in captivity reach 17 years.

SIGN

Track most frequent sign, conspicuous on sandy lakeshores, in mud near ponds, dust of dirt roads and trails. Tracks of large wolf easy to see, measuring 5¼ inches long by 4¼ inches wide, and areas well tracked up because most travel in family groups. On tundra or rocky riverbeds where tracks impossible most conspicuous sign is scat, measuring 1 inch in diameter and 3–5 inches long, composed mainly of hair and bone fragments of prey. Scats do not disintegrate readily but bleach with age. Feeding little on vegetation, wolves void less often than other canids. In winter urine stains of scent posts and boundary markers easily seen. Dens identifiable by pile of earth removed to make it, large entrance holes, and considerable skin, hair, and bone fragments in area.

ENEMIES

Adult's only enemy is man. Bears and mountain lions can be outfought by pack or outrun by wolf's size, speed and strength. Pups taken occasionally by large predators. Wolves susceptible to mange, tularemia, distemper, encephalitis and rabies. Most attacks on humans in Europe by rabid wolves. Among internal parasites are tapeworms, roundworms, and flukes. Wolf also afflicted by lice, fleas, ticks, flies and mosquitoes.

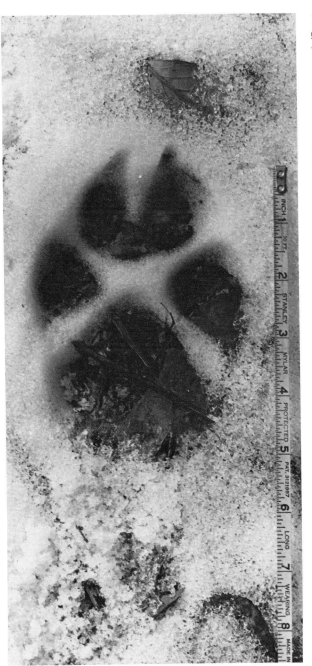

The huge size of a wolf can readily be seen in its large tracks.

HUMAN RELATIONS

The early Europeans brought their fear of wolves to North America with them. They had learned to fear the rabid ones in Europe. C. H. D. Clarke, a wolf expert from Canada, offers strong evidence, however, that the most famous European killer wolf, known as "the Beast of Gevaudan," was actually two wolf-dog hybrids and that there was no evidence of rabies in either of the animals when they were killed.

There is also no denying that in the period of 1764–67 these two hybrids and their cohorts killed more than 100 persons and ate most of them.

And there is no denying that the wolves in North America wreaked havoc on the domestic livestock of the early settlers. The settlers replaced the wildlife with their domestic animals and the wolves did the same in their diet. Some of the famed individual "lobo" or buffalo wolves killed $25,000 to $50,000 in livestock. This large wolf, *Canis lupus nubilus,* is extinct in the wild although offspring have been preserved by Jack Lynch in "Loboland" near Gardiner, Washington.

The controversy over the wolf continues. It is an incontrovertible fact that the population of wolves will continue to decline as our human population increases. Wolves need wilderness and so do humans and for many of us the quality of the wilderness is enhanced just by knowing that there are wolves there sharing such places with us.

COMMERCIAL VALUE

IAFWA statistics: 1,076 wolves taken in Alaska, 1976–77, $200 average price, $215,200 total. In Canada: 6,150 taken, $63.18 average price, $388,569 total (most Canadian wolves taken in Quebec, where they are smaller then Alaskan, which may explain difference in price).

ARCTIC FOX, *Alopex lagopus*

INTRODUCTION

The Arctic fox is not a true fox, although it is a canid and is closely related to the foxes. Red foxes have been crossbred with the Arctic fox but the offspring are sterile. It had originally been named *Vulpes lagopus* in Latin by Linnaeus in 1758 but was changed to *Alopex lagopus* by Johann Kaup in 1829 to show that it is not a true fox. *Alopex* is the Greek word for fox. *Lagos* is Latin for "hare" and *pous* means "foot." This part of the fox's name came about because in the winter its feet have a dense covering of hair for better insulation and to increase its foot size for ease in traveling over soft snow, like the hare's foot.

DESCRIPTION

The Arctic fox is a small, chunky, short-legged fox having small, rounded ears. Its body shape and short ears are adaptations to the polar regions, its home. The body shape conforms to Bergman's Law: a larger, compact body size in relation to weight and extremities conserves heat loss. Allen's Law limits the size of the extremities because the smaller they are, within functional ability, the less heat loss. Dr. William Pruitt of the Department of Biological Sciences, University of Alaska, claims that the Arctic fox's body is unaffected by temperatures as low as −60° F.

The Arctic fox weighs 8 to 10 pounds with a top weight of about 15 pounds. There is one record weight of 21 pounds. They stand 11–12 inches high at the shoulder and have short legs, about 6 inches from the armpit to the toe tip. They have a total body length of 32–36 inches overall, of which 11 inches is tail length. The fur of the Arctic fox is extremely dense as befits a creature living in the Arctic. The guard hairs

are about 3 inches long and the undercoat is 2 inches long.

The Arctic fox has 2 distinct color phases in its winter coat, pure white and blue. The white phase is the most common. The blue phase is a distinct contradiction. The white phase provides the Arctic fox with useful camouflage in snow. The only black parts are the eyes, lips, nose and claws. The blue phase runs from a slatey-blue to almost black. That both color phases are successful is proven because the blue phase has not disappeared. If it were a serious handicap, the fox-

The Arctic fox's white coat provides excellent camouflage.

The soft dense fur of the Arctic fox enables it to withstand the biting cold of the winters in the far north. (Photo: Irene Vandermolen)

es having those genes would have been eliminated through evolution years ago. A saving factor, perhaps, is that in the winter, darkness blankets the northern regions for 20 or more hours out of every 24. The blue phase is dominant on the Aleutian Islands and the Pribilof Islands, where there were many blue fox farms during the early 1900s.

The blue phase, because it is a more luxurious fur and scarcer, comprising only one to 2 percent of the total Arctic fox population, commands a price of three to five times the white phase. The blue fox phase is more common on islands and along the seacoast while the white phase is more common in the colder interior areas.

In the summer both white and blue color phase foxes turn a brownish-gray color and are indistinguishable. The Arctic fox is the only canid in the world that goes through a seasonal color change.

The Arctic fox goes through two complete molts per year; most foxes have only one. In April or May the winter coat is shed and the short-haired coat is worn throughout the summer. In September the foxes molt again and the winter coat is then acquired. As is true with most mammals having a two-season molt, the adults usually go through the change before the young of the year do.

The Arctic fox has 42 teeth—12 incisors, 4 canines, 16 premolars and 10 molars. As with all canids, the fourth premolar and the first molar are the carnassial or shearing teeth.

It has 5 toes on its front feet, 4 being functional and the fifth toe, corresponding to our thumb, is up on the inside of the leg and is known as a dewclaw. There are 4 toes on the hind feet. In the summer, only 4 toes show in the tracks of any of the feet. In the winter, no toes show at all. The hairs on the feet become so long that the pads are completely covered and protected.

All foxes have scent glands on the top of their tails and the Arctic fox is no exception. When I wrote of the Arctic fox in 1968, I said that it had no offensive odor because no researcher ever reported it, and some observers still claim they have none. Since then,

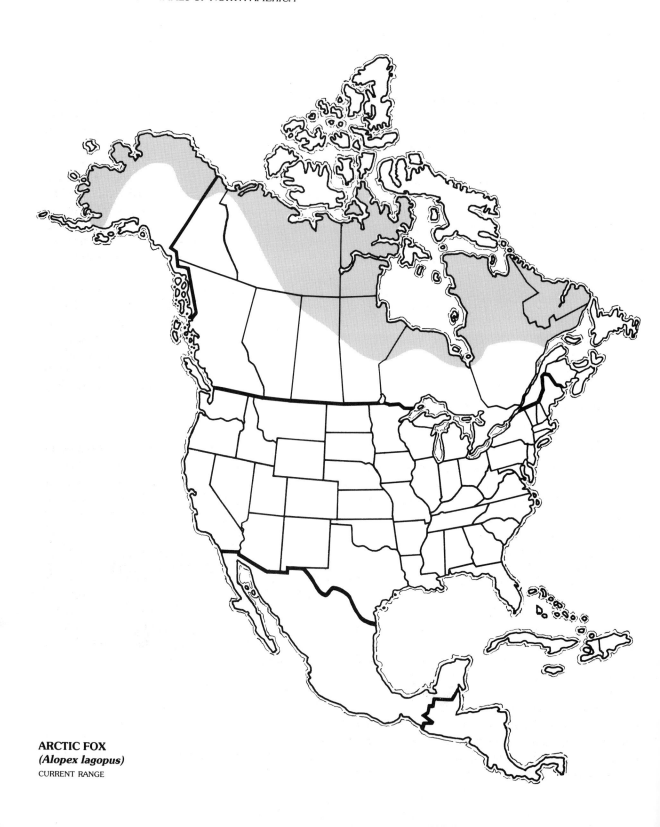

ARCTIC FOX
(Alopex lagopus)
CURRENT RANGE

through personal experience, I have learned differently.

Friends of mine had obtained an Arctic fox in Alaska as a pup. They kept the fox in their apartment in New York City and walked it on a leash in Central Park. Problems developed when a policeman realized that the "dog" looked different from any dog he had ever seen. Forced to get rid of their fox, my friends gave it to me. My first reaction was to the reek of its odor. Red foxes are famous for their penetrating, acrid, offensive odor. Gray foxes do not have this heavy odor but the Arctic foxes definitely do. I don't see how my friends stood the odor of the fox in their apartment. Their apartment must have reeked, too.

DISTRIBUTION

Found in treeless tundra throughout world in polar and subpolar regions. In North America found from Labrador to James Bay and from Greenland to Aleutians.

TRAVEL

The Arctic fox travels more than any of the other foxes; it often ranges hundreds of miles. In the summer, when the living is good, the foxes have a very limited range. They usually establish just enough territory in the spring to guarantee that they, as parents, can secure enough food to feed their young. Where den sites are common, the foxes may live as much as 5 miles apart. Where den sites are scarce or localized, the foxes may live in fairly close proximity to one another. Sometimes the foxes live in what be called communal villages.

The distance that the Arctic fox travels is not usually determined by choice but by necessity.

Wildlife researcher Herbert Spencer first recognized the cyclic occurrences in some types of mammals, particularly those in the Arctic. This work was later refined and expanded by Robert Collett, Gordon Hewitt, Ernest Thompson Seton and Charles Elton.

The voles and lemmings of the polar regions are on a 4-year cycle, fluctuating wildly between periods of great abundance and scarcity. The Arctic fox is also geared to this 4-year cycle because these rodents form the bulk of its diet. However, as is usual in such prey-predator relationships, the crash for the predator occurs one year after that of the prey. When the populations of the rodents of the north crash, the Arctic foxes and the snowy owls emigrate hundreds of miles to the south in search of food. In most instances, neither the foxes nor the owls survive to make the journey back north, hence my use of the word emigrate.

At other times the foxes may travel hundreds of miles on floating ice masses. In the winter of 1970–71, ice masses brought the white Arctic foxes to the Pribilof Islands, which had a resident population of blue foxes. Polar bears are inveterate travelers and the foxes often tag along after the bears to scavenge upon whatever food scraps the bears may leave after filling their own bellies.

LOCOMOTION

On many of the islands where the Arctic fox lives, it is the tip of the food chain pyramid; it is the top predator. Because of this and because of its comparatively short legs, the Arctic fox does not have to, nor is it able to, run as fast as most foxes. It has been estimated that the top speed of an Arctic fox is about 25 miles per hour. It is very light on its feet and seems literally to float along. Much of this fox's food is obtained on the ice cliffs and it is very nimble and surefooted. When pursued by larger predators, the Arctic fox will frequently escape by climbing on the cliffs or seek refuge deep among the jumble of rocks at the foot of the cliffs.

The Arctic fox usually trots and can keep up this pace indefinitely.

It can swim but, like all foxes, prefers not to. Its fur is not waterproof and the frigid ocean water penetrates to the skin. The increased weight of water that saturates its fur soon destroys the fox's flotation abilities.

The Arctic fox follows the polar bear in winter to feed upon the carcasses of seals that the bear has killed and fed upon.

Many times Arctic foxes are trapped on ice pans that are a hundred miles or more from land. As these sheets of ice move southward and into warmer water, they break into increasingly smaller pieces. In time the foxes either die of starvation or drown.

FOOD

Food supply often feast or famine. Mostly eats animals, although some berries eaten during long Arctic summer. Each day 1–2 pounds of food eaten. Beaches patrolled regularly in search of sea urchins, clams, oysters and mussels exposed at low tide. Sea fleas, small crustaceans, favored food. Dead fish and bodies of marine mammals form large part of diet. Dead whales attract foxes from miles away—Eskimos report over 300 Arctic foxes taken in vicinity of one whale carcass. Such a carcass provides food for that many foxes for many months. Birthing sites of fur seals and sea lions provide food in form of placentas discharged after birth and pups themselves on occasion.

May, June and July bring abundance of seabirds, and birds nesting in less desirable spots away from cliffs easy prey for fox, which takes eggs, young and adult birds. With food plentiful foxes gorge themselves and cache remainder in holes in tundra, crevasses of cliffs and under rocks. In Alaska fox cache revealed 65 crested auklets, 37 least auklets, 1 whiskered auklet, 1 parakeet auklet, 1 pigeon guillemot and others. On Bobrof Island 103 petrels, 6 tufted puffins, 4 least auklets and 1 pigeon guillemot in cache. On one island of Semisopochnoi group 107 least auklets, 18 crested auklets, 3 tufted puffins, 1 horned puffin, 1 murre and 7 fork-tailed petrels in one cache. Arctic fox an efficient hunter, industrious at caching, and eats many types of birds.

During winter foxes move onto ice where they scavenge. On ice they follow polar bears; in some areas on land they follow wolves, but this is dangerous because fox can become prey for wolf. Seabirds have disappeared by this time, and small animals snug beneath snow. Fox will follow polar bear until bear kills a seal, eats only half of prey, and leaves to sleep, when fox can move up and feed on carcass. If hunting is good bear will move on to hunt another prey without returning to seal carcass. If hunting is poor, bear will kill and eat fox if possible, although fox generally too fast for this to happen. During starvation foxes have been known to eat each other.

BEHAVIOR

The activities of the animals in the north are geared entirely to their stomachs. Daylight and darkness plays no part. In the summer it is daylight all the time and dark most of the time in the winter. When the foxes are hungry, they hunt; when they are fed and are sleepy, they sleep. Most of the Arctic animals' activities are seldom influenced by man because men are infrequently seen.

Because the Arctic foxes live where the earth is permanently frozen beneath the surface, they have a ready-made ice box. By digging to the permafrost, the fox's stored food is kept fresh and preserved for long periods of time. These caches, although perhaps not sufficient to last the fox throughout the winter, are tremendously important to its survival.

Usually the Arctic fox has no fear of man, and thus it is comparatively easy to trap, especially when food is scarce. When food is plentiful, fewer foxes are trapped but more are shot because, although they may not respond to food, their curiosity is as great as ever. On several of my trips to Alaska I had these foxes follow me, barking and squalling. I do not know if I was near a den area but they followed me much farther than was necessary for that reason.

Its dense coat of fur gives the Arctic fox such good insulation that it does not have to seek shelter in even the bitterest of storms. With its large, fluffy tail held over its face and feet, the Arctic fox remains curled in a ball and is often covered by the snow. Of course the snow then also acts as a blanket of insulation.

Water is never a problem for the Arctic fox because it can lick ice or eat snow in the wintertime and drink the fresh water from the snow melt-off in the summer.

SENSES

Smell most important, fox able to relocate cache under drifted snow. Foxes claimed to have gathered from 30 miles away when whale or other large mammal is beached.

Hunting in or near bird rookeries done mostly by sight because smell of birds and excrement overpowering.

Hearing highly developed despite small ears. In vast flat habitat with little protection, necessary for foxes to hear soft footfalls of bear or other predator.

COMMUNICATION

The first time I heard an Arctic fox bark, it startled me. It sounded as if someone were strangling a goose. It was a long, raspy, drawn-out vocalization that descended in notes. It was a call that I was to hear many times in many places in Alaska because the Arctic fox barks frequently at what it considers intruders into its area. It also makes other, more foxlike whines, yelps, growls, howls and hisses.

BREEDING

Arctic foxes that live on islands or live inland probably remain mated for life. The foxes that move out on the ice probably seek new mates because they may end their winter's wandering hundreds of miles from where they started. Dens on the Pribilof Islands have been used continuously by known foxes over a period of many years.

The breeding season commences in late February when the foxes pair up or reunite. There is much barking, chasing and fighting. Rival males fight viciously over unmated females. The female Arctic fox does not discharge vaginal blood, which marks the preestrous period in all other canids.

Copulation takes place in March or early April depending upon the latitude of the foxes. After this cementing of the nuptial bond, the foxes turn their attention to locating, preparing or renovating a den before the pups are born. The den is usually dug into a gravelly stream bank, esker or south-facing slope or it may be located in among the broken rocks of a talus heap.

BIRTH AND YOUNG

After the crash of the Arctic fox population, the rebound is swift. Two factors account for this—an almost unlimited, increasing food supply, and the fox's fecundity. One Arctic fox female had 23 embryos in her body. Naturally, even with a superabundance of food, it would be impossible for a female to raise that many young. Litters of 10–12 are fairly common, although 6 to 8 is the usual number of pups that can be successfully raised.

The pups are born after a gestation period of 52 days and the pups weigh 2 to 3 ounces at birth. The fur on the pups is short, fuzzy and brown. Their eyes open somewhere between the 9th and 12th days.

The parents are very good providers and the male is exemplary, feeding first the female and later the pups, until the female is able to join in the hunting again.

By the time the pups are a month old, sooner than other foxes, they crawl out of their den to play in the sunlight. It is as if they instinctively know enough to take advantage of the very limited sunshine that is available in the north, soaking up the additional vitamin D. The pups soon follow after their parents when they have to hunt food, thus learning how to hunt for themselves.

The drastic shortening of the days portends the coming of winter with its darkness and food shortages. At this time the fox families split up voluntarily or else the young are driven from the area by the parents. It is important for the foxes' survival that they spread their population over the widest range possible. This forced dispersal is also crucial to guarantee that the food cached by the adults is available to them when they need it.

LIFE SPAN

Potential: 12–14 years, as learned from extensive records of foxes grown in captivity. Few wild foxes achieve this age.

SIGN

Arctic foxes themselves the most common sign; being curious and fearless they watch humans' activities while sitting on ridges, barking almost constantly.

Tracks easily identifiable, smaller than wolf's and slightly larger than red fox's, larger than house cat's, and nail marks show. Dens easily seen by earth pulled out and spread near entrance. Scats contain feathers of birds or fur of voles, lemmings or hares.

ENEMIES

Two major natural enemies are starvation, when population peaks the year following crash of prey population, and disease, rampant among foxes weakened by starvation and who come in frequent contact with each other. Man the next major enemy, and wolf, wolverine, lynx and polar bear all capable of killing adult and pup foxes when they can catch them. Snowy owl known to have killed fox pups. Foxes plagued by mosquitoes, fleas and lice.

Encephalitis a major disease especially among northern foxes. Also the northern dog disease, apparently a form of distemper, which periodically wipes out populations of sled dogs, afflicts foxes. Immunity to encephalitis does not give immunity to northern dog disease. Rabies occasionally infects Arctic fox, but said to be a type not harmful to man, although does affect dogs. Frequent reports of "crazy" foxes appear throughout polar regions.

HUMAN RELATIONS

The beautiful pelt of the white Arctic fox has always been sought by the fur trade and its prices have usually been high. The first blue Arctic fox was recorded by Georg Steller, who, with Vitus Bering, was shipwrecked in 1741 on what is now known as Bering Island. When the sailors got ashore they found that the island was swarming with blue foxes. Many of the men were dying of scurvy and the foxes had to be kept from eating the sick men. Bering died and is buried on the island. Eight months after the shipwreck, the survivors had fashioned a boat and finally reached Kamchatka. Bering's voyage was of great interest to the Russians because through it they laid claim to Alaska and began to colonize it. One of the major interests was the great value of blue fox skins that Bering's men had brought with them. The Russians enslaved the Aleut Indians and forced them to hunt and to gather furs for them. In 1754 one ship alone had 7,000 blue fox pelts as part of its cargo.

Even today man's relation to the Arctic fox is one of constant exploitation.

COMMERCIAL VALUE

IAFWA statistics: 1976–77, 4,261 taken in Alaska, $36 average price, $153,396 total (no breakdown between white and blue phases). In Canada: 36,842 taken, $54.20 average price, $1,317,612 total (again no breakdown).

RED FOX, *Vulpes vulpes*

INTRODUCTION

People perceive not only foxes but everything else in their world according to the manner or degree in which it affects them. Farmers who allow their chickens to run loose and have them stolen by the fox hate them. Orchardists, who are plagued by rabbits and mice damaging their trees, love the fox because it feeds upon these pests. The grouse, quail and pheasant hunters are sure that the fox is responsible for every dip in their favorite game bird's population. The fox hunter, whether he be the hound-dog man or the red-coated horseman, thinks that the fox is the grandest animal in the world. The fox plays all of these roles and plays them well. He is an admirable animal, intelligent and adaptable. These qualities are universally recognized as portrayed in song, story and fable about the fox throughout the centuries.

The Latin name for the fox is *vulpes*. This generic name applies to both the European and North American red fox. At one time the species name for the former was also *vulpes* while for the latter it was *fulva*. Today, it is generally accepted that both of these foxes are the same and *fulva* is now used as a subspecific name.

The controversy stems from the fact that when the European settlers first came to this continent the red fox was found throughout Canada and most of New

The alertness and intelligence of the red fox can readily be seen in this portrait. (Photo: Irene Vandermolen)

England. It was not known from the southern regions of New York on south. Red foxes were imported for hunting by the plantation owners to Maryland around 1650 and released along the Eastern Shore. By 1670 the red fox had spread to Virginia. Around 1750 red foxes from England were released on Long Island and in New Jersey. At the same time the settlers had opened up the solid stands of forest throughout all of eastern North America, creating conditions favorable to the native red fox. It quickly expanded its range and has continued to do so even today.

DESCRIPTION

The European red fox is a larger, stockier animal than our native fox. As this body size difference and the distinctive skull characteristics are still apparent, it has been concluded that the European red fox has contributed nothing to the native species.

The size of a red fox is very deceiving. Its body, deprived of its fur coat, looks like a whippet or greyhound but is much smaller. However, the red fox, like those two dogs, is designed for running, having a long, lean body.

It is hard to convince people that the average red fox weighs 9 1/2 pounds. That is the average weight for the hundreds of red foxes that I have personally weighed in New Jersey. The largest red fox I ever caught weighed 11 3/4 pounds. The largest red fox I have ever weighed was given to me by my friend Joe Taylor in April 1967. This large male weighed 14 pounds 12 ounces, stood 16 inches high at the shoulder, was 42 inches in total length and had a heart girth of 15 3/4 inches. Its body size was no larger than most of the other large males I have measured; but it was in excellent condition and weighed more.

It must be remembered that of the 12 subspecies of red foxes found in North America, those in the North will be slightly larger and weigh more than their southern counterparts. Fox studies done in Indiana showed males weighing between 8.4 pounds and 13.4 pounds, averaging 11.57.

The female reds in that study weighed from 7.4 pounds to 12.5 pounds and averaged 9.28 pounds. Studies in Virginia had 11.7 pounds as the greatest weight for the males with 8.75 pounds being the average.

Walter Lasch of Conneaut Lake, Pennsylvania, shot a wild red male on January 15, 1967, that weighed 16 pounds 1 ounce. Ernest Thompson Seton wrote of a

Red foxes have exceptionally long silky coats. The long fur and bushy tail in wintertime make the fox appear to weigh much more than its average 9½ pounds.

red male raised on a fur farm that weighed 16 3/4 pounds. This exceptional weight is the result of unending food and a lack of exercise.

The tail of the red fox is 13–16 inches in length, is very bushy and cylindrical in shape. It is usually white-tipped with the amount of white varying from just a few terminal hairs to a distal tuft of 2–3 inches. All red fox pups are born with a white tail tip but the tip is sometimes bitten off while playing or fighting.

The color of the red fox varies greatly with the southern foxes usually being a sandy blond while those of the far north are a deep cherry red. And even those two different shadings may be found in a single litter no matter where they may be.

The red foxes have white chins, necks, chests, bellies and are white on the inside of their upper hind legs. Their front legs and hind feet are black. Their ears, which are about 3½ inches long, are light-colored on the inside and black on the outside.

The silver fox, a color phase of the red fox. This color variation occurs only in the north.

The fox's eyes are yellow with elliptical pupils that contract in the bright sunshine.

In the northern portion of its range, the red fox may be found in 4 distinct color phases. Why these variations occur and why they only occur in the North has never been satisfactorily explained. A red female giving birth in the North may have all 4 variations in one litter. The cross fox is a brown rather than reddish color with a very dark brown band of hair going down its spine and another crossing its shoulders. A black fox has all-black hair while a silver fox has black hair that is tipped with silver. The silver fox has always commanded the highest price paid for any of the red fox pelts.

A bastard fox is one that has dark bluish-gray fur instead of red. A Samson fox is one that has no guard hairs, just the short woolly undercoat. This name comes from Samson's method of routing the Philistine army by tying fire brands to foxes and setting them loose in the ripened grain fields. The foxes were thought to have had their long guard hairs singed off by the fire, hence the name.

Foxes shed their coats just one time per year. The coats begin to look "rubbed" on their hind parts in February when the fox pulls out the guard hairs that freeze into the ice and snow when it sits. The flanks slough large patches of hair in April. The hair is then lost in a gradual line that starts at the head and progresses steadily toward the tail. By July most of the old coat is gone and the fox is much slimmer in appearance than at any other time of the year. Their short hairs continue to lengthen and by October the fox is in good coat, although not usually prime till November.

A red fox has 5 toes on each of its front feet and 4 toes on each of its hind feet. Only 4 toes show in the front feet tracks because the fifth toe, corresponding to our thumb, has shrunken and is located high up on the inside of the fox's foot. Foxes walk in a manner called digitigrade because they do so on just their toes or digits. The toe pads of the red fox are much smaller than those of the gray fox. In the wintertime, the hairs on the red fox feet grow so long that the toe pads are seldom seen. These hairs provide good insulation from the cold and also help to give the fox traction on smooth surfaces, such as ice.

Like all members of the *Canidae* family the fox has 42 teeth—12 incisors, 4 canines, 16 premolars and 10

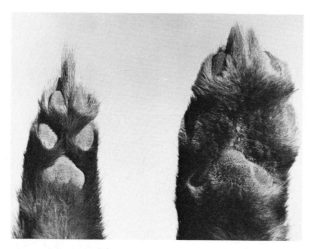

Gray fox's front foot on left, red fox's on right. Note difference in the size of the toe pads.

molars. The first molars in both the top and bottom jaws are referred to as carnassial or shearing teeth. A fox does not chew its food. Small prey is swallowed whole while pieces too large to be swallowed must be cut to a smaller size. To do this the fox turns its head sideways and scissors off a piece of meat from the larger mass using the carnassial teeth.

DISTRIBUTION

Found in all states except Hawaii, only recently in Florida, but increasing steadily there. Absent from portions of high plains and from most of Nevada, southern California and Arizona.

TRAVEL

I learned a great deal about foxes by following their trails. As a kid, starved for more information about all wild creatures, I had the motivation and the time to do a lot of tracking. It was and still is an exciting experience but it takes a lot of time.

A red fox's home range is about one square mile. The distance it travels within that area or beyond it will be determined by the season and the abundance or shortage of food. In the late winter when most wild-

life species are at their nadir, the fox just keeps going till it can secure food. At such times the fox may travel 5 miles or more in a single night.

Each fall the foxes disperse from their natal den. They usually move only far enough to acquire a territory that is not already occupied. The older, stronger, more dominant foxes inhabit the best areas and the younger foxes have to be satisfied with the fringe areas. As mortality takes the older foxes, the young foxes will move into the vacated areas. Nature abhors a vacuum and unless a population of wildlife is declining, all available habitat will be occupied. The better the habitat the denser the population it can support and the smaller the home range of each individual fox.

Nelson Swink, a biologist at Virginia Polytechnic Institute, recovered one tagged fox 150 miles from its release point and although we have no idea how long it took to make the trip we do know it took less than 8 months. Researchers Paul Errington and R. M. Berry tagged a number of red fox pups during a study program in 1937. One was shot 160 miles from its release point.

Of even greater interest were the two red fox pups that were tagged on August 19, 1962, at the University of Wisconsin's Wild Life Refuge at Madison. One fox was shot in March 1963 in Indiana after having traveled a distance of 245 air miles. Its litter mate was killed in June 1963 just 300 yards from their original den site. There are no hard-and-fast rules about the dispersal distances.

LOCOMOTION

The long, lean body of the red fox is built for running and this fox actually seems to enjoy a good chase. This can be proved by the number of authenticated records of foxes deliberately coming down to seek out the dogs to chase them.

The red fox is a faster animal than most people realize. Ernest Thompson Seton told of a red fox that ran at 30 miles per hour for half a mile in front of his automobile. Dr. Schrenkeisen clocked a red fox at 45

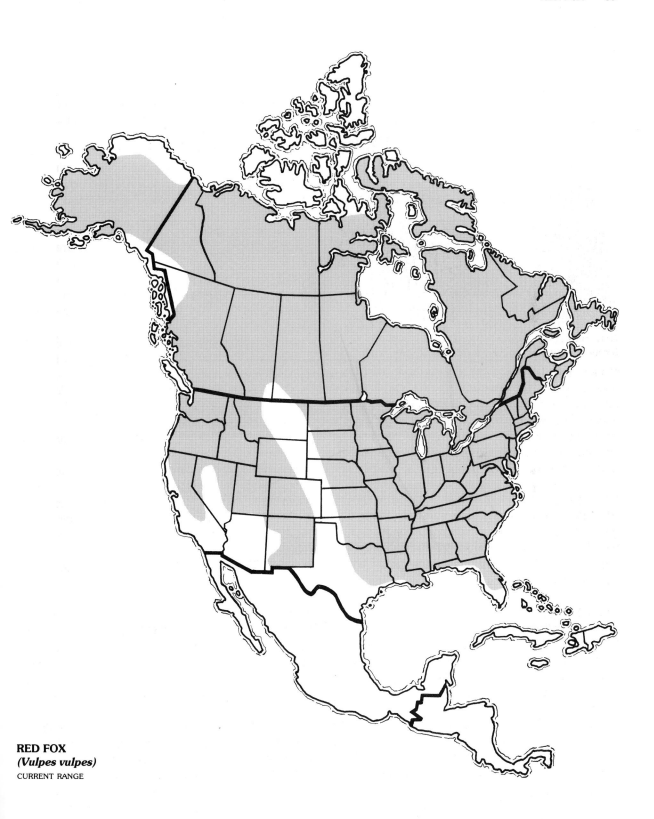

RED FOX
(Vulpes vulpes)
CURRENT RANGE

A red fox running at full speed.

miles per hour. Harold Morton, of Winstead, Connecticut, also clocked one at 45 miles per hour. I personally clocked one at 35 miles per hour but I know they can do better. I saw a frightened red fox outrun a frightened deer. The fox was just a red blur of motion.

When foxes trot, which is their usual gait and they can do it forever, they travel about 6 miles per hour. They also lope.

Foxes can and do swim but they don't like it. They have been clocked at 4 to 5 miles per hour swimming.

FOOD

Red fox's diet (or public beliefs about it) spur controversy over the animal. Many food studies have been done, which to repeat show only what a particular fox ate at a given time and place. Reports show meadow mouse or vole the main prey species in most areas, a plus for humans because these mice are destructive. In hunting mice fox hones in on prey by hearing it squeak or rustle in grass, and when pinpointed fox leaps in an arc and pins mouse to ground with its forefeet, next biting down to crush grass, mouse, etc., and then pulling mouse free of grass, or tosses mouse and grass aloft and catches mouse on its way down. Fox eats mice and rats of all types; the white-footed mouse a winter mainstay because it travels on the snow sur-

face, while meadow mice tunnel beneath the snow.

Long, sharp, rear-curving canine teeth of fox enable it to prey on larger animals than mice, and rabbits and hares thus important fox foods. A 1934 study by Adolph Murie, biologist with the National Park Service, on Edwin S. George reserve near Pinckney, Michigan, showed a very high cottontail population and fox predations. Trail of two foxes was followed and found that they killed 7 cottontails in a single night. None had been eaten, signifying foxes had probably fed before finding rabbits' trails. Since fox requires about 1 pound of food per day, 1 full-grown cottontail would be enough for 2 foxes. Foxes often kill far more than they can eat when hunting is good and surplus is cached and dug up later when hunting is poor. Generally foxes return to eat most of cache although sometimes crows discover and feed there.

According to old-timers, foxes cache their food because they like it "ripe" or tainted. Although true that foxes are attracted to the more powerful smell of tainted meat, burying it actually helps to preserve it. Buried meat does not become infested with blowflies' eggs and resultant maggots, and in north the earth acts as a refrigerator, keeping meat fresh for considerable time. Caching also protects food from other predators, such as other foxes, crows, vultures, etc. To cache food fox digs hole with front feet, drops the food in hole, and covers it by pushing dirt in with its

Although mice are the red fox's most important food, they prey upon rabbits when they can catch them. (Photo: Irene Vandermolen)

nose. Most caches deep enough to cover food completely.

Woodchucks are frequently prey for red fox and also provide burrows the fox converts to its own use. During drought, stranded muskrat populations can be nearly annihilated by foxes, a meal ordinarily denied them by deep water. Foxes feed also on opossums, moles, shrews,—probably on all types of creatures including cold-blooded snakes, frogs, even earthworms.

Fox has been persecuted for feeding on game birds such as pheasants, quail, grouse and wild turkey, but studies show that although it does feed on these birds it is not a major factor in their declining population. Foxes wreak havoc on domestic fowl—in fact I am a naturalist today after turning to trapping foxes when their depredations nearly forced us out of chicken farming. Today poultry plays small role in fox's diet as most poultry now kept fenced or housed.

During summer foxes eat great number of insects of all types, but mostly grasshoppers, crickets and beetles. Fruits and berries eaten in season.

Carrion important to fox in winter. Every deer dead of gunshot wounds and unfound or dead of starvation becomes a bonanza for foxes from all around. Fox's habit of scavenging causes it to be blamed for predations it did not do, when carcasses of animals it had found dead are later found in fox's den.

BEHAVIOR

Foxes usually move around only under the cover of darkness in areas where they are disturbed. I have been fortunate to have been in areas where I could watch foxes go about their activities in the early evening and mornings. And in Alaska, in 1966, I spent weeks living with foxes round the clock.

Except during the birthing period, foxes do not den up. Inclement weather will cause them to seek some shelter from the rain by getting under a tree or a rock ledge. Foxes hate to get wet. They repeatedly and vigorously shake their tails to rid them of the excess water and weight. In the winter they sleep out despite the cold and are often buried by the snow. They will seek out high, sunny, sheltered spots that will be warm even on cold days. Their fluffy tails are used as a muff to keep their noses and feet warm while they are curled up. The red fox prefers open country to dense forest. Even in the Canadian bush country they seek out clearings made by man or fire. Such clearings let them take advantage of their speed if they must escape enemies, and when the clearings grow back into brush they hold far more wildlife than do virgin or climax forests, which means more food for the fox.

At the risk of sounding anthropomorphic, I want to state that I believe that foxes, coyotes and wolves think; that they can reason out many things, that their actions are not just reactions.

As I mentioned earlier, I considered myself to be a good trapper, not the best (Joe Taylor was that), but I was a good one. Yet I encountered some trap-wary foxes that I never could catch. I spent so much time and effort attempting to catch these Ph.D's of the fox world that it was ridiculous. I set traps upside down, I backed up sets, I made blind sets, gang sets, combination sets—all to no avail. The foxes could not have been using instinct, because they were encountering things they had never encountered before. They mastered the situation and thoroughly enjoyed themselves. I know they enjoyed the game as much as I did because they kept coming back for more when they could just as easily have stayed clear of the area.

Red foxes are active all winter, hunting for food, despite the cold, wind and snow.

Discounting all the myths, fables, or tall stories, there is still irrefutable evidence of the high degree of intelligence of red foxes. I don't mean to say that all red foxes are smart. Young foxes are easy to catch, because they haven't lived long enough to get the experience needed to cope with man and his ways. Those that make it through their first winter usually have a good chance of surviving.

Foxes are very inquisitive but they temper this with wariness. They do not like to approach anything that can't be seen from all sides. When their curiosity is aroused they approach the object and circle it so that the breeze will waft any telltale clues to them. If *anything* moves or makes a sound they are off like a shot. Then back they come. They are so alert and so cautious they seem to float rather than touch the earth; they are as light as thistledown on their feet. Most wild creatures know that eternal vigilance is the price of life.

SENSES

As with other canids smell most important, although no studies exist to show just how keen it is. Weather conditions affect scenting—warm air currents raise and dispel scents; cool misty nights keep scent near ground for breezes to carry.

Hearing acute. Squeak of mouse or similar sound made by kissing the back of the hand will be heard by fox at 300 feet if air is still. Once photographing a den in New Jersey the fox pup I was watching located me 150 feet away after I had slightly moved my foot.

Eyesight good at all distances. Pupils appear as slits in daylight, opening wide at night, the sign of a night hunter. Foxes in Alaska I've seen able to spot mates at over half a mile away.

Touch not greatly important but fox is attuned to vibrations in earth made by movements of other animals.

Taste well developed, as seen by food preferences—weasels, shrews, moles and snakes, while often killed, seldom eaten because all have musk offensive to taste buds.

I believe that animals, and people as well, have a sixth sense. As I have written in other articles and books, when we better understand psychic phenomena we will better understand animal sense capabilities and communication.

One of the best examples I can give for this belief occurred in McKinley National Park, where I was working on foxes. I had a large red male under observation. The fox was sleeping in a gully that was about 6 feet deep. A slight breeze was blowing parallel to the ditch. The fox knew I was there but was not concerned and I was sitting motionless.

Suddenly, the fox exploded from his bed and took off at full speed going up a nearby high hill. I was baffled. What had scared the sleeping fox?

Out on the tundra, about a quarter-mile distance, a wolf was trotting our way. The fox could not have seen the wolf, he could not have heard it or smelled it, yet he knew it was there. Some sixth sense warned him of impending danger.

COMMUNICATION

Red foxes scream, squall, yap, bark, growl, hiss, whine, cry, and I've run out of words to describe their vocalizing. They have scent glands on top of their tail and on the pads of their feet. They employ scent posts, urinating on sticks, clumps of grass and stones in the same manner that dogs urinate on car wheels and fire hydrants. These scent posts mark territory and act like the Chinese wall posters. They give off a wealth of information, proclaiming individuality, sex, well-being, food eaten, passage of time and things we cannot even guess at.

BREEDING

The first evidence of the approaching breeding season is the intertwining of two foxes' tracks in the snow in late December. By January the previously mated pairs are together constantly and the young foxes have sought out and found mates.

Foxes usually do not fight except to settle territorial disputes and for the possession of a mate. Fighting foxes circle each other, their bodies curved and with their bristling tails jabbing at each other's face. When a fox has his vision temporarily blocked it allows his opponent a chance to bite him before he recovers.

In January red foxes pair up and the tracks of the male and the female will be seen traveling together.

Foxes will also frequently charge into one another trying to knock the other off its feet by using their shoulders. At times the foxes rise up on their hind feet, striking out with their front feet and snapping and biting at each other. The vanquished fox usually leaves the area with little damaged besides its ego.

The foxes are more vocal during the breeding season than at any other time of the year. Hunting pairs keep in touch with each other by frequent barking.

Male red foxes produce motil, viable sperm from the middle of December through February. The female red fox has an estrous period of about 3 weeks, yet evidence points out that, like dogs, the 9th to 12th days are the most fertile. Most red foxes are bred the last 2 weeks of January.

BIRTH AND YOUNG

The red fox's gestation period is between 52 and 53

days with most of the pups being born about the middle of March. There are records of birthing times as much as 6 weeks earlier or later than this period but they are exceptions.

The usual litter for the red fox is 6 to 8 pups. The largest litter ever recorded for a single female was discovered by Larry Holcomb in Calhoun County, Michigan—17 pups. The pups were of one size and badly emaciated because they were not getting enough food.

I have found that fox litters tend to be smaller in the north country and I'm not sure whether it is because the winters are longer and less food is available or because smaller litters can still keep the population stable there.

When first born the fox pups are 6 to 8 inches in body length and have tails that are 2 1/2 to 3 inches long. Each hind foot is over one inch long and the erect ears are about one-half inch long. The pups weigh between 3 1/2 to 4 ounces with the males being larger. The pups are dark brown in coloration but the tail tip is white. The pups' eyes are sealed shut. The eyes begin to open at the ninth day and are blue in color. The sex ratio favors the males with 52 percent to the females' 48 percent. Population studies done on adult foxes usually show a much higher ratio of males but I believe this is because the males travel more and are more apt to be caught and thus counted. So in reality, because mortality is higher among males, there are probably more adult female foxes than males.

For the first week, following the birth of the pups, the female stays with the pups and is fed by the male. After this period both parents hunt for food for the puppies. Prey up to the size of rabbits and woodchucks are brought back whole and torn to pieces for the pups; anything larger would be eaten and then regurgitated.

Warden Lowell Thomas of Maine saw a fox carrying something. His shout startled the fox into dropping its load. The fox had been carrying a rabbit, two woodcocks and a red squirrel back to its den for the pups.

Red fox natal dens are easy to recognize because of the large apron of earth at the entrance, the tracks and the remains of prey species.

At 5 weeks of age the pups begin to venture out of the den but tumble back inside to its safety and darkness at the least disturbance. Both adult foxes are now sleeping elsewhere, returning only with food for the young. Weaning takes place at about 2 months of age.

The young now spend hours each day outside the den. They play, they fight, they run around, they stalk each other, they chase insects, they are a study in perpetual motion.

The pups at 3 months of age are following after the parents to learn the art of hunting and the den is abandoned a short time later.

LIFE SPAN

Mortality high among pups during first year. After this period potential span is 12 years, although few reach this age. One red fox in captivity reached 16 years; a silver fox made 18 years.

A female red fox bringing in a ground squirrel to feed her puppies.

SIGN

Tracks easily identified in snow, looking like dotted line because hind foot placed directly over track of front foot. Front track about 1¾ inches long by 2 inches wide, hind track slightly smaller. Tracks usually 12–14 inches apart when fox is trotting. Urine stains mark scent posts. Scat about ½ inch diameter by 2–3 inches long and usually sharply pointed. Feces often left standing on end. Consistency depends on fox's diet. Feces usually lighter colored than those of gray fox.

Den most conspicuous. Dirt pulled out of burrow is spread around entrance in an apron about 2–3 times larger than that of woodchuck dirt spread. Prey remains scattered profusely around den area.

ENEMIES

Man the major enemy, although man's hunting and trapping prove beneficial for red fox, because without it to keep population in check parasites such as sarcoptic mange often decimate the population, depleting entire areas. Red fox contracts rabies, as do many other types of wildlife. Also plagued by fleas, mites, lice and ticks. Internal parasites are roundworms and tapeworms. Diseases are distemper and encephalitis.

Second to men as enemies are dogs. In outback, wolves, coyotes, bobcats, lynxes, mountain lions, bears and fishers will kill pups and adults. Golden eagle known to kill pups and adults; great horned owl takes pups.

HUMAN RELATIONS

I love foxes and I know there are many who feel just as I do. I also know there are many who feel just the opposite. Foxes are watched, photographed, hunted and trapped and everyone doing his thing has a different view and puts a different value on the fox.

Millions of dollars are spent annually by wealthy hunt clubs whose members pursue the fox with horses and hounds. They dash across the countryside at breakneck speeds, their horses hurdling the fences and stone-rows. The object of this hunt is the chase. Fox hunting for these people is a great social and sporting event.

Hundreds of thousands of dollars are spent on good trailing hounds by hunters who just like to hear the music of the chase. They, too, are not interested in catching the fox. Hundreds of thousands of dollars are also spent for trail hounds by hunters who shoot the fox. Hunters without dogs try to walk up on a fox by trailing it in the snow. Other hunters try to call the fox by using predator calls. These people hunt for the sport and the rewards from selling the fox skins. Trap-

ping is a business, often a sole means of sustenance in backwoods areas. It is also a tremendous challenge.

In the past, millions of dollars have been spent on bounties. Today bounties are in disfavor, as they should be. They have never done the job and have always squandered tax money. The most effective way to eliminate problem foxes is to have professional government men go to the problem area and catch those particular foxes. That method controls the problem but does not eliminate the population.

COMMERCIAL VALUE

Fur prices higher today than ever. Red fox skins bring

Note the characteristic white tail tip on this 8-week-old red fox pup.

as much as $95 in northeastern U.S. and $135 for northern pelts. IAFWA statistics: 356,249 taken in U.S., incomplete because 12 states keep no records, and of these Alaska, New York, Michigan and Vermont are top red fox producing areas, especially New York. National average price, $48 per pelt, $17,099,952 total. In Canada: 65,456 taken, $37.41 average price, $3,096,147 total. Fur value of North American red fox is over $25,000,000.

At 10 weeks of age the red fox pups still seek the safety of their den if threatened. They will soon leave the natal den for good.

GRAY FOX, *Urocyon cinereoargenteus*

INTRODUCTION

The gray fox is unique among our North American foxes in that it has stiff pelage instead of soft fur. This fact was recognized by Schreber in 1775 when he gave this fox its scientific name. *Urocyon* is a combination of the Greek words *oura,* meaning "tail," and *cyon,* meaning "dog." This name applied to the fox because its stiff, bristly hair is like the hair on a dog's tail. For this reason, this fox's pelt has always been less valuable than the red fox's long, silky fur. *Cinereoargenteus* means ashy-silvered, which does describe the gray fox's overall coloration.

DESCRIPTION

The gray fox is often confused with the red fox by those unfamiliar with the animals because of its beau-

and the ruff framing its face makes this more apparent. The gray fox seems smaller than the red fox because its legs are shorter but it has a stockier body. An adult gray fox stands about 15 inches high at the shoulder and measures up to 45 inches overall. Its tail is 12–15 inches long and is not as cylindrical as the red fox's. The musk gland on the top of the tail is about 4 1/2 inches long. An adult male gray fox will weigh 8 to 11 pounds, with the greatest weight recorded at 19 pounds. Gray foxes are not as active as red foxes and when food is plentiful they gorge themselves beyond need, becoming very fat.

Note the characteristic black streak on the top of all gray foxes' tails.

In the northern part of the gray fox's range, the animal is larger and heavier and develops a thicker coat of hair, as do most animals in response to Bergman's Law. This fox was photographed in the mountains of northwestern New Jersey.

tiful rusty-red ruffs and ears. The fox's throat, chest, belly and the inner sides of its legs are white. The general coloration of the gray fox is best described as being a salt-and-pepper gray on the top of its head, back, sides and tail. A black streak extends down the fox's back, along the top of its tail and ending in a black tail tip.

Two very odd gray foxes have been reported. George H. Wagner, of McClure, Pennsylvania, shot a gray fox that had an all-white face, although the rest of the fox had normal coloration. Another gray fox was hit by a truck near Mohawk, New York. The fox was almost pure white on the head, legs, shoulders and belly. The back was light gray and the tail had the regular black stripe down the top. Around the pupils, the eyes were as white as a human's.

The gray fox has a shorter muzzle than the red fox

The gray fox of the southwestern desert areas is small, lean and has a thin coat of hair.

The gray fox has 42 teeth—12 incisors, 4 canines, 16 premolars and 10 molars.

The gray fox, being an animal with origins in the warmer regions of North America, has large exposed toe and heel pads on its feet. Four toes show in the tracks of each foot. Although there are 5 toes on the front foot, the dewclaw, the shrunken fifth toe on the inside of the foot, does not register.

The eyes of a gray fox are dark with elliptical pupils that open wide in dim light.

DISTRIBUTION

Range expanding steadily for years, now found in all contiguous 48 states except Montana and Idaho, but presence there only a matter of time. Some found in southernmost parts of Manitoba, Quebec and Ontario.

Requisite habitat contains brush, trees, cactus, swamps or mountains, plenty of cover because fox averse to running. Being chased fox will escape into burrow, cave or crevasse or up a tree.

TRAVEL

Foxes do not migrate and do not usually even shift their ranges except under the most severe conditions.

Within their home range, which they know intimately, the gray foxes will concentrate their activities according to whatever food supply may be in abundance. The fox does not want to leave its home range. As it holes up quickly, it is seldom pushed beyond familiar ground by dogs or hunters and this is an important survival factor.

Dispersal time in September or October will force young foxes to seek new territory and that they do emigrate to new territory and that they do expand their range has been proven. Far less research has been done on the gray fox than on the red fox and I can find no really long-distance records for it. One study showed that 56 tagged foxes were recaptured within a half-mile of their original capture point.

LOCOMOTION

Gray foxes are seldom seen except at night as they cross roads. Their preference for heavy cover precludes their being seen as often as are red foxes, which prefer open country. The gray fox is usually active only after dark. When something disturbs a gray fox, it is less likely to dash away. Most of the time it slinks into cover and waits for the disturbance to pass it by. If pursued, the gray fox seeks protective cover

GRAY FOX
(Urocyon cinereoargenteus)
CURRENT RANGE

The gray fox is the only member of the dog family that can easily climb a tree.

and many times it gets that protection by climbing.

The gray fox is the only member of the dog family that I know of that can climb. Red foxes can scramble up a many-branched tree, such as an evergreen, but they don't really climb. I saw a gray fox shin up an 8- to 10-inch, branchless, smooth, black birch tree to a height of 20 feet or more. My cousin Levi Kries, of Washington, New Jersey, saw a gray fox climb up a large walnut tree and perch on the first branch about 12 feet above the ground. What made this achievement all the more remarkable was that the fox had lost its left front foot.

Gray foxes have often been seen sleeping up in trees and on occasion hiding or sleeping in old hawk nests. There are also records of them living and raising their young in large hollow trees, some of the trees being smooth-barked and with the entrance hole 20 feet above the ground.

Gray foxes walk, trot and gallop. When they trot, their narrow chest allows their feet to be placed in almost the exact center of their body so that their tracks appear as a dotted line. Their hunting is done with a purpose but their tracks seem to meander all over the place because of the dense cover that they frequent. When trotting they travel at about 3 1/2 to 4 miles per hour.

When running full speed, the gray fox has a rocking-horse motion and carries its tail curved into an arch. When turning a corner, the tail is whipped about as a counterbalance. The top speed of the gray fox is about 28 miles per hour and it does this for only short periods. John Terres once timed a running gray fox with an automobile that was doing 35 miles per hour. For a short distance gray foxes can be fast, but their speed just doesn't last. When chased by dogs, the gray foxes run a maze of circles and backtracks, they run on top of fences, up inclining trees, they employ a great assortment of ruses and when all else fails, they go to earth or climb a tree. The gray fox can swim but is most reluctant to do so.

FOOD

Preferring native wildlife, thus not ordinarily enemy of farmers. Heavy predator of ruffed grouse, eating adults, young and eggs. Personal experience includes seeing wild turkey killed by gray fox that weighed more than fox itself. In brush fox takes quail; in the East, the bobwhite; in West, the scaled, Gambel's quail, and California quail. Cottontail, swamp and brush rabbits a mainstay, and takes snowshoe hare

The gray fox will sleep inside a den in the winter, but it will sleep out in the open during the summer, as this one was doing in New Jersey's Worthington State Park.

when in area. Also important foods are bushy-tailed wood rats, white-footed mice, woodland voles. Gray squirrels, active at dawn when gray fox is still hunting, frequently taken. Fox squirrels seldom taken, being later risers and preferring open country. Carrion eaten often. Insects encountered also eaten, although fewer found in forest than in grassland. Gray fox eats more plants than red fox because vegetation is more easily obtained. In season fox eats all fruits, melons, berries, nuts and acorns, occasionally domestic crops. Seeds of wild black cherries appear in droppings. Gray fox also known to scavenge at garbage dumps.

BEHAVIOR

Although the gray fox is shyer than the red fox, and

less seldom seen, it is the aggressor when the two foxes meet. A little-known fact is that when gray foxes expand their territory, they invariably force the red foxes out. I have seen this happen on many pieces of territory and it was not that the habitat was forcing the change.

My friend Leon Kitchen once saw a gray fox attack a red fox that was caught in a trap. I have seen gray foxes best red foxes when both species were in the same enclosure. Red foxes are not afraid of gray foxes but they do avoid them and the grays are dominant. Although red foxes have longer teeth, they also have a very thin, easily torn skin. The skin of the gray fox is much thicker and stronger and in a fight it is the red fox that is soon slashed open and bleeding.

The gray fox will sleep out for a good part of the year but it dens up more frequently than the red. In New Jersey I have found that the gray usually seeks shelter during the time there is snow on the ground. Gray foxes are very clannish and frequently male, female and some of the past season's pups will den up together during the winter. The tumbled fields of talus on the mountain's southern slope, the split ridges of uptilted sandstone slabs on the north slopes are ideal denning areas for the fox. I have also seen them utilize large fallen trees. The silver-gray bodies of the fallen giant American chestnut trees at one time provided many mammals with den sites. Unfortunately, even this extremely long-lasting wood has eventually succumbed to the ravages of time and most of them are now in the process of adding soil to the forest floor.

SENSES

Smell most important, able to smell game several hundred feet away when breeze bears scent. Foxes seldom track prey, preferring to course back and forth until scent of actual prey detected. Hearing is good, better at high frequencies; slight sounds heard several hundred feet away, and squeak of mouse at over 100 feet. Sight is good, but hunts more by scent. Able to recognize a stationary man as potential danger, which canids can do but most animals cannot.

Most foxes are right-footed, according to records kept by Joe Taylor in which 90 percent of foxes trapped were caught by their left feet, having extended the right foot to reach for the bait. Figure closely matches 87 percent right-handedness in humans.

COMMUNICATION

Gray foxes bark, growl, whine, squall and generally are more vocal than red foxes. Many of the unidentified caterwaulings heard in the mountains at night are done by either gray foxes or raccoons. Gray foxes have a much lower-pitched bark than the red fox and it is often part-bark and part-squall; a raspy sound. The gray foxes do a lot of barking during their courtship and breeding period and then are almost silent after the young are born. They do nothing that would attract attention to their den. In late August and early September, they again become vociferous as they teach the pups to hunt and attempt to keep track of their family group.

BREEDING

Adult gray foxes usually mate for life but even mated pairs go through a courtship period that is accompanied with much vocalization. The pair becomes inseparable, their tracks in the snow show that they are seldom out of sight of each other and almost never out of hearing range. Gray foxes hunt cooperatively throughout most of the year and even more so during courtship.

Den sites are reused year after year by the older pairs and are eagerly sought by the juvenile pairs. If it is a new den, it must often be enlarged where needed (and if possible), or at least cleaned out. Foxes carry in no bedding material. When the foxes sleep now during the daytime, the female will often use the den while the male will curl up on the rocks above. The gray foxes' coloration blends in with most rocks so well that they are exceedingly difficult to see. Copulation will take place a number of times during the 3 or 4 days that the female is most fertile.

BIRTH AND YOUNG

Between the last of March and early May the pups will be born after a gestation period of 53 days. The average litter consists of 3 to 4 pups and occasionally 5. This small litter size is reflected in the female gray fox having only 6 nipples compared with the red fox having 8.

The pups weigh about 4 ounces at birth and have

Gray fox pup. Gray foxes usually have about 3 pups to a litter.

dark skin that is almost hairless. The pups' ears are closed and their eyes are sealed shut. The female stays with her pups to attend to them for the first 3 or 4 days; nursing them frequently and keeping them warm with her own body heat. She leaves the den just long enough to rid her body of waste material and to eat the food that the male has brought in. She will stay away from the pups for longer periods of time after their first week.

When the pups are 10 to 12 days old their eyes open but there is little for them to see within the confines of the dark den. Their world consists of smelling, touching and hearing each other and their mother; a warm, comfortable world. At 5 weeks of age the pups venture out of the den for increasing periods of time. At 3 months of age they are strong enough to be able to accompany their parents on their hunting forays. At 4 months of age the pups are almost perfect miniatures of the adults. The pups' training period lasts from 2 to 5 months. The pups may stay with the adults or at least associate with them till under their hormonal stimulations they go off to seek mates and territories of their own.

LIFE SPAN

Potential: 10–12 years, a level reached by few. Record age in captivity: 14 years.

SIGN

Scats conspicuous along roadsides. Gray fox voids more frequently than red because of more vegetation in diet, which also makes scats darker than red fox's. Fox scat usually sharply tapered at end. Urine scent posts visible in snow.

Gray fox track has larger visible toe pads but smaller foot than red fox; differs from track of house cat because no nails visible in cat's tracks.

Dens usually well hidden, but some sign left by passage because dens used more frequently than other foxes'; careful inspection of suspected den will reveal a few hairs.

Gray fox tracks are easy to identify because of the large toe pads, and although they are about the same size as a house cat's tracks, the fox's claw marks show.

ENEMIES

Man the main enemy, followed by dog, which likes to chase and often kills fox. Pups and adults taken by coyote, mountain lion, bobcat and bear. Great horned owl known to take pups; records of golden eagle taking adults. External parasites include fleas, lice, mites and ticks; internal parasites, roundworms and tapeworms. Gray fox does not get mange as does red fox; in tests mange deliberately introduced but foxes recovered in about a month. Gray foxes more susceptible than red to encephalitis and canine distemper, diseases not transmissible to man but potentially fatal to dogs. Foxes can contract rabies from dogs or other animals and can transmit the disease to man, dogs and other animals. Any wild animal appearing "tame" could be diseased—avoid contact and report to a conservation officer.

HUMAN RELATIONS

For many years the price paid for fox pelts was so low that, except for the sport of hunting, the gray fox was left virtually alone. That has all changed over the past several years with the soaring prices that are now being paid for long-fur pelts.

Gray foxes are generally considered to be less intelligent than red foxes. They are easier to trap, not because they are less intelligent but because they usually don't encounter man and his devices as often. A gray fox that has been caught by the toe and has managed to pull free from the trap becomes super smart. I have always said that an adult, trap-wise female gray fox was the hardest fox of all to catch.

The gray fox competes less with man because of the areas it frequents and the food it eats. The fact that it does not put up a good run for hounds, and that its pelt has always been worth a fraction of that of all the other foxes, are factors influencing man so that little pressure is put on the gray fox.

In many cases the gray fox is beneficial to man because of the large number of rodents it eats. The gray fox feeds heavily upon cotton rats in the South. The rats in turn prey heavily upon quail eggs. Every cotton rat eaten by the foxes removes a major predator of the quail and the rats do far more damage to quail than the fox does.

Today a very popular method of hunting the gray fox is the use of a predator call. When blown, the sound of a dying rabbit that is produced is music to the ears of most foxes. Even foxes that have full bellies often respond to the call. There are many instances of foxes that were carrying prey who dropped it to investigate the call.

COMMERCIAL VALUE

IAFWA statistics: 1976–77 winter, 225,277 total, $34 average price, $7,659,418 total. Fifteen states not reporting, due either to lack of animals or records.

ORDER:

CARNIVORA

FAMILY:

URSIDAE

The bears are the largest four-footed carnivores. Their long, strong canine teeth have classified them as carnivores but their flat-topped molars are designed for grinding vegetation. The polar bear feeds almost exclusively upon flesh, while flesh is a sometime treat for the black bear. With the exception of the polar bear, the other bears are more omnivorous.

The young of all bears are very small at birth compared to the tremendous size achieved by the adults. The females usually breed every other year.

The bears become very fat in autumn and most retire to dens where they become lethargic and sleep for extended periods of time during the coldest weather, although they do not hibernate in the true sense of the word. The polar bears spend less time denned up in the winter than do the other bears.

The bears are plantigrade, have 5 toes on each foot, and strong claws. The black bear climbs trees readily; the others do not. All bears can swim but the polar bear excels as a swimmer.

Because of their large size, great strength, teeth and claws, the bears can be formidable and dangerous. They usually try to avoid any contact or conflict with humans and cases of bear attacks are usually results of the bears being provoked.

GRIZZLY/BROWN BEARS, *Ursus arctos*

INTRODUCTION

When you see a grizzly bear in the Rocky Mountains and then view a brown bear on the coast of Alaska, there can be no doubt that you are looking at two different bears. Or are you?

It's a good question and one that has puzzled many people for many years. The controversy will never be settled to everyone's satisfaction. Originally they were thought to be different species and were so named.

The grizzly bear was named *Ursus horribilis* by Ord back in 1815. *Ursus* is the Latin word for bear and *horribilis* means just what it says: horrible. This name was given to the grizzly bear because of its ferocious nature.

The brown bear of Alaska was named *Ursus gyas* by Merriam in 1902. *Gyas* is the Greek word for "gigantic," a fitting name for this huge bear. Merriam then went on to split these two groups into 86 species and subspecies, with 77 for the grizzly bear and 9 for the

102

brown bear. It was found, however, that his divisions did not stand up to scrutiny and only added to the confusion.

The latest scientific classification recognizes that the grizzly-brown bears are the New World representatives of the Old World brown bears. Linnaeus named the European brown bear *Ursus arctos* in 1758 and this is the correct scientific designation for both of our bears today. The two North American races interbreed freely where their ranges overlap. Today, it is generally accepted that the brown bear is found along the coast of southeastern Alaska for a 1,400 mile arc to the end of the Alaskan Peninsula. The bears found along the coast, on the offshore islands and for 50 miles inward from the coast, are designated as brown bears and are designated *Ursus arctos middendorffi*.

Any of these bears found other than in the brown bear's range are classified as grizzly bears and are known as *Ursus arctos horribilis*.

A large silver-tipped grizzly bear (above), and a huge male Alaskan brown bear. Note the shoulder hump that typifies both the brown and the grizzly bears.

DESCRIPTION

Both the grizzly and the brown bear have the "dish-faced" or convex appearance to the skull and the shoulder hump that typifies these bears. An adult grizzly bear stands 3 1/2 feet high at the shoulder and is 6 to 7 1/2 feet in overall length. A large male brown bear stands 4 1/2 feet high at the shoulder and is 9 to 10 feet in total length.

The study done on the grizzly bears in Yellowstone Park by John and Frank Craighead is one of the most complete ever done and much of the new information that I have included here is taken from their reports.

They found that the average adult male grizzly bear weighed 500–575 pounds. The females averaged 300–380 pounds. The largest bear weighed in the years of study was a male that tipped the scale at 1,120 pounds. This was an accurate scale weight and is the greatest weight that I can find for a wild grizzly. A grizzly in the Union Park Zoo in Chicago weighed 1,153 pounds.

The average adult male brown bear weighs between 800 and 1,200 pounds, with the female weighing between 500 and 800 pounds. The greatest scale weight for the brown bear is 1,656 pounds. When a big male brownie stands erect, he measures 8 1/2 feet in height. Roy Lindsley shot the number-one brown bear on Kodiak Island in 1952. The bear was weighed in pieces for a total of 1,190 pounds. The hide weighed 157 pounds and, when laid flat, measured 11 feet 2 1/4 inches in length by 9 feet 8 1/2 inches in width. The mounted bear stands in the Los Angeles County Museum and measures 8 feet 8 inches in height. Bob Reeve, owner of Reeve's Aleutian Airline, showed me a photo of a brown bear that he shot in 1948 at Cold Bay, Alaska, which measured 12 feet from claw tip to claw tip. Unfortunately, there was no way to weigh this giant.

Friends of mine own and operate the Space Farms Zoological Park at Beemerville, New Jersey. They have a huge brown bear that measures 5 feet high at the shoulder and I have seen it rub its head on the 9-foot bars overhead. Its estimated weight is well over 2,000 pounds.

There are 5 toes on each of the bear's feet. The claws on the front feet are much longer than those on the hind feet. These claws are excellent tools for digging and much of the food of these bears is obtained in this manner. The brown and grizzly bears do a lot more digging for roots, tubers and ground squirrels than does the black bear. Although a young grizzly can climb a tree, the older, heavier bears cannot unless there are branches that can be utilized. These claws also become deadly weapons when powered in a slashing attack by the bear's fantastic strength.

The claws on a brown bear skin that I have are 4 1/4 inches in length on the front feet and 2 inches on the hind feet. I have seen bears with claws longer than these and although I couldn't measure them (the bears were alive), I am sure they were at least 5 inches long following the outside curve. The claws of a big grizzly bear are 3 1/4 to 3 1/2 inches in length on the front feet and 1 1/2 inches on the hind feet.

The bear's claws are usually black or very dark brown with light-colored tips. As the bears age, their

Canine teeth of Alaskan brown bear. The large canine teeth of the bears are used for grasping prey but their flat-topped molars are designed for grinding vegetation.

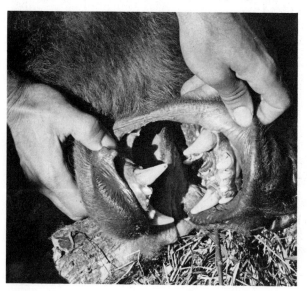

Grizzly bears come in a wide variety of colors. This one has a blond coloration.

er, in both plains and mountains. Range has shrunk drastically due to loss of habitat to man; remnant populations remain in Wyoming, Montana, Idaho, Washington, perhaps Colorado. Classified as threatened, population in these states between 200 and 400. Glacier National Park (Montana) maintains good population. There are 8,000 grizzlies in British Columbia, 1,250 in Alberta, 5,500 in Yukon, no figures for Northwest Territories, but barren ground grizzly increasing there in numbers and in range, and in recent years has moved eastward to Hudson Bay. Figures from Alaska report brown and grizzly bears together, to 20,000 total; half would be brown bears, which biologists say may be increasing, although trophy-size bears becoming scarcer.

Many of the grizzly bears in Alaska's McKinley National Park, such as the one shown here, look exactly like the coastal brown bears, but are smaller in size.

claws become lighter in color and some of the old bears that I have seen had pure white claws.

The bears have 42 teeth—12 incisors, 4 huge canine teeth, 16 premolars, some of which are rudimentary or missing entirely, and 10 molars. The molars are flat-topped for grinding vegetation.

Most of the brown bears are brown in color, shading from a light russet to a very dark burnt umber. The pelage of the grizzly bears varies from the very light blond bears of the Toklat Valley in McKinley National Park, through all shadings of brown, to almost black with frosted hair tips producing the so-called silver-tip grizzly coloration of the Rocky Mountains. The guard hairs on these bears measure about 3 inches in length, with the undercoat being about 1½ inches in length. The hair on the bear's belly is more sparse but measures up to 6 or 7 inches in length.

DISTRIBUTION

Formerly found in most states west of Mississippi Riv-

BROWN BEAR
(Ursus arctos)
CURRENT RANGE

Brown bear found along coast of southeastern Alaska, along Peninsula to Aleutians. Large concentrations on islands of Kodiak, Afognak, Admiralty, Baranof and Chichagof. Kodiak Island most famous hunting spot where most world record bears taken, skulls of these bears larger in proportion to body size than are those from elsewhere. Large-bodied, heavier bears found on Peninsula. McNeil River on Peninsula is a photographic preserve and famous spot for bear photographs. I saw 28 bears congregated near falls at one time; researchers noted 89 bears using area in one season.

TRAVEL

Some of these bears are homebodies, staying on a very limited area when food is plentiful, while others travel just because they want to. The bears are not territorial in that they will fight to defend a given piece of ground. They may fight to defend the carcass of a large animal that they have killed or found. At other times they will share their kill when dominance has been established.

The Craigheads found that the grizzly bears had a home range of 20–125 square miles, with one bear having a range of 168 square miles. This particular bear made a circle of 50 air miles in 7 days. The actual miles covered would be much greater because of the exceedingly rough topography of the area.

One sow with 3 cubs stayed within one square mile for an extended period of time so long as the food supply was ample. On the average, it was found that the females traveled about 3 miles per day while the males traveled 9 miles per day.

The bears' homing ability is strong. One female that was captured and transported to the other side of Yellowstone Lake returned to her point of capture, which was 53 air miles, in just 62 hours.

The traveling that bears do is not generally considered a migration, yet they do considerable traveling to go to their preselected den sites each fall. In the spring the bears usually reappear on their favored feeding grounds.

LOCOMOTION

Bears usually walk from place to place, sniffing and snuffling as they go, always searching for food. When they have a destination in mind, they have a determined walk that is a little faster than a human's, being about $3\frac{1}{2}$ to $4\frac{1}{2}$ miles per hour. When they are in a hurry, but not going flat-out, they have an easy lope or gallop that allows them to cover the ground in short order. When a grizzly is chasing something or is being chased, 30 miles per hour is considered their top speed. People who have been charged by a bear swear that the bear could go faster than that and they are right. Just recently, three wardens in Banff National Park, in Alberta, had the opportunity to clock a grizzly running flat-out at 40 miles per hour.

The bears swim well and use all 4 feet. I have watched the brown bears swim the swift McNeil River, even though the current carried them downstream. The Craigheads found that the grizzly bears had no trouble swimming across the surging Yellowstone River.

Brown bears often swim because they have to and, at times, just because they want to. I have watched them paddle around for no other purpose than to be in the water and perhaps to cool off. It was ludicrous to see some of the bears swimming around with their heads beneath the surface so they could watch the salmon that lay beneath them. Occasionally they would dive underwater in an attempt to catch a fish but I never saw a salmon caught in this manner. They were more like kids with their noses pressed against a candy store window.

FOOD

Will eat anything edible they can capture or find. Would prefer meat but are too cumbersome to catch healthy alerted game animal. Will kill game when handicapped—bison and elk mired in mud, a cow elk struggling up riverbank after swimming—and also take young of all creatures, from mice to moose. Grizzlies hunt mice either by digging them out or waiting near tunnels the mice frequent, smashing them with their paws when they pass by. Ground squirrels and marmots important to diet. Marmots generally dig burrows beneath rocks to prevent bears digging them out, although ground squirrels often do not do this and bear will move a ton of dirt to dig it out. I have seen alpine meadows riddled with craters where bears sought squirrels. Carcass of any animal, even another bear, readily eaten. Also frequents garbage dumps, camps and cabins for food. Most grizzlies avoid contact with man but those who conquer their fear will go after domesticated animals, which can be killed easily. Some bears notorious as stock-killers.

Grizzly and brown bears feed in late spring mainly on grass shoots and sprouts, preferring some roots and tubers.

Salmon runs in mid-July bring both bears to spawning streams' riffles, pools and falls. Salmon run upstream only on incoming tide, making 2 fishing periods every 24 hours. First fish taken, when bear is hungry, will be consumed entire. After 5 or 6 fish, bear eats only fish steaks, leaving rest for lesser bears or

Alaskan brown bear with salmon, the brown bear's most important food item in the summertime.

An Alaskan brown bear standing upright to search for salmon. (Photo: Len Rue, Jr.)

Glaucous-winged gulls gather to scavenge on any scraps of salmon left by the feeding Alaskan brown bear. (Photo: Len Rue, Jr.)

gulls. After 10–12 fish, only female salmon sought and bear eats only roe. Bears learn to fish from their mothers, employing whatever method she uses, thus some more adept at it than others. Best fishing spots occupied by highest-ranking bears. McNeil River studies show average bear caught 2–4 fish per hour, 7.8 per hour for a ranking male. Many can catch 12–15 fish in 4–6 hours. Fish are caught in the mouth, by pinning fish on stream bottom, or grabbing to chest with the paws. Fish not thrown onto bank. Some dead fish eaten after spawning, but most left to rot. By late summer bears leave for hills and meadows to search for ripe berries. Deprived of berries in dry summers.

Perhaps brown bear developed into larger bear because salmon plentiful for it each summer, whereas many mountain grizzlies are deprived of this food.

One grizzly bear, nicknamed Old Mose, was finally killed April 30, 1904, by J. W. Anthony, in the Black Mountains of Colorado. This bear ranged over a 75-mile area and had been consistently hunted for 35 years. His track was recognized because of 2 missing toes on his right front foot. He had avoided traps, snares, poison and hunters till he was finally brought

to bay with a pack of hounds. Even then, it took 8 bullets to drop this giant bear. The skin of Old Mose measured 10 feet 4 inches in length by 9 feet 6 inches and he weighed 875 pounds, hog-dressed. In his years of destruction, Old Mose had killed more than 800 head of cattle, worth an estimated $30,000. He had also killed 5 of the men who were hunting him.

BEHAVIOR

Grizzly and brown bears are much more social than are the black bears. They will fight to establish a hierarchy based on dominance but will then tolerate others of their kind when each bear knows its place. Dominance is based on many factors. The social structure of dominance is very fluid. Ordinarily the largest, strongest male is the kingpin. All other bears defer to him until a younger male can displace him.

A fight between two big males is an awesome sight. I have seen them stand up on their hind feet and slash out at each other with their forepaws, their murderous claws raking chunks of fur, skin and flesh from their opponent's body. At other times they will lock jaws

Bears sometimes fight vicious battles but they usually try to avoid doing so by threat and bluster. Note the defensive gesture of the bear on the left.

and hammer away at each other. At all times, they are alert to any possibility to do deadly damage with claw or fang.

The fights are not usually to the death, and the bears are not normally vindictive. When one bear is beaten, it breaks away and, although the victor may chase him for a short distance, he is not intent on killing him.

A bear that is wounded by a human may be another matter. Some wounded bears may run; others will attack. A mother bear who feels that her cubs are threatened, either by a human or by another bear, will charge with unrelenting fury. Berserk is a good word to describe these charging bears.

The word berserk was first used to describe the Norsemen when they went into battle. They fought with such a fury, a frenzied violence, with total disregard for their own lives, that they were called berserkers. It means to be like a bear; i.e., to put on a bear's sark or skin and to fight as a bear fights.

When a bear attacks a human, it does not stand up and "hug" him. If the bear stands up, it is to use its paws to pull the human close so that it can use its teeth. Grizzlies often kill by smashing with their paws while the brownie usually kills by biting.

The strength of a bear is phenomenal. There is a record of one big bear picking up another bear that weighed perhaps 700 pounds and shaking him like a terrier does a rat.

There are a number of records of grizzlies dragging

moose or cattle that weighed 800 pounds. I was in Yellowstone one spring trying for grizzly bear photos. A grizzly had killed a cow elk near one of the warm springs. The area was too open to suit the grizzly. The elk probably weighed about 300 pounds. The bear first fed upon the carcass, which gradually stiffened with rigor mortis. The bear then picked up the carcass and walked through the snow without leaving any drag marks from the elk it carried. It was a frightening show of strength. The bear carried the elk into heavy timber and stayed with the carcass to guard it and to feed upon it.

This is a common practice with both the grizzly and brown bears. Sometimes they will cover the carcass as if to hide it, but the job is usually incomplete. They usually stay very close to the carcass to prevent other bears or animals from feeding on it. Any time you stumble upon the carcass of a large animal that has been fed upon and covered, you have stumbled on trouble.

Females with cubs rank high in the hierarchy. A female with newborn cubs ranks higher than a female with yearling cubs because she is more defensive. A female that has had cubs ranks lower than those with cubs but higher than the young females that haven't bred at all. Of the two females with newborn cubs, the older bear ranks the highest. Although females with cubs try to avoid males, they will even attack the dominant male, if they feel their cubs are threatened. The male usually gives way before the female, not because he has to but because the males usually don't stand up to females with cubs. The rest of the males are scattered throughout the hierarchy according to their size and strength. Young bear siblings that present a united front and concerted action are dominant over a single, larger bear. The siblings drop in status when they split up. The subadult bears are at the bottom of the totem pole and are the most vulnerable and it is this age group that suffers the highest mortality. These bears may be killed by the larger bears and they do not have access to the best or easiest sources of food.

Ben Lily, who was one of the greatest bear hunters of all time, stated that a grizzly under 2 years old would fight only to escape, even if wounded. A female grizzly 3 to 6 years old would attack to defend her cubs but a male of that age would fight only to escape. After 6 years of age, any grizzly would attack anything that it thought was an enemy.

At times, a dominant grizzly will chase all other bears from a large carcass until he has fed. Then, if the other bears are properly submissive, with lowered head and averted face, he may allow them to eat.

It is usually the same with the big brown bears. If fish are scarce, the dominant male takes over the best fishing spot and allows no other bears to approach. If fishing is good, the lesser bears rotate. As soon as one catches a fish, it carries the fish up the bank to eat it while another bear takes its place. On the McNeil River, this feeding pattern creates two large circles of

Alaskan brown bears fighting. The bears develop a social hierarchy based on size, strength and aggressiveness.

bears fishing, going up in the bushes with fish, eating and going back to fish. This cuts down on the competition for the best fishing spots. Only the largest, most dominant bears eat their fish right where they catch them and this disrupts the pattern. Even if there are other bears fishing, when the dominant males come in they go to the best fishing spots as is their right, and the lesser bears scatter. One huge male, Old Scarface, would not tolerate any other bears within 200 feet while he fished, but he was the exception. Usually after dominance is established, the bears try to avoid conflict, not even looking at one another, so that they can settle down to fishing in earnest.

Grizzly bears are most active in the early evening and at night and retire shortly after sunup, if the weather is warm. If the weather is cool, they may be active any time of the day, because their light-colored coats do not absorb the sun's heat as does the coat of the black bear. The grizzly loves to feed in the open mountain meadows.

The pattern for the brown bear is the same except when the salmon are spawning and then they are active during the 2 periods of the incoming tide when the salmon are running.

Starting in August, the bears begin to gain weight rapidly, putting on as much as 150–250 pounds of fat in a 3-month period. One grizzly male was 7 feet in total length and weighed 520 pounds liveweight when first captured and tagged. He was caught and weighed again 14 months later and was found to have gained 320 pounds.

A fact that greatly interests doctors is that the biologists have discovered that despite the tremendous amount of fat that the bear accumulates each fall, there is no corresponding build-up of fatty deposits in the bear's blood vessels and arteries.

In September the bears leave their feeding areas to go to the spot where they excavate the dens they will use later during the winter. The brown bears usually go to the headwaters of the streams they have been frequenting and usually dig their dens at altitudes of 1,100–1,500 feet, on north-facing, open slopes. Some of the dens are very easy to see as the tons of dirt

from dens form an apron as much as 25 feet long by 6 feet wide. The actual dens are about 4½ feet high and extend back into the bank 6 to 11 feet.

The grizzly bears also utilize north-facing slopes. The bears choose the north-facing slopes because the snow drifts deeper there, effectively covering over the entrance to the dens. There is also less chance of the snow melting during a warm winter spell with the resultant dripping water.

The grizzly bear usually digs its den beneath the base of a large tree hidden in a dense stand of vegetation. The dens discovered by the Craigheads were all above the 7,000-foot elevation. The average den was 5 feet deep by 4 feet wide and 3 feet high. Several of the dens sloped upward so that the bears had no problem with drainage and, being higher than the opening, the animal's body heat was trapped inside.

Both the brown and the grizzly bears carry dead leaves, boughs and grass inside to make a soft nest and to provide insulation from the ground. After their dens have been dug, the bears return to their feeding areas and continue to gorge themselves.

All wildlife seems to be able to predict the weather at least 24 hours before it occurs. Until the Craigheads were able to equip the bears with radio transmitters, they were not able to follow the bears to their dens because they always went into their dens during a snowstorm so their tracks could not be followed.

Bears do not hibernate in the true sense of the word, although they do become lethargic and sleep for extended periods of time. Some of the bears actually become lethargic and sleep in day beds before entering their dens, waiting for the snowstorm needed to cover their tracks.

Prior to denning, the bears stop eating, which allows their stomachs and intestines to become empty. Then the bears eat a small quantity of pine needles, dead grasses and dry leaves. This material passes through the bear's body and forms a fecal plug that may be 2 to 3 inches in diameter and up to 12 inches in length, blocking the anus.

After the bears enter their dens and drop off to sleep, their heart rates drop from a normal of 40–50 beats per minute to about 10. Their body temperatures drop from a normal of 100°–102° F. to about 94°–96°. The temperature inside the den often drops below freezing but it is much warmer than the −50° F., or more, of the outside temperature. If the bear's body temperature drops below 89° F., it will wake up automatically and move around a bit to bring the body temperature back up. When 94° F. is reached, the bear will doze off again.

If the bears are disturbed while denning, they usually awaken very quickly and will dash out of the den. At times in the early spring, they wake up and voluntarily leave the den to walk around. They may even make nests of evergreen boughs and bark outside the den, curl up, sleep and be covered with drifting snow. When they awake, they may go back into the den and continue to sleep.

The adult grizzly males usually leave their dens permanently about the end of March. The grizzly females with yearling cubs usually leave their dens before mid-April. Females with newborn cubs are usually out of their dens by the end of April.

The brown bears come out of their dens in April. Once the bears leave their dens they do not return to them but construct new ones next year.

When the bears first come out of their dens in the spring, they are in good condition, having lost only 25 percent of their weight. Each pound of fat yields about 3,500 calories and the bears' metabolism is very low while they are lethargic. The balance of their fat is utilized after the bears leave their dens and are busy searching for food. The bears are at their lowest weight of the year in late May and June. They usually shed their winter coats during this same period so they appear very scraggly.

The big males may have difficulty in walking as they break through the softening snow. The bears prowl the stream bottoms first and search for the new blades of grass and for the carcasses of winter-killed animals.

SENSES

Smell most important to grizzly and brown bears for detecting food and danger. Some grizzlies radio-tracked heading for carcass 19 miles away. Unscrupulous outfitters used to kill a horse just outside Yellowstone, partially cook meat, and lie in wait for bears to be coaxed out of park by the smell where they could legally be shot.

Hearing important, and bears hear potential danger before it arrives—one of the reasons bears bed down in dense cover. Long hair makes ears appear short but in fact they are 4 inches long, well-rounded and with a broad base. Advisable when traveling through dense brush in bear country to make sure you make some noise—talk, shout, sing, wear bells on the pack—to advertise your whereabouts.

Bears myopic—distant objects are blurred—and a man (not smelled) will be unrecognized at 100 yards. Movement is usually seen, or perhaps only heard. Bears see well close up because much of their communication is by sight.

COMMUNICATION

Bears inform each other of their intent by the various positions of their body, head, mouth and actions. A threatening bear will usually drop its head lower than normal but with its eyes fixed on its opponent and with the head held straight in front of its body. It walks with a stiff-legged gait as it approaches its opponent. A submissive bear turns its body sideways, drops its head and turns it away from the dominant bear to avoid making eye contact. There are many other signs given in the bear's body language that are under investigation.

Bears rear up on their hind feet to see better but also to be seen better; they want to show off their size.

Bears whine, cry, bawl, roar, make a whooshing sound when surprised and a warning HUFF-HUFF.

Grizzly bears mark "bear trees" by scratching and biting as high as they can reach. As I mention in my next chapter, on black bears, the exact meaning of these signs are pure speculation on the part of humans.

A really angry bear snaps its jaws together, the teeth

making a very loud sound, drooling strings of saliva in the process. Once heard, it is a sound not easily forgotten.

A bear cub separated from its mother bawls lustily. The female gives the cubs both audible and visible commands and expects to be obeyed at once. The cub that disobeys is usually knocked sprawling by a blow from mom's paw. A cuffed cub hastens to obey, although it may whimper and whine while doing so.

BREEDING

The grizzly bears breed from late May through the month of June with the peak being the first two weeks in June. The brown bears breed through June into July. I saw a big bear following a young female that was about to come into estrus in the last week in July. She kept running off and he kept following but he would be there when she was ready.

Bears are polygamous. Although most of the breeding is done by the dominant males, the younger males take advantage of any opportunity that presents itself. One witness reports that while the two large males were fighting, a smaller male copulated with the female they were fighting over.

At times the female has been seen to initiate copulation by turning around and backing into the male. She is in estrus for a period of between 13 and 27 days. If she has not conceived in that period, she goes out of estrus but will have a second period after a short interval.

One female grizzly who had not yet come into estrus was seen to dig a hole like a small den and back into it to resist the constant advances of an amorous male.

Two biologists in Banff National Park watched a large male grizzly bear herd a female onto a grassy ridge and keep her there during a 2-week period of courtship and copulation.

The big males travel almost constantly seeking receptive females. Bears stimulate one another by rubbing their bodies against each other, caressing the other with their tongues and engaging in gentle wrestling matches. The male stays with the female for perhaps a week and then is off to seek another mate. One female grizzly was seen to copulate with 3 different males in a period of a couple of days. Copulation lasts 20–60 minutes and one observer stated that the bears become fastened as do members of the dog family.

Female bears become sexually mature at 3½ to 4½ years of age, the males a year or more later. Most of the grizzly and brown bears breed every third year, with some breeding in the second year. Most of the cubs stay with their mothers till they are over 2 years old.

Bears experience delayed implantation in that the female is bred and her eggs are fertilized, but they do not fasten themselves to the wall of the uterus until late October or early November after she has denned up. As soon as the blastocysts (fertilized eggs) become implanted, growth and development are rapid and the young are born about 3 months later. Because of the delay in the implantation, the gestation period for the bear is about 7 months.

BIRTH AND YOUNG

The female grizzly bear, owned by my friends the Spaces, gave birth to 3 sets of twins and I was fortunate to see 2 sets while they were very young. As there is almost no research available on the newborn young of wild grizzlies, let me give you the statistics from my personal notes:

Grizzly bear cubs born 1/9/71, viewed 1/11/71. Cubs about 8–10 inches in total length; weight estimated at 8 ounces. Hair about ¼–½ inch in length, blue-gray in color. Feet and nose light pink. Eyes sealed shut. Claws perfectly formed. Hind feet about 1½ inches long, tail about one-half inch. Little ones make a noise like a female mallard's feeding call while they are nursing contentedly. At other times they make a squall of protest. Mother very gentle with little ones and usually lifts them up with her very dexterous claws. She licks them constantly while they nurse, making a loud slurping noise. She cleans up their body excrement in this fashion. When the mother lies on her side, she curls around so that the babies are in the warm hollow formed by her body and legs. At times she will put both babies on her extended forelegs and turn her head backward toward her chest so that her exhaled breath warms the cubs. She also picks up the babies by their heads with her mouth.

From the sketchy records, it appears that baby brown bears are a few inches longer at birth and a few ounces heavier than grizzlies. The cubs' eyes open about their 40th day, at which time the cubs weigh about 3 pounds.

I was able to get some accurate measurements of the cubs when they were removed from their mother on 3/6/71. At this time, they were 22 inches in total length and stood 9 inches high at the shoulder. Their ears were about 2 inches long. Their claws were one-half inch in length, their front paws were 2 inches in

Around the last of March the 2-month-old cubs, the age of the one pictured here, are brought out of the den by their mother.

These day-old grizzly bear cubs are about 10 inches in length and weigh less than one pound.

width, their hind feet were 3½ inches in length by 1¾ inches wide. Their fur was still blue-gray in color, with one cub having a white *V* on its chest, the other had a complete white ring like a collar. I did not get a scale weight but estimated it at about 5 pounds.

The Craigheads took milk samples from a number of the females that they captured and found the milk was low in lactose but high in protein, minerals and fat. Unfortunately, they did not give the butterfat content, saying only it was much higher than cow's milk, but almost all animals' milk is.

The cubs weigh about 10–12 pounds when they leave the den with their mother the last of April or the first of May. They grow very rapidly throughout the summer and weigh up to 100 pounds by fall.

I have watched both grizzly and brown bears nurse their cubs and at times they do so with the mother sitting upright and at other times she will lie flat on her back while the little ones clamber all over her chest. The cubs often sleep draped over the mother's back, if she is sleeping on her belly.

Female bears are famed as being good mothers and

An Alaskan brown bear sow and her 5-month-old cubs.

they deserve the accolade; most of them will willingly fight for their cubs. Yet studies done by the Craigheads on the grizzly bears and studies I have personally done on the brown bears show that mothers of equal age cubs are always losing some of their own cubs or adopting those of the other females. And it never seemed to make any difference to the cubs.

The Craigheads found that the grizzly bears average 2.2 cubs per litter. I found that most of the brown bears had 3 cubs and a number of them had 4. Both bears have been known to have as many as 5 cubs, although it is unusual.

On the McNeil River, there were a number of females that had 3 or more newborn cubs. While the mothers fished, the cubs would intermingle. If some-

thing frightened the bears, pandemonium reigned as the cubs dashed off in many directions. Each mother may have come in with 3 cubs apiece but often went off with 4 and 2 respectively. Females that were distinctively marked, so that they were easily recognized, had a constantly shifting number of cubs following them. No matter the number, the mother accepted any or all of the cubs willingly and took care of them.

I realize that both of the locations where the bears were studied had exceedingly high populations and this exchange of cubs probably would not have taken place where the bears were more scattered. The Craigheads studied at the Yellowstone dump area which, after decades, had become a natural location for the grizzlies, and I studied on the McNeil River, which probably has the greatest concentration of brown bears in the world.

The Craigheads record one female grizzly whose cubs were all adopted by another female. When this happened, the first female stopped lactating at 17 months and bred again a month later. This stepped up her personal reproduction by a full year. Ordinarily grizzly and brown bears lactate for 18–22 months and keep their cubs with them till they are over 2 years old.

Long before the cubs are weaned, they are feeding upon whatever food their mother is eating. Yearling cubs weigh about 145 pounds in June and have gained another 100 pounds, and usually much more, before denning for their second winter.

Grizzly and brown bear populations are vulnerable because of their low reproduction rates. The bears in Alaska have not experienced the habitat destruction that is rampant in the lower 48 states but it is increasing there as well. And the grizzlies in the Yukon average only 1.7 young per litter.

The Craigheads figured that the Yellowstone grizzly bears averaged 2.24 young per litter and bred every third year. The females are capable of breeding at 3 to 5 years and are productive up to the age of 22 years. This gives an annual average reproduction potential of 0.658 cubs per female year for 18 years or 11.84 cubs per lifetime. Taking into account the high mortality of the subadult bears, they figured one female could successfully raise 6.6 cubs per lifetime. A reduction in the number of adult female grizzlies can decimate the population.

An Alaskan brown bear sow and her 17-month-old cubs fishing for salmon.

LIFE SPAN

Potential: 30 years, although few fulfill this potential. Captive grizzly in Druid Hill Park Zoo in Baltimore lived to be 33 years 8 months 7 days, and brown bear there lived 36 years 10 months 6 days. Old Mose, killed in Colorado in 1904, thought to be at least 40 because he was full-grown when his depredations began and was hunted for 35 years.

SIGN

Tracks most common sign. Huge weight puts imprint on most surfaces. If ground very soft front foot heel pad will register, but not ordinarily. Both grizzly and brown bears create trails formed by thousands of bears walking in same tracks, creating hollows. Measurement from center of left hollow to center of right is 28 inches or 56 inches from center to center of tracks on either side. One awe-inspiring track of brown bear that I saw (of the largest bear in the vicinity) was 17 inches from claw tip to rear of heel pad and 11 inches wide.

Other sign includes marking trees, scat, torn stumps, covered carcasses and sites where they had dug ground squirrels, all previously described.

ENEMIES

No natural enemies, the biggest threat being the larger bears. Adults sometimes kill each other in fights, and adults kill subadults. Bears occasionally killed by big game attacked as prey, one grizzly gored to death by large bison bull. External parasites include flies, mosquitoes, ticks, fleas and lice; internal parasites, roundworms, flatworms, tapeworms. Occasional cases of rabies. Man the greatest threat of all, mainly through habitat destruction.

HUMAN RELATIONS

The greatest threat to all bears is the invasion and destruction of their habitat by man. It is not only the de-

The tracks of the male and female brown bears are seen together during the breeding season. The male's much larger tracks are on the left.

velopers moving in to change the wilderness; it is the tremendous influx of nature lovers who backpack into the bears' areas and cause conflict with the bears by doing so. In recent years there have been more bear-people contacts, conflicts, attacks, deaths, and some of the people have been eaten. The chances of any of this happening are extremely remote but it's always a possibility when you are in bear country.

To give the bears greater protection from people and from the park and refuge authorities, I believe that anyone entering bear country should sign a release so that the government can't be sued if he is injured by going into such country. Anyone not willing to sign such a release should stay out of the country in which bears might be found. Perhaps if people can be made to realize that they are responsible for their own actions in a confrontation with a bear, the bear will be given the respect it so easily commands and so rightly deserves. The bears were there first and I would like to be assured that they will be there for all time to come.

In hunting areas there is less danger from the bears because, where hunted, they are more wary of man. And the hunter has a weapon for protection.

The largest grizzly bear skull was picked up by James S. Shelton in 1970 in Bella Coola Valley, British Columbia. It measured 17 6/16 inches long by 9 12/16 inches wide for a total of 27 2/16 inches. There is no grizzly bear among the top 30 heads that were taken in the lower 48 states.

Twenty of the top 30 heads for the brown bear were taken on Kodiak Island. The skulls of the Kodiak Is-

land bears may be a little bit shorter than average but are much wider, which puts them high in the record book. The bears also have a distinctively high-domed forehead.

The skull of the brown bear killed by Roy Lindsley measured 17 15/16 inches in length by 12 13/16 inches in width, for a total of 30 12/16 inches.

COMMERCIAL VALUE

IAFWA statistics: average price grizzly or brown bear skin, 1976–77, $225, although no state reported sale of any skins and figure probably represents average price paid for 6 skins in Alberta, Canada. Such a price much too low from sportsman's viewpoint: cost of skin achieved through 10-day hunt with outfitter in British Columbia, including air fare, outfitter's fee, license, etc., would be nearly $6,000—explaining why bear skins are not sold.

BLACK BEAR, *Ursus americanus*

INTRODUCTION

The Latin name of the common black bear is *Ursus,* which means "bear." Some scientific writers use *Euarctos,* but most do not. The family name for all of the bears is *Ursidae.* The *americanus* is Latin for this American bear, which although found only in North America, did not originate here. The black bear came from Asia about 500,000 years ago by crossing the Bering Sea land bridge. As if all this were not confusing enough, the black bear is not always black but has five color phases.

The black bear has always been referred to as the clown of the woods. It is usually depicted as being a coward, always running from man. Fortunately, in the vast majority of encounters between the bear and hu-

man beings, this is true. Unfortunately, in recent years the number of attacks on humans by black bears has increased. It is not known if these attacks are the result of a change in the temperament of the bears or if they reflect the law of averages in more frequent encounters between the bear and man.

DESCRIPTION

The black bear is a medium-sized bear with the average adult male weighing between 300 and 400 pounds. It stands 27–36 inches high at the shoulder and measures 4 1/2 to 5 1/2 feet in length. The females are usually considerably smaller. Bears always appear to be much larger than they actually are because of their long hair. The guard hairs are 3–4 inches in length, with the hairs of the undercoat being between 1¼ to 1½ inches long. A dead bear is exceedingly difficult to move. They are so bulky, so hard to get hold of, that they seem to be a sack filled with lard. Most hunters so greatly overestimate the weight of their bears that only scale weights are reliable. However, the scales show some tremendous weights.

It is very difficult to get a scale large enough to weigh a bear out into the woods where the bear is located. Usually the bear is eviscerated in an effort to lighten the weight so the bear can be moved more easily, and as much as possible of the entrails, stomach, heart, liver, lungs, blood and fat is removed. Bear research has shown that these organs and other matter usually constitute 15–18 percent of the bear's total weight. When the hog-dressed bear is brought out and weighed, the 15–18 percent is added and the total is very close to what the bear weighed when alive.

In recent years some gigantic black bears have been taken. In 1953, Ed Strobel shot a black bear near Land O' Lakes, Wisconsin, that weighed 585 pounds, hog-dressed weight on a scale. The estimated liveweight is usually given at 700 pounds, but if the 15 percent calculation is used, the weight comes out to 669 pounds—still a mighty big bear.

On September 21, 1974, Holly Rhew, of Carp Lake, Michigan, dropped a huge black bear in Emmet County, with a single arrow. Certified scale weight was 613 pounds, giving this bear a live weight of 702 pounds.

In September 1968, Dean Kerscher shot a black bear near Land O' Lakes, Wisconsin, that scale-weighed 643 pounds. That gave an estimated liveweight of 733 pounds for a bear that was just starting to put on its accumulation of fat. What this bear would have weighed just before it denned up can only be speculated.

In November 1963, Otto Hedbany, of New Berlin, Wisconsin, shot a black bear near Glidden, Wisconsin, that was weighed on a certified scale at 652 pounds hog-dressed. The estimated liveweight of this bear was 749 pounds.

On September 13, 1975, Sam Ball, of Batavia, New

The black bear.

York, shot a black bear at Altamont, New York. Gary Will, bear specialist on the staff of the Department of Environmental Conservation's regional office at Ray Brook, New York, weighed the bear. Field-dressed, the bear weighed 660 pounds for an estimated 725 pounds liveweight. If the standard 15 percent had been used, the bear's estimated weight would have been 759 pounds.

The greatest verified scale weight for a black bear that I can find is one shot at Steven's Point, Wisconsin, in 1885. This bear was weighed without being dressed at 802½ pounds. Unfortunately, I cannot find a record of who killed the bear.

Although a black bear weighing 600 pounds is an exceptionally large bear, there are quite a few accurate records of live bears going over this weight. In 1957, two New York State biologists livetrapped, tagged, weighed and released a 605-pound black bear at Tupper Lake. One bear that they had trapped in 1956 weighed 332 pounds. When retrapped in 1957, the same bear weighed 562 pounds, for a net gain of 230 pounds in one year. Researchers for the Wisconsin Game Department recorded a weight gain of 130 pounds on one male bear from mid-August to mid-October. They claimed that on good food males will usually gain more than 100 pounds each fall, with females gaining 70–80 pounds on the average.

One other interesting note is of a 633-pound black bear killed by Herman Crokyndall, near Milford, Pennsylvania, in 1923, which measured 9 feet from nose tip to tail tip.

The black bear lacks the shoulder hump that typifies the brown-grizzly bears. The face of the black bear is comparatively straight or even slightly convex in profile, while the face of the brown-grizzly bear is concave or dish-faced.

The eyes of the black bear are small in comparison to the size of its head and are a very dark brown in color. The ears are quite large and well-rounded. The black bear has 42 teeth—12 incisors, 4 canines, 16 premolars and 10 molars. The canines are long, strong and sharply pointed; the premolars are rudimentary and some may be missing; the molars have flat-topped grinding crowns. The bear has loose, facile lips and a very long, flexible tongue.

The bear, like a human, is plantigrade, walking on its entire flat foot, although the rear tip of the heel pad of the front foot does not show unless the foot sinks in about 2 inches of snow or mud. The track of an adult black bear's front foot is about 5 inches in length by 4½ inches in width, from nail tip to heel pad; that of the hind foot is 8 inches long by 5½ inches in width.

There are 5 toes on each of the feet, with the claws on the front feet being about 1½ inches in length. They are curved, sharp and strong. Because of the shape and the size of its claws, the black bear can climb trees readily.

The black bear has 5 different color phases with a wide range of shadings in between. East of the Mississippi River, most of the black bears are black with a splash of white on their chests. In some individuals there is a definite white V. On rare occasions, some of the eastern bears will be brown in color.

In the Rocky Mountain region, the bears are as frequently brown as they are black and, in some areas, more of the bears are brown than black. The white on the chest is usually smaller in size or almost entirely absent. The shading of the brown phase* of the bear runs from a light tan, through a cinnamon-red, to a very dark brown. Occasionally a very light blond bear will be seen. Many biologists claim that as the blond bears get older, their color darkens. In Yellowstone National Park, I have photographed adult bears that had retained this blond coloration.

The Kermode Islands, off British Columbia's Pacific coast, are the home of the white black bears. These bears are not true albinos because they have dark eyes and a shading of brown around their muzzles. Their claws may be light colored. Most of the Kermode Island black bears are black, with these white "sports" being a genetic minority. These white bears are completely protected from hunting.

Along Alaska's coastal regions of the St. Elias Alps, the Yakatut and Glacier bays and in the extreme northwestern corner of coastal British Columbia, are found the rare "blue" or "glacier" black bears. Again, most of the glacier bears are black, with a few of the genetic blue ones being seen occasionally.

DISTRIBUTION

Through cunning, adaptability, tolerance of man and omnivorous diet black bear survives where other large predators have not. Recent better protection has increased population in some areas. Wise game management essential to its survival.

Needs dense cover by nature and physiology—to escape enemies and for shade. Black fur absorbs too much heat in strong sun and during warm weather bear will appear in open only at dusk or daybreak.

Found throughout most of Canada and Alaska, except for tundra, and all of western states with mountains; also in most of northern and northeastern states,

*A *phase* as used here is a characteristic form (i.e., color) that distinguishes some individuals of a species.

BLACK BEAR
(Ursus americanus)
CURRENT RANGE

along Appalachians and in swamplands of Virginia, North Carolina, South Carolina, Georgia, Florida, Alabama and Louisiana—adaptable to both sea-level swamps and 9,000-foot mountains, wherever there are large areas of dense cover and food. Northwestern New Jersey has small population of black bears.

TRAVEL

Bears do not migrate, but they are great wanderers. They may have seasonal shifts due to pressure put upon the bears by hunters or by a change in food supply. If there is an ample amount of food, a bear may confine its activities to one square mile. They do not have a den area that they return to each night but eat, sleep and wander about according to the dictates of their stomachs. When they are sleepy, they seek out dense cover for concealment. They may rake dead leaves and grasses together to form a bed or they may sleep wherever they happen to flop down. On occasion, they may climb up a tree and sleep on a large limb with their feet hanging down on both sides. The small size of some of the limbs that these bears sit and sleep on is amazing, some only 2 to 3 inches in diameter.

Under normal conditions an adult black bear female will have a home range of about 10 square miles, while a male will have about 30–40 square miles; the size always depends upon the amount of food that is available.

When a bear is moving about looking for food, it meanders unless it has a destination in mind. Bears love to walk upon and along the top of downed logs. They do not do this to enjoy the scenery because their eyesight is not that good.

Bears, in areas where they are hunted heavily, will often circle back on their trails and lie where the breeze will carry the scent of anything following them.

A great deal of study has been devoted to the homing abilities of the black bear. Bears that become a nuisance in national parks, because of people feeding them, usually have to be livetrapped and removed. In most cases the bears are drugged, weighed, tattooed, tagged and their age determined before being released again. Records on such bears are thus easily obtained.

Studies done in Michigan showed that one black bear traveled 64 miles to return to its home. One sow with cubs traveled 98 miles in 35 days and was within 6 miles of being home when she was killed. One bear traveled 57 miles in just 3 days to return to the dump where it had originally been captured. No matter what we humans think of bears eating garbage, that was one bear that knew exactly what it wanted.

A study by bear researchers in Virginia showed one bear returned 100 air miles after being released. The bear holding the traveling record was a black that was captured at Pawley Springs, Virginia, and taken to Loft Mountain, 130 air miles away. The bear was recaptured in Pawley Springs just 12 days later.

LOCOMOTION

Bears ordinarily walk with a flat-footed shuffle at about 3 miles per hour. They are always stopping to sniff about for food. When they are in a hurry, they just walk faster; they don't trot. When a bear runs flat-out, it goes in a rolling gallop that will hit a speed of about 30 miles per hour with 12–15 foot jumps. At a slower speed, but using this same bounding gallop, bears can run for hours without stopping.

Bears can't jump very high, being just too bulky and heavy but they can climb up almost anything unless the surface is too smooth or steep. Anyone who thinks they can escape from a black bear by climbing a tree is in for a shock; a black bear can climb up a tree faster than a person can fall out of it.

When a bear is climbing leisurely, it may use its feet alternately as a man would. If the tree has branches, the bear will take advantage of them. When a bear climbs a tree quickly, it uses its front feet to hold its body upright and in position and powers its climb with both hind feet working in unison. It literally gallops up the tree. In climbing, the bear's claws often slip until they dig in through the outer bark of the tree. These scars usually darken, permanently marking the smooth-barked trees such as birch and aspen.

The short, strong claws of the black bear allow it to climb trees easily. The adult grizzly and brown bears cannot climb.

At times, when frightened, a bear will jump out of a tree. There are many records of them jumping out at heights of 20–30 feet. Niles Fairbaine, of Margaretville, New York, saw a bear jump out of a beech tree, where it had been feeding on the nuts at a height of 40 feet, land on its rump unhurt and run off.

Bears are strong swimmers and I have often seen them cross large lakes in Canada. When a bear swims, it usually goes in a straight line, even though by turning to a point of land the swimming distance could be shortened. Never approach closely a bear that is swimming. Many people who have done so learned quickly to regret it as a bear will scramble up into any boat or canoe that gets near. They have a swimming speed of between 3 and 5 miles per hour.

FOOD

Bears classified as carnivores but actually omnivorous, as revealed by large canine teeth (for grasping prey) and flat-topped molars (for crushing vegetation). Will eat everything found or captured, ants beneath rocks or within rotting trees, all types of berries, fruits, and melons (blueberries, blackberries and lingonberries mainstays during summer). Blueberries consumed as bear sits amid bushes raking in berries, leaves and stems to its mouth and tons of berries eaten by single bear in good season. Berries pass quickly through bear's system and leave heaps of large, soft round dung.

Beginning in 1945 in Washington (with highest

Many trees have scars from the claws of the bears that have climbed them.

black bear population of 48 contiguous states at 30,000–35,000) bears began chewing bark from Douglas firs, silver firs, western hemlocks and western red cedars to consume sugar-rich cambium layer, which killed trees. Although begun in a season short of berries, the diet became habitual and now bears feed on these trees from the time they emerge from the dens in the spring until berries ripen 6–8 weeks later. Some areas have lost 90 percent of tree plantations to bears, a loss of millions of dollars in lumber. Some bears destroy 40 trees a day.

Like raccoons, bears crave sweets and satisfy this craving by eating honey. Bears able to wreak havoc on apiary—raccoons settle for wild honey while bears can invade commercial beehives. Thick fur protects against stings. Bears also eat bees.

Bears eat all types of vegetation: corn (when fields border on wilderness areas), most vegetables, grains, grasses (which make up the bulk of the diet) and hay crops. Bears able to extract as much protein from vegetation as the herbivores. During autumn, black bears feed on acorns, beechnuts, hickory nuts, pecans, piñon nuts, etc. Blight of American chestnut in 1920s and 1930s a blow to bears and other wildlife.

Small creatures eaten include snakes, frogs, salamanders, turtles; suckers and salmon also eaten. Eggs, young and adult ground-nesting birds eaten if they can be captured, as are mice, rabbit nestlings, ground squirrels, newborn of deer, elk and moose. Large game eaten if injured, sick or aged. Carrion, no matter how spoiled, also consumed. Among livestock pigs are a favored food, and some nuisance bears develop taste for young lambs, calves, colts and poultry, although most bears avoid livestock. Black bears extirpated from their primal range because seen as threat to livestock. Bears often destroy wilderness camps and cabins, making a shambles in their search for food. Precautions to campers to minimize the problems between people and bears:

1. Do not leave food lying about or keep it in your tent.
2. Burn or bury all garbage.
3. Keep food in tightly sealed plastic containers to cover odors.
4. Do not sleep close to areas where you have done your cooking.
5. Suspend your food between trees at least 12 feet above the ground and 5 feet from nearest tree trunk or limb.

Bears love apples and they can be very destructive to the trees. Not content to pick up just the fallen apples, the bear climbs up into the tree to gorge itself and to shake down the apples that it can't reach. Usually the bear sits up in the crown of the tree and pulls all of the outspreading branches into the center, breaking them to get the apples. My neighbor's trees, victims of this technique, look as if some big bird had

It is amazing how small a limb a big black bear will sit on.

made a giant nest in the top of each apple tree.

After a hard windstorm has knocked most of the apples from a tree, the bears may get drunk from eating the fermented fruit. Two bears in Massachusetts, in 1969, became so intoxicated from eating apples that they were unable to walk. The State Game Commission closed the bear hunting season from October 28 to November 1 to give the bears a chance to sober up. Three game wardens were detailed to baby-sit with bears around the clock so that they would not be killed while in a stupor. When the bears finally sobered up and staggered away, the bear season was reopened.

BEHAVIOR

Bears are usually very shy and avoid all possible contact with man. Most problems bears have become that way because they have been fed by man. Bears, contrary to television shows and movies, are not big, lovable, cuddly creatures. They are interesting, sometimes comical, but they also are individualistically unpredictable. *Don't feed the bears.*

As it is with some people, so it is with some bears, they are just bad. These are the bears that are constantly getting into trouble and the reason behind it may never be known or understood. These are the bears that may attack without apparent provocation because it is sometimes next to impossible to know what has provoked an animal or has made it feel threatened.

Mother bears with cubs are particularly dangerous because they usually rush to protect their cubs from anything that might be considered dangerous. And you, on the receiving end, may not even know what triggered the reaction. Let me give you an example.

My son Lenny and I were backpacking up the trail to Sperry Glacier in Glacier National Park in Montana. Suddenly we were startled by a loud crashing of bushes and then branches as two 6-month-old bear cubs went scrambling up a nearby tree, whining all the time. Believe me, we had done nothing to the cubs, we hadn't even been aware of them till they panicked,

but our greatest hope was that we could convince big momma bear of that. We had backed off the trail and got in among some trees by the time the mother bear dashed onto the scene. She popped her teeth and made her presence known, while we tried to shrink out of sight. Evidently she figured, rightfully so, that we were not really a threat either to her cubs or to herself and she called the cubs down from the tree and left. But that's how easy it is to get into trouble in bear country.

Bears are essentially loners. The male and female consort with each other only during the breeding season; at most other times they are rivals or antagonists. The mother bear usually keeps her cubs with her till they are $1\frac{1}{2}$ to 2 years old. The cubs den with their mother for their first winter and some cubs may den with her for their second winter. While with their mother, the cubs are well protected by her knowledge and strength. She frequently has to defend her young against the adult male bears in her area, including the father of her cubs.

The greatest mortality occurs to the young bears in the period of their first year after being abandoned by their mother in the spring. Adult male bears do not hesitate to attack any young bear, particularly young males. The adult bears frequently eat any younger bears that they kill.

The younger bears have to compete with the older, larger bears for territory, den sites and food. All of this is no problem in areas or during years when food is plentiful. If food shortages occur, the young bears are driven into the most undesirable areas where many of them die or are killed.

Den sites are not usually a problem because so many types of shelters can be used. Most people think of bears living their lives and spending the winters sleeping in caves. Some bears retire to caves in the winter, but the vast majority do not. Most bears spend the winter beneath the roots of blown-down trees, in dense brushy tangles or in hollow trees. The bears prefer the dens to be on a north-facing slope so that there is not much of a temperature change and little chance of melting snow. The bears usually carry varying

A huge black bear that is exceptionally fat just prior to denning up.

amounts of dead leaves, dead grasses or chewed-off stick into their dens for bedding. At times, the bears will have carried in enough vegetation to plug up the hole they crawl through before they go to sleep.

Bears do not hibernate. All during the summer and the fall months, bears gorge themselves in order to store as much fat on their bodies as is possible. For a week prior to denning up, the bears stop eating in order to thoroughly empty their stomachs, intestines and bladders. The bears then eat several fistfuls of dead pine needles, grasses and leaves. This material passes through the body and forms a fecal plug in the bears' anuses. Then, with the coming of severely cold weather, they den up and go to sleep.

The bears become lethargic but they do not go into the deep sleep of hibernation. Their breathing rate slows down and their heartbeat rate drops from a normal of 55 beats per minute to 30 heartbeats or even slightly lower. The bears' body temperatures drop from 100° F. to about 89° F. No waste material is voided as the digestive system is empty except for the fecal plug. Although the bears' kidneys continue to function, the small amounts of water are reabsorbed back into the bears' systems while there is a slight build-up of uric acid in the bears' blood.

Black bears that are disturbed during denning react in different ways; most are just too sleepy to do more than move about. Occasionally a bear may be roused enough to bound out of its den but this usually occurs only in the late spring. Almost all of the bears give some indication that they are aware of being disturbed but most do nothing about it.

Bears in the warmer regions may wake up and leave the den to wander about before returning to their dens again. In the Deep South some of the bears don't den up at all.

There are times in the North, when food is exceedingly scarce, when the bears will den up without the amount of fat on their bodies that they really need. Denning up, which lowers the bear's metabolism and reduces its caloric needs, is a tremendous survival factor with the bears that did so evolving and surviving up to the present time.

In a season when food has been plentiful, the accumulation of fat on the bear is nothing short of incredible. In some cases the fat on a bear's back may be more than 5 inches thick. There are also generous deposits of fat in the abdominal cavity. A bear killed in Wisconsin had a blanket of fat that weighed 212 pounds. Rendered out, this would have produced almost 20 gallons of bear oil. In our country's early days, and even today, this oil was highly sought for cooking, frying, baking, in the tanning of leather, lubrication, as medicine and for many other purposes. In Colonial days, it was worth $5–$6 per gallon and that was at a time when a day's wages were about $1.

Usually less than half of the bear's accumulated fat is reabsorbed during its denning period to feed its flickering furnace of life. Most emerge from their dens in good condition. The remaining fat is usually quickly burned up after the bears emerge from their dens in late March or April.

When the bears do emerge from their dens, they seem to wander about quite aimlessly at first. Their first need is water. When the bears begin to feed, they seek out the newest green sprouts and shoots. It is at this time that skunk cabbage is heavily fed upon, where found. Bears are at their lightest weight about two weeks after emerging from their dens.

During the winter the pads on a bear's feet slough off, just as we humans lose the calluses on our hands when we don't work with them for a week or more. Until its feet begin to toughen up, a bear does not do extensive walking.

SENSES

Sense of smell most important, bear relying on its nose for its safety and its food. Bear often stands erect to search air for scents and walks with head swaying from side to side, snuffling constantly. It usually walks upwind to receive advance notice of danger or food. One bear in California reportedly traveled in a straight line for 3 miles to find deer carcass it had smelled. Bears have been known to swim large lakes, attracted by the smell of frying bacon on other side.

Hearing is very keen, and any noise in their dense habitat alerts them. Bears usually move away from unidentified sound before it can become a threat.

Sight is poor, bears being nearsighted, and they stand erect principally to improve their view. Bears often approach people in order to see them. Bears can detect motion readily.

Because of its preferred foods bears' sense of taste probably keen, but appetite overrules taste because they will eat nearly everything.

COMMUNICATION

An adult black bear, under most circumstances, is a solitary and very quiet creature. A confrontation between two adult male bears or an adult faced with other potential danger is occasion for many vocalizations. At such times the bears growl, snarl, roar, make a whooshing sound and chop their jaws. This popping of their teeth is a frightening sound and an effective threat. The sheer size of a large bear's body spells danger to any lesser bear. The various positions of the head and the way it is held all have meaning to other bears; a subordinate bear usually lowers its head and turns its face away.

An injured bear sobs, cries and wails, with most humanlike sounds. Bear cubs whine, bawl, squeal and, when contented, make a humming or buzzing sound.

On occasion bears will roll in foul-smelling substances to get the putrid odor on their head, neck and shoulders in the same fashion as the canids do. This is a means of communication but I'm not sure what it means.

Controversy swirls about the meaning of the bear "marking" trees. I have seen bears stand upright against trees and rub their backs and extend their heads as high as possible. Was the bear just scratching an itch or was it deliberately marking the tree to show its size to other bears?

Many of the trees marked by bears have been bitten. Did the bear do this to get the sweet cambium layer or is it marking the tree?

Some of the bear trees are raked with the bear's claws with the bear reaching as high as is possible. Is the bear trying to show his rivals how big he is or is he just stretching and sharpening his claws, as cats do? Many stories have been written about these bear tree markings. We do know that the bears mark the trees but we really don't know why, and the bear experts can't agree either.

BREEDING

Young female bears become sexually mature at 3½ years of age. Young males are capable of breeding at that age but are usually kept from doing so by the larger adult males.

The breeding season for the black bear occurs during the latter part of May, through June and into early July. A female that has grown cubs with her will lose them at this time or the male bear will drive them away.

Bears are monoestrus with one period in the year when the female comes into heat, and this is the only time of the year that the male consorts with the female. At other times, she will avoid him. The female must be stimulated before copulation takes place and the bears are most affectionate. They stroke each other with their claws, caress one another with their tongues, rub their bodies against each other and roll and tumble about in light wrestling matches. For a short period, they put the cares of the everyday world aside and regain the playfulness they displayed as cubs. The male stays with the female for perhaps 2 weeks, copulation taking place a number of times, and then he leaves to seek another female.

Bears are subject to delayed implantation, which means that although the female's eggs have been fertilized, they develop very little and do not become attached to the wall of the uterus until late October or November. After attachment to the wall occurs, the blastocysts develop rapidly. Because of many factors, the actual time of implantation varies and the gestation period is said to be about 7 months.

BIRTH AND YOUNG

The young of the black bear are usually born in the latter part of January or early February, while the female is denned up. At one time it was thought that the female was not awake when the young were born but this has been proved untrue. A bear mother is very solicitous of her young and carefully cleans them, keeps them warm and nurses them.

Twins or triplets are common, although 4 cubs are not uncommon. There have been a number of litters consisting of 5 cubs and records exist for 2 sets of 6 cubs each.

Bear cubs are fully formed at birth but are exceedingly small. The average black bear cub weighs about 8 ounces, compared to a human baby's weight of 6 pounds. A human baby weighs about $1/20$th of its mother's weight, a baby black bear weighs about $1/250$th of its mother's weight or less. When we remember that many black bear males get to weigh over 600 pounds, which means that the cub is $1/1200$th of its future size, you can readily see that its growth potential is phenomenal.

At birth the bear cubs are almost naked with a fine tan fuzz visible, their claws are developed but their eyes are sealed shut and they measure 8 to 10 inches in nose to tail tip length.

Although the female does not leave the den for water or food during the winter, her body fat is metabolized into milk for her young. I can find no record of the butterfat content of a bear's milk but it must be very rich as the young grow very rapidly.

The female has 6 teats, 4 located on her chest between her front legs and 2 between her hind legs. The cubs nurse primarily at the breast because the mother usually cuddles the young to keep them warm.

The cubs' eyes open about 6 weeks of age. At this time the cubs are well furred with glossy hair and they weigh about 6 pounds. At 2 months they weigh about 8 pounds and are ready to follow after their mother when she leaves the den.

Mother bears are strict disciplinarians. They tell the cubs just once, and a second telling is accompanied with a clout that sends the young ones sprawling. When a mother bear is confronted with what she considers danger from another bear, or from a human, she most frequently sends the cubs scrambling up a tree while she makes a determined stand on the ground. The cubs are not allowed to come down till she tells them to do so. Cubs have been known to stay up in trees for 20 hours or more until the mother returned for them.

Although wild animals do not make good pets, this 2-month-old black bear cub looks as soft and cuddly as its namesake, the teddy bear.

The cubs have an almost idyllic, protected life. They are well fed and cared for and their waking moments are filled with play. The cubs are constantly wrestling, playing and fighting. If the play or fighting gets too rough, the mother puts an end to it.

Although some females have been known to lactate

for 12 months or more, most of the cubs are weaned by 6 to 8 months. Long before this time, the cubs are imitating their mother in securing and eating natural foods. By September the cubs weigh about 40–50 pounds.

I can find no record of two adult bears denning together. A mother bear does take her cubs into the den with her for at least their first winter and at this time the young will weigh between 70 and 90 pounds.

The young bears usually stay with the female during their second summer. She does not breed that year. When the young bears are ready for denning at 1 year 10 months, the males will average 154 pounds to the females' 118 pounds. These young bears will usually seek out dens of their own or they may den up with their mother. If they do the latter, they will be driven off soon after they emerge from their den in the spring.

Extensive studies were done by the Pennsylvania Game Commission on the continued growth pattern for the black bears of both sexes. At 2 years 10 months, the males will average 223 pounds; the females 159 pounds. At 3 years 10 months, the males will average 280 pounds, the females 179. At 4 years 10 months, the males will average 312 pounds, the females 195 pounds. For 5 years and older, the males will average 400 pounds, the females 205 pounds.

LIFE SPAN

Potential: 20–25 years, many captive bears living to this age and more. Most accurate method of aging bears and other mammals is to slice and stain a section of incisor teeth and count number of annual cementium layers by microscope observation. Game Commissions in New York and Pennsylvania have aged wild bears at over 30 years. Oldest on record: 41.75 years, a bear killed in Newcomb, Essex County, New York, in 1974.

SIGN

Tracks in mud, soft earth, snow, sand and dusty roads

conspicuous by their large size. Droppings vary in shape, size and color depending on diet: fruit and berries produce droppings as large as a cow's and very loose; grasses produce droppings greenish-brown color and more compacted; meat produces droppings like humans' but twice the diameter. Other sign includes torn-apart stumps, upturned rocks, broken fruit treetops, bear tree markings.

ENEMIES

Adult black bear has no natural enemies in eastern half of U.S. In western mountains grizzly bear is an enemy where it remains. Dogs chase bears on occasion. External parasites: fleas, lice and ticks in dense hair. Also plagued by flies and mosquitoes. Internal parasites include tapeworms, lungworms, and flukes. Bear meat must be thoroughly cooked because, like pigs, bears carry trichinosis. Sometimes black bears contract rabies.

Major predator of black bear is other black bears. Large males kill each other during breeding season and will kill any younger males they encounter and can catch. At times bears gored or kicked to death by hooved prey animals.

HUMAN RELATIONS

Let me reiterate what I have touched upon briefly before. The vast majority of black bears will run from humans as soon as they hear or see one. Unfortunately, of late, there has been an increase in the number of attacks upon people by black bears for reasons that are unknown to us. And more bears have eaten a part of the human that they killed.

Our national parks, such as the Great Smokies, Yellowstone and Yosemite, all contain populations of black bears but only a fraction of the bears that formerly lived there. Despite the admonitions of park officials and rangers not to feed the bears, the general public, blissful in the ignorance of their actions, feeds the bears. So many accidents have occurred to people, through their own stupidity, that many bears have

had to be destroyed or moved elsewhere. In 1960, I saw 56 bears in one day in Yellowstone Park, but in recent years I have not seen a single bear there. The only protection a human has against a bear is the bear's unreasonable fear of humans. When this fear in the bear has been destroyed by the proximity of man, through feeding or at dump sites, then all advantages belong to the bear. In the parks the bears are kept wild by forcing them to live on their own in the back country. On the rest of the bear's range, the bear has learned to fear man because of hunting, as it has been since the day when both of us slept in caves.

The status of the bear has changed drastically in the last 20–30 years. Formerly the bears of most areas had a bounty on their heads and could be killed at any time and in any manner. Today, the bear has been granted protection in most states by being classified as a game animal to be hunted only during a specified season. In some states, where the bear is scarce, it receives complete protection.

The black bear population in the United States today is estimated at about 194,635, with Canada having approximately 200,000 more. In most areas, due to increased protection, the bear population is holding its own or increasing slightly. The continued destruction of its habitat by man is the largest question mark in the black bear's future.

A total of 1,102 black bears was killed in the United States in the 1976–77 hunting season. The trophy bears are determined not by their size and weight but by length and breadth of the skull.

The number-three black bear in the record book was taken by Richard R. Barney and Hal E. Booker, in 1968, in Apache County, Arizona. The skull measured 13 9/16 inches long by 8 11/16 inches wide, for a total of 22 4/16 inches.

The number-two skull was taken by Joseph A. Waite, in 1975, on the San Carlos Indian Reservation in Arizona. The skull measured 13 12/16 inches long by 8 9/16 inches wide, for a total of 22 5/16 inches.

The number-one black bear was taken by Rex W. Peterson and Richard S. Hardy, in 1970, in San Pete County, Utah. The skull measured 13 11/16 inches in length by 8 11/16 inches in width, for a total of 22 6/16 inches.

COMMERCIAL VALUE

In 1976–77, with only 4 states reporting, 1,102 black bears taken (a low, inaccurate figure), average price $44 per skin, $48,488 total. In Canada, 3,402 black bears taken, average price $43.93, $149,444 total. Cost of bear hunt, including license, food, lodging, transportation, rifles, etc., averages to $40 per day per hunter, thus the peripheral commercial value runs into millions of dollars per year.

POLAR BEAR, *Ursus maritimus*

INTRODUCTION

The great white bear of the Arctic is king of all it surveys. Shuffling along on its huge padded feet, the polar bear appears and disappears among the broken ice like a wraith, its white coat rendering it almost invisible.

Formerly designated scientifically as *Thalarctos maritimus,* it has now been changed to *Ursus maritimus. Thalassa* is a Greek word meaning "sea," while *arctos* is "bear." *Maritimus* is Latin, meaning "of the sea." The new form *Ursus* is Latin for "bear" and this bear is of the sea. Many of the polar bears spend most of their lives on the frozen ocean. It has been found that this bear is closely related to the brown bears and interbreeding between the two species produces offspring that are fertile. Nanook is the Eskimo name for the great white bear.

DESCRIPTION

The polar bear is the only all-white bear in the world, although its fur takes on a very yellowish tinge in summer. The polar bear's hair is waterproof and about 2 1/2 inches in length.

There is constant debate over whether the polar bear or the Alaskan brown bear is larger. The greatest scale weight for a wild brown bear is 1,656 pounds, from English Bay, Alaska. A polar bear that is in the Carnegie Museum display in Pittsburgh, Pennsylvania, was weighed in pieces and tipped the scale at a verified weight of 1,728 pounds. A polar bear shot at Cape York, Alaska, stood 4 feet 6 inches high at the shoulder and weighed 1,800 pounds. Its skin measured 11 feet in total length. A Russian report states that one polar bear measured and weighed there stood 4 feet 9 inches high at the shoulder, had a 9 foot heart girth and weighed 2,100 pounds. Of that weight, 430 pounds was fat. Dr. Bernhard Grzimek, director of the Frankfurt Zoological Garden, states that some exceptional polar bears in the Siberian Arctic weigh up to 2,200 pounds.

A polar bear shot near Kotzebue, Alaska, in 1960, weighed 2,210 pounds. The bear was mounted in a standing position and measured 11 feet 1 1/2 inches. This should prove that the polar bear is larger than the Alaskan brown bear.

Now that we have looked at the records, let's look at the average polar bear. Female polar bears usually attain full body size at the age of 4 years. At this time they average about 3 1/2 feet high at the shoulders, 6 feet in total length and weigh 700 pounds. Male polar bears reach maturity at 6 years of age and will stand 4 feet high at the shoulders, measure 8 to 9 feet in total length and weigh between 800 and 1,000 pounds. They have a 6- to 8-inch tail.

The polar bear is the largest carnivore in the world. Note bear's long sinuous neck and big feet. (Photo: Len Rue, Jr.)

The polar bear has an elongated, pear-shaped body accentuated by the large, heavy hindquarters. The bear's neck is long and sinuous, tapering from the small, pointed head. There is a slight hump to the shoulders. Polar bears, while standing, are constantly shifting their weight from one front foot to the other, their long necks swaying from side to side.

The polar bear's feet are large, with forepaws up to 12 inches across, and the feet are covered with long, thick hair that insulates its soles and provides traction on smooth ice. Bears that come on land frequently wear this hair off. There are 5 toes on each foot and the bear walks on its entire flat foot surface. The polar bear's claws are about 3 inches in length, strongly re-curved, sharp and black in color. Again, those bears that come on land dull the claw tips that are needed to grip the ice. The sharp claws allow the bears to climb up almost sheer ice columns and slabs that dogs cannot negotiate.

The polar bear's fur is dense and waterproof. The guard hairs measure about 2½ inches in length, while the undercoat is about 2 inches long. When the young male bears reach 4 years of age, they begin to develop longer hair along the back of their necks, over their shoulders and along the rear portion of their front legs. The bears molt their winter hair in May through July. The better the condition of the bear, the earlier it molts.

The skin of the polar bear is rather spongy and oily with fat. A bear that has been feeding well will often have a layer of fat 3 to 4 inches thick beneath its skin. Instead of having a dense lardlike marrow in the center of its bones, the polar bear's marrow is of a more oily consistency. The liver of the polar bear has a tremendously high concentration of vitamin A. So high, in fact, that it is toxic to man. A 3-ounce portion of the bear's liver will supply all the vitamin A that a man would need for a year. Many explorers became very ill and some died from eating polar bear's liver.

The eyes of a polar bear are dark brown. To protect its eyes from the glare of the sun on the vast expanses of snow and ice, the polar bear has almost transparent eyelids that serve as sunglasses by filtering out the excessive brightness. These eyelids also act as waterproof goggles when the bear is swimming. The bear's ears are situated low on the sides of its head and do not protrude above the crown.

The polar bear has 42 teeth—12 incisors, 4 two-inch canines, 16 premolars and 10 molars. The last premolar and the first molar teeth of the polar bear are more nearly like the carnassial teeth of the canids than any of the other bears because this bear is almost a complete carnivore.

DISTRIBUTION

Found around the world at southern edge of Arctic Ocean, rarely in the interior reaches. There are about 5 million square miles of Arctic and sub-Arctic area, but location of bears depends upon time of year and corresponding extent of pack ice. In North America, polar bear found from Bering Sea in Alaska to Labrador and Newfoundland off eastern coast. First polar bear noted in New World caught at Funk Island in Newfoundland in May 1534 by Jacques Cartier. Recent research indicates heaviest concentrations of polar bears are in Hudson and James Bay areas of Canada.

TRAVEL

Some polar bears travel more than any other land mammal in the world. A good deal of the travel is deliberate because some of the large males have no home but keep moving to be near the openings in the ice so that they can secure food. Some researchers claim that hunting bears travel average distances of 75 miles per week.

Much of the distance traveled by the bears is done inadvertently because the Arctic pack ice turns clockwise, or from east to west, and moves on the average of 2.4 miles per day. Occasionally the bears are on a section of ice that moves southward as a field, carrying the bears hundreds of miles before it breaks up.

In Alaska, some of the bears are near the Kotzebue–Point Barrow area in April and are then carried toward Siberia in June and July. Some of the bears are carried through the Bering Strait as far south as St. Lawrence Island and occasionally even to the Pribilofs in the winter and then back up to the Chukchi Sea in the summer, a distance of 600–700 miles. There is one record of a polar bear, which I cannot verify, being killed on Kodiak Island. This would entail a distance traveled of about 1,100 miles.

On the eastern coast of North America, some of the polar bears are both carried and travel from Baffin Bay down to Labrador, following the harp and bladder-nosed seals. This is a distance of about 1,000 miles.

I can give an extreme example of the possibility of the tremendous distance traveled by polar bears. A polar bear was killed on Lake St. John in Quebec. The bear could have come down the eastern Canadian coast and into the Bay of St. Lawrence, as polar bears occasionally do. It would have then had to travel up the St. Lawrence River to the Saguenay River and from there northwestward up the river to Lake St. John. That would have set the all-time distance record at about 1,888–2,000 miles just from Hudson Strait. Or, the bear could have come down from James Bay, up the Rupert River, eastward to Lake Mistassini and south to Lake St. John. This would have entailed a trip of 600–800 miles, according to the route the bear had taken.

Studies done on polar bears do not really contradict each other when the results differ. They do illustrate the fact that any study done on any creature shows only what that particular animal is doing in that particular spot at that particular time. Jack Lentfer, biolo-

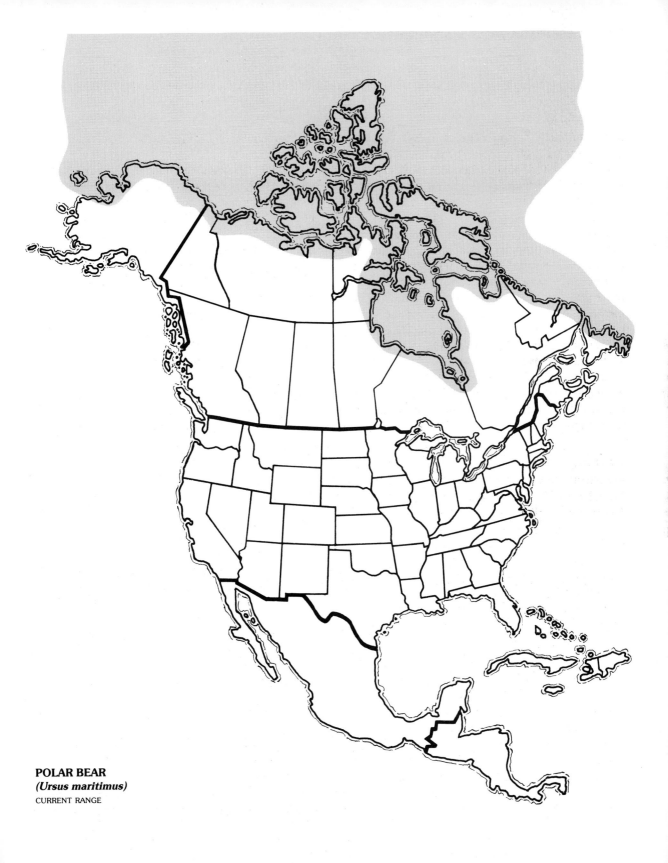

POLAR BEAR
(Ursus maritimus)
CURRENT RANGE

gist with the Alaska Department of Fish and Game, made a study of the polar bears in Alaska which showed that most of the bears that he tagged stayed in the general vicinity in which he tagged them. He also tells of one tagged bear that was shot 700 miles away on the Russian coast.

The homing ability of the polar bear is well illustrated by the two bears that were making a nuisance of themselves around Churchill, Manitoba. The bears were drugged, tagged and transported by helicopter to a release point 300 air miles away. Fifteen days later both bears were back at their point of capture.

The polar bear's range expands with the coming of frigid weather and shrinks when warm weather causes the ice to recede.

LOCOMOTION

All bears have a shuffling walk but this gait is accentuated with the polar bear because its feet look like the large furry floor mops that some women wear as slippers. They have a trot that sets their flaps of belly skin swinging from side to side. Their gallop is rolling and bounding, emphasized by the hind legs being so much longer than the front legs and the fact that most of the bear's weight is in the hindquarters.

Despite their bulk, polar bears are exceedingly nimble and can cover a lot of terrain in a short time. When the bear gallops, it covers the ice in 12-foot jumps at speeds of up to 25 miles per hour. What makes the bear so fearsome in the Arctic is that there is nothing a man can get behind or up on to get away from a bear that is charging.

The polar bear can jump up and over a 6-foot block of ice. With its sharp claws, it can scramble up an extremely steep ice slope. The bears often climb up on tilted ice hummocks or pressure ice, only to slide down again. They often do this in a sitting position with their front feet extended like skis. The bears will also climb up these hummocks to use them as lookout posts, scanning the area for seals.

The polar bears are excellent swimmers—as they would need to be to survive in the region they inhabit.

They frequently have to swim from floe to floe to secure food or to get back to the land or the main ice pack when the floe they are on breaks loose and drifts away. Their waterproof fur and their insulating fat make them impervious to the most bitter weather. Polar bears are often seen hunting when the temperatures are −50° or −60° F. Seawater freezes between 28° F. and 30° F. so the water is actually much warmer than the air. When the polar bear climbs out of the water, it shakes itself vigorously, cascading the water droplets from its fur.

While swimming, the polar bear usually uses just its front feet, leaving its hind feet extended behind the body and using them as rudders. The bear's huge front paws, some having as much as a 34-inch circumference, provide excellent propulsion. The toes are partially webbed and this increases the foot's surface. When the bear swims leisurely, it travels at about 3 miles per hour but it has been clocked at over 6 miles per hour. It has also been seen to surge or lunge forward in the water for distances as much as 15 feet.

The bears are excellent long-distance swimmers because when tired, they can float on the surface of the water without any exertion. Their buoyancy is attributed to the layer of fat on their bodies and the air trapped in their hair.

One female polar bear and her small cub were seen swimming 35 miles off the shore at Cape Barrow, Alaska. Polar bear cubs, when they tire while swimming, will hold on to their mother's tail with their teeth and be towed along. Or they may hold on to her rump with their paws or even climb up on her back.

Bob Bartlett, Admiral Robert Peary's ship captain, saw one polar bear swimming in the open ocean 60 miles from land. He figured that a polar bear could swim 75 miles in 24 hours.

Alf Olsen, a Norwegian ship captain, reported a female polar bear and her half-grown cub 200 miles out in open water. He did not say she had swum that far but that she was 200 miles from land. She was headed for the nearest pack ice which he knew to be 100 miles to the north of the bear's position.

Ordinarily, the bears plunge into the water headfirst

when it is not in their interest to be quiet. If they enter the water to swim out to an ice floe which has a sleeping seal on it, they lower themselves into the water backward and silently. When they swim toward a sleeping seal or walrus, they often swim underwater, coming up every so often to get a breath of air and to check their position and their sleeping prey. Polar bears have been timed at remaining underwater for two minutes. When they reach the floe, they spring out of the water and attempt to kill their prey before it can escape.

Norwegian explorer Otto Neuman Sverdrup was once hunting a polar bear with dogs. When cornerd, the bear dove off an icy cliff into the water 50 feet below and swam toward the nearest land which was 22 miles away.

FOOD

Seals—the bearded, harp, harbor or hair, bladder-nosed or hooded, gray and ringed—the polar bear's main food. Storms and presence of seals determine where polar bears will be found. With good hunting bear will eat only skin, viscera, and blubber of seal; when hungry bear will eat meat as well until belly is full. Polar bears eat as much as 50 pounds of seal at once; one polar bear found with 156 pounds of walrus meat and blubber in stomach. Distended bellies sag to within 6 inches of the ice. Bears shot shortly after eating seal found to have no meat in stomachs, but a thick, oily greenish fluid and some hair. Seal's blubber rapidly converted to oil for quick absorption into body, producing energy and heat.

After gorging itself polar bear sleeps several days, then hunts again. Sometimes returns to carcass of seal it has killed, but usually not. Average polar bear kills 50 seals per year.

Polar bears followed by Arctic foxes, which scavenge upon seals left by bears. Often remaining carcass consumed completely by foxes.

Polar bears also scavenge on large carcass, such as walrus, and will congregate at a whale carcass. Food sources such as whale carcass or garbage dump make for only time bears found in numbers together. In one afternoon in 1896 35 killed on Mackenzie Island in Canadian Arctic when they came to feed on a beached whale. In 1863, 75 polar bears killed on Spitzbergen Island after congregating to feed on walrus carcasses.

Generally only fish eaten are dead ones. Rarely polar bears will catch spawning salmon.

Bears also eat mice, lemmings, young hares, ground-nesting birds' eggs and brooding birds if caught; eggs and young of flightless ducks and geese also eaten.

During summer polar bears crave vegetation, and bears on land eat grasses, sedges, sorrel and seaweed. Bears in Hudson Bay area rely on vegetation as main food source for 2–3 months of summer. Polar bears also eat ripe berries.

Cannibalism is rare but does occur, one report stating observation of large male killing and partially eating adult female.

One might think that creatures, and people, living in the Arctic would be free of toxic wastes but this is not so. There is no place on earth that man has not polluted with his chemical contaminants. Polar bears, and the Eskimos, have been found to have substantial levels of DDT, Dieldrin, mercury and other poisonous substances in their bodies because they both eat seals. The seals, in turn, have fed upon migratory fish. The fish have picked up the chemicals from the food they have eaten that live in the ocean and at the mouths of the rivers that are often merely running sewers for industrial wastes.

BEHAVIOR

The seal remains the "staff of life" to the polar bear. Tens of thousands of years of dependency upon this food source have produced extremely efficient hunting methods by the bears. It has also produced an inbred caution among the seals. They can never really relax and sleep. They sleep fitfully, dozing for a few minutes, only to wake up and look around carefully for danger before dozing for a few minutes more.

The polar bears patrol the edges of the pack ice or the lightly frozen cracks in the ice made by tidal currents. Krill, microscopic crustaceans, swarm in the less saline water off the edges of glaciers and icebergs. The krill is eaten by many kinds of fish, which produce a superabundance of food for the seals. Where the seals find good hunting, so do the polar bears. Seals also prowl the new leads made in the ice as the mass moves and shifts, creating the open leads in the water and the pressure ridges on the ice. The seals frequent such places because though such open spots may freeze over, the new ice is much thinner than the pack ice and can more easily be broken through.

Seals can break ice that is 4 inches thick by bumping it with the tops of their heads. They chew through thicker ice with their teeth. The seals, being air-breathing mammals, must be able to get through the ice to breathe every 7 or 8 minutes.

As the ice thickens, the seals keep chewing away at the bottom portion so that the hole looks like an inverted bell. These holes are known as aglos, which is the Eskimo name for them. Each seal usually has four or more aglos situated in its feeding area so that it has a source of air over a large area. Usually one of the aglos will be made large enough so that the seal can pull itself out on the ice to rest and to sleep.

The bears stalk the sleeping seals by crawling upwind on their bellies. When possible, the bears try to keep a landfall or an ice hummock behind them so that their body is not silhouetted against the horizon. The Eskimos claim that the stalking bears cover their black noses with their paws so that the seals can't see them.

The bears stealthily creep closer to the seals until the seals raise their heads to look around for danger. At the first movement of the seal, the bear freezes, not moving a muscle. When the seal's head goes down, the bear resumes its stalk. When the bear is within 50–60 feet of the unsuspecting seal, it springs to its feet and dashes forward to bring one of its huge forepaws crashing down on the seal's skull, crushing it. There are times when the bear is discovered and the seal quickly pops through the hole and is gone.

At times the bear will sit at an aglos and wait for the seal to pop its head up to take a breath. Then, quick as a flash, the bear will reach down and hook the seal with the claws of its forepaw and pull it up on the ice. A large male bear can easily snatch a 500-pound bearded seal out of the water and up onto the ice with one fluid motion. There are records by Haig-Thomas, British wildlife researcher, of polar bears filling a lot of aglos with snow and ice to force the seals to come to the ones that they are watching.

Some of the fierce snowstorms will cover the aglos to a depth of 3 feet or more. The bear can still locate the seals beneath the snow by the sound of the water in the hole and by smelling the seal through the snow.

In March or April the seals give birth to their young. The mother seal will make an aglos to the lee of a pressure ridge of ice where the snow is of the greatest depth and firmly compacted by drifting. She then makes a chamber up on the ice which will serve as a nursery for her pup.

Most newborn seal pups cannot swim for the first 2 weeks of their lives. Their natal coats of hair are not waterproof and if the pups get wet, they will become waterlogged and drown. Pups in this stage are known as "white-coats" because of their pure white natal hair.

Despite the depth of the snow, the polar bear can locate the seal pup beneath it and, by smashing down into the nursery, can easily get the pup and sometimes even the mother. During this period, when the seal pups cannot swim, the bears glut themselves on this almost unending source of food. Arctic explorer Peter Freuchen tells of one polar bear that had killed five seal pups and had eaten only a portion of two of them. The bear was playing with the carcasses by throwing them around, up into the air, and carrying them about. Other explorers and researchers have reported witnessing similar displays.

The bears do not always have things their way and bears that have had a seal escape from them have been seen to fly into a rage, smashing at the ice with their forepaws and throwing chunks of ice about. One enraged bear, which was later shot, was found to have broken all the bones in its one forepaw when it had

The polar bear's white coat is excellent camouflage against the snow but makes it conspicuous against rocks, dirt and trees.

smashed its paw down on some rocks. It is amazing how human the reactions of some animals are.

Polar bears also occasionally hunt small walruses that are up on the ice. They avoid the large males at all times but particularly when they are in the water. Walruses have been known to attack and kill bears in the water and the big males are not afraid of the bears, even when they are up on the ice. The bears usually make a detour around the walrus. The walrus remains alert, watching the bear carefully, but often refusing to give way before it.

The Eskimos claim that the polar bear can kill a walrus by crushing its skull with a large chunk of ice. This has never been witnessed by scientists and has been generally discredited. In 1962–63, polar bears in the London Zoo often threw huge chunks of ice about. Such a chunk could easily be used to kill a walrus. The Eskimo story of the bears killing walrus with chunks of ice may be just a story. Again, it could be fact. The Eskimos have lived with polar bears for thousands upon thousands of years and have witnessed many things the scientific community has not.

The bears may be active at any time of the day or night because they are not geared to periods of daylight and darkness. In the Arctic, the sun disappears from the sky about October 26, not to be seen again for almost 5 months. In this perpetual semidarkness, the bears hunt when they are hungry and sleep when their bellies are filled. It has been found, however, that they are the least active during the hours of 2:00–7:00 A.M.

The bears avoid the freshwater ice and pools formed by melted snow and glaciers because this type of ice, unlike sea ice, forms sharp crystals which can cut the soles of their feet.

The bears do not usually hesitate to swim but on thin ice they will spread-eagle themselves to distribute their body weight over the largest possible area to avoid breaking through.

Some of the most interesting research has turned up the fact that more polar bears den up in the winter than was previously suspected. Some of the large males may not den up but it is now known that most of them do, although for much shorter periods of time than do the immature bears. They may den up for no more than 2 months. Females with newborn young remain in their dens for the longest periods of time, up to 5 months. Bears that are fat may den up sooner and for longer periods, while those that are lean will continue to hunt.

Where possible, the female bears come off the new ice in October or November to hunt for a den site. Most sites are used year after year by either the same bear or succeeding generations of bears. Where there is no suitable earthen bank, the bears will seek out the hardest-packed snow in the lee of a rocky cliff or iceberg to excavate their dens.

One study showed that only 2 out of 104 dens were actually out on the ice, the bears much preferring to den on land, even if the den itself was dug into snow. Even the snow dens offer good protection from the cold because the snow is very good insulation and the dens have been found to be 40 degrees warmer than the outside air. Drifting snow soon seals up the entrance to the den. In the winter, the dens can often be located by the steam from the animal's breath escaping through the ventilation hole that was formed by the bear's body heat. This vapor often appears like smoke in the frigid air.

Whether dug into snow or earth, the dens are similar in construction and size. A study done by the Russians, on Wrangell Island in 1964, gives the following dimensions as an average for the 116 polar bear dens they had under observation. The entrance to the den had a 28-inch diameter leading into a tunnel that extended for 6 to 9 feet back into the den's chamber. The chamber measured 7 feet long by 5 feet wide and 5 feet high. Occasionally a den may have 2 chambers.

In the Manitoba-Ontario region of Hudson Bay, the polar bears also dig dens by tunneling into the earth down to the permafrost to escape the heat of summer. Pilots flying over the area have reported seeing the bears stick their heads out to watch as they fly over.

It is now known that some of the polar bears of that region go into estivation, a period of inactivity, to escape the heat and the scarcity of food during summer. The adult males usually have their dens the closest to the coast, and the females with cubs are farther back. Barren females and the immature males are the lowest in the hierarchy and their dens are the farthest from the sea. Some of the bears range inland as far as 100 miles, but 87 percent of all of the dens are within 10 miles of the sea.

When the bears den up in the wintertime, they become lethargic but do not go into hibernation. The bears' body temperatures drop to the low 90° F. range and their heart rates and breathing rates slow down. The bears can be easily awakened.

The Eskimos claim that the bears have an anal plug as do all other bears when they den up. Excrement is not found in the den proper, although it may be found outside the den. This excrement is most likely deposited there after the bear comes out of the den in the spring. At that time, the bear may remain in the vicinity of the den for several weeks, returning to it periodically before finally abandoning it.

In the winter the bears often dig temporary dens in the snow wherever they happen to be. Eskimos, while traveling in the winter, often construct temporary igloos. Perhaps they got the idea from the bears.

Polar bears are extremely curious about anything strange in their habitat and particularly about man. The polar bear has no enemies on the ice, so it has no fear.

Some explorers claimed they had a great deal of trouble with the bears because the bears considered everything in their terrain as a potential meal. Other explorers claimed that it was the bears' curiosity that brought them into camps and that they were not really dangerous. Bud Helmericks, of Alaska, has probably guided as many hunters for polar bears as any other living guide. He claims that he has never seen the bears attempt to hunt anyone, regardless of the provocation. Most polar bears are shot mainly because they just get too close to people. There is usually no way to get away from a bear out on the ice and there is probably no time left to find out if the bear is just curious or about to attack.

SENSES

Sense of smell very keen, as demonstrated by congregations of bears from miles away drawn to a whale carcass by the scent. Hunters capitalize on this by burning seal blubber to attract bears, some of whom come from 20 miles distance. Bears also able to smell seals beneath 5–6 feet of snow.

Hearing also good, bear able to distinguish noises of seal barking, diving, and exhaling through the often raucous din of ice in motion that grinds, rings and roars.

Sight very good, one researcher claiming bears can

see a motionless object at 300 yards. Others find polar bears can spot a seal on the ice a mile away.

COMMUNICATION

Polar bears do not have a large repertoire of vocal sounds. When angry, they growl; when annoyed, they hiss. Bears that have been hurt often whine or roar. The cubs whimper and whine when hungry or cold and bawl when separated from their mother.

BREEDING

The breeding season for the polar bear occurs primarily in late March, April and the early part of May. It is the one time of the year that the male and female seek out each other's company. Female bears reach sexual maturity at about 5 years of age, the males at 8.

The big males often battle for the right to breed with a receptive female; lesser males are driven off by the presence of a dominant male. The battles are often bloody, although death seldom results.

When dominance has been established, the courtship period lasts for about 2 weeks. The couple builds strong bonds of attachment by caressing one another with their paws and claw tips, by body contact and playful wrestling and chasing about. During this period males could not be driven away from the female, even if she were killed. Copulation occurs a number of times. When the female will no longer accept the male, he departs to seek another female that will.

BIRTH AND YOUNG

All bears are subject to delayed implantation. The bears breed, the eggs are fertilized, but they do not attach themselves to the wall of the uterus for about 6 months. This implantation takes place about mid-October when the females are about ready to den up. The gestation period is considered to be 8 months.

The polar bear's cubs are born in December while the female is snug in her winter den. Although most bears have twins, Jack Lentfer's studies show that the average litter size in Alaska is 1.68 cubs, while litters in Ontario average 2.4. Bears having their first young usually have a single cub. Triplets are rare.

The cubs at birth are about 10 inches in total length and weigh between one and 2 pounds. Their eyes and ears are sealed shut. Their body is covered with a short white fuzz. The mother cleans, cuddles and nurses her babies; she has 4 nipples. She will hold their bodies against hers to warm them with her body heat and she also usually exhales her warm breath on them. At 5 days of age, the cubs' lips, noses and bare foot pads darken.

At 2 months of age the cubs' eyes open and their teeth begin to irrupt through their gums. Now, when the mother nurses the little ones, she usually sits upright. The young will nurse 6 to 8 times in a 24-hour period.

At 4 months of age, the little females are about 29 inches long and weigh about 24 pounds; the little males are about 30 inches long and weigh 27 pounds. This size discrepancy will continue and increase with age.

For the first summer, the female will make her cubs stay in one spot while she hunts for food. In their second summer, the cubs learn to hunt with their mother.

In April, the mother is usually ready to leave the den with her young following after her. They may stay in the vicinity of the den for the first couple of weeks and then leave it till the following winter.

Although the little bears can swim, the mother tries to avoid getting them into the water till they are at least 2 months older. The cubs molt into their adult coat of fur in July. The mother will take the young out on the ice as soon after leaving the den as is possible because more food is available there and, for the polar bear, it is the area of greatest safety.

The polar bear's cubs will stay with their mother through the next two winters, at which time they will weigh about 400 pounds. The mother will not hesitate to fight to protect her young but most of the time will try to avoid dogs and man by running away with the cubs. If the cubs tire, the mother will push them along with her head. The cubs nurse till they are about 21 months old.

When the cubs are a little over 2 years old, they leave the female or are driven off by the amorous male as the female comes into estrus. The cubs usually stay together then for 2 or 3 months. Polar bears breed until they are about 25 years old.

LIFE SPAN

Potential in wild: 32 years. Sultana, female in Milwaukee Zoo, destroyed at age 35 with old age infirmities—had been first polar bear to rear young successfully in captivity. A male in Chester Zoo, England, lived 41 years.

SIGN

Most common sign the bear itself. Tracks visible only when snow soft enough to receive impression.

ENEMIES

Polar bear at peak of its food chain pyramid, although wolves have been known to kill cubs when bears on land. In water, adults occasional prey of killer whales and rarely of walrus. Ectoparasites few in winter as cold kills most of them. In summer bears plagued by fleas, lice, flies and mosquitoes. Mange occurs occasionally. Polar bears harbor trichinosis and bear meat must be cooked thoroughly before eating. Bears may contract rabies from canids.

HUMAN RELATIONS

Man is the polar bear's nemesis. Unrestricted shooting in the past and perhaps overshooting now, plus man's invasion of the Artic areas, have caused a drastic decline in the number of polar bears. There is no accurate census of polar bears; it is estimated that there are between 10,000 and 12,000 of the bears circumpolar.

Russia allows no hunting of the bears along its entire coast. Canada allows only the Eskimos to hunt the bears as they have done traditionally. The bears are still hunted north of Norway and Greenland and about 300 bears a year are being taken. Alaska has a kill of about 400 polar bears each year. The bears may no longer be hunted from airplanes. The Boone and Crockett Club no longer recognizes the polar bear as a trophy and this has decreased pressure on the bear. Still, between 1,200 and 1,300 polar bears a year are presently being killed, a take that is far too high for the safe continuance of the bear's population. A moratorium should be declared to give the bears complete protection until more is known about their numbers.

Polar bears will continue to be shot for the safety of the men working in the Arctic. And men, in increasing numbers, will continue to flood into the Arctic in the search for oil and minerals.

With the advent of oil exploration in the Prudhoe Bay area of Alaska, there is no denning being done there by the polar bears. This type of steady encroachment will also cause the bear's population to continue its decline.

A bright side to the coin is the complete protection given the bears by the Russians and the establishment of two parks set aside for the polar bears. One park has been established on Norway's Kong-Karls Island, the other is the 7,000-square-mile Polar Bear Park, which is located 165 miles north of Moosonee, on James Bay in Canada.

COMMERCIAL VALUE

No skins reported sold in U.S., but Alaska figures hunting the bear there generates $300,000–$400,000 annually. In Canada: 530 skins sold 1976–77, $585.25 average price, $310,165 total.

CARNIVORA

PROCYONIDAE

The family *Procyonidae* contains the ringtails, raccoons, coatimundis and kinkajous. With the exception of the kinkajou, these animals have alternating light and dark rings on their tails. They all have great manual dexterity in their forepaws. All have 5 toes on each foot, walk on the soles of their feet, have sharp claws and are excellent tree climbers. The raccoon does not hibernate but it does spend extended periods of time in its den during the coldest winter months. The southern raccoons and the other members of this family do not den up.

All of these animals have sharp canine teeth for grasping prey but flat-topped molars for grinding vegetation. Although classified as carnivores, these species are omnivorous, eating far more vegetable matter than flesh. Raccoons raiding sweet corn or other crops are very destructive.

Raccoons are frequently hunted for sport and both animals are trapped for their fur.

RINGTAIL, *Bassariscus astutus*

INTRODUCTION

The ringtail is one of our most elusive and least known animals, not because it is rare but because it is strictly nocturnal. Many other so-called nocturnal creatures, eager to be about their feeding, often move about as the light is fading. Not so with the ringtail. It waits till the world is completely shrouded in darkness before it bestirs itself and sets about its activities.

Confusion is usually rampant about anything that is not well known. The many different names that are given to this creature are the result of this confusion and misinformation.

The name ringtail is perhaps its most frequently used and most generally accepted common name. It is a good name, apt and very descriptive. The long, bushy, beautifully banded tail is almost as big as the animal itself, particularly when the animal has the hairs fluffed out.

Cacomixtle or cacomistle are two other names given to the ringtail. Cacomixtle is the Aztec Indian name for the delightful little ringtail, and the animal has shown up in their ancient pictographs. Cacomistle is another version of the Aztec word, although it is incorrect. Most of the Mexicans still use the name cacomixtle today and it is also often used by the Spanish-

The large, bushy ringed tail gives this animal its name and shows that it is related to the raccoon. (Photo: Irene Vandermolen)

speaking people of our southwestern states. In Baja, California, the natives there refer to the ringtail by the name babisuri.

This animal's original scientific name was given to it by Lichtenstein in 1831. He named it *Bassaris astuta. Bassaris* is the Greek word for "fox" while *astutus* is Latin for "clever." The *cus,* which was added to *Bassaris* by Coues in 1887, means little, which gives us a translation of "clever little fox." The name bassarisk is a takeoff on its Greek name.

The ringtail is not related to the fox and got its descriptive name because of its beautiful foxlike face. However, the ringtail's face never portrays the craftiness of a true fox's face. The ringtail's face always depicts an air of mild bewilderment and curiosity. It is an appealing face, enhanced by its oversized black eyes.

The ringtail is sometimes called civet-fox or civet-cat. Again, these names only add to the confusion because the ringtail is not related to the Eurasian civets or to any member of the cat family. The civets do have long banded tails and are famed for the penetrating odor of their musk. The ringtail also has anal musk glands but its musk has a sweetish odor and cannot be directed as a spray.

The names coon-cat, ring-tailed raccoon or rac-coon-fox show the obvious linkage between the ringtail and the raccoon. For years, the ringtail was classified with the raccoons and the coatimundis in the family *procyonidae*. Today, it is recognized that, although the ringtail and the raccoon are closely related, the ringtail is sufficiently unique to qualify for its own family classification, *Bassarisidae.*

DESCRIPTION

The ringtail is a small, short-legged, long-bodied, long-tailed omnivore. An adult male ringtail will stand 5 to 6 inches high at the shoulder and measure 28–34 inches in total length. The tail will be 14–17 inches of that length. Weight is between 2½ to 2¾ pounds. The female ringtails are slightly smaller than the males in both size and weight.

The basic body color of the ringtails shades from a light gray through yellow to an occasional dark brown.

The nose of the ringtail is a pinkish-tan color; the large liquid eyes are jet black. The eyes are the face's most prominent feature. The eyes protrude more than normal as do those of the flying squirrels, another truly nocturnal creature. The bulge gives the eye more surface area for the diameter of the orb and this may be an aid in light-gathering. There is a conspicuous white ring around each of the ringtail's eyes that would help reflect light into the eye as do the feathered facial disks of owls.

A creamy-white band of fur about 2 inches wide starts beneath the ringtail's chin and extends in a slightly widening wedge to the animal's chest. The light-colored band is bordered on each side by a slightly yellower, darker strip that is about one inch wide. The sides of the ringtail are slightly darker shading to gray, while many of the tips of the guard hairs on its back are dark brown or black, forming an indistinct dark dorsal streak. The guard hairs on the belly are about three-quarters of an inch in length while the underfur is about one-half inch in length. On the ringtail's back the guard hairs are about one to 1¼ inches in length. It is the guard hairs that give the animal its general color. The underfur on both the belly and the back is almost uniformly dark gray at the base and a yellowish-tan on the tips. I can find no record of albinism or melanism in the ringtails.

The hair of the tail is almost pure white, broken with 7 to 9 bands that are almost jet black. The bands are incomplete as they do not meet on the ventral surface. The hairs on the tail are 2 to 2¼ inches in length and are erectile so that an excited ringtail can fluff its tail up like a giant bottle brush. The tail helps the ringtail maintain its balance as it scampers over the rocks and through the trees.

There are 4 rows of vibrissae with the longest whiskers measuring between 3½ and 4 inches in length. Above the inner corner of each eye there is a small tuft of about 6 hairs that are about 1½ inches in

The large eyes of the ringtail allow it to see well at night. It is almost never active during the daytime. (Photo: Irene Vandermolen)

length. A few one-inch hairs are situated slightly behind the outside corner of each eye. The whiskers of the ringtail are very important to it when it hunts at night.

The ears of the adult ringtail stand sharply erect and help to create its foxlike look. The ears are about 1½ inches in length by one inch in width at the base. The tips of the ears are fairly sharply pointed. There is a very noticeable notch in the outside contour of the ear about one-third up from the animal's head. The color of the hair on the inner surface of the ringtail's ear is much lighter than the hair on the back of the ear, being an off-white.

The ringtail has 5 toes on each of its feet, each armed with a strong, sharp claw that is semiretractable. The ringtail is digitigrade and walks on its toes and not on its entire foot. The pads of its feet are bare, the heels covered with hair.

The dentition of the ringtail is designated as 12 incisor teeth, 4 canines, 16 premolars and 8 molars, for a total complement of 40 teeth. The last premolar and the first molar teeth have sharp, shearing ridges similar to the carnassial teeth of the canids.

The anal glands of the ringtail produce a clear amber fluid that cannot be discharged at will. This gland does ooze a drop or two of the sweetish-smelling musk when the ringtail is highly excited.

DISTRIBUTION

Primarily a creature of warm, desert rimrock areas, but never found over ¼ mile from water source, even a spring or seep if larger bodies not available. May also be found in brushy areas, draws with scrub cedars, woodlands and conifer-deciduous forests, below sea level in Death Valley, California, and 9,000 feet above sea level at rim of Grand Canyon in Arizona, and among 7,500 foot peaks of Mogollon Mountains of New Mexico. Now found in Oregon, California, Nevada, Utah, Arizona, New Mexico, Colorado, Texas and Mexico, and occasionally in Wyoming. *Bassariscus sumichrasti,* a slightly smaller ringtail, found from Mexico through Central America to Costa Rica.

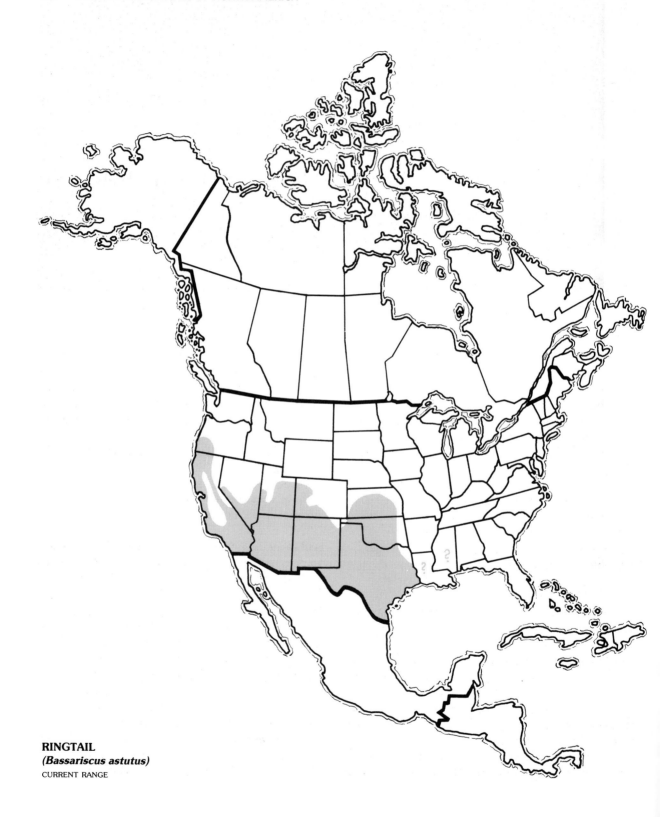

RINGTAIL
(Bassariscus astutus)
CURRENT RANGE

The ringtail is an agile tree climber.

TRAVEL

The ringtail is pretty much of a stay-at-home. The actual size of its range is always dependent upon the availability of food. In good areas the population of ringtails may be 5 to 10 animals to the square mile. Poorer areas may only support one ringtail to the square mile. It is most unlikely for a ringtail to have a home range as large as one-quarter of a mile in diameter. Over most of its range, snow depth and extreme cold are seldom a problem so there is little need for the ringtail to have to shift its range seasonally to seek food. What it does do is to change its diet to take advantage of the most plentiful food supply that is available in each season.

LOCOMOTION

The ringtail is an especially surefooted climbing animal on both rocks and trees. Ringtails have been seen hanging from tree limbs by just their hind feet. It does most of its traveling about on the ground but its den may be in either rock crevasses or ledges or in hollow trees. The ringtail also usually climbs to escape from almost any or all of its predators. It has been known to leap 10 feet horizontally.

The ringtail usually walks when hunting because it catches its prey by ambushing it or occasionally by stalking. It does not have the need for traveling fast nor for long distances. When frightened or pursued, the ringtail gallops. In this gait the 2 front feet come down almost simultaneously and then the 2 back feet come down together. The ringtail's long body compresses into a humped position before lengthening out as it springs forward. When the ringtail walks or runs, it carries its tail straight out behind with just the tip drooping.

Almost all animals can swim but I can find no record of anyone who has seen a ringtail swim.

FOOD

An omnivore, but closer to carnivores because more successful at catching prey and possesses carnassial-like teeth. Ringtail consumes 2–3 ounces of food per day. Study on Edwards Plateau in Texas showed ringtail's most important food was insects: grasshoppers, moths, butterflies, beetles, ants, bees and dragonflies. Also eats good deal of spiders, millipedes, centipedes and scorpions—how it eats scorpion without being stung is unknown. In summer, insects constitute up to 56 percent of total diet; 35 percent average through the year. Arachnids make up 6 percent. Mammals second in preference, 24 percent of total diet. Wood rats an important food source—sometimes lack of them will mean lack of ringtails as well. Whitefoot, pocket and harvest mice also important. Ringtails in caves feed on bats. The desert cottontail, the smallest U.S. rabbit, also eaten, as are various ground and tree squirrels. Vegetation makes 18 percent of yearly diet, 25 percent in fall when other foods scarce and berries and nuts are ripe. Cedar berries consumed, enabling ringtail to thrive on heavily overgrazed, cedar-studded draws and sides of plateaus. Also consumed are hackberries, persimmons (preferred over all other foods when ripe and sweet), mistletoe, barberry, acorns, cactus seeds and fruits, wild plums, dogwood berries and others. Ringtail also takes smaller birds and their eggs when it can, including the blue jay, Texas jay, towhee, white-throated sparrow, cardinal, mourning dove, some woodpeckers, thrashers, robins and others. Edwards Plateau study showed ringtail not a threat to wild turkey there. Birds represent 12 percent of total diet and less than 25 percent in winter. Ringtail also frequently eat carrion, a habit that makes it vulnerable to poison baits put in southwestern border areas to control influx of rabid dogs from Mexico. Where poison baits have been used, ringtails have been annihilated.

BEHAVIOR

One other name that is frequently given to the ringtail is "miner's cat." In that capacity, the ringtail was more than welcome around the mines, caves, root cellars and cabins of not only the miners but of most of the people living in the Southwest.

A very common rodent living in the southwestern states, in fact some species are found in most states, is the wood rat. The wood rat also has been given the name packrat because it carries off any shiny, bright or metallic object that it can move. Money, jewelry, watches, false teeth, nuts, bolts, spare parts and even sticks of dynamite, have all been carried off by the wood rats. Sometimes, some of these objects could be retrieved from the wood rat's nest, more frequently they were never seen again. The ringtail is the wood rat's nemesis.

I have always found that whenever anyone takes food into the wilderness, the animals living there are willing to share it. Mice usually infest wilderness cabins, not only eating the food but also chewing into everything, searching for more food or using it as bedding.

Any cabin with a resident ringtail has none of these problems.

Because the ringtail was such an efficient predator against all types of rodents, they were frequently raised as pets or were encouraged to live in or around the cabins and mines. Not only did the ringtail pay its way by destroying rodents but its beauty and playful antics made it a welcome diversion to people living where they had little or no contact with other humans.

The ringtail is easily tamed. It is a very shy and retiring animal and usually retreats before loud noise or quick motion, particularly if the motion appears threatening. Almost anyone with patience and time can win the confidence of even adult wild ringtails.

Literature is filled with stories of people who have befriended or have been befriended by a ringtail. Such animals that have responded to kind treatment will eat from the person's hand and often allow themselves to be stroked and even picked up. Many times the ringtail will climb up on the person's lap and even sit on his shoulder.

Where the ringtails are not actually tamed, but are not molested, they become accustomed to people and to noise. Ringtails often live in the attics or basements of people's houses even in small rural towns and despite the constant threat from dogs and cats.

In the wilderness cabins, the ringtail seems to be as curious about the person as the person usually is about the ringtail. Ringtails often stand erect on their hind feet to get a better look at what interests them.

Some people, to encourage the ringtail, not only tempt it with food but also put a box beneath or even inside their cabin. Some people cut a small hole in the cabin to facilitate the ringtail's entry. And some ringtails have responded to these overtures by having and raising their families in the boxes provided for them.

One disadvantage to the ringtail as a pet is that it just never gets over the habit of being active all night and sleeping all day. The main advantage to a resident ringtail is that the cabin will be rodent-free.

When feeding pet ringtails, it has been found that they will eat a tremendous variety of food. Like the raccoons, to which they are related, the ringtail eats almost anything edible.

Although ringtails are truly nocturnal mammals, they may occasionally be seen sunbathing high on a rocky ledge or up on a large limb of a big tree.

Ringtails are always elegant. They spend a lot of time grooming. Like a cat, they will clean themselves with their tongues, licking their fur. To wash their faces, the ringtails lick their paws and then scrub their faces. If they have an itch, they scratch it with either their front or hind feet.

SENSES

Ringtail a sight hunter and oversized eyes well supplied with rods (cells sensitive to low-intensity light). Eyes reflect red when shined with strong light, yellow when shined with weaker light.

Large ears also essential and acute hearing enables ringtail to hear slightest rustling signifying food or danger.

Working along with ears, and possibly of greater importance, are ringtail's long whiskers. In almost constant motion, whiskers let animal know the size of any opening they enter, and sensitive whiskers like those of ringtail respond to vibrations in air, acting as a sort of radar.

Taste well developed as demonstrated by its fondness for sweets, fruits and berries. The related sense of smell may also be well developed.

COMMUNICATION

The ringtail is quite vocal, having a large repertoire of sounds. Baby ringtails make, and keep up, an almost constant metallic squeaking. Some biologists claim that it sounds like the squeaking of a rusty hinge. Even while nursing, the young squeak or make a whining sound.

The adult ringtails have a birdlike twitter when they communicate among themselves. If they are separated from one another, they call OO-YE, OO-YE in an attempt to locate each other.

The most commonly heard sound is the short explosive bark that the ringtails make when they are surprised. The barking of a ringtail is very similar to the rough, raspy barking of the gray fox. An angry or frightened ringtail will grunt, growl, spit, hiss, chatter and scream.

Like its cousin the raccoon, the ringtail will frequently climb up a tree and deposit its scat on the limbs or in a heap at the base of a large tree or even on a large conspicuous rock. Thus, the piles of excrement are a notification of territory.

There is no record of the ringtail depositing its anal scent to mark territory but the scent is discharged when the ringtail is frightened or angry. As such, it would be an olfactory warning between rival males.

BREEDING

The ringtail is undoubtedly polygamous because researchers have reported several females being in a given territory feeding in one spot but with only one male ever present. The male may actually den with one of the females, but it is most unlikely that two females would tolerate each other in a communal den. Except when they are actually feeding at a food concentration, ringtails are solitary. Actually very little is known about the breeding of the ringtails.

BIRTH AND YOUNG

Each ringtail has a main den that it lives in and usually several other escape dens to be used in emergencies. They prefer their dens to be high up in a tree or in a rock ledge and to have an opening that they can just squeeze through. This precludes large predators from entering the den. In the Edwards Plateau area of Texas, it was noted that many of the den trees were in the midst of thickets, adding additional protection. Most

Ringtails often live in hollow trees, such as this ringtail emerging from its den.

of the dens are lined with soft grasses. The ringtail's main den will be the natal den.

The gestation period for the ringtail is between 50 and 60 days, and the young are born between mid-May and mid-June. If a male ringtail is using the same den as the pregnant female, he will be driven out 3 or 4 days before she gives birth.

The ringtails have only one litter of young per year and 2 to 5 young are born. Most frequently, the female has 3 and occasionally 4 young. As she has only 4 nipples on her lower abdomen, having more than 4 young at a time would cause a hardship for the babies.

At birth ringtails weigh about one ounce and measure about 5 1/2 inches in total length. The baby ringtail's eyes and ears are sealed shut, although its body is covered with very short, whitish hair. The hair is so sparse that its cream-colored skin shows through. The bands on the tail are discernible because, although the hair is lacking, the skin itself has the dark pigmentation.

The umbilical cord usually drops off in 2 to 3 days.

At this early age, the young have difficulty in righting themselves should they be turned over on their backs. The female, while nursing the young, will often push those that are not nursing or are searching for a nipple toward her nipples with her front feet. The female may sit in a hunched position over the young with her hind legs spread or she may lie on her side. In either position, she does everything to make it easy for the young to nurse. The female has been seen licking the anal region of the young, as they nurse. This is common with most mammals as it stimulates the bowels. The female consumes both the excrement and the urine as it is voided so that the den does not become soiled. When the mother ringtail wants to move her young about, she does it in the same manner as does the raccoon. She will pick up the youngster by putting its entire head in her mouth. Occasionally, she will pick the youngsters up by their shoulders and at other times by their bellies. She seldom picks them up by the nape of the neck as a cat would do.

The baby ringtail's ears open on about the 29th day, but the tips bend in the middle and droop downward. Even though the ears are drooped, the babies have enough muscle control to twitch them. The ears stand erect at about 8 weeks of age.

The eyes of the young ringtails open between the 31st and 34th days. At first they are mere slits and it takes another 2 weeks before they open fully.

At 5 weeks of age the young ringtails have attained the coat coloration of the adults but it has a fuzzy appearance due to the shortness of the hair. At this age, the young stop crawling and are able to walk about, clumsily, with their bellies raised off the ground. It is also at this time that the female begins to bring solid food into the den to feed to the young. Fruit and small prey are brought in and as the young begin to feed upon this new material, it lessens the demand for their mother's milk.

When the young ringtails are 6 weeks old, they gradually stop making their squeaking sound and begin to make the explosive, coughing bark of the adults.

From here on, the development of the young ringtails is very rapid. By 7 weeks, they can climb with agility and the young climb and jump with abandon. With the increased agility has come the ability to twist catlike in the air and to land on their feet every time. They have no fear of falling; it seldom happens.

No one is sure just when the young are completely weaned but it probably occurs when they are about 3 months of age. At 4 to 4½ months, they have shed their juvenile coats and are now just smaller editions of the adults. The young have ceased following after the mother and are now hunting for food on their own.

Dispersal takes place about this time. Some leave on their own and the adult male will drive out any of the young males that remain in the area. Young males at this age have been seen going through the motions of copulation with their mothers, although breeding is not possible at this time of the year. Nevertheless, the adult male will not allow any future competition to remain in his territory. Young ringtails are sexually mature at one year and are capable of breeding when they are 10 months old.

LIFE SPAN

Potential: 5–6 years, typical of animals of this size and development. Record: 8 years, a captive animal.

SIGN

Droppings most conspicuous sign, placed on tree limbs, rocky ledges, and conspicuous rocks. Scat 4–6 inches long, about ⅜ inch in diameter. Diet of birds or mammals includes feathers and hair which keep scats intact. Diet of insects causes scats to crumble before drying.

Tracks often difficult to find due to rocky habitat. When found, appear similar to house cat's except rightail's track shows 5 toes and house cat's only 4. Ringtail's semiretractable claws usually do not register in track. Front and hind tracks nearly identical, about ⅞ inch long by ⅞ inch wide.

ENEMIES

Major enemies are domestic dogs and cats when ringtail is in small rural towns or lives beneath farm or ranch buildings. Other enemies include coyotes, bobcats, and great horned owls. From most enemies ringtail can escape through small crevasses in rocks. Rattlesnakes can enter cravasses but generally take only young ringtails because adults can move faster than snake. Predation not limiting factor for ringtail.

Continuous use of one den makes ringtail susceptible to minor ectoparasites of fleas and lice. They probably have usual complement of roundworms, flatworms and tapeworms. I find no record of rabies in ringtail, but they do live in areas where other creatures are rabid, increasing their chances of contracting the disease.

HUMAN RELATIONS

The fur of the ringtail has never brought high prices so that trapping has never been deliberately intensive for this species. The ringtail is most often accidentally caught in traps set for more valuable furbearers. The poison campaigns that men have waged so constantly against other species have also taken their toll inadvertently against the ringtail. However, the greatest damage that has been done to the ringtail is for men to move into the areas in which these animals formerly lived. Many biologists have remarked about the steady decline in the numbers of ringtails as we humans constantly urbanize what used to be wilderness.

The ringtail is finally being given better protection by many of the states in an effort to check their declining populations.

COMMERCIAL VALUE

IAFWA statistics: 88,329 ringtails taken 1976–77 trapping season; average price $5.50; $485,810 total. Although fur remains prime until April 1, when most other furbearers have begun to shed and are unprime, ringtail fur does not make a good coat.

RACCOON, *Procyon lotor*

INTRODUCTION

In the early 1600s Captain John Smith wrote a report on the Virginia Colony. In it he wrote of "a beast they call the aroughcun, much like a badger, but useth to lie in trees as squirrels doe." Aroughcun or arakun was the English version of the Algonquin Indian name for the raccoon.

The scientific name for the raccoon was given it by the taxonomist A. S. Desmarest in 1819. *Pro* is Greek for "before" and *cyon* means "dog." It is thought that the name was derived from a group of stars that rise in the summer sky just before the Dog Star, Sirius. The name *lotor* is Latin for "washer" because most people think that the raccoon always washes its food before it eats it. This is further reflected in the German name for the raccoon, which is *waschbar*.

The raccoon feeds around water, it gets a lot of its food from the water, it likes to play in the water, but it does not have to wash its food in water before it eats it.

For years it was a common belief that raccoons had to wet their food before they could swallow it because they did not have the necessary salivary glands. This misconception was dispelled by Dr. Leon F. Whitney, veterinarian and instructor at the Yale University Medical School. Dr. Whitney proved conclusively that the raccoon's salivary glands are sufficient for its needs.

It is now known that when a raccoon puts its food in water it is responding to an inherent trait known as a "search and seizure" pattern. Other animals, notably the clawless otter, do the same thing. These animals are accustomed to finding their food by searching beneath the surface of the water. They find the food by overturning rocks, feeling in underwater crevasses in the bank and under submerged tree roots. These are the spots for crayfish, minnows, frogs and newts, all food for the raccoon. When a captive raccoon puts its food in water, it is still acting out this search and seizure of its prey, but most captive raccoons do not put their food in water.

DESCRIPTION

The two main features that everyone recognizes about a raccoon are the black mask across the animal's eyes and its ringed tail. Raccoons vary greatly in both color and size depending upon the section of the country that they inhabit. As a general rule, the raccoons from the northern part of their range are the darkest, those from the south are much lighter. Raccoons taken from the salt water coastal marshes are usually more reddish. We are not sure whether this is from a greater exposure to sunshine and the resultant bleaching or whether it is a reaction to the salt spray.

Although the above generalization usually holds true, it is not an absolute. In New Jersey I have found diverse shadings from light to dark in a single litter, although the dark pelage is more common. In the 1950s and 1960s the raccoon populations soared throughout most of the country creating untold problems for the growers of sweet corn. Control men had to remove hundreds of raccoons that were doing damage. It was suggested that all the light-phase raccoons be destroyed and all the dark-phase raccoons be transplanted. This would have improved the stock of raccoons because the dark pelts have always commanded the highest price. The suggestion was never followed.

It is true that the raccoons in the north are much larger than those in the south. This is a response to Bergman's Law that the farther an animal of one spe-

Raccoons do not have to wash their food before they eat it, but they do catch a lot of their food around water. This one is feeling for food with its paws in what is known as a "search and seizure" activity.

cies is found from the equator, the larger its body size will be because the mass, relative to the surface area, conserves heat.

An adult raccoon in the north will stand 9 to 10 inches high at the shoulder and measure up to 34–38 inches in total length. Of that length, 10–13 inches will be its tail length. I have the skin of a huge raccoon that is 47 inches long. Southern raccoons are almost as big, but they don't put on the weight or the body fat that the northern raccoons do.

The average weight for a northern adult male raccoon is 15–18 pounds. The largest I ever caught weighed 21¾ pounds. The female northern raccoons weigh between 12 and 15 pounds. A male southern raccoon will weigh about 15 pounds and the female about 12 pounds.

Raccoons raised in captivity have been known to reach some really fantastic weights. The largest male raccoon I ever raised weighed 24 pounds, but I know of others that weighed over 30 pounds.

There is nothing like an accurate scale to reduce the weight of a raccoon. Any hunter carrying an adult raccoon by its tapered feet for a couple of miles is no judge of its weight. However, enough really large raccoons have been accurately weighed to prove that some raccoons do grow to be monsters.

Dr. Whitney, hunting near Orono, Maine, took 18 raccoons in 5 nights. Eight of these raccoons weighed over 23 pounds with the largest weighing a little less than 27 pounds. On later hunts he took 5 raccoons that weighed between 29 and 30 pounds. He claimed there was such a difference in the raccoons of that area, not only in weight but in their pelage, that they should be established as a subspecies.

Let's look at several of the top raccoon weights. Oliver J. Valley of Grant County, Wisconsin, shot a raccoon that weighed 54 pounds.

Tolla Brown and Glen King of Sterling, Colorado, shot a raccoon on November 11, 1960, that weighed 54 pounds on one scale and 56 pounds on another. The scales were never verified to give the proper weight.

The raccoon that Albert Larson of Nekon, Wisconsin, shot on November 4, 1950, is the greatest weight I can find. This giant weighed 62 pounds 6 ounces and measured 55 inches from nose tip to tail tip.

The guard hair on the back of a raccoon is 2 to 2 1/4 inches in length and is usually dark-tipped. The dense undercoat hair is about 1 1/2 to 1 3/4 inches in length and dark brown in color. The undercoat hairs are very wavy, which helps to trap air and to provide better insulation.

The guard hairs on the raccoon's belly and sides are about the same length as those on its back but are white-tipped. Both the guard hairs and the undercoat are sparse on the belly.

The raccoon's tail is almost perfectly cylindrical and on a big raccoon will measure 3 to 3 1/2 inches in diameter. The dark bands vary in number from 4 to 8 with the terminal tip being dark.

There are 4 to 5 rows of vibrissae with the longest hairs being 3 1/2 inches in length and they are white. Some of the shorter hairs are dark.

The black mask across the raccoon's face is not a complete band. There is a dark ridge down the raccoon's muzzle, then 2 thin, white stripes join the white band that goes across the forehead to the one that goes over the muzzle. There are 2 elongated black patches that make the raccoon look more like it is wearing goggles rather than a mask.

The raccoon's nose is black, as are the eyes. When the raccoon is angered, the eyes blaze with a greenish film.

The raccoon's ears are 1 3/4 inches to 2 inches in length. They are dark on the inside but have a light-colored edge for about one inch in the front and back.

Albinism in raccoons is fairly common. In most of the albino raccoons the pelage is not pure white. All the albino raccoons that I have seen had faint light brown or orangey-colored markings where their normal conterparts were black. Having pink eyes is considered proof of albinism and the albino raccoons that I have seen passed this qualification. There are several records of melanistic raccoons.

Ray Jones of Pecatonia, Illinois, caught a young male raccoon that was absolutely hairless. A local conservation officer said it would have undoubtedly died as soon as cold weather set in.

J. C. Hyde, land management assistant for the Pennsylvania Game Commission, reported that in the fall of 1972, near Huntington, he caught three raccoons almost entirely red, one almost entirely black, two with no tails and two with no teeth at all.

Three years later another toothless raccoon was caught on November 26, 1975, by William T. Reyan near Everett, Pennsylvania, 35 miles away. There were no details on the first two raccoons but the third was carefully examined and the jaws preserved. The raccoon female had had teeth but had lost them several years before and the jaw sockets had filled in. All three raccoons were in good flesh despite their handicap. With three raccoons coming from the same area there is the possibility that this is a genetic deficiency.

Raccoons have 40 teeth—12 incisors, 4 canines, 16 premolars and 8 molars. The canine teeth have an elongated, pyramidal shape. They are needle-sharp and strong, making them tremendous weapons. The molars have somewhat flattened tops for the grinding of vegetation as befits an animal with an omnivorous diet.

The raccoon, like the bears, rodents and humans, is plantigrade and walks upon its entire foot. There are 5 toes on each foot. The toes, including the nails, on the front foot of a large individual are about 1 1/2 inches in length and can be widely spread to support the raccoon's weight or to be used in grasping. The palm pad is also about 1½ inches in length. Many people refer to a raccoon's hind foot as making a track like a human baby's foot. There is some resemblance but not really that much. The toes, including the nails, are 1¾ inches long while the foot pad is about 2 inches long. Our human heel is broad and well rounded, that of a raccoon is tapered. The claws on the feet are about one-half inch in length and are slightly longer on the forefeet than on the hind feet and are nonretractable.

DISTRIBUTION

Found from Panama through southern tier of Canadian provinces, from Atlantic to Pacific coasts. Raccoon has thrived where other species have suffered from man's usurpation of habitat. Raccoon has moved northward in Canada as forests open up and farms take their place. Now at about 52° latitude in British Columbia, up to 54° in Alberta, Saskatchewan, Manitoba and Ontario. Some have been imported to Alaska's southeastern panhandle. In U.S. raccoon limited only by lack of water and thus is not found in true desert areas.

TRAVEL

Raccoons do not migrate. The amount of food available to them determines the size of their home range. Prior to radiotelemetry, most work on the range and movements of animals was done by tracking in the snow. Most northern raccoons den up during the periods of snow so there was really a lack of information. It has now been found that the raccoon's home range covers 2 to 4 square miles. The actual shape of its range is not uniform but adapts itself to the contour of the countryside, centering on whatever brooks, streams, rivers, lakes, ponds and marshes are in the area. Raccoon males do not have a den as their focal point as do the female and young. The males travel at night, as much as 3 to 5 miles, hunting for food and

retiring for the day wherever they may end up. As the raccoon knows its territory intimately, it usually has many oft-visited spots for sleeping.

Research in Illinois showed that the raccoons being studied there had an average home range of 136–168 acres. One large male spent all of his time in 122 acres.

Tagging of raccoons has shown that there is actually little movement even among the young at dispersal time. Most of the tagged raccoons have been recovered within 5 miles of where they had been captured initially. A major reason for this is that dispersal usually occcurs in late winter, after the hunting season. Hunters usually take a large percentage of the fall raccoon population, greatly reducing the competition for food and den sites and the stress of overpopulation, all of which are the reasons for dispersal. Where raccoons are protected, dispersal occurs. This is why when raccoons move into a new area, and receive protection, their colonization and extension of the area occurs in a short period of time.

It has also been proved that to import raccoons into an area is a waste of time and money. They just don't stay in the release area. Out of a shipment of 150 raccoons from Texas into Indiana only one was ever recovered. It was shot 38 miles from the release point.

LeRoy W. Giles, in 1941, tagged 256 raccoons and removed them from the White River Migratory Waterfowl Refuge to other refuges in Arkansas. One female wandered only 2 miles, one 16 miles, one 32 miles and another 130 miles. As a whole, the males wandered farther with some traveling 3, 33, 75, 82, 92 and 132 miles.

South Carolina transplanted 789 raccoons, of which only 14 were ever recovered. Two of the raccoons were found near the release site. The rest were recovered at distances of 20–180 miles. That latter record is the greatest distance that I can find for the travels of a raccoon.

LOCOMOTION

Raccoons always present a hunchbacked appearance

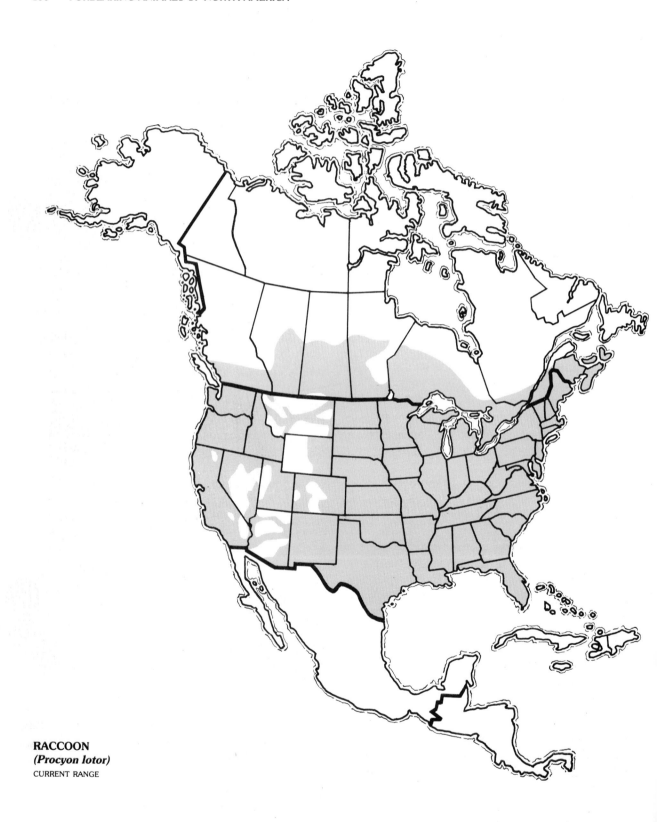

RACCOON
(Procyon lotor)
CURRENT RANGE

when they stand or move about. This is partially due to the hind legs being longer than the front but the spine is also flexed upward in front of the hind legs.

Raccoons usually walk and, because of the flexed spine, they seem to roll sideways and if they are fat, they waddle. Unless they have a definite destination, they stop every few yards to investigate something of interest. When more speed is needed, the raccoon trots. When the raccoon walks or trots, it holds its tail out behind at about a 60-degree angle from the body. Knowing this helps to identify a raccoon at a distance when seen in silhouette or crossing the road ahead of you. Most other large-tailed animals, such as a fox, carry their tails much higher.

The front foot of a large raccoon is about 3 inches in length; the hind foot is 4 to 4 1/2 inches long. When walking, the distance from hind foot to hind foot is about 12 inches. When the raccoon trots, this lengthens to about 15 inches. When the raccoon is really moving, it bounds.

In bounding, the raccoon, like all tree-climbing animals, hits the ground with its 2 front feet placed side by side. Then the 2 hind feet touch the ground in front of the front feet, but also to the outside. The track looks like two lopsided exclamation points.

A raccoon cannot outrun a dog. A raccoon chase with dogs is possible if the raccoon has a head start. In an open area I have run down raccoons. I would say that a raccoon's top speed would be about 15 miles per hour but it cannot maintain this pace.

When hard-pressed, a raccoon takes to a tree. It can climb very well. If it is climbing leisurely, it climbs using its front feet alternately. When it is in a hurry, it literally bounds up a tree using its feet in unison. Raccoons may descend a tree by backing down it or by climbing down headfirst. They usually come down headfirst if they are in a hurry.

If the raccoon really wants to get out of a tree fast, it just jumps. I have often seen them jump from heights of from 35 to 40 feet. As they jump, they spread their legs out so that the increased air resistance helps to slow them down. Like a cat, the raccoon always lands on its feet when jumping. It usually

Treed raccoon. Raccoons are very good climbers and use this method to escape from most of their enemies. (Photo: Irene Vandermolen)

This raccoon is eating a frog. Raccoons also love crayfish. (Photo: Irene Vandermolen)

hits the ground with quite a thump but scampers off, apparently uninjured.

Spending a lot of time around water, raccoons swim very well, but they do not swim just for the pleasure of it.

When feeding along the edge of a lake or river they often are in water up to their bellies, yet will wade back to shallow water rather than swim across a deep finger of water. They don't hesitate to swim if it is to get to a destination or to escape from their enemies. I figure that raccoons swim at about 3 miles per hour. As soon as raccoons get out of water, they shake themselves vigorously to get rid of the accumulated weight of the water.

FOOD

Although classified as a carnivore, a raccoon will eat almost anything it can find or capture. Freshwater snails eaten when pond levels drop and snails exposed. Raccoons feed often in small streams in search of a favorite food, crayfish; also eat mussels, clams and oysters, as well as fish, frogs, salamanders, snakes, earthworms, ground-nesting birds and their eggs, baby mice and rabbits. Turtles safe from raccoons when in water but vulnerable when out on land to lay eggs. Eggs and turtles themselves eaten, the raccoon pulling out flesh from either end of shell. In some marshes raccoons invade duck nests, even getting into wooden duck nest boxes on poles. Will also feed on baby muskrats, although seldom can catch an adult. Some raccoons live and sleep in marshes, moving from muskrat house to house. Insects an important food: grasshoppers, crickets, beetles; aquatic insects such as hellgrammites, dragonfly larvae, caddis fly larvae.

Throughout year vegetation makes up bulk of diet, eating in season all types of fruits, berries, most grains and some grasses. Wild grapes a favored food, and when sweet or field corn comes into milk raccoons consume large quantities, ruining more than they eat by taking only a few bites from each ear and moving on to another. Devastation of corn a serious farm problem. In fall nuts sought avidly, especially acorns which while low in protein are high in fats and starches and are easily digested. American chestnut had been favored food of raccoon before tree's blight.

Will feed readily on carrion. I watched them eat rotten shad without washing them. Also scavenge on highway for animals killed there and are often killed themselves.

Raccoons raid suburban garbage cans and can deftly open doors, latches and pry off lids. Will also eat seeds and suet at bird feeders, and raid chicken coops for birds and eggs.

Raccoons glut themselves in autumn to put fat on their bodies. I have charted captive raccoons eating up to 5 pounds of food per day at this time.

BEHAVIOR

The raccoon is a very curious creature, investigating everything it discovers and everything discovered has to be handled. Anything that is shiny has to be picked up. Trappers often take advantage of this trait by placing something shiny on the pan of a trap that they then conceal in shallow water. The raccoon, not seeing the trap but only the shiny object, can't resist trying to pick it up and is caught.

Curiosity is also a sign of intelligence and an adult raccoon can be an extremely clever animal. When hunted by dogs, the raccoon is quick to lay down a maze of tracks. It will run in and out of the water, it may even swim across a river. It will "tap" a tree, that is, it will run to a tree, climb up a short distance and then jump off again. Many dogs will then bark "treed" while the raccoon scampers off. A really wise raccoon will not climb a tree at all but will seek refuge by going underground in a groundhog's burrow or by getting in a fissure or split in the rocks or beneath the jumble of a talus rock slide. Underground, the raccoon is safe from almost any pursuer.

When a raccoon does seek refuge in a tree, it may be one that does not have a protective hollow. Then, when the hunters gather below, the raccoon's curiosity causes him to look down as the flashlights are used to search out its position. The reflective gleam of the raccoon's eyes give his position away and are a target for the hunters' guns.

Sometimes a hunter may climb the tree and shake or force the raccoon to jump out. The raccoon is a strong, courageous fighter. Pound for pound, a raccoon can whip any dog it faces. Unfortunately for the raccoon, most dogs that are used for hunting them outweigh them two to four times. And as the dogs are usually run in packs, they also outnumber the raccoon. Still, the raccoon will slash and bite like a buzz saw and always gives a good account of itself, even though the outcome is usually a foregone conclusion.

If the raccoon is cornered near water, it may do more than just give a good account of itself. As a dog swims out to grab it, the raccoon will often climb up on the dog's head and may drown it.

The lack of protective den trees also results in the raccoon frequently sleeping in less desirable spots. When the sun begins to light up the world, the raccoon will cease its feeding and seek shelter for the day. Lacking an underground den or den tree, the raccoon will often climb to the top of a tree and sleep in the crotch of the branches. I have seen them do this many times. Sometimes as many as two or three young raccoons will sleep in the same crotch. At other times they lie outstretched on a large horizontal tree limb and sleep with their legs dangling. I have also seen them sleep in abandoned hawks' and crows' nests.

Raccoons do not hibernate, contrary to the popular belief. After putting on all the weight possible, the raccoons retire to their dens to sleep away most of the cold weather. Raccoons in the Deep South remain active all year, the females denning only when they give birth.

From personal experience, over many years, I have found that when the temperature drops to between 26° and 28° F., raccoons den up. In true hibernation the animal's body temperature drops dramatically as do its heart and breathing rates. Hibernating animals are difficult to awaken. Raccoons become lethargic, but they don't hibernate. Their body temperature is only slightly lower than normal and they are easily roused. Because of their inactivity and the heat-retaining qualities of their coats, raccoons have a much lowered metabolic rate. While sleeping, their bodies' fuel needs are met by the reconversion of their body fat. It has been figured that a raccoon loses about three-quarters of an ounce of body weight per day while in its den in winter.

If the temperature should rise above freezing, and there is no snow on the ground, the raccoon may rouse itself and wander about for a while. It will eat food if it is available. If the temperature rises but there is more than a 6-inch depth of snow, the raccoon will remain in its den.

The depth of snow cover and the length of time it remains on the ground is a critical factor in the raccoon's survival and its northward range expansion. Although adult males will leave their dens to search for the females during the breeding season, snow or not, the young raccoons will not. If deep snow lasts longer than the young raccoons' supply of body fat, they starve to death. This is a major cause of death among young raccoons in the north.

SENSES

Touch most important, raccoons having thousands more nerve endings in skin of forefeet than humans in skin of hands. Research shows raccoon brain case designed to accommodate increased size of area that receives tactile impulses from front feet. Wetting of food and feet improves feeling for catching or eating. Raccoon will sit in water trying to catch minnows hiding in its fur. In searching for crayfish, it will gaze into sky, its paws moving rapidly about in the water.

Raccoons very alert and difficult to say whether hearing or eyesight is next in importance. They look constantly for danger and respond to slightest noise.

Smell not well developed by my observations. Taste either subjugated or poorly developed, raccoons eating bitter acorns that humans could not.

COMMUNICATION

Raccoons make a great variety of sounds. I am firmly convinced that many of the "panther screams" or "wildcat wailings" heard by so many people are actually some of the sounds made by the much more common raccoon. Raccoons churr, whimper, whine, growl, snarl, and have a coughing bark and hiss. Baby raccoons make so much noise right after they are born that it is a wonder that their whereabouts are not discovered. An angry adult makes a whining growl that leaves no doubt about its feelings. The young and adults churr. This sound, which sounds like a human saying "churr," has many modulations and evidently has many meanings. It is one of their most commonly made sounds. The mother makes this sound when she is looking for her young, or trying to keep them together while feeding. It is used when the little ones are warm and contented. The adult raccoon also has a call that sounds like a coarser version of the plaintive, whistling notes of the screech owl.

BREEDING

The breeding season of the raccoon is determined primarily by latitude; those in the South breed at least a month or even more before those in the North. Most raccoons breed in February.

Raccoons do not have mates. The males are polygamous and will breed with as many receptive females as they can find. The female will accept the first male that finds her but only if she is agreeable. If she does not like a certain male, she will drive him from her den.

Although female raccoons do not travel through the cold and snow, the males do, when the breeding season arrives. I saw the tracks of one large male in the snow during the last of January when the temperature was $-4°$ F. Most males know where the females are denned and make a beeline for them.

Female raccoons are capable of breeding when they are 10 months old, the males do not usually breed until they are 22 months old.

The female raccoon has a long estrous period and this period is announced by the vaginal swelling and a bloody discharge. If the female is not bred during her first estrus, and most of them are, she will come into another estrous period 4 months later.

When the male finds a receptive female, he moves in with her if she will accept him. Copulation occurs a number of times and lasts from 20 minutes to one hour per session.

Nine-day-old raccoons in their den in a hollow tree.

BIRTH AND YOUNG

The female raccoon, after breeding, usually goes back to sleep for several weeks, then wanders about as much as the male until it is time for the little ones to be born. As the time of birth approaches, the female again seeks out what will be the natal den. Gestation for the raccoon is usually 63 days, although there are accurate records of both longer and shorter periods.

When born, the baby raccoons have both their eyes and ears sealed shut. Their face and tail markings are plainly visible. Each baby will weigh 2 1/2 to 4 ounces and be 8 to 9 inches in total length, of which 2 1/4 inches are its tail.

The average litter in the South is 2 to 4 young, while 4 to 6 is more common in the North. Occasionally 7 young are born to one female but this is rare. Most of the young are born in April.

The mother raccoon is very devoted and very defensive of her young. Other wildlife mothers, including bears, will sometimes abandon their young if danger threatens but the raccoon almost never does so. She leaves the young just long enough to feed, then hurries back to her babies. The male does not help to raise the young and would be driven off by the irate mother if he came to the den.

The young raccoons keep up an almost constant chattering whine. They can crawl about quite well before they are one week old, even though it is done spiderlike. They can climb before their eyes open at 22–24 days.

At 5 weeks of age the baby raccoons begin to venture out of their den for the first time.

A mother raccoon teaching her young ones how to hunt for food.

At 4 weeks of age the little ones weigh over a pound and are 13 inches in length. By 8 weeks of age they are starting to climb around and peer out of the den. They are not allowed out as yet and if one does crawl out, the mother promptly carries it back inside. She carries the little ones by their heads or by the nape of their necks. At 12 weeks of age the young are clambering all over the den tree and will frequently sleep in the upper branches.

The female usually starts to wean the little ones at about 4 months of age. Now the mother takes her entire family along when she goes searching for food. This is a particularly dangerous time because the young are in constant motion and are going in all directions.

The family group stays together until autumn, when some of the young may go off on their own for either a short while or for good. Most of the young stay with the mother and occasionally some of those that wandered off earlier return to sleep in the communal den. The young will weigh 12–15 pounds at this time.

LIFE SPAN

Normal life span: 10 years. Most raccoons in wild do not reach this age, those in captivity often live much longer. Oldest on record: Old Jerry, captive raccoon in Wisconsin, lived 22 years.

SIGN

Tracks along shore of water bodies the most common sign. Tracks of adult raccoon are distinctive, while those of young raccoon about the same size as a large woodchuck, although woodchuck tracks not likely to be found near water, as are raccoon's. Feces of raccoon common as diet includes much fruit and animal voids often. Feces larger in diameter than those of most other animals in the area and more frequently appear on fallen logs or tree limbs. Trees with holes in them have silver-tipped hairs clinging to bark if raccoon has climbed it.

ENEMIES

Bobcats, coyotes, fishers, bears, mountain lions, large owls, golden eagles and alligators take young raccoons, but only larger predators can take adult. Most medium to large dogs will chase and kill raccoons if opportunity comes. External parasites plaguing raccoon are lice, fleas, ticks, flies, mosquitoes and mange mites. Also have usual internal parasites such as roundworms, flatworms, and tapeworms. Subject also to cat and dog distemper and encephalitis. When infected with encephalitis raccoons appear tame, and if people pick them up the disease will spread to their dogs, but not to the people themselves. Eventually raccoon's eyes fill with matter, the nose runs, and hind-leg motor paralysis develops, and it dies shortly thereafter. Raccoons also infected with rabies, and recent reports state rabies on the upswing in South Carolina, where 67 rabid raccoons found in 10 months, and in other southeastern states. Vaccination of domestic cats and dogs would help curtail disease, transmitted to man by bite or scratch of rabid animal.

HUMAN RELATIONS

No wild animal makes a good pet. I fully realize there will be thousands of people that disagree with me on this, because there are thousands who have raised raccoons as pets and think they are the greatest. The raccoon is probably the most popular of all wildlife pets. I have probably raised more than 50 raccoons of my own, but still from personal experience I maintain that wild animals do not make good pets. Sooner or later, everyone who raises raccoons will have the scars to

Raccoons are very adaptable and many have learned to live in urban areas by raiding garbage cans for food.

Hollow trees are very important to raccoons as den sites that can be used year-round. The family may stay together during their first winter. (Photo: Irene Vandermolen)

Raccoons do not hibernate, but they do sleep in their dens for extended periods of time in the winter. If the weather moderates, the raccoons will awaken and may even come out of their dens to look for food, as this one is about to do.

prove what I am saying. Wild animals belong out in the wilds. Even my good friend Sterling North, who wrote the delightful book *Rascal,* had to return his raccoon to the wild after it turned on him. Raccoons are delightful at an early age, although they can make a shambles of a home in a matter of minutes with their investigations and their desire to climb on everything.

During the 1920s raccoon coats were in demand; everyone had to have one and the population of raccoons went down. After the fad passed, raccoons increased in numbers and their value dropped. In the 1950s the demand for coonskin hats developed as all the kids emulated their television hero, Davy Crockett. Prices again went up and then dropped as that fad passed.

Around 1949–50, an irruption of raccoons was noted across the nation; their populations skyrocketed and complaints of their damage poured in. The price of raccoon fur dropped as the irruption continued; pelts hit an all-time low about 1968 of $1.80. Only the most fervid coon hunters still hunted them, as it was just too costly to maintain a pack of hounds with such low monetary returns for the pelts. Again, the pendulum had swung in the other direction.

Today, the price paid for most furs is higher than ever. Raccoon hunting has regained its popularity with tens of thousands of hunters going forth at night with their hounds. It has been calculated that 80 to 90 percent of all the raccoons are taken by hunters, the balance by trapping.

COMMERCIAL VALUE

Raccoon the most important fur animal in U.S. today. IAFWA statistics: 3,832,802 taken 1976–77; $26 average price; $99,652,852 total (genuine total even higher because 5 states did not report). Top 6 states: Texas, 430,510; Michigan, 357,570; Ohio, 294,079; Iowa, 264,819; Louisiana, 254,435; Missouri, 247,671. In Canada: 99,339 taken; $22.27 average price, $2,212,625 total. Latest figures certain to show increase in monetary value, good pelts in 1978–79 season selling for $40.

Raccoons also a food source to many, with young roast coon a favorite. All excess fat must be stripped away before roasting.

VI

ORDER:

CARNIVORA

FAMILY:

MUSTELIDAE

The weasels, stoats, polecats, ferrets, minks, martens, fishers, tayras, grisons, wolverines, badgers, skunks and river and sea otters are all members of the weasel family. The least weasel is the smallest carnivore in the world, with adults weighing between 2 and 3 ounces. The sea otter is the largest member of the weasel family, weighing between 80 and 100 pounds.

All of the various forms have a long body and comparatively short legs, although some have a slim body and others are heavy and stocky. They all have the two anal scent glands, although none of the others are as well developed as those of the skunks.

Some, like the badger, excel in digging, the marten and fisher excel in climbing and the otters excel in swimming. The sea otter is a truly oceanic mammal, spending most of its life in the sea.

The canine teeth of all members of the weasel family are needle-sharp and are used for grasping their prey. None of their teeth is modified for the extensive chewing of food. Food is cut into pieces small enough to be swallowed.

Most of these animals are solitary most of the year, with the exception of the sea otters. Delayed implantation occurs in most of these species. Some of the weasels turn white in the wintertime; none of the other species does.

MARTEN, *Martes americana*

INTRODUCTION

Larry should have known better. The six ptarmigans that he had left lying on the ground, outside his tent, were gone when he got up in the morning. A few feathers marked the spot where the ptarmigans had been but their whereabouts and what had taken them was a mystery. At least until the following night.

That night a loud scratching on our tent roof woke us up. Irene and I could see the shadow of some crea-

ture dash along the ridge pole, slide down the roof and then scamper back up. My first thought was that a flying squirrel was the culprit but the shadow was too large. The creature was evidently enjoying its repeated tobogganing down the tent roof.

I got up, slipped on my boots and grabbed a flashlight. As silently as I could, I opened the tent flap and stepped out into the frigid night air. When a dark form came bounding along the ridgepole toward me, I impaled it with a shaft of light. There, 4 feet away, stood a marten. Anchored by curiosity, its little foxlike face alert, its bright eyes trying to see beyond the light, the marten refused to flee.

In the high country of British Columbia's Cassiar Mountains, the marten is fairly common but so seldom seen that to see it is always a thrill. Now we knew what had carried off the ptarmigans.

The American marten is usually referred to as the pine marten but to do so is to give it the name of its European cousin, *Martes martes*. It is also sometimes called a sable but that is the proper name of another Eurasian mammal, *Martes zibellina*. There are 8 species of marten found throughout the world.

Our American marten, *Martes americana*, was given its current scientific name by Miller in 1912. Earlier, in 1806, Turton had called our marten *Mustela americana*. The marten is a member of the weasel family and *Mustela* is Latin for "weasel." The name was corrected to *Martes*, Latin for "marten," and *americana* is appropriate because this particular member of the weasel family is found only in North America.

To further add to the confusion, up until 1953, 3 distinct species of marten were recognized as inhabiting this continent and they were designated as *Martes americana*, with 6 subspecies; *Martes atrata*, being restricted to Newfoundland; and *Martes caurina*, having 6 subspecies. Additional taxonomic work by Philip L. Wright proved that all of these martens were conspecific and they are all classified today as subspecies of *Martes americana*.

DESCRIPTION

All members of the weasel family are always extremely alert but because the marten has large, more erect and more forward-placed ears than any of its relatives, it seems superalert. And its little fox face seems super-inquisitive.

The marten is truly a beautiful animal.

In total length, an adult male marten is 24–30 inches. Of that length, 7 to 8 inches are tail bone. The marten usually appears much longer than it actually is because the hair on the end of its tail is 3 inches long.

Martens prefer to den in hollow trees. This one has found a snug home in an abandoned woodpecker's hole. (Photo: Irene Vandermolen)

Martens, like all members of the weasel family, are digitgrade—standing on the soles of their toes and feet. Standing, the marten is about 7 1/2 inches high at the shoulder.

In weight, the adult males weigh between 2 and 3 pounds, with 4 pounds being exceptional. The adult female martens are smaller in overall size and weigh about 30 percent less than the males.

The dentition of a marten is classified as 12 incisor teeth, 4 needle-sharp canines, 16 premolars and 6 molars. The molars are fairly flat-topped so that the marten's food can be thoroughly chewed before being swallowed.

The marten's nose and eyes are jet black. The eyes sparkle, showing the interest that the marten has in everything in its surroundings. As the marten turns its head, the refraction of the sunlight turns the eyes to a bright green. When a bright light is shined, the marten's eyes have rods that reflect a bright yellow.

The marten's ears stand erect and are about 1 1/2 inches in length. The fur on the outside of the ear is usually a dark brown while the inner surfaces, facing the viewer, are an off-shade of white. There are two short, dark vertical eye bars standing above the inner corners of the marten's eyes.

There are 4 neatly stitched rows of sparse vibrissae, with the longest whiskers being about 2 1/2 inches in length. There is a row of 5 or 6 long hairs projecting from the eyebrow. There are also a few straggly chin hairs.

There is a tremendous variety of color and shading in the marten's fur. Some of the martens have a basic, very light, silvery-gray color, some are golden yellow, others are as dark as burnt umber. There is also a tremendous variation in the size, color and extent of the marten's conspicuous throat patch. On some martens the throat patch is a creamy-white, on most of them it is a very bright burnt orange. The color of the throat patch has no correlation to the sex of the animal.

Most martens are lighter colored on the head than on any part of the body, with the exception of the throat patch. The throat patch starts beneath the chin, widens out to encompass the entire throat and breast

Although the marten is a member of the weasel family, it has a foxlike face. Its curiosity about the photographer kept this marten from running away before its picture was taken. (Photo: Irene Vandermolen)

area, continues as a narrow streak down the belly and flares out widely to encompass the male's genital area. On the female, the streak is narrower on her lower inguinal region.

I am struck by the reflective beauty of coloration of the golden guard hairs on this belly strip of the marten study skins that I have before me. The sunlight hits the hair tip's burnished gold and when the pelt is turned, each individual hair becomes prismatic. The primary colors are reflected but toward the yellow end of the scale. The beauty beggars my attempt to describe it.

The marten's body fur shades from light to dark, from the belly to the back, with a definite darker dorsal strip running from the head to the tail. The tail has the darkest coloration. I can find no record of albino martens. The underfur of the marten is about one inch in length and is tricolored, shading from a basal white to gray to cinnamon. The guard hairs range between 1¼ to 1¾ inches in length. The marten has a very bushy tail and the hair on the tip is 3 to 3½ inches in length. In November 1958, Al Lysker, of Alaska, caught a "Samson" marten that had no guard hairs at all. Such a pelt is worthless.

The marten has 5 functional toes on each foot, although the toe corresponding to our thumb is greatly reduced and often does not leave an imprint in the animal's tracks. The claws are almost one-half inch long, following the curve, and are semiretractable. Although not going back into sheaths, the claw tips are raised off the ground so the tips, needed for climbing, are not dulled by making contact with the ground. In the wintertime, long hairs grow on the marten's feet between the toe and sole pads, giving the foot protective insulation and blurring the registry of pads in the tracks.

The 2 anal scent glands of the marten are not as large or as well developed as those of the skunk and it cannot "shoot" the scent. Nor is the marten's musk as acrid and as offensive as that of the mink or weasel. It is true that when the marten is excited or angered it discharges some of this scent but I find that it cannot be directed, is not foul-smelling and dissipates rapidly in the air. Even material that comes in contact with

this scent will be relatively free of its odor within 10–12 hours.

The marten also has an abdominal, sebaceous skin gland that is elliptical in shape. The gland is about 3 inches long and three-quarters of an inch at its widest point. This gland is used primarily for communication, particularly during the breeding season.

DISTRIBUTION

Marten population increasing today and range expanding steadily back into areas where it had been extirpated. Marten prefers forests of mature spruce and fir; mixed conifers and hardwoods also good habitat. Mature stands of hardwoods acceptable provided enough blowdowns to ensure good cover. Marten will avoid mature stands of second-growth aspen and birch, bean-pole forests of miniature softwoods or jackpine, due to lack of cover. Dense cedar swamps make good habitat, having excellent cover and abundant food. In most areas martens found at 2,000–4,000 foot elevation and higher, and 20–30 years ago they appeared only on mountain peaks because man had overrun habitat. Adequate protection today enables them to live at sea level where habitat is good, along coasts of Maine, British Columbia and Alaska. Generally martens stick to highest peaks in summer, moving to low elevations when deep snow drives them down in search of food. Found across Canada and Alaska where good stands of evergreens and ample food, also in Maine, New Hampshire, Vermont and New York. In West: in mountains of Montana, Idaho, Washington, Oregon, California, Utah, Nevada, Wyoming and Colorado, and several found recently in Minnesota. In most of these states martens have been imported or restocked with animals caught within their own borders.

TRAVEL

The first marten I ever saw was running along the sandy beach edges and over the portage trails of the

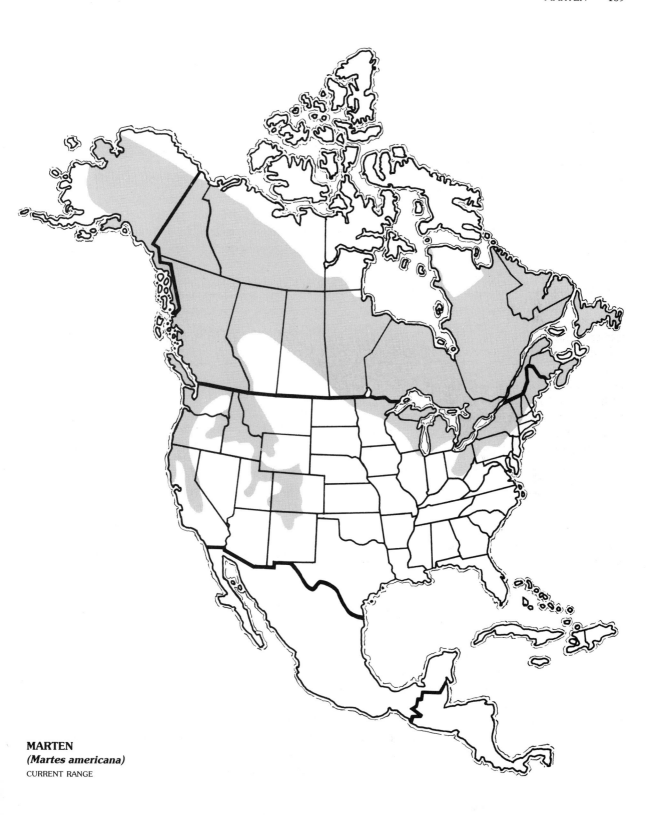

MARTEN
(Martes americana)
CURRENT RANGE

Martens are active in the coldest weather despite the snow-laden tree branches.

wilderness area of Quebec where I used to guide canoe trips years ago.

It is true that the marten is the most arboreal member of the weasel family but it is also true that martens spend most of their time on the ground. Any movement of potential prey up in a tree, such as a red squirrel, chipmunk or a bird on its nest, will cause the marten to ascend the tree in a flash. When threatened by any predator, the marten heads for the nearest tree. When frightened by man, the marten may as often dash away on the ground as climb a tree.

Like all members of the weasel family, the martens have their own individual territories and are even more solitary than some of their cousins.

The size of a marten's territory depends entirely upon the availability of food and the amount of cover to be found there. Areas that have been opened in the forest by clear-cutting large blocks of timber, or that have been burned out by fire, are of little or no use to a marten. The marten will not even cross such areas if they are more than 300 yards across, particularly in the winter. In the summertime such areas usually produce an abundance of grasses, bracken fern and berry bushes, providing a protective screen from predators. Areas of new growth of jackpine or the bean-pole stage of softwoods, such as aspen and birch, provide little cover and have almost no food potential and are thus avoided or skirted.

The adult male marten has a much larger individual territory than does the mature female. His territory may be 5 to 10 miles across and perhaps more. The female's territory will be one to 5 miles across and one male may overlap the territory of 3 or 4 females. Immature females travel much more than adult females and have larger territories.

It has been calculated that one marten to the square mile of good habitat is about all that the territory can hold. In late summer and early fall, the ratio may go as high as 3 or 4 martens to the square mile. As dispersal takes place, the younger martens spill over and colonize adjacent territories, expanding their range if the martens are protected. Where part of the marten population is harvested by trapping, the range expansion is much slower because the young martens then usually fill in any areas left vacant when the resident martens are removed.

Martens can travel through the treetops without coming down to the ground if the trees are large and close-standing. Usually the marten travels on the ground and prefers to follow along the edge of such natural watercourses as lakes, rivers and streams.

Martens, in their constant circling, over and throughout their territories, usually do not follow a definite path, although they will visit specific spots where they have secured food previously. Their apparently aimless drifting about is in reality a thorough coverage of their territory. How far a marten travels in any particular day depends entirely upon its success in hunting and on the weather.

Martens that have been followed by biologists have been known to travel 5 miles or more per day. Most of this traveling will be done from one piece of cover to the next with no definite goal or distance in mind. When the marten has caught enough food to fill its belly, it seeks out a tree cavity or den and curls up to

Although the marten catches most of its food on the ground, it can outclimb the tree squirrels. It is more at home in the treetops than it is upon the ground.

sleep. When hungry, it hunts and travels again. Ordinarily a marten makes a circuit of its territory every 8 to 10 days.

Martens detest getting wet because their fur is not waterproof and will mat. Heavy rains will cause them to den up and they won't travel again until forced to because of hunger. Active all winter, the martens will also seek shelter during a severe, prolonged snowstorm.

LOCOMOTION

When martens walk they have a stride that is about 6 inches in length with the track of the hind foot registering on top of that of the front foot. Martens usually bound with the humpbacked, rocking-horse-type gait which is typical of the weasel family. While bounding along, the distance between the tracks varies between 24 and 31 inches. When hard-pressed, the distance is even greater. The tracks of the feet are staggered because each of the 4 feet touch down in a sequence. The right front foot may touch down first, then the left front foot comes down slightly ahead of it. The right hind foot touches down slightly ahead of the left front foot and then the left hind foot comes down still farther ahead. As the hind feet come in contact with the earth, the body is compressed, then catapulted ahead into the next bound by the hind feet.

In climbing, the marten may use its front and hind feet, each pair in unison, and it literally gallops up the tree. Or it may climb using its front feet alternately. Most of the time the marten climbs in evergreen trees and on the smaller trees or in the tops of the big trees where the branches are close enough so that it can climb from branch to branch. On smaller branches, it climbs as a man would, hand over hand.

The marten can climb down a tree headfirst, being able to turn its hind feet outward and reversed as a squirrel can. Occasionally, the marten will hang from the tree trunk or from a tree branch by just its hind feet.

A large marten can jump about 9 feet horizontally from one tree to another or from branch to branch.

Martens have been known to jump from heights of 20 feet without hurting themselves. Martens have also been seen jumping out of trees, repeatedly, into soft snow, apparently just for the pleasure of it.

Martens can swim but hate to do so. When they swim, they are much slower than the mink, which has hair webs on its feet to aid propulsion. However, the marten swims with its back and tail held much higher out of water than the mink does. This may be due to the fact that martens hate to get wet and expend more of their efforts to keeping as high in the water as is possible. I have noticed that humans who dislike and fear the water usually swim much higher in the water than do those people who like and can relax in the water.

Anton DeVos, who has made extensive studies of the marten in Ontario, has seen martens swim across the Chapleau River, although he does not mention how far that might be. He has also seen a marten swim underwater for about 100 feet.

Martens have a limited homing ability. Researchers have found that a marten, that is livetrapped, then moved 8 to 10 miles from its point of capture, will return to its original territory. The greatest distance recorded for a return by a marten is 12 miles. Moved beyond that range, the marten evidently just seeks out a new territory. They may travel much farther in establishing their new territories but this cannot be proved because such marked martens have yet to be retrapped.

FOOD

Fast metabolism and high activity level make martens always hungry. Concern for food overrides concern for safety—caught in live traps they frequently accept food and eat while remaining trapped, and on release would stop to eat proffered food or immediately begin search for food on their own. Some martens become tame enough to venture into backwoods cabins and accept food from occupants; in Adirondack Park martens accustomed to presence of hikers raid their food packs at night. Not strictly carnivorous, martens known to have eaten candy, pancakes, cooked cereal, canned fish and meat, fruit, jams and jellies, but in the wild the mainstay is red-backed and meadow voles. Wood rats and occasionally deer mice also eaten.

Red squirrel not a major source of food despite claims to the contrary. In Alaska 446 martens examined and it was found that red-backed vole were eaten 336 times, meadow mouse 62 times, brown lemming 3 times, red squirrel 2 times. In Montana and Washington red squirrel the most important food item, although no more common there than in Alaska. Red squirrel able to escape marten by jumping from tree to tree from the ends of thin branches where marten's greater weight would cause branches to bend, or by disappearing down crevasses too narrow for marten to enter.

In western mountains marten may hunt above timberline or live among rock slides feeding on marmots and pika. Determined adult marmot could stand off marten attack, but martens easily kill and eat young. Pika easily killed because marten is faster and can follow pika anywhere.

Birds, eggs and young eaten at every opportunity, even tree-nesting birds. Grouse burrowed beneath snow also caught and eaten. Marten tunnels beneath snow to feed on mice, a favored food. Snow is less deep beneath mature stands of conifer, making tunneling easier, one reason conifer stands are good habitat. In British Columbia and southeastern coast of Alaska martens forced down to sea beaches by deep snow in mountains. Tides keep beaches freer of snow and ice and deposit various live and dead marine life on beach. Martens also eat frogs and snakes occasionally, but not toads and salamanders, whose skin secretions are offensive. Insects eaten in large quantities: grasshoppers, crickets, wasps, bees, flies, moths, butterflies, underground nests of yellow jackets and wasps dug up and pupating larvae eaten. Insects were number-one food in Washington State study in summer. Also eat honey of wild bees. Martens eat great deal of vegetation, particularly berries. In Alaska martens observed with blue-stained lips from eating blueberries—also eat crowberries, wild cranberries, currants, raspberries, fruit of mountain ash, seeds of various spruce and pinecones. Martens also scavenge on anything edible, carcass of moose, caribou or deer. Martens will revisit spots where carcasses lie even when bleached bones have been scattered.

Prey usually killed by biting point where neck meets skull, sometimes piercing skull itself with canine teeth. Larger prey such as hare and squirrel bitten in throat, severing carotid artery. Prey attacked with great speed, seizing throat with teeth, and neck and body with claws, wrapping itself around prey, biting and slashing. Marten and prey tumble about until prey succumbs. Fearful itself of an attack, marten drags prey away into hiding—within tree or underground den, or beneath thicket, copse of grass, or blowdown. Small prey consumed entirely, bones, feet, meat, feathers, fur. With larger prey the feet, fur and larger bones cleaned but discarded. When prey too large for one meal, remainder cached or stored. Marten eats 4–6 ounces per day.

High activity level keeps marten lithe. When food plentiful, small amount of fat may form on abdomen. Cycles of prey availability determine population cycles of marten where the population is stable in true wilderness areas. Although one study shows snowshoe hare account for only 9 percent of marten diet, a cycle coinciding with snowshoe-hare cycle ran 1867, 1876, 1887, 1896, 1904, when cycle disrupted due to overtrapping; cycle resumed with 1926, 1939, 1946, according to figures of the Hudson's Bay Company. Since 1946 cycle disrupted again. Another study said marten in Labrador was on a 4-year cycle coinciding with cycle of mice and voles, common prey of marten.

BEHAVIOR

Martens are most active during the late night and early dawn period and again in the late afternoon till night. Again, the length of their activity is determined by their success in hunting. In true wilderness areas where the marten does not encounter man, or in areas where they have complete protection and have grown accustomed to man, the marten may be abroad at any time of the day. I have found almost no activity by the marten between the hours of 10:00 A.M. and 2:00 P.M.

During the daylight hours, if the weather is overcast and cold or wet, the marten will curl up in a snug tree or earthen den, if it can find one. On sunny, cold, windy days, the marten will curl up on the ground, in the sunshine, beneath some brushy cover. On sunny, cool, calm days, the marten will often sleep up in the top of a tree, stretched out along or draped over a limb, soaking up the sunshine. The deciding factor is always the strong wind, which all animals avoid because it causes the cold to penetrate their fur and to chill their bodies.

Lying out like this, the marten is frequently plagued by jays, crows, ravens and magpies. These birds always set up a clamor whenever they discover a predator, diving at it and disclosing its whereabouts with their raucous calls.

Martens are a study in contrasts. They either avoid man at all costs, leaving the area as man passes by, or else, drawn by curiosity, they make a nuisance of themselves.

One marten at Mount Adams, in New York's Adirondack Park, just couldn't be kept out of the biologists' live trap. The first time the marten was caught, it was ear-tagged through both ears, weighed, measured and had a small premolar tooth removed. This tooth would later be decalcified, sliced, stained and used to provide the accurate age of that particular marten.

Biologists usually administer a tranquilizing drug to the marten so that it can be handled with no chance of injury to the biologists or to itself. The effects of the drugs seldom last more than 30 minutes and in that length of time the biologists are finished with the marten and are ready to release it.

After that kind of treatment, one would think that the marten would promptly leave the area. Not so. That particular marten was caught 7 times in 8 successive days in the same live trap. Although most animals struggle wildly when caught in a trap, the marten usually accepts its fate with equanimity.

Martens are perhaps the easiest of the wild animals to catch. Traps set for most wild animals must be skillfully concealed but not for the marten. It will step into a bare, visible trap to get at an enticing piece of bait. This "dumbness" was a chief factor in the marten's threatened annihilation a few decades ago. Today, the marten is protected by set seasons and limits because the marten has proven that it can easily hold its own in the natural world but just as easily falls prey to man.

Martens will usually run on any downed log that lies in the direction of their travels. They cannot seem to resist running up inclined logs and perhaps they do so to get a better look at their surroundings. Trappers often take advantage of this trait by cutting a notch in the inclined log and placing a trap there. A trap, so placed, can be successful with or without bait.

SENSES

Smell and hearing probably equally keen, marten depending upon both in hunting. Difficult to prove whether marten hears or smells mice beneath snow—probably both.

Vision very keen, being primarily a sight hunter, and takes notice of all surrounding it that moves. Immobile man not recognized as danger and may go unnoticed unless he makes even slightest of movements.

Sense of taste revealed in fondness for honey. No evidence available concerning sense of touch.

COMMUNICATION

Many creatures give out with vocalizations that can be heard for long distances and by which they may be identified, but not the marten. I don't want to give the impression that the marten does a lot of vocalizing but it does give an almost continuous staccato, rasping growl when angry, disturbed or even when it is just curious about something. Martens also squeal and have a loud, piercing scream when they are angry or hurt. They squeal, snarl and whine. Researchers report the female makes a clucking sound during the breeding season.

Marten scat is usually deposited upon very prominent logs or rocks and undoubtedly some of the anal scent is deposited at the same time. These scent posts are an important means of communication between the martens in the same way that fire hydrants are to dogs. Every marten that passes such spots will turn aside to visit them to add its own contribution.

Martens are frequently seen stretched out on a branch or log, dragging their bellies on the wood. In this manner they distribute scent from their abdominal scent glands.

Before and during the breeding season, the male marten's testicles enlarge so that the scrotum almost drags on the ground. With the rubbing that the marten does to deposit its scent, the hair is usually worn off the bottom of the scrotum.

BREEDING

Prior to the breeding, which occurs in July, the martens travel extensively throughout their territories, and the males and females try to make contact with each other. At this time, they engage in depositing scent on as many tree branches and limbs as possible. The female calls to the male with her soft clucking.

All competition and animosity between the males and females are subjugated as the more important, pressing need of mating becomes dominant. Rival males show even more animosity toward each other than at other times of the year. Fights between the males are common and vicious until dominance is established.

During the courtship period, the male and female martens become very playful with each other, chasing each other about on the ground and up through the trees. Mock fighting and wrestling matches are indulged in with the martens rolling and tumbling about.

The females are usually in estrus for about 15 days, starting just before the middle of July and extending into the first part of August. The male stays with the female for a week or more, till conception is assured. The male then leaves to seek another receptive female.

After breeding, the female prepares what will be the natal den. She will choose the most secure den that is located near a good food supply because the male does not assist with the feeding of the young. Tree dens are preferred. The female then carries in dead grasses and pieces of moss to make a soft, warm bed.

BIRTH AND YOUNG

The marten is subject to delayed implantation. Breeding takes place in July or early August but the fertilized egg does not fasten itself to the wall of the uterus till late January or February. Development is then rapid and the young are born in late March or early April. This gives a gestation period of approximately 260–268 days.

Several researchers carried out a very interesting experiment. They kept captive, bred, female martens subjected to continuous artificial light for 24 hours a day. This forced the implantation of the blastocyst to the uterus in a much shorter period of time, and the females gave birth to normal young in 4 1/2 months instead of the regular 8 1/2 to 9 months.

These conditions cannot be duplicated in the wild where most living things are controlled by photoperiodism, i.e., the amount of light in a 24-hour period. The experiments may be of some value to game breeders who raise martens commercially for their fur.

A litter of martens may contain from 2 to 5 young, with 3 being the most common number. At birth the babies measure between 9 and 12 centimeters or 4 to 5 inches in total length. They weigh about 30 grams, about one ounce. They are covered with short, gray hair, although the throat patch is already visible. The eyes of the little ones are closed.

The female marten is a devoted mother, quick to fly to the defense of her young. She will leave them only long enough to secure the food that she needs. The young are washed, and suckle at the 4 teats located on the female's lower abdomen. The young whine when hungry and occasionally squeal.

After one month, the young are arrayed in coats

that are similar to the adults' in coloration. At 5 weeks the eyes of the young open.

Now the female begins to give the little ones their first taste of meat. The young martens had pushed and shoved each other when they were nursing, but now they begin to fight actively among themselves. Each time the mother brings back a prey species, the young growl and fight with each other for sole possession of the food. By 6 to 7 weeks, the young martens are weaned and are feeding almost exclusively on meat. Between 7 and 8 weeks the young have developed sufficiently so that they now climb out of the den and follow after the mother as she hunts. In their eagerness for food, they often spoil their mother's attempt to sneak up on her prey.

At 3 months of age, the young martens are almost full-grown in both size and weight. The young males weigh about 26 ounces, the young females 23 ounces. The fighting between the young becomes more intense as they become more competitive, although they don't usually hurt one another. By midsummer, by the time the female comes into estrus, the family unit has broken up and scattered. Any young males that remain in their mother's area are soon driven off when the adult males come courting. At this time, the young males weigh about 41 ounces, while the young females weigh about 33 ounces.

The young are sexually mature at 15 months and most of the young females breed their first year, although a few may not breed until they are 27 months of age.

The most accurate method of aging mammals is by sectioning one of their teeth as has been described. Immature martens can be told from adults by the sagital crest on the top of the head. This ridge of the skull becomes very pronounced after the animal is one year old.

LIFE SPAN

Potential of 10 years in wild. European pine marten recorded at 17 years, and American species could probably reach such an age under favorable conditions.

SIGN

Tracks most common sign, those of adult being about 1 3/8 inches in length and width. Four of 5 toes show prominently, with the fifth, corresponding to our thumb, seldom registering in track. Claw marks seldom show unless track is in very soft mud. Most tracks appear in soft snow in winter, usually as sets of 4 holes punched in snow, each set about 26 inches apart. Marten tracks may be confused with mink, although mink tracks will disappear into water, marten's will not. Marten tracks will end at a tree more often than those of any other weasel family member. Scats easily seen displayed on prominent rock or log. About 3/8 inch in diameter, 3–5 inches long, they usually lie in a semicircle and appear twisted. Scats generally dark when fresh and contain hair and feathers. Scats become larger, straighter, and filled with seeds when marten feeds on berries, which also act as laxative and make scats more numerous.

ENEMIES

Fisher is an enemy, although fishers kill martens far less often than has been supposed (only 5 recorded instances). Marten can escape fisher by climbing out on branches too thin to support fisher's weight. Nevertheless, when fisher population is high, marten population is low. This fact due more to the competition of the two for food, the fisher being such an efficient predator that it often drives itself out of areas it has depleted of food. Marten also competes with weasel, bobcat, lynx, fox, coyote, great horned owl and goshawk. Beyond fisher, marten relatively free from predation, able to escape in cover and seldom venturing beyond cover. Occasional predator, particularly great horned owl, takes young marten. Marten comparatively free from internal and external parasites and disease because it is solitary, antagonistic with other martens and constantly moving from den to den. Fleas and ticks appear occasionally, and flies and mosquitoes more bothersome to martens in lower cedar swamps than to those in high country. One case of mange in marten reported.

HUMAN RELATIONS

In the past, uncontrolled fires, lumbering, trapping and the encroachment of man upon its habitat extirpated the martens over most of their normal range and drove the remnants back into the most inaccessible of mountains. Today, with better fire control, systematic logging and strictly enforced trapping seasons, we have found that the marten can survive side by side with man.

Fire and lumbering are disadvantages to the marten where entire areas are cleared; both work to the marten's benefit where small spots are opened, allowing the brush to come back with the resultant increase in food species.

While the damage that man has done is revocable, our invasion of habitat, in most cases, is not. The marten is surviving and in many areas thriving, despite man's alteration of the environment.

COMMERCIAL VALUE

Marten a conservation success story. In 1875 in North America total take was 118,000 martens, a figure that dropped to 800 martens in 1930. Population continued to decline for a decade after that. From 1920s through the 1940s states and provinces gave marten complete protection to save the species, and those efforts have succeeded. IAFWA statistics: 1976–1977, 130,530 taken in North America. In 8 of 50 states, 27,898 martens taken, average price $14, total $390,572. In Canada: 102,632 taken, $19.92 average price, total $2,044,210.

16

FISHER, *Martes pennanti*

INTRODUCTION

The fisher is a little-known animal to most people. It is a will-o'-the-wisp that appears and disappears in the dark forests before you are sure that you have even seen one. And up till a couple of years ago, it is not likely you saw one in the wild. Not many people ever have.

Nowhere abundant at any time, the fisher all but disappeared from the face of the earth between 1930 and 1940. In 1920 fisher pelts brought a price as high as $345 apiece and, at such prices, the trapping and hunting pressure on this animal was relentless. If the tracks of a fisher were seen in the wilderness, particularly of the female whose pelt was worth more, hunters would strap on their snowshoes and follow the trail, though it often took days, until the animal was killed. Between overhunting and trapping and the destruction of its habitat by lumbering and fire, the fisher retreated to a few isolated, inaccessible pockets in the mountain vastness.

Besides being scarce, a great deal of misinformation about the fisher's name, habits, and habitat only added to the confusion.

The fisher's Latin name was given to it by Johann Erxleben in 1776. *Martes* is Latin for "marten" and *pennanti* was given to this animal in honor of the Welsh naturalist, Thomas Pennant.

The fisher does not really catch fish, although it does love to eat them. The only authentic account of the fisher actually catching fish was given by Rae Hunt, of the New Hampshire Fish and Game Department, in 1934. He had been following a large male fisher by its tracks in the snow. The tracks led to a stream where trout often concentrated. The tracks led directly to the water where the fisher dove into the wa-

The fisher's long, lean body shows that it is a relative of the weasel.

ter and caught a trout. Remnants of the trout and fresh blood on the snow showed that the fisher had been successful.

Fishers have been known to steal fish and it is one of the best baits for this animal. In wilderness areas where people smoke or freeze fish for later usage, fishers often raid their caches.

Ernest Thompson Seton pointed out that perhaps the name derived from fisher-marten. Both the marten and the fisher are of the *Martes* family. The marten is usually referred to as a pine marten and frequents the high, dry ridges and mountain tops. The fisher-marten prefers the big timber forests, the higher wooded swamps, lakes and watercourses.

Or, it may be that the fisher reminded some of the early settlers of the European polecat. Some of the common names of the polecat are fitchet, fitche or fitcher. Many North American creatures were erroneously named after similar-appearing, although not necessarily related, European counterparts.

The French Canadian name for the fisher is pekan. In the United States it is also called fisher-cat, tree-fox, Pennant's marten or black cat, each locale having its own colloquial name.

Although the use of the name fisher is confusing, it is the name we will use to avoid confusion because it's the most commonly used name.

DESCRIPTION

The fisher is a large, lithe, muscular member of the weasel family. The measurements and weights given by Dr. William J. Hamilton, former professor of mammalogy at Cornell University, for an average of 27 males taken in the Adirondack Mountains in New York State, were 37½ inches total length, with 13¾ inches being tail length; average weight 8.18 pounds, with the largest one being 12 pounds 1 ounce. In 1962, Forrest Smart, of the Maine Fish and Game Department, livetrapped a large male fisher near Sebic that was scale-weighed at 20 pounds 2 ounces. James Knight of Effie, Minnesota, claims to have taken several males that scale-weighed 28 pounds. From weights averaged from all over the continent, most male fishers weigh between 10 and 12 pounds.

The female fisher is a much smaller animal, not being much larger than the largest mink. Hamilton averaged 42 females at 31½ inches in total length, of which the tail was 11¾ inches long. The females' weights averaged 4.6 pounds, with the heaviest being 6 pounds 15 ounces.

An adult male fisher stands about 9–10 inches high at the shoulder, and its humped back is several inches higher.

The adult female fisher weighs about one-third the weight of the male and is much smaller in size but has a much greater value than the male because the fur of her pelt is so much silkier and darker in color. The male fisher's pelt varies in color from a light tan to almost jet black. It is this latter coloration which led the northeastern trappers to call the fisher the black cat. Most of the males are dark brown but some have a grizzled coloration or are light-colored around the face, the head and over the shoulders. This grizzled coloration varies widely with the individual. The fisher is darker on its belly than it is on its back, although there is a dark streak down the center of the back that starts behind the shoulder. There are two small white patches of fur in what would be the fisher's armpits. The fisher's tail and legs are almost black and are the darkest parts of the animal.

The guard hairs on the fisher's body are 1½ to 2 inches in length, the underfur is about 1¼ inches long. The tail hairs are 2 to 2½ inches in length. The tail is thick and tapers toward the distal tip.

The fisher has the typically weasellike, pointed, alert face. The nose is black. The eyes are also jet black and beady; they reflect green when a bright light is shined in them. The fisher's ears are about one inch in length, rounded and, although situated on the sides of the head, the tips do extend up over the crown. There are 4 rows of vibrissae, the whiskers being very stiff and from one to 4 inches in length.

The fisher has a total of 38 teeth—12 incisors, 4 canines, 16 premolars and 6 molars. The molars are flat-topped to allow the animal to chew its food. New York State biologists have developed a method of sexing the fisher just by its teeth that is 99 percent accurate. Using this method the sex of the fisher can be determined when only the skull is found. It is also easier for the trappers to just send in the lower jawbone of any fisher they catch, rather than the entire carcass, to the New York Fish and Game Department. The biologists extract the canine tooth from the jaw and measure its width. Any tooth width that is under 5.6 millimeters is that of a female. Any tooth 5.65 millimeters in width, or more, comes from a male.

There are 5 toes on each of the fisher's feet with the inside toe being very small and situated well behind the other four. This toe registers in the track. Stiff hairs grow between the toes and the hairs on the bottom of the feet are long enough to cover the sole pads. Each toe is armed with a strong, sharp claw that is about three-eighths of an inch in length. The claws are nonretractable and the tips may be worn where they come in contact with the ground. However, they are sharp enough to allow the fisher to dig easily into the bark of a tree. Although the fisher does not spend as much time in trees as it does on the ground, nor does it climb as much as most people believe, it is the fastest tree-climbing animal in North America. The marten is an excellent climber; the fisher is the best.

Being a member of the weasel family, the fisher also has a pair of anal musk glands that are not developed to discharge scent in a spray as does the skunk. When angry or frightened, the fisher will discharge some of this foul-smelling liquid.

The constant activity of the fisher precludes its ever

The fisher is the fastest tree-climbing animal in North America; its strong sharp claws give it a good hold even on smooth tree bark.

being very fat. When food is superabundant, the fisher may build up a trace of fat beneath its skin in its abdominal region.

DISTRIBUTION

Found today in Maine, New Hampshire, Vermont, Massachusetts, New York, West Virginia, Wisconsin, Michigan, Minnesota, North Dakota, Montana, Idaho, Wyoming, Oregon, and California; British Columbia, Yukon and Northwest Territories, Alberta, Saskatchewan, Manitoba, Ontario, Quebec, New Brunswick, Nova Scotia, with protection range slowly but steadily expanding. In prehistoric times fisher found in Appalachians as far south as Georgia; excavations of Indian burial mounds show fisher was hunted there by Indians A.D. ca. 1100–1500. By time of European exploration fisher no farther south than North Carolina. After 1870 fisher extirpated from much of former range, and high fur prices in 1920s nearly wiped it

out. States and provinces then began total protection of fisher and a few remained in isolated areas of New Brunswick, Maine, New Hampshire, Vermont and New York.

Baxter State Park in Maine served as a reservoir for fisher population. Given complete protection there at park's opening in 1923, fisher population overran park boundaries when fisher afforded protection throughout the state in 1937, and in 1940 had begun repopulating the wilderness. From 1950 to 1955 spread from remote areas to more populous ones, and in 8 years the range had doubled—in 1960 fisher could be found in 73 percent of the state, on a range of about 23,000 square miles. In 1939, 88 of 90 Maine wardens said fishers very rare or absent from their territories, but by 1949, 124 wardens said fishers common to abundant in northern and western Maine. In Nova Scotia last fisher killed in 1940, but fisher transplanted there after being livetrapped in New Brunswick in 1947 and 1948. Transplant successful as young fishers caught in Nova Scotia a few years later. Minnesota gave fisher complete protection in 1933, and since 1940 population in northern part of state has increased steadily. The fact that fisher returned to areas where second-growth timber had reforested cutover, burned-out areas disproves the notion that fisher requires virgin forest to thrive. Fisher also reintroduced to Oregon in 1961 (24 from British Columbia released) and to West Virginia (23 from New Hampshire released), after considerable public-relations work to satisfy apprehensions of local people over the introduction of a predator. Fortunately both conservation program and public-relations efforts have been successes. In New York, fisher increase began in Adirondacks in 1950 and population stabilized around 1960. Adirondacks contain about 6,000 square miles of good fisher habitat, and with an estimated 3,000–4,000 there (and in some areas one fisher per square mile), exceeds normal rule for a good population of one fisher per 10 square miles. Department of Environmental Conservation began restocking fishers in Catskills in 1975, buying most from trappers who had livetrapped them, releasing 30 in 1975, 15 in 1976

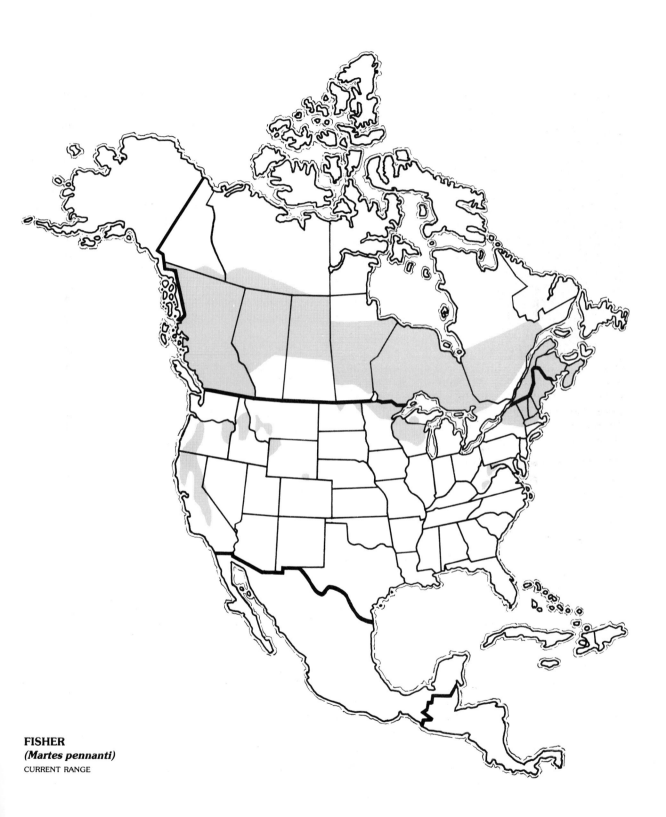

FISHER
(Martes pennanti)
CURRENT RANGE

and 15 in 1978. Latest reports say fishers again well established there after an absence of 100 years.

TRAVEL

One of the fishers of that restocking either didn't like the Catskill Mountains or else it was truly a wanderer. It set a record for the longest distance traveled by a fisher. This particular fisher was donated by the University of Vermont to New York State and was released in the Catskills in 1977. In February 1978 it was captured alive in Hampton, New Jersey, a distance of 85 miles. Taken back to the Catskills, it was released at its initial release site. It still didn't like the area. In April 1979 it was shot, north of Allentown, Pennsylvania, near New Tripoli, a distance of more than 100 miles.

Fishers usually stay in their home territory winter and summer. The size of their territory and the amount of traveling done by an individual fisher each day is based solely upon the amount of food that is available. Ordinarily a female fisher will have a home territory of about 10 miles square. The male fisher's territory will be about three times that size. All of the fishers travel farther and more continuously in the wintertime when food is scarce, often 10 miles or more in 24 hours.

Fishers travel circuitously, but they do not follow exact paths or trails, they just go in the same general direction. They tend to concentrate along lakeshores, creek and stream sides and up on ridges. All these places usually offer easier traveling. In the summer the fishers like the open sandy lakeshores and they often walk in the shallow water. In the wintertime they walk on the ice and may even cut directly across large lakes. When traveling, they usually go directly toward their destination, meandering more while hunting.

Nyman, a wildlife biologist, followed a female fisher for three days near the Fire River in Ontario. There was 3 feet of snow on the ground which made the going difficult for both. During that time the fisher fed on a cached rabbit and denned up only once. When he finally caught up with the fisher, he figured they had traveled about 40 miles but in a circle with a 10-mile diameter. The circle ended within 200 yards of where he had first started following the fisher.

Female fishers usually make a 3- to 7-day circuit, while some of the males take 2 weeks to complete a round of their territory.

During dispersal, the young fishers travel until they find a suitable territory that is not occupied. Tagged females that were released in Montana were recaptured from 3 to 35 miles from their release site. Two males were captured 45 and 64 miles from their release sites. The actual travels of the fisher are determined primarily by its prey concentrations, the topography of the terrain, the location of suitable dens and by weather conditions.

LOCOMOTION

Fishers walk, walk fast or trot and bound. The long muscular body, the short legs and arched spine make bounding a natural. When bounding, fishers usually cover 5 feet at a time. Helen Hoover, who had lots of experience with wild fishers in Minnesota, even got the animals to eat from her hand. She has measured their bounding leaps at 16 feet, when they were running at top speed, and she thinks they could actually do more. Deep snow hampers the fisher, forcing it to walk instead of bound.

At all times the fisher will walk on top of downed trees when they lie in the direction of its travels. Snow seldom is as deep up on these logs as on the ground and they are often blown free of snow by the wind. At such times, the fisher uses them as a major pathway.

Right after a deep, soft snow, the fisher may remain denned up for a couple of days till hunger forces it to hunt again. Usually the snow will have settled a bit and this facilitates the fisher's travel.

As mentioned before, the fisher is undoubtedly the fastest tree-climbing animal in North America. It does, however, spend most of its time hunting on the ground. The fisher can climb any tree and it has been seen to travel by leaping from one tree to another, jumping distances up to 9 feet. It has also been seen to lose squirrels that it was chasing in the treetops. Its greater weight did not allow it to travel on the thin twigs that the squirrel could travel on with ease. One fisher was observed traveling about half a mile through the treetops by jumping from one close-growing spruce tree to another.

There are numerous reports of fishers leaping out of the tops of trees. John Bachman tells of one fisher that leaped 50 feet out of a tree to the snow-covered ground without injury. Fishers, like cats, always land on their feet when they jump. And like a squirrel, a fisher can climb down a tree headfirst. It can even run down a tree headfirst.

Although the fisher does not enter the water as readily as a mink, it will swim across streams, rivers and lakes when it has to. It swims well and uses all 4 feet, with a speed of between 2 and 3 miles per hour. Paul Smith, of New York, reported a fisher swimming across Spitfire Lake, which is one mile wide.

FOOD

Although a carnivore, fishers eat some vegetation by choice and not necessity. Major food is snowshoe hare, common in fisher habitat and the reason fishers frequent swamps and thickets, which provide the hare food and shelter. Hunting by sight and scent, fishers try to sneak up on hare before it escapes from its form, but if it escapes fishers can track hare by scent like a hound. Fishers also run hares, staying inside the circle made by running hare so less distance must be covered. Possessing great stamina, a fisher usually catches the hare, and needing only 1–1½ pounds of food per day, it will cache half the hare. Red squirrels, flying squirrels and less frequently gray squirrels, all fisher prey. Often they can escape from fisher by jumping farther than fisher can from tree to tree, or by hiding in a hollow tree—an effective escape when hole is small and tree is alive, but not when tree is dead, because fisher can tear rotten wood apart and capture squirrel.

Mice, voles, rats and shrews also eaten. Unlike most predators fisher will eat shrews despite their musky odor. Fisher also eats beaver and muskrat when caught on land, and woodchuck on rare occasions when encountered in forested areas. Fisher also kills and eats raccoon even though a large raccoon will outweigh fisher by 50 percent, fisher able to wear raccoon down. Raccoon populations depressed or absent when fisher population is high. Records also show fisher killing foxes, otters and, in one exceptional case, a lynx. Also eats large and small ground-nesting birds and their eggs, especially ruffed and spruce grouse and ptarmigan. Frogs and salamanders eaten (one report of fisher digging through 34 inches of snow to catch a frog), and fish, although as mentioned earlier only one record exists to show fisher fishing. Also eats larger insects.

A surprise to many, including biologists, is that fisher often eats vegetation, and by choice, since eaten when other foods available. Mountain ash berries, blueberries, and beechnuts the favorites, but also eats cranberries, wild cherries, currants and salmon berries. Dr. Clark Stevens of University of New Hampshire found apples in stomachs of 178 fishers examined.

Fishers also eat carrion, concentrating on carcass of winter-killed deer, moose or caribou, and return to the site even after all meat is eaten and most of the bones cracked open for marrow. Despite claims by hunters, fishers do not kill deer, unless in rare circumstances when deer is starving and near death. Deer hair in fisher diets usually the result of scavenging. One record exists of fisher attacking deer fawn, in Long Lake, New York, in 1957. Five recorded instances of fishers running down and eating martens by chasing through treetops. With fisher population high, marten population is low, and vice versa. While fishers the major predator of martens, some must escape as some martens always in evidence near fisher habitat. Fishers also a major predator of porcupines, and in fact have been imported to areas where forest damaged by porcupines in order to control damage. Previously some states had protected porcupines because it was argued they could be used as food in an emergency, while others paid a bounty on porcupines. Most northern states now regard porcupines as a nuisance and have fishers control the population. Coyotes, lynxes, mountain lions and others occasionally kill porcupines, but fishers generally kill all they encounter, attacking the porcupine's face to avoid the quills in the tail, circling more quickly than the porcupine and eventually tiring the porcupine so the fisher can flip it over and attack the unprotected belly and throat. As fisher feeds it often rolls back porcupine skin, leaving it as neat as if the animal had been skinned by a trapper. When fisher at times eats skin as well, quills pass through its system and are voided intact, but softened. One report tells of fisher that ate a small porcupine and left only a splash of blood on the snow. Occasionally porcupine will slap quills into a fisher, though one researcher claims most quills penetrate only the outer layer of skin, and are then turned parallel to flesh, not entering deeper. M. J. Daniel, in British Columbia, found 3 of 25 fishers examined had quills in their bodies. One male had a quill in thin layer of fat under skin, 5 had penetrated stomach walls into peritoneal cavity and 2 penetrated the small intestine. All quills were softened and fisher seemed healthy. While other researchers have never seen a fisher injured by quills, another found a fisher starving, with head and body riddled with quills. A Maine researcher examining 242 fishers found one-quarter had recently eaten porcupine. Of 350 carcasses of fisher, one-third had quills in body, some deep, glancing off bones, some penetrating stomach and other vital organs, although no inflammation was apparent.

Fisher is such an efficient predator that its natural food supply can dwindle to starvation levels, forcing fisher to abandon range and seek new areas. During scarcity fisher has been known to raid suet at backwood-home birdfeeders and to kill domestic cats.

Fisher population in parts of the Adirondacks dropped in mid-1970s, coinciding with near-extermination of porcupine there and the low of snowshoe hare cycle of 1974–75.

BEHAVIOR

In the wilderness areas that the fisher most commonly

Natural hollows in large trees like this one make good homes for fishers.

frequents, it may be active either day or night. Where it could encounter people, it is most active at night. During the summer it is usually active only at night to escape from the heat of the day.

Fishers prefer heavy timber and big trees. They have expanded their range as the second-growth forests have reclaimed many of the old, abandoned mountain farms. They avoid areas that have been opened up by lumbering or by fires. In the Adirondack Mountains in 1903 and 1908, fires burned over 850,000 acres, completing the job of total devastation that had been started by the lumbermen. The fishers not killed by the fires completely abandoned the burned-over areas for many, many years. Balsam, white spruce, jack pine, large aspen and large white birch forests are preferred areas. Cedar swamps are frequented because of the snowshoe hare.

I'm not sure whether the fisher requires high mountains or lives in the higher mountains because of its isolation from man and the fact that mountains are more likely to be clothed in mature forests. Fishers are seldom found below the 1,000-foot elevation.

Fishers do not like rain. A downpour will cause them to den up till they are forced out by hunger. Lowland swamps are usually avoided.

When traveling in deep snow, the fisher does not make as good time as usual and may not reach a favored spot to den up. Then the fisher will tunnel down into the snow and sleep in a snow cave.

Most members of the weasel tribe are a paradox. Some of them are extremely easy to catch in a trap, others become extremely trap-wary. An inexperienced fisher may be caught in a bare trap, others will discover every trap set for them. The wise fisher will often destroy the cubby sets made by trappers and spring the traps.

Many times a fisher will cause tremendous loss to a trapper by following his trail made as he checks his traps. The damage is done when the fisher is ahead of the trapper, killing and destroying all of the fur animals that the trapper has caught. The loss of 4 or 5 martens in one day is a great financial loss to any trapper.

The fisher struggles wildly in a trap when caught, often chewing off the trapped foot. Wildlife biologist David Mech, trying to release a fisher caught in a trap, had his boots, pants and long johns bitten and clawed through by the fisher in the process. One trapper from Berlin, New Hampshire, lost two fingers, bitten off by a trapped fisher.

The stories of a fisher attacking a man are just stories. A trapped fisher is an injured, frightened creature that lashes its tail about, snarls and hisses and is ready to die fighting. An unharmed fisher may even be reluctant to cross a man's tracks in the snow.

Charles Roth, of the Massachusetts Audubon Society, raised a fisher from a baby and it was affectionate, playful and full of grace. Henry Laramie, of the New Hampshire Fish and Game Department, also raised one and found it to be very friendly, playful and clean.

One time he supervised the live-trapping of 26 fishers that were to be shipped to West Virginia for restocking. Laramie claimed that after the wild fishers were in their cages for about two hours, he could touch them on their noses with his bare hands and not be bitten.

Fishers are curious and often stand erect to get a better look at what they are investigating. Ade and Helen Hoover had one fisher that learned to push down the thumb latch on their cabin door and let itself in. This was the same wild fisher that learned to take food from Helen's hand.

SENSES

Very keen sense of smell, able to track prey by scent and locate prey deep beneath snow. Hearing also acute—responds quickly to sounds of prey or enemies. Stationary man not recognized as danger but is quick to notice movement.

COMMUNICATION

Fishers make a soft TCHEEK, TCHEEK, TCHEEK sound when they are curious or contented. When angry, they snarl, growl, spit and hiss, arching their backs like frightened cats.

Of all of the weasel family, the fisher's musk is one of the least offensive, although it has been known to put this scent and urine on a large carcass to claim it as its own.

Fishers do rub their anal glands on logs and pieces of wood, depositing musk particularly just prior to the breeding season.

BREEDING

Male fishers are usually solitary animals for most of the year. In January, and on through April, the tracks in the snow often show where the male and female have started to travel together. The tracks may be one behind the other or they may separate, only to rejoin again as the fishers begin to sleep with one another.

Most of the female fishers may breed when they are one year old, some of them do not breed until they are 2. Male fishers do not breed during their first year. The bulk of the breeding of fishers is accomplished between March 23 and April 13. The females come into estrus and are capable of conceiving for 2 or 3 days. The fishers have a unique breeding period. Virgin females come into estrus and are bred; nothing different about that. Mature females give birth to their litter of young and 6 to 8 days afterward come into estrus and are bred. Because of delayed implantation, they have a mean gestation period of 352 days, the minimum being 338 days, the maximum being 358 days. The fertilized eggs, or blastocysts, do not become fastened to the wall of the uterus till late in January.

Copulation lasts for about one minute; the male clasps the female around the body behind her shoulders with his forepaws.

BIRTH AND YOUNG

Although the fisher is capable of digging, it does not like to do so. Long before the female gives birth to her young, she will have selected a den site to be used for a nursery. Hollow trees, logs, any hole or crevasse in or under a rocky ledge, an abandoned beaver house or even a woodchuck's burrow can be used. Most of the dens will be in trees if these sites are possible because they are preferred sites.

E. Raymond Hall published data from Harold James, of Fraser River, British Columbia, who kept as many as 28 fishers in captivity at one time. James stated that most of his baby fishers were born about March 31. Each female gives birth to one to 4 young at a time, with the average of 26 litters being 2.7 young. Of 13 litters that he sexed, there were 13 males and 20 females. This discrepancy is true in later life with most fur animals, but only because the males travel farther and are caught more frequently—most creatures start off with a near 50/50 sex ratio.

The baby fishers are born blind, helpless and have some short fuzzy hair on their backs. When they are 3 days old, their entire bodies are covered with fine gray hair.

The female has 4 nipples located on her lower abdomen. She is a devoted mother but when the little ones are 6 days old, she leaves them temporarily to go search for a male as it is time for her to breed again.

The baby fishers' eyes open on or about the 53rd day and they are better able to scramble about. In another month, the young fishers come out of the den to play and in a short time follow after their mother as she searches for food. Weaning takes place at about 4 months. Usually the young stay with the mother till December when the family splits up, each going its own, solitary way.

LIFE SPAN

Potential: 10–12 years. Record: 18 years, although no information on where this animal lived.

SIGN

Tracks most commonly seen sign when animal is on the ground, but difficult to find if animal has taken to trees. Tracks about $1\frac{1}{2}$–$2\frac{1}{4}$ inches in diameter; all 5 toes show, eliminating possible confusion with small dog or large cat, because with them only 4 toes show. Tracks paired when animal bounds. When it walks, tracks 6–7 inches apart; leisurely bound, 32 inches apart; top speed (according to one report), 16 feet apart. Scat often contains porcupine quills. Scat similar to marten's except larger, being $\frac{5}{8}$ inch as opposed to $\frac{3}{8}$ inch.

ENEMIES

One record exists of fisher killing lynx, but lynx more often preys on fisher. Fisher remains found in bobcat's den, and Metogami Indian chief in Ontario reported 3 wolves killing (but not eating) fisher on frozen lake—away from cover that would have provided escape. Young killed by great horned owls, bobcats, lynxes, coyotes and wolves.

Fishers remarkably free of internal and external parasites, being solitary most of year and having numerous dens. Do have some fleas, ticks, nematodes and tapeworms. One fisher found in 1959 heavily infested with scabies mites, was thin with badly encrusted skin and open lesions. Unknown why such mites do not appear more often as porcupines are often infested with them. No record of rabies in fisher. Animals trapped and used for restocking usually inoculated against feline and canine distemper.

HUMAN RELATIONS

Fishers have never been numerous but overtrapping, extensive logging, forest fires and settlement of the country in the years gone by, all combined to bring their numbers down drastically. The value of the pelt has also come down drastically. Today, the fisher is valued not only for its fur but as a prime controller of the numbers of porcupine. With an appreciation of this animal's value as a natural predator and for the esthetic value of returning the fisher to many of its former haunts, the fisher has been given the protection it needs to hold its own. The future of the fisher looks bright.

COMMERCIAL VALUE

In 5 years up to 1976 over 4,000 fishers taken in U.S. each year. In 1976–77, take dropped to 2,893, the drop believed due to food shortage during low of snowshoe hare cycle. Those pelts sold for $95 average price, $274,835 total. In Canada: 9,664 taken 1976–77, $95.38 average price, $921,795 total. Fisher also valuable for timber saved from destruction by porcupines.

SHORT-TAILED WEASEL, *Mustela erminea*
LONG-TAILED WEASEL, *Mustela frenata*

INTRODUCTION

The *Mustela* in the name of these two weasels is the Latin word for "weasel." It was given to this genus by Linnaeus in 1758. The *Erminea* was also given by Linnaeus, designating it as the European weasel. In 1838, Charles-Lucien Bonaparte named this, the short-tailed weasel, *Mustela cicognanii* after an Italian friend. The weasel, however, came to be called the Bonaparte weasel. The scientific name was again changed back to the original name by Hall in 1945.

The long-tailed weasel was designated as *Mustela frenata* by Lichtenstein in 1831. *Frenata* is from the Latin word *frenum,* meaning "bridle." Lichtenstein's type specimen came from near Mexico City. This particular subspecies ranges up into Texas. The name was given because the long-tailed weasels in the southern part of their range have individualistic white facial markings, some of which resembled the bridles used on horses. The various subspecies of this weasel found over most of its northern range do not have these markings. One thing that was found on all of the subspecies was its long tail. In 1838, Bonaparte named it *Mustela longicauda. Longus* is Latin for long and *cauda* means "tail"; a most appropriate name. What used to confuse me when I was a kid was that this weasel was called the New York weasel. In 1912, Miller reviewed all of the subspecies and proved that they were closely related and changed the name back to its original form, *Mustela frenata.* The easiest way

This photo shows the long, thin snakelike body of the long-tailed weasel in its summer coat.

to classify the weasels is as short-tailed, long-tailed or the rare little least weasel, *Mustela rixosa*. If in winter, the tail that is between 2.8 and 4 inches in length has a black tip, it is that of a short-tailed weasel. If the tail is between 4.5 and 6 inches in length and has a black tip, it is that of a long-tailed weasel. If the tail is between 1.2 and 1.5 inches in length and lacks the black tip, it is that of the least weasel.

DESCRIPTION

The adult male short-tailed weasel measures between 10.9 and 13.4 inches in total length. Of that total, the tail will measure between 2.8 and 4 inches in length. This weasel stands about 2–2.25 inches high at the shoulder. It will weigh between 3.1 and 6 ounces. Adult female short-tails measure between 9.4 and 10.2 inches in total length, of which the tail will be 1.6–2.7 inches. Females weigh between 1.8 and 2.8 ounces.

The adult male long-tailed weasel measures between 13.8 and 17 inches in total length. I have a specimen in my collection that measures 20 inches in total length. The tail will measure between 4.5 and 5.9 inches. This weasel stands about 2.75–3 inches high at the shoulder. It will weigh between 6 and 8.7 ounces. Adult female long-tails measure between 11.2 and 13.4 inches in total length, of which the tail will be 3.3–4.8 inches. Females weigh 3–3.5 ounces.

A weasel's body can go through any hole that it can get its head through. An adult female long-tail and both male and female short-tails can go through a one-by-one-inch wire mesh, the adult male long-tail can go through 1 1/4-by-1 1/4-inch mesh.

The color of these two weasels depends upon the latitude, altitude and the season in which they are found and on heredity.

Both of these weasels, in the summertime, are brown on the tops of their heads, on their sides and backs, and have brown tails with black tips. Their chins, throats, breasts, bellies and the inner sides of their legs are a creamy white.

In the wintertime, both weasels, if they are from areas where snow lies on the ground all winter, every winter, turn white to match the snow. The higher the altitude, despite the latitude, the more snow. In areas where the snow is sparse, or lacking entirely, both weasels will stay brown all winter.

My home area of northwestern New Jersey is in the transition zone; some of our weasels turn white, some change partially and some don't turn at all. I know of a deep valley, just a few miles from my home, where the weasels always turn white whether we have snow or not. Over the years the snow in that area has always stayed longer than in any other area. It will be fascinating to see if the change in the national weather pattern of the last 20 years produces a change in the weasels' winter coats.

Formerly our winter weather came out of the north and west, but it is now blowing farther south before blowing east. Now the southern states, as far south as Georgia, are getting more snow than the New Jersey, New York and Pennsylvania areas. If this weather shift is permanent, I wonder if the southern weasels will begin to turn white.

Long-tailed weasel in summer coat.

The changing, or the retention, of the color of the weasel's summer and winter coats is the result of two complete moltings of the hair in spring and autumn. The hairs are shed and replaced; the change is not a result of the hair itself changing color.

We know that heredity plays a very important role in the weasel's changing color. When weasels from areas where they always turn white are moved to areas where others of the same species always stay brown, the imported weasels turn white as they or their ancestors did. Conversely, when brown weasels are moved north, they continue to molt brown in winter, despite cold, snow or elevation.

Ordinarily, the weasels start their spring molt about the middle of March. The first brown hairs appear on the back of the neck, then behind the ears, between the shoulder blades and down the middle of the back. Gradually, the spots between the ears meet and expand up over the head to the nose and down toward the shoulders. The areas on the back merge and start down the legs and extend up the tail. Finally, all of the brown coloration is completed and the white hair on the undersides is replaced with creamy-white hair. The molt takes about 2 months to be completed.

The weasel's summer coat has undercoat hairs that are about one-quarter of an inch in length, while the guard hairs are three-eighths to one-half of an inch in length.

About the middle of October, the fall molt is underway but the replacement is reversed. The hair on the tail, except for the tip, and the undersides is the first to turn white. Then the sides rapidly whiten, leaving just a dark streak down the weasel's back. The streak is finally separated into patches over the hips, shoulders and back of the ears. The fall molt takes about 70 days and is completed before the end of December. In my area, many of the weasels never complete the change to all-white, despite the winter molt, and are known as "graybacks" with the fur being almost valueless.

William J. Hamilton found that in areas of New York State where part of the weasel population changed white and part did not, those that did not change would invariably be males.

Toward the end of winter, many of the white weasels, particularly the males, acquire a yellowish cast to their hair. The cause of this yellowing is not known for sure. Some researchers claim it is caused by the weasel's urine, some claim it is from its musk. The yellow is darker on the weasel's belly than it is on the back, but it is so uniform that I personally don't think that staining is the answer. Polar bears don't have the type of musk glands that the weasels have but their white coats, particularly those of the males, also turn yellowish in late winter.

The molt in both the spring and fall is triggered by photoperiodism, i.e., the amount of light received through the eye in a 24-hour period. As the light hours lessen in the fall, the pituitary gland at the base of the animal's brain stops producing the hormone needed to produce pigment. This causes the new hair growing in to be white.

Conversely, increased light in spring stimulates the pituitary gland into producing pigment in the new hair follicles and the weasel turns brown.

Researchers have done many experiments with weasels and snowshoe hares and have caused these species to turn white or dark at any time of the year by exposing them to artificial light or by shutting them up in darkness. Under normal conditions, the weasels farther north change at a different time than those farther south because of the amount of light available. The length of time it takes an individual weasel to change is variable.

Experiments have also been done with the weasels by controlling the temperatures. The white-coated weasels exposed to higher temperatures started to change sooner but the ones kept at colder temperatures changed faster when they did start. All the weasels in the experiment finished their molt at about the same time, proving again that it is the amount of light available each day which controls the process.

I can find no record of melanism in weasels. There are several records of albinism, where the eyes were pink and even the tail tip was white.

The black tail tip on the weasel is diversionary. Researchers have found that birds of prey, attracted to the white weasel against the white snow by its movements, often dive at the black tail tip and miss the weasel's camouflaged body.

The underfur on a weasel's winter coat is about three-eighths of an inch in length, the guard hairs are about five-eighths of an inch. The hair on the tail tip is about 1 1/2 inches in length.

The weasel has 4 rows of vibrissae, with the longest whiskers being 2 inches in length. There are a few eyebrow hairs and a small cluster located behind the eye. Even when the weasel is in its white winter coat, some of the whiskers remain black.

The weasel's nose is pinkish in coloration. Its eyes are jet black and reflect a greenish light when shined with a light. The ears of a short-tailed weasel are about one-half inch in length, those of the long-tailed weasel are five-eighths of an inch. The ears are very broad-based, well rounded and project slightly above the crown of the head. Their erectness helps to emphasize the weasel's alertness. The ear's opening is large.

A short-tailed weasel in its winter coat. (Photo: Irene Vandermolen)

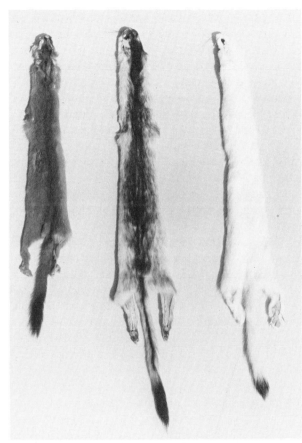

Left to right: Pelt of short-tailed weasel in summer, a long-tailed weasel changing color and a long-tailed weasel's winter coat. Note also the size difference in the two species. (Photo: Irene Vandermolen)

Both weasels have 34 teeth—12 incisors, 4 canines, 12 premolars and 6 molars. The tips of the canine teeth project below the upper lip and can readily be seen. The last premolar and the first molar teeth of the weasel are shaped like the carnassial teeth of dogs and cats and are used for shearing off pieces of meat from its prey.

There are 5 toes on each of the feet, although frequently the toe corresponding to our thumb, on the forefeet, does not show in the tracks. The claws are nonretractable and sharp. In the wintertime, in the

north, hair covers over the soles of the feet, although the tips of the toe pads remain bare.

The weasels are also equipped with 2 anal musk glands. Although the weasels cannot direct the discharge of the musk, they are much more excitable than the skunks and release it at the slightest provocation. The weasel's musk has a more offensive odor than that of the skunk but the amount discharged is much smaller. This musk does not have the lasting quality of that of the skunk.

DISTRIBUTION

Short-tailed weasel found throughout Alaska and Canada, including Arctic. Range extends south to about 40° parallel in eastern and middle U.S. In West, found in Rockies, south through Colorado, into New Mexico and along Pacific coast to central California. New Jersey is on the southern fringe of weasel's range.

The more common long-tailed weasel is more southern, found in Mexico, all contiguous 48 states, and in southern tier of Canadian provinces from coast to coast. Scarce in Florida, Oklahoma, and dryer sections of Texas, New Mexico, Arizona, California, Utah and Nevada.

Has been found at elevations up to 12,000 feet.

TRAVEL

Weasels are inveterate travelers but only within a small area. They do not migrate nor do they even have seasonal shifts. Their movement within their home ranges is determined by the food and water available. Weasels, although they do not drink a lot of water at one time, are never found far from a source of water, be it free-flowing or in the form of ice and snow.

Extensive studies have been done on the weasel to determine habits, home ranges, populations, and so forth. It has been found that a weasel usually uses just one den at a time, living in that den and circling out to hunt and returning. The maximum diameter of a weasel's range is usually less than a half-mile. Weasels

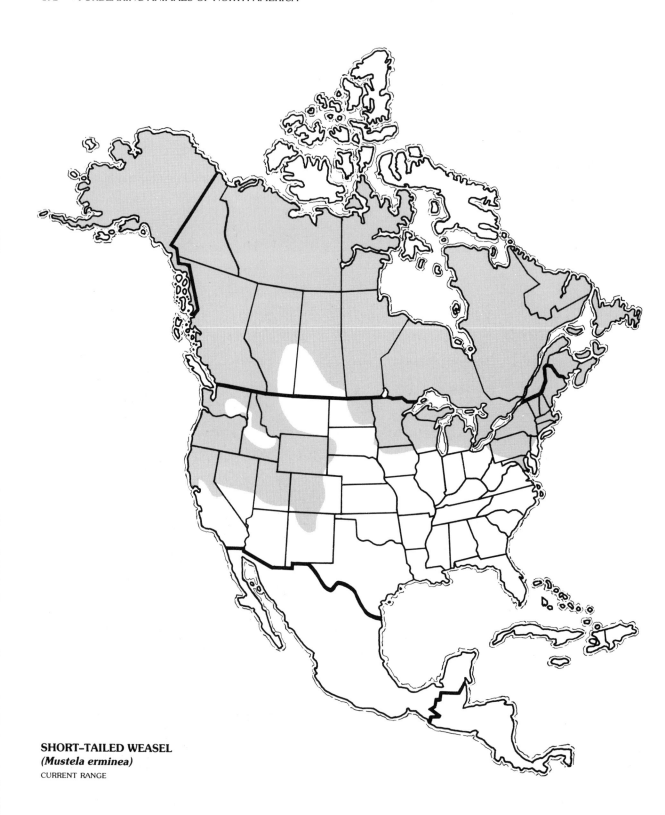

SHORT–TAILED WEASEL
(Mustela erminea)
CURRENT RANGE

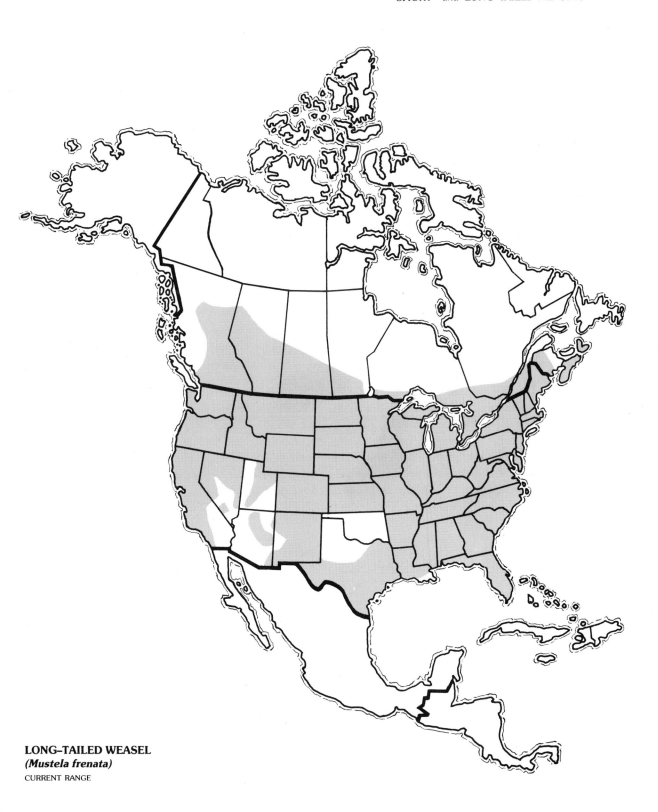

LONG–TAILED WEASEL
(Mustela frenata)
CURRENT RANGE

may travel over 80–400 acres as a home range, averaging about 300 acres apiece. However, weasels are not strictly territorial and their ranges usually overlap those of several others, although weasels do not usually use the same area at the same time. Research shows that on the average weasel territory, there are 4 weasels to 640 acres, or to the square mile.

The density of weasels, and most other mammals, depends upon the food available, which depends upon the terrain and the type of habitat. Glover, a game biologist doing studies in Pennsylvania, found that where the forests had been opened up and piles of slash made for good cover and the grass and underbrush were abundant, that the weasel population was as high as one to 6 1/2 acres. Bogs or grassy areas, making ideal habitat for mice, surrounded by trees, made ideal habitat for weasels. Grain fields also make good habitat for weasels, if cover is available.

Although weasels may not go more than 600–800 feet in distance from their dens in one night, they may actually travel 2 1/2 to 3 1/2 miles doing it. Weasels loop or zigzag back and forth in covering their territories while hunting. Powell found that on the average, a weasel travels one and a half times the straight distance in reaching its destination. Often it may travel three to four times the straight distance. This allows the weasel to more thoroughly check the area for prey and it is also an evasive action, making it difficult for avian predators to catch the weasel.

Male weasels usually travel twice as far as do the females. The males are almost twice the size of the females and need almost two times the amount of food to satisfy their hunger and so must travel twice as far to obtain it. Short-tailed weasels travel less than do the long-tailed weasels because they need less food. The longest distance traveled in one day by one long-tailed weasel was 3.43 miles.

LOCOMOTION

Weasels can walk but they seldom do. Their regular mode of traveling is bounding and they go slow, fast or flat-out. In bounding, their hind feet come down almost exactly on top of the spot where their front feet have just been. As their body bunches up, prior to springing forth into the next bound, their back is arched upward like an inchworm. Their tail is held either straight out behind or elevated about 45 degrees above the ground level.

When bounding leisurely, they cover about 15–18 inches with each bound. This distance stretches out to 3 to 6 feet when they get up a head of steam. E. Raymond Hall measured one leap of 8 feet two inches.

Weasels are as quick as a flash. One male weasel I had in captivity would come out of its nest box, run down the wire, across the floor, around the pen and back up again in such a blur of motion that no one could get a look at him. Weasels, in hunting, use that same blinding speed to attack and seize their prey before it really has a chance to know what hit it.

Weasels are not fast distance runners. I can easily outrun a weasel, but they can dodge, twist, zigzag and reverse position so fast that it makes them almost impossible to catch.

Although not considered arboreal, the weasels climb well and fast. They often go up into trees to rob the nests of birds that have caught their attention. They have been seen climbing trees in pursuit of chipmunks and squirrels. One weasel chased a chipmunk that jumped out of a tree to the ground 10 feet below. Without hestitation, the weasel did the same. Again, the chipmunk scampered up the tree and jumped out and again the weasel followed. The third time the chipmunk scrambled up the tree, the weasel caught it before it could jump out. Weasels have been seen climbing trees to get away from enemies that can't climb.

We had a weasel come into our barn, undoubtedly to hunt for mice in and around the feed box. Seventeen chickens had just been killed by a weasel and we set out to dispatch this one. You never saw such a commotion; the weasel was running like a blur up, over and around the feed box as my sister, Virginia, my Uncle Tom and I flailed at it with shovels, brooms and sticks. At one point, the weasel ran up the outside of my sister's overalls leg to her shoulder and jumped off. The weasel wasn't attacking her, it was just trying to escape.

Weasels do not ordinarily swim but they can and are good at it. One weasel, chasing a chipmunk, plunged into a stream after its prey. When both animals were about 8 feet from shore, they forgot about each other and turned and swam back to shore. Franklin W. Sturges tells of a weasel he saw dive into a stream in the Columbia River gorge in Oregon and come up with a larval giant salamander in its mouth. Several researchers have reported weasels jumping into water and swimming to get away from them. I have no record on the distance that a weasel can swim but most rivers do not act as natural barriers to the species.

FOOD

Earlier studies showing poultry high in weasel diet nullified by modern indoor poultry-raising practices. Recent study in Michigan shows mammals comprise 83 percent of diet, birds 9 percent, insects 7 percent. Mammals included meadow mice, 31 percent, white-footed deer mice, 24 percent, cottontail rabbits, 14 percent, shrews, 11 percent and moles, 2 percent. A New York study gives similar results: meadow mice, 34.5 percent, cottontail rabbits, 13.1 percent, deer mice, 11.3 percent, shrews, 11.2 percent, rats, 6.7 percent, chipmunks, 3.6 percent, undetermined small mammals, chiefly mice, 16.4 percent and birds, frogs and snakes, 3.2 percent. In Pennsylvania: meadow mice, 31 percent, deer mice, 22 percent, cottontail rabbits, 17 percent, short-tailed shrews, 9 percent, and 21 percent made up of other mammals, poultry and game birds, and insects.

Thus in each study meadow mouse (vole) made up one-third of weasel diet, and together with white-footed deer mice, mice constitute 45–55 percent of total. Other studies show mice make up 85 percent or more of diet. A single pair of field mice could produce 2,200 descendants in one year. Predators such as weasel keep their population in check—adult male long-tailed weasel eating 3 or more per day, or 1,200

per year. Control of mouse population beneficial to orchardists, whose trees are girdled by mice eating bark beneath snow cover, and to grain, dairy and poultry farmers. Lower population of white-footed mouse also reduces food competition for other birds and animals, including song birds, ruffed grouse, wild turkeys, bobwhites, squirrels, deer, etc. One mouse nest found containing 1 peck (8 quarts) of beechnuts; mice also gather acorns, chestnuts, seeds of basswood, wild cherry and dogwood.

Rabbits form 12–18 percent of diet, and as a rabbit (depending on size) provides food for 2–3 days, the total kill might be 18–25 rabbits per year. There are many reports of rabbits defending themselves against attack by a weasel, usually by kicking the weasel away (and sometimes to death). Weasels can and do kill adult rabbits, but are more successful if rabbits are babies or immature.

Will eat nesting birds and their eggs, particularly ground-nesting birds. In south weasels catch occasional bobwhite quail but are more beneficial than harmful to quail because they eat cotton rats, a major predator on quail eggs.

Weasels feed on pikas in mountains, wood rats in mountains and deserts, pocket gophers in farms and plains, and snowshoe hares in far north. Eat frogs, salamanders, lizards but not toads because of their poisonous skin secretions. Although many predators will kill but not eat shrews and moles because of their musky odor and taste, shrews are an important food item for weasel.

Weasels kill and eat snakes, with one record of weasel eating 41-inch snake. (Snakes also eat weasels, but only young as adults too quick for snakes to catch.) Also eat butterflies, moths, grasshoppers, crickets, beetles, in small amounts. Although weasels prefer fresh meat they have killed themselves, they will eat carrion, and have been known to eat putrid meat. Also eat berries occasionally, but they are not a major food item.

On the farm we would frequently flush weasels when we moved shocks of corn. In those days, the cornstalks would be cut by hand, after the ears had dried. Each big armful of stalks would be tied together

A long-tailed weasel in its winter coat and its prey. (Photo: Irene Vandermolen)

with binder twine. Then the corn bundles would be stood on end, leaning against each other to form a shock 8 to 10 feet in diameter and the shock would be tied with binder twine. Throughout the fall and winter, the shocks would be brought into the barn where the corn ears would be husked and stored and the stalks chopped up and fed to the cattle.

Mice of all kinds flocked to the shocks. They made soft nests out of corn silk and the corn ears provided an unlimited amount of food. Hawks, owls, foxes and so on knew the mice were in the shocks, but they could only catch them if they left the safety of the shock. The weasel was the only predator that could follow the mice through the compacted stalks. The weasels would live inside the shock on the mice.

BEHAVIOR

The weasel's long, lithe, trim, thin shape makes it appear like a furry snake with legs and it was designed that way. The main item of food in any weasel's diet is mice. Its present shape evolved to allow it to go down the tunnels of the mice and to kill them in their underground burrows.

The process of evolution has its attendant cost. In defiance of Bergman's Law which states that the larger the mass of the body in relation to its surface area,

the less heat loss there will be, the weasel evolved long and thin. To compensate for this heat loss, the weasel has a very high metabolic rate, which in turn requires a high food intake. Weasels will eat one-third to one-half of their own body weight in food every day. Hand in hand with a high metabolic rate is efficient digestion and weasels defecate about 10 times every 24 hours. This combination means that weasels are almost perpetually hungry.

William Hamilton had a young male long-tailed weasel in captivity that weighed about 5 ounces. The weasel ate an entire chipmunk, bones and all, that weighed about 3 ounces, in a 24-hour period. The next day, the weasel was fed a partly grown rat weighting about 4 ounces. The weasel consumed the entire rat within 24 hours, which was the equivalent of four-fifths of its own body weight.

The weasel cannot eat all of this food at one time because its stomach cannot hold this volume. After gorging itself, the weasel will sleep for about 3 hours, then eat, then sleep again. When the prey has been consumed, the weasel will hunt again.

Weasels hunt primarily by scent. They are also intensely curious. As they hunt, they zigzag back and forth across the terrain, investigating every hole, crevasse, nook, cranny and runway they encounter. All weasels are exceedingly persistent. Intent upon tracking, the weasel may dash by its prey if it remains motionless.

Adolph Murie, a biologist with the National Park Service, tells of sitting on a stump and watching the interactions of a weasel hunting a snowshoe hare. The hare knew that the weasel was hunting it so it laid down a conflicting maze of tracks, then sat and waited for the weasel to unravel them. The weasel dashed along the trail, its nose close to the ground. When the hare saw that the weasel was gaining on it, it dashed off and made another circular maze of tracks, then stopped and waited. At one time, the weasel, following the scent of the tracks, passed within 3 feet of the motionless hare without discovering it. Several times the weasel went the wrong way on the trail but discovered its error and backtracked until it was going in the

Weasels pop in and out of every hole, nook and cranny, as this one is doing in its search for food.

right direction. Three times the hare led the weasel on a wild chase before the weasel finally gave up to seek easier prey.

Park Service biologist Joseph Dixon watched a group of pikas frustrate a short-tailed weasel high in a talus slope in the mountains of California. The weasel could go anywhere the pika could go in among the broken, jumbled rock slides. The pika's main advantage was that it was on its home range and knew the area intimately.

The weasel was pursuing a young pika, which was beginning to tire, and was steadily closing in on it. Suddenly, an adult pika dashed down from its observation post where it had been watching the chase. The adult pika got in between the young pika and the weasel, who then followed the adult pika. The young pika dashed out of the race to hide. After several rounds, another adult pika dashed in front of the weasel. The weasel did not fall for the ruse and continued to follow the original adult. Then a fourth pika intercepted the weasel, which followed it and allowed the first adult to get a much needed rest. The weasel never did catch a pika and finally gave up and left the area.

While coursing back and forth searching for prey, the weasel also responds to the slightest sound or squeak. With its keen hearing, it can hear the squeak of a mouse or the slightest rustling in the grass or leaves at distances of 50 feet or more. Weasels can easily be decoyed by anyone making a high-pitched squeaking by "kissing" the back of the hand.

When the weasel gets close to its prey, it begins a careful stalk. When its prey is seen or its location noted in the grass, the weasel pounces like lightning striking. Many times the weasel will be on top of its prey before the prey even has a chance to react. The weasel usually bites its prey at the base of the neck, piercing the skull or severing the head from the neck. Weasels have exceptionally heavy masses of jaw muscles allowing them to inflict powerful bites.

At the same instant the weasel bites into the prey's neck, it also grasps the prey with its front feet. Hanging on with its teeth and forelegs, the weasel kicks and scratches constantly with its hind feet. With small prey, like mice, rats, shrews, the weasel and its prey usually tumble and roll about like a furred ball until the prey's last violent reflex actions cease. Larger prey may run about in an effort to dislodge the weasel and at times they may be successful. On larger prey, the weasel may shift its attack to the prey's throat where it will attempt to sever the carotid artery or jugular vein, causing the prey to bleed to death.

Once the weasel has seized its prey, it will not release its hold until it is thrown off or the prey is dead.

Because of its high metabolism and its corresponding high demands for food, the weasel will kill all the

Weasels are extremely alert and they will usually dash into a hole at the first sign of danger. However, their intense curiosity soon causes them to peer forth to see what had alarmed them.

This short-tailed weasel in its winter coat of white is standing erect to see over the surrounding vegetation. (Photo: Irene Vandermolen)

prey possible at one time. It is not killing this prey for the pleasure of killing it, but out of necessity. The fact that the weasel will occasionally kill far more than it can eat is not the result of a deliberate action but of a definite need.

Although most weasels will not attack chickens, some individuals will. There are many records of a single weasel killing 30, 40, even 70 chickens at one time. In these instances the weasel did not stop to think that it could not eat so many chickens at once; it was responding to an inherited trait of self-preservation which had programmed the weasel to kill, kill, kill while the prey is available.

When all of the available prey has been killed, then the weasel will begin to eat. It may lap some of the blood, if any has flowed from the wounds made on the neck and the head. The weasel is not a "blood-sucker," feeding exclusively on blood. It will lap or lick the blood from a bleeding wound before it starts to eat but so do most of the other mammalian predators. Then the weasel will usually bite into the skull and eat the brains of its prey. When its immediate hunger is assuaged, the weasel will then carry, or attempt to carry, any uneaten prey back to the safety of its den.

The weasel has absolutely no trouble carrying the largest of mice. Usually it doesn't have to carry the mice anywhere because often the weasel will just live in the mouse's den until the mouse or mice are consumed.

Prey such as large rats, chipmunks and small squirrels are picked up by the weasel and carried to a safe den. Heavier prey such as large squirrels, rabbits and hares will be dragged to a safe spot. The weasel is very persistent and very strong. A weasel can drag prey that is 10–12 times its own weight.

I discovered a long-tailed weasel dragging a three-quarters-grown cottontail rabbit toward a woodpile. As I approached, the weasel stopped pulling the rabbit and dashed to the safety of the woodpile. When I retreated, the weasel ran back to the rabbit to claim its prize. When I advanced, the weasel retreated but this time it did not go as far. When I backed off again, the weasel ran back to the rabbit and commenced tugging

on it. When I again approached, the weasel refused to give up its rightful prey. It screeched at me and released its powerful musk but continued its tugging. Even when I held the rabbit by its hind legs, the weasel refused to let go. When I picked the rabbit up, the weasel held tight, swinging in the air, holding on with its teeth.

Wishing to get photographs, I tied the rabbit with a piece of nylon cord to a nearby tree and left while the weasel pulled on the tethered rabbit. It was as if I had tethered the weasel. When I got back, it was still trying to pull the rabbit to the woodpile. I did get good photos of the weasel in the woodpile, some of which illustrate this chapter.

When a weasel takes over a mouse burrow, it will usually utilize the burrow as its own as a base for forays against the dens of other mice in the area. A mouse family may provide food for one weasel for a day or perhaps two days at the most. In warm weather, even though the weasel may bury some of its prey to preserve it, much of the prey will spoil before the weasel can eat it. One farmer, in trying to locate a weasel in his chicken coop, discovered more than 100 rats and mice, freshly killed, that the weasel had stockpiled beneath the floor. Many times a weasel will visit a chicken coop only to feed on the rats and mice that are attracted to the area by the chicken feed.

Several researchers have noted where a female weasel had a natal den in the same vicinity as a chipmunk's den and never molested the chipmunk. Many predators will not hunt in their own backyard.

Weasels are very determined and, although an occasional prey species escapes from the weasel by tiring it out, most do not. Usually, once a weasel has committed itself to a chase, it continues until it has caught the prey to be used as food to replace the energy it has just expended.

A researcher discovered a weasel in among high grass and grabbed the weasel with his bare hands. Immediately the weasel latched onto the researcher's hand and would not let go. Its jaws could not be pried open. The researcher did not want to kill the weasel as he wanted it kept for study. Walking about a quarter of a mile to a small stream, the researcher plunged his hand and the weasel beneath the surface. Only when the weasel was about to drown did it open its mouth to struggle for air. And only then was the researcher able to free himself.

Attacks by weasels on humans, although not common, have occurred on a number of occasions. The weasels had no intention of killing the human, or any delusions about their ability to do so. When humans have been attacked, it was because the person got between the weasel and its intended prey. When a weasel is intent on securing its supper, it brooks no interference, not even by man.

Weasels are absolutely fearless. They will run from large predators because their lives depend on it, not because they are frightened. It is a good thing that weasels are not the size of dogs or there probably would be no humans. And if a weasel was the size of a lion, *it* would be the undisputed King of Beasts.

The least weasel, weighing between one and 2 ounces, is the smallest carnivore in the world. Compared to the giant brown or polar bears, which can weigh up to 1,600–2,200 pounds, this weasel is tiny indeed. Its weight is 1/12,800 to 1/20,000 times that of the giant bears. What it lacks in size, it more than makes up for in courage.

Weasels may be active at any time of the day or night, depending on their hunger. They are usually more active at night. Many mammals like to bask in the sun but the weasel does not. Although weasels do not sleep for long periods at a time, they are hard to awaken when asleep.

Despite their comparatively short coats and their lack of a heat-retaining body form, weasels continue to be active during even the coldest weather. A good supply of food will minimize their excursions but weasels seldom remain in their dens for more than 48 hours.

During the winter, weasels often hunt by traveling beneath the snow and there are three major advantages to this. The most important is that meadow mice, their major food, will also be beneath the snow. The white-footed deer mice tend to travel on top of the snow. By being under the snow, the weasel is protected from most of its own predators. Third, the snow also acts as a blanket of insulation, keeping the weasel warmer, which reduces its caloric expenditure.

SENSES

Have very keen hearing and smell, two senses used in conjunction in hunting and probably of equal importance. Eyesight not good at detecting stationary objects, but quick to see slightest motion. Food preferences evidence well-developed sense of taste. No information on sense of touch.

COMMUNICATION

One of the weasel's main means of communication is dependent on scent. Weasels, both male and female, often lie down on their bellies and, with their hind feet extended, drag themselves along over logs, sticks, rocks and grass depositing scent. I can find no evidence of an abdominal gland so they evidently mark with their anal glands.

The musk given off by a weasel at any provocation announces its presence emphatically. It usually accompanies this discharge with squeals or screeching. Both sounds are high-pitched and loud, the latter sounds more raspy. They also have a raspy bark. One of the most commonly heard weasel sounds is their loud hissing. Weasels make most of the foregoing sounds when they are disturbed or angry and most weasels, most of the time, feel disturbed or angry. A female with young makes a chattering or twittering sound.

BREEDING

Weasels are solitary, the sexes getting together only for the breeding season. Although the ratio of males to females is close to 50/50 at birth, there is a preponderance of males from that time on. When the weasel population is low, more females are encountered, as if the nurturing of additional females is nature's way of guaranteeing the increase in population. In my collection of over a dozen study skins of weasels, there is only one female. Any fur buyer will tell of similar discrepancies. The males do travel longer and farther and are exposed to more trapping. With most other species this means that the population that is left is predominantly female but this is not true of weasels, and we don't know why.

The competition among weasels is keen because of the larger proportion of males. However, one factor is of help. Female weasels become sexually mature at the age of 3 to 4 months, while the young males do not. This eliminates the young males from the sexual competition for their first year. Weasels are probably monogamous, primarily because of the sexual ratio disparity. Monogamy lends credence to the idea that the male weasel, in some cases, may help to raise the young.

The male adult weasels are capable of breeding from May through to the beginning of August. Their testicles are about 8 times larger than they are in the winter months when they have regressed and both sexes of the weasel are incapable of breeding.

The adult female comes into estrus 65–104 days after giving birth to her young in April. The young females born in April are also capable of breeding at about 90–100 days after being born. Most breeding takes place in July.

During the breeding period the weasels do not really show affection for one another, they usually just show less enmity. The male seizes the female by the back of her neck and drags her around. Then clasping her body with his forelegs and maintaining his hold on her neck with his teeth, the male throws the female to the ground on her side. Curved around her, intromission is possible, although it may not be accomplished at once. Actual copulation takes anywhere from 20 minutes to 3 hours.

The short- and long-tailed weasels are subject to delayed implantation with the blastocysts attaching themselves to the wall of the female's uterus about 27 days before the young will be born. This gives a gestation period of approximately 270–279 days.

The den of a weasel is usually very snug and warm. Most weasels carry quantities of grasses into the nest area and many of them pluck the hair from mice to line the nest. Some nests have been found to be almost like a soft fur felt about one-half inch in thickness. These warm nests conserve the weasel's body heat at any time and provide an exceptional nursery for the young.

BIRTH AND YOUNG

The short- and the long-tailed weasels give birth to their annual litter in the last part of April or in early May. Four to 6 young per litter is common, the record number of young is 12. This latter litter would have really taxed the female as she has only 8 nipples.

The baby weasels, at birth, are flesh-colored and almost naked with just a few sparse, fine white hairs on the tops of their heads and the backs of their necks. The short-tailed weasel babies actually grow a little mane. At birth the young weigh between 1½ and 3 grams and measure about 1½ inches in total length. The young squeak lustily and constantly.

The young develop very rapidly with their ears opening at about 24 days and their eyes between 30 and 35 days. By this time they are also fully furred.

The young play with each other, looking like a can of worms in constant motion. The mother will play with the young when she is not busy bringing in food.

The female is an excellent provider. Judge Walter Fry had a weasel den under close observation in the Giant Forest in California's Yosemite National Park. The female weasel, by actual count, carried in to her young 78 mice, 27 gophers, 2 moles, 34 chipmunks, 3 wood rats and 4 ground squirrels for a total of 148 prey species in 37 days. Undoubtedly the female also carried in some food at night when she could not be seen.

Some biologists claim that the male assists the female with the feeding and rearing of the young, but other biologists doubt it.

It is currently thought that the female's small size is an advantage to her during the time she is feeding her

A young long-tailed weasel about 3 months of age.

young. Because of her smaller size, the female requires less food to supply her own body requirements and can thus deliver more food to her young. I contend that her small size is not an advantage. If she were as large as the male, she would be capable of killing larger prey which would produce greater amounts of food for the energy expended in obtaining the food.

At the age of 2½ to 3 months, the young weasels are full-grown. The young males are already larger than their mothers. At this time, the young are weaned and can hunt for themselves so the family breaks up and scatters. With the approaching breeding season, young males, although incapable of breeding, would be driven from the female's den by the adult male.

LIFE SPAN

Potential: 5–6 years. Record in captivity: 10 years.

SIGN

Scat not normally seen because frequently deposited under earth of tunnel of the den near the nest, but occasionally found near the den's entrance. Scats about 2–3 inches long, ¼ inch in diameter, composed chiefly of hair and bone fragments of prey. Scats sometimes deposited on stones.

Tracks seldom seen, except in snow. With normal bounding gait only one set of tracks visible because hind tracks usually obliterate tracks of front feet. Weasel's foot about ⅜–½ inch wide by ½–⅝ inch long.

ENEMIES

Among many enemies is mink, which not only kills weasels but competes for food. Where mink population high, weasel low. Snakes occasionally prey on weasels. House cats kill weasels and bring them home but do not eat them. Martens, fishers, bobcats, dogs, coyotes, and red and gray foxes kill weasel but latter four do not eat them. One fox den had 8 weasel bodies lying at entrance, uneaten. Pennsylvania bounty records show enemy-prey relationship of fox and weasel. From 1930 to 1939, 15,000–20,000 foxes bountied each year while 65,000–88,578 weasels bountied. After fox population explosion of 1939–mid-1940s, in 1945–46, 50,000 foxes bountied and weasels bountied dropped to less than 20,000. When fox population dropped again in late 1940s, weasel population rose.

Great horned owl a major predator of weasel, and weasels killed also by barred, snowy, and great gray owls. Hawks such as the sharp-shinned, coopers and goshawk kill weasels, one witness reporting an instance where a sharp-shinned hawk grabbed a weasel and flew off with it, only to have weasel turn, grab the hawk's throat, and kill it, the weasel escaping after crashing to the ground with only talon wounds.

Weasels have lice, fleas and ticks, being more susceptible to these parasites than other members of weasel family because they have only one den. Also plagued by flies and mosquitoes. Internally weasels have usual flatworms, roundworms and tapeworms.

HUMAN RELATIONS

The winter fur of the weasel, when it is known as ermine, has always been highly regarded as the trappings of the high and the mighty. Warbonnets of western Indian chiefs were festooned with tails, and sometimes with the entire skins, of white, long-tailed weasels. In Europe, ermine was the sign of royalty and the skins were used as trimmings for their crowns and their robes. It has been estimated that 50,000 ermine skins, mainly those of the short-tailed weasel, were used at the coronation of King George VI of Great Britain in 1937.

Recent studies done on the weasel have proved that this little mammal is of tremendous benefit to mankind. Consequently, our attitudes on the weasel have changed. It has been a long, hard conversion and the education of the general public has a long way to go. It is hard to overcome long-held, time-honored myths.

For many years, due mainly to public pressure, the Game Commission in Pennsylvania, and some other states as well, paid a bounty on weasels. Most bounty programs have been discontinued now for a number of years. Over the years, Pennsylvania had paid out more than $1.5 million in weasel bounties without ever curtailing the population. Most game commissions know that bounties don't work but political decisions, under the pressure of public support, often force their continuance.

COMMERCIAL VALUE

IAFWA statistics: 18,374 weasels taken in U.S. 1976–77, average price $1, total $18,374. In Canada: 102,698 weasels, $1.03 average price, $105,778.94 total.

In the light of what we now know, the weasel deserves more appreciation of the good it does. It's going to be a hard job to make a hero out of the same weasel that was portrayed as a villain for so many years.

MINK, *Mustela vison*

INTRODUCTION

The mink cannot climb as well as a marten. Nor can it swim as well as an otter. It cannot fit into as small a hole as a weasel. Like all members of the weasel family, it gives off a very fetid secretion from its anal glands but cannot direct it or use it for defense as does the skunk. The mink is not the specialist that these other animals are but it is capable of doing all of these things very competently. Its niche in nature's scheme of things has produced in the mink a composite.

Its scientific name was given to it by Schreber in 1777. *Mustela* is the Latin word for "weasel." *Vison* comes from a Swedish word used by Peter Kalm from a "type of marten that lives in water." The common word mink comes from either the Old English word *mynk* or the Swedish word *menk*.

DESCRIPTION

Minks are medium-sized weasels that have the typical short legs and the long, lithe, supple body and tail. An average adult male mink has a total length of 20–30 inches, of which 7–9 inches will be tail length. Minks stand about 3 1/2 to 4 1/2 inches high at the shoulder and their spines are humped in front of their hind legs.

The female minks, are much smaller than the males of the same subspecies. Adult females measure 16–21 inches in overall length. Males average between 1 1/4 to 3 1/4 pounds in weight, with the record being about 4 pounds. Female minks weigh between 1 1/4 to 2 pounds.

The mink's head is small and the face expresses alertness. There are 4 rows of vibrissae with the whiskers being sparse and varying in length from one-half to 1 1/8 inches. They are not conspicuous. The nose and muzzle are pointed.

The mink's eyes are small, brightly beady and black. The eyes reflect an emerald green when a light is shined into them. The ability to reflect light proves the presence of numerous rods situated in the rear of the eye itself. However, the mink's eyes are also generously supplied with cones.

The ears of the mink are about seven-eights of an inch in length, are rounded and situated on the sides of the head below the crown.

There are 5 toes on each of the mink's feet that are connected by a skin web for about half their length. There is hair on the toes and the foot, except for the small bare pads where the ground is touched. The small inside toe on each foot is almost entirely covered with hair and these toes very seldom show in the tracks.

The mink has 34 teeth—12 incisors, 4 canines, 12 premolars and 6 molars. The canine teeth are one-quarter to three-eighths of an inch in length and are needle-sharp. The single molar in the top of the skull is dumbbell-shaped and fairly flat-topped for chewing.

The mink is famed for its fur, its sheen, luster, silkiness and beauty. The guard hairs are between 1 1/8 and 1 3/8 inches in length, the soft underfur is about one-half inch in length. The tail appears bristly, like a bottle brush, because of the guard hairs. The guard hairs of a mink, when viewed in sunlight, are almost prismatic, reflecting primary colors of green, blue and red; each hair repeats these colors several times in its length. The overall effect leans toward a bluish tint.

Minks basically are a deep brown, to almost black in general color, being much darker on their backs than on the bellies. The tail is usually darker than any other part of the body. The coloration of mink varies

Minks are closely related to weasels, as shown by their long, thin bodies.

widely in just one area and there are geographic extremes according to the 14 subspecies.

All minks have a white patch beneath their chins that varies with the individual. There may or may not be white patches in various sizes and shapes on the mink's throat, chest and belly. All of these white markings are highly individualistic and as unique to a particular mink as are fingerprints. These markings, when recorded, are used for the identification of particular mink during biological studies.

Occasionally the underfur of a mink will be white instead of having the normal brown coloration. These mink are called "cotton" mink and have very little value in the fur trade. Minks were never plentiful in my area and I will never forget my disappointment to find that one of the minks I caught was a "cotton." Both melanism and albinism occur in wild mink.

Raising minks in captivity began to be commercially feasible in the early 1900s; there were numerous mink

farms in Canada by 1913. All of the original breeding stock came from minks that had been livetrapped in the wild. Pacific coast and Alaskan minks were the most avidly sought because they were the largest in size and the darkest in coloration.

The mutant minks, those being of many different colors, dominate the production of those being raised commercially. The first mutant minks, those that are now called platinum or silverblu, were first found on two small mink farms in 1931 and 1935. William Whittingham, of Arpin, Wisconsin, discovered that one female mink born in 1931 was of the silverblu color. From that start, through genetic control by breeding, he produced more of the same silverblu color and established a true breeding form.

Charles Whitaker of Union Grove, Wisconsin, produced two silverblu females in 1935. Since that time minks have been evolved that reproduce consistently as albinos, jet black and pastels. Although these colors can occur among wild minks, when minks of these colors are seen, they are almost sure to be escapees from mink farms.

One species of mink, *Mustela macrodon,* the sea mink, was never plentiful and is now thought to be extinct. The last reports of this mink were from Governor's Island, Connecticut. It was the largest mink in

This curious mink pauses in its search for food to investigate the photographer.

North America, measuring up to 38–40 inches in length. It was a light reddish-brown in color and its fur was coarse. It was found primarily along the New England coast.

DISTRIBUTION

Found in all contiguous 48 states and Alaska, and all Canadian provinces, although not in Newfoundland before 1934. Since then game farm escapees and government releases have established viable population. Never found far from water, minks prefer wooded stream sides but also inhabit streams without forest but with jumbled rocks that provide shelter. Found in almost every swamp, bog, marsh, pothole, pond, lake and river. Prefer fresh water but many inhabit saline estuaries and sometimes found along seacoast. Not found in Arctic tundra. Because North American minks have higher fur value than European *Mustela luteola,* many were imported for fur farms. Those that escaped or were released by governments flourished and today North American mink well established in Northern Europe.

TRAVEL

Minks travel almost constantly. The female, during the time that she has newborn young, has a main den to which she, and later they, retire each day. If food is in good supply, the female's range may be restricted to about 20 acres. If food is scarce, she may be forced to cover 3 to 5 times as much territory. During the wintertime the female may become as nomadic as the male but covers a smaller area.

The male mink's circuitous route may cover 25 square miles or more. The male will have a number of dens that it will utilize, sleeping in whichever one is handy at the time. Minks are small enough to be able to enter almost every hole and crevasse and finding dens is seldom if ever a problem. Minks do prefer bedding for sleeping, and dens that they use frequently while on their travels will be lined with grasses, leaves, feathers, bits of fur and remnants of prey.

MINK
(Mustela vison)
CURRENT RANGE

Livetrapped minks that are later recaptured provide good records on the movement of the animals. In one study, the farthest distance moved by a female from her initial captive point was 400 yards. Males were recaptured most frequently between one-half and one mile. The greatest distance for the travels of a mink was 20 miles.

From personal observations, I have found that most male minks travel on a 5- to 7-day circle. In marshes and swamps, a female may not leave the area at all. If males traveling along streams, rivers and lake systems would leave their tracks today, you could count on finding their tracks again in almost the exact same spot a week later. This is, providing some predator had not permanently interrupted the mink's travels.

LOCOMOTION

Minks walk with the alternating placement of feet that is common to most mammals. Minks often stalk their prey by flattening themselves against the ground and sliding forward on their bellies like serpents. However, minks usually bound. While bounding leisurely, the space between their paired tracks is from 12 to 18 inches. When the mink is bounding at full speed, the distance is stretched out to 24 inches or a little more. The tracks of the hind feet register ahead of the tracks of the front feet. The tracks of a mink traveling leisurely at 2 miles per hour are in the form of a rough square. When the mink is bounding at full speed of 6 to 7 miles per hour, the tracks tend to be on a more diagonal line.

Minks can climb trees, although they selom do except when hunting. When they are the hunted, they prefer to go underground to hide rather than up a tree. The rougher the bark of the tree, the easier it is for the mink to get a claw-hold.

Minks are as much at home in the water as they are on land and are strong swimmers. When swimming, a mink uses all its feet, with the left front and the right rear working in unison and vice versa. The partial webs increase its foot surface and are a great aid to propulsion. It has been figured, over measured courses, that minks swim at about 2 miles per hour.

Minks are able to outswim many fish, particularly small ones and those such as sunfish and suckers. They have been seen to swim underwater for distances of up to 50 feet and can remain submerged for about 2 minutes.

Even when the streams are choked with ice, the minks will unhesitatingly dive through a hole and swim underwater to reappear at another hole. They can outswim a muskrat mainly because the muskrat uses only its hind feet for propulsion whereas the mink uses all 4 feet.

When the snow is deep and fluffy, the mink may travel beneath it for short distances. It dives down through the snow and uses the same motions as it does while swimming. It pops up through to the surface every so often to look around and to get its bearings. The mink's feet, in comparison to its body size and weight, are not large enough to support its weight on the top of soft snow.

Minks have been known to make slides on hillsides in the snow, like the otter, just for the pleasure of sliding down them.

FOOD

Many food studies of mink prompted by game farmers as well as sportsmen and farmers because mink is a rival of muskrats, game birds and animals, fish and poultry. Minks eat all of these but in most cases minks do not constitute conflict with human interests. Minks eat frogs, muskrats, fish, crayfish, mice, rabbits, small birds, eggs, insects such as grasshoppers, crickets and greater diving beetles, salamanders, snakes, turtles, squirrels, chipmunks, poultry, freshwater mussels, clams, crabs, ducks, pheasants, etc., and scavenge on carcasses.

North Carolina study of 335 minks showed fish made up 61 percent of diet, mammals 34 percent and the balance miscellaneous. New York study at Montezuma Marsh showed muskrat in 49 percent of samples taken, fish 41 percent, diving beetles 39 percent. These three made up 79 percent of diet. Amount of

When ice covers the ponds and lakes, the mink is forced to feed more heavily upon land creatures.

beetles surprisingly high. Prevalence of muskrats due to circumstance, muskrats being more common in the area. Another New York study examined summer, fall and winter diets, and fall and winter percentages from 630 minks are 34.1 percent fish, 33.2 percent mammals, 21.9 percent amphibians, 14.4 percent crustacea, 6.8 percent insects, 2.7 percent birds, 2.4 percent earthworms, 1.6 percent mollusks, 1.4 percent reptiles, 0.3 percent vegetation. Muskrats had been eaten 5.4 percent of the time. Summer percentages: mammals 44.0 percent, fish 32.4 percent, insects, 29.2 percent, amphibians, 18.9 percent, crayfish, 12.7 percent, birds, 9.3 percent, reptiles, 4.1 percent and snails, 0.7 percent.

It must be remembered food studies show only what particular animals eat at a given time and place, showing what food is most common or most easily obtained (which may not be the same). Minks eat about 3½ ounces of food per day.

Captive minks must have fresh food or they sicken and die. Eating of carrion a trait lost to the ranch mink. To ensure that food is fresh mink rancher puts food on top of wire mesh cage, which mink pulls through. Uneaten scraps fall through mesh at bottom to ground, preventing chance of mink's eating spoiled food.

BEHAVIOR

Paul Errington has undoubtedly done the most extensive study ever on the muskrat-mink relationship, spanning more than 20 years in the same areas of Iowa. He found that muskrats that had an individual home range during the breeding months were virtual-

Hollow logs are important to this mink because its prey species may live inside them, and also because the log may provide shelter for the mink itself.

ly safe from mink predation so long as the habitat was in good condition. Severe drought conditions prompted mink predation upon the muskrats which had lost their protective cover of water and vegetation.

Adult muskrats that did not have individual territories and had no permanent residences were subject to high mink predation simply because the muskrats were constantly exposed to danger. They had nowhere to hide.

The study found that young muskrats were subject to little mink predation until their increasing population caused overcrowding, which forced them into poorer habitat where encounters with predators became more frequent.

Dispersal in the fall, caused by overcrowding, prompted high mink predation because the muskrats are particularly vulnerable on land. Errington found that although the mink is a semiaquatic mammal, it patrols only the edge of ponds, lakes and marshes.

The muskrats living on the shore or close to it were subject to mink predation while those farther out in deeper water were relatively safe because the minks did not venture there.

Minks, like all predators, are opportunists. As an example of minks taking advantage of a situation, Errington tells the following.

A female mink and her young lived in good muskrat territory but did not prey upon the muskrats, there being ample sources of other food. In July an exceedingly severe windstorm blew loose many deep-water muskrat houses and pushed them up on the shore. Intraspecific strife broke out immediately between the rats that lived along the shore and the now homeless rats forced into their areas. Fighting was savage and many of the muskrats were badly cut with their skins slashed open. Some muskrats were killed and these were eaten by the mink. Then the wounded, homeless muskrats, suffering from shock and wounds, were attacked as they offered little or no resistance. Between scavenging and predation, the mother mink brought 16 muskrats back to feed her young in one day. From that time on the mink family fed primarily upon muskrats.

Disease, overcrowding, stress and starvation among prey species invites predation. Healthy prey lives relatively untouched. When a periodic epizootic disease was rampant, the mink fed upon the dead, dying and decaying muskrats. Sixty-five to 70 percent of all mink predation upon muskrats in Errington's study was prompted by this disease, which Errington was the first to study and which carries his name. Out of 13,176 mink scats that Errington examined over a 10-year period, 2,415 had muskrat remains in them. He figured 1,344 scats were deposited after the minks had been scavenging on muskrats dead from the epizootic. After the muskrats had been subjected to drought and freeze-outs, 343 more scats were picked up. Out of the entire 13,176 scats only 674 scats, or 19.6 percent, were the result of actual predation by mink upon healthy muskrats.

Healthy adult muskrats just don't make easy prey for minks. It has been found that male minks kill the bulk of the muskrats that are taken because of their larger size. An adult muskrat is often larger than an adult female mink. Muskrats are fighters and a large healthy adult backed into a tunnel or against some other protective backing is too formidable an opponent for most minks.

I once watched a mink attack a muskrat in the pond in front of my home. The pair rolled about in the water, but the muskrat broke away and escaped. When the muskrat crossed my lawn to go to the pond behind it, it was limping but very much alive. The mink, which was running up and down the bank of the front pond looking for the muskrat, was only frustrated.

Albert Jacob was on Loon Lake in Warren County, New York, hunting for ducks. He was sitting concealed on a huge fallen tree in the lake watching a mink approach. Suddenly a large muskrat, which he had not noticed, darted out of a hollow log and pounced on the mink. A wild melée followed and the mink was glad to escape.

At a later date, on the same lake, Jacob was hunting with a friend. They watched as a mink attacked a small muskrat. Suddenly 2 adult muskrats dashed out of their nearby house and attacked the mink. The young muskrat dashed back into the house and the mink just barely got away from the parents.

When minks attack their prey, they usually bite through the back of the neck near the base of the skull or grab for its throat with their teeth. Holding on with their forefeet, minks scratch with their hind feet much as cats do.

With mice, rats, chipmunks and muskrats, this usually results in the mink and its prey rolling and tumbling about like a blurred ball of fur. Rabbits and hares seldom offer resistance, except to try frantically to escape by trying to run off with the mink hanging onto their throats. Minks have been known to frequent garbage dumps to feed upon the rats living there.

Minks seldom attack poultry today because most farms do not allow their chickens to roam about as they used to do. The proper housing of poultry has just about eliminated it from the diet of most wildlife.

Occasionally, minks will attack wild ducks, particularly the females brooding their eggs, ducklings or flightless ducks during their eclipse period when they lose their primary flight feathers in the summer. However, duck remains usually show up in mink scats most frequently as soon as the duck hunting season opens. Any ducks that are crippled and cannot be found by the hunter will probably be found by the mink. There have been many instances of hunters shooting ducks, only to have minks steal them. Fishermen have often been robbed in the same manner. One fisherman, not having a creel to hold his fish, was throwing the fish up on the bank as he caught them. When he had his limit of 8 fish, he went to gather them up only to discover that a mink had already done so and had carried them all off.

Although minks do not kill as wantonly as does the weasel, they do frequently kill more than they can eat at one time. Most surplus food is carried back to the den for later usage. In warm weather, the meat spoils rapidly and the dens become foul. Some mink dens have been found that contained from 12 to 24 prey species of different kinds.

During the winter, the cold weather preserves the food for long periods of time. Under these conditions a mink may spend days or even weeks in one den feeding upon the stored food. A severe storm, or being well fed, will also cause a mink to spend several days curled up sleeping before hunger forces it out to hunt again.

Minks are not fussy eaters. Usually they eat the fur, feathers, scales, bones, and ectoskeletons (such as the hard shells of crayfish) of their prey. Digestion is rapid because the mink's metabolism is high. Food material is passed through the stomach and the digestive system within hours so that the material that the scats contain is of local origin.

Minks are a contradiction. They are shy and retiring and because of this, they are seldom seen. On the other hand, they are curious and often approach closely to whatever interests them. Minks often sit upright for a better look.

Minks do most of their traveling and hunting during the late evening, the night and at dawn. These hours are not theirs by choice—they are forced into them because of pressure by man. The large number of cones in the mink's eyes are those of a creature that should ordinarily hunt by daylight. Minks in wilderness areas, or in areas where they are not molested, can be found almost any hour of the day or night. I have seen many minks in the daytime in the wilderness regions of Canada, along the Delaware River in New Jersey and in southern swamps.

If you ever have a chance to watch a wild mink, you will soon note that it investigates every den, hole and crevasse it encounters. It is constantly sniffing about for food, poking its nose in every small hole and crawling into every hole that it can fit into. The investigations of a mink are more direct than those of a weasel. A weasel is all over the place, it can't seem to contain itself and seems to lack direction. The mink, if it has been through the area before, knows where it wants to go and goes there. However, as author and naturalist H. Preston said, "A mink is liable to go anywhere, and just as liable not to."

SENSES

Sense of smell very keen. Minks able to trail prey like a hound, scenting the tracks. Most food located by scent.

Hearing very good, able to hear faint squeak or chirp up to 100 yards if air still or wind favorable. Minks can be called by making such noises. Hearing most important sense for detecting danger.

Minks are color-blind but have been trained to recognize and respond to colors in laboratory, an ability of uncertain advantage to wild mink. Immobile man not recognized as danger, but any motion instantly detected.

COMMUNICATION

An angry mink, and most of them seem to be angry most of the time, squeals like a rat. Minks also screech, snarl, growl and hiss. When angry a mink also discharges scent from its anal glands. Almost any type of a disturbance will cause this discharge; the mink does it with lots less provocation than a skunk. Although the mink does not eject as much scent as a skunk, nor can it squirt it in a specific direction, it is a foul-smelling odor to most people but evidently not to other minks.

When minks travel about, they leave their scats and some of their scent deposited on prominent rocks and logs. It is a means by which minks keep in touch with one another.

BREEDING

At no time are minks sociable but the increased use of scent prior to the breeding season is an attempt by the mink to contact those of the other sex. Males that happen to meet usually avoid each other unless a female is in the area. The fights between the males, over the females, are fierce and bloody. Even a female that has not come into heat is not safe from the fury of an aroused male.

The breeding season usually occurs during the last week in February or the first week in March. Adult females usually breed on the exact same day each year and it is usually the exact same day as when their mothers were bred. They are in estrus for about 8 days.

With minks it is not so much courtship as it is conquering. The male is very aggressive to the female and she frequently is equally vicious. The male approaches the female from behind and seizes her by the back of her neck with his teeth, and drags her around. This really does not hurt the female as much as it seems that it might. The female is protected by a thickened pad of skin on the back of her neck. The minks then lie on their sides with the larger male wrapped around the female. Copulation may take 15 minutes to 2 hours. During this entire period the male does not loosen his hold on the female's neck. Copulation may occur several times. Six days later the female may breed again.

Baby minks are hairless and have their eyes sealed shut at birth. This one is one day old.

There are always more adult female minks than males, as more males are caught each year in the trapping season because they travel more and are exposed to more danger.

One male mink will mate with as many females as he can locate but this would usually be no more than 2 to 4. In most cases the male is a "love 'em and leave 'em" type, but he usually stays with the last female that he breeds.

I personally have never seen a mink family with both the male and female present with the young. Most of the researchers stated that the male stays with the last female he breeds, while other researchers claim that the male would kill the young if he stayed.

Fred Space, of Space Farms, raises 10,000 minks a year. He said that an old male mink, except in the breeding season, will kill any other mink that it can get at. It may not kill an adult female, but it definitely would kill any juvenile mink of either sex. Fred has seen such males try to tear nest boxes apart to get at the baby minks. As he said, perhaps the minks raised in captivity have lost the paternal instinct. I realize that I am offering two conflicting views but each animal is an individual and there are no concrete rules that apply to them all.

After being bred, many of the females leave the open areas of the big lakes and rivers and seek out small streams that have more protective cover.

BIRTH AND YOUNG

The den which the pregnant female chooses may be an abandoned muskrat house or bank den. If muskrats are living in the den that the female wants, she kills them and then considers the den abandoned. These dens will have their entrances beneath the water so that they can be entered only by diving and swimming underwater. More often, the mink will tunnel a hole through the walls of the house so that it can be entered from above the water level. Minks don't like to dig, and they are not really equipped to do so, but they can and will dig a den if forced to.

Many times the natal den will be in a woodchuck's burrow, a hole in a stone fence row, in a fallen hollow log, or even up in a hollow tree. The mink's long, lean body allows it to fit into most of the natural cracks and crevasses so that a den site is really no problem. The female will carry dry grasses and leaves in for bedding.

Because of delayed implantation, the fertilized egg does not become fastened to the wall of the uterus at once; hence the gestation period for minks varies between 40 and 70 days. Almost all baby minks are born between April 25 and May 15. There is only one litter per year.

A litter of newborn minks will consist of between 3 and 8 young, with from 3 to 5 being the norm. Most of the baby minks are hairless but some have a very fine, very short coat of white fuzz on their bodies. The baby minks weigh about one-fifth of an ounce and are $3\frac{1}{2}$ inches long or about the size of a man's ring finger. They are blind and absolutely helpless at birth.

Minks are usually very devoted to their young and they are good mothers but they are high-strung. If a mother mink is disturbed shortly after giving birth, she may worry the young ones to death by carrying them about in her mouth or she may kill and eat them. Their maternal instincts are so strong that most female minks will adopt any orphan mink they can get.

The female mink cleans and cares for her babies and keeps them warm in their grass-lined den. She leaves them just long enough to secure food for herself. As early May is the time that most wildlife have their young, the female finds food in abundance. She will carry the surplus back to her den to eat it there as she needs it. She has 8 nipples and her young grow rapidly on their diet of rich milk.

At 2 weeks of age the baby minks are covered with dark reddish-brown hair that lacks the luster of the adults' coats. Between 3 and 4 weeks of age the mother begins to feed the young their first solid food. They usually begin by feeding on pieces that are remnants of food that the mother is eating.

At about 5 weeks of age the young minks start to wander about on legs that are still wobbly. Their eyes open now and for the first time they can see the world that they had previously known only by their other four senses. They weigh about 4 ounces.

The young minks now begin to venture out of the den, scurrying back into it at the first hint of danger.

If the young have to be moved or brought back into the den, the mother carries them by the skin on the nape of their necks. The young play by pouncing on each other, fighting over their food or fighting for no specific reason. They swim well and soon play in the water. The young minks are weaned at about 8 weeks of age.

If the male is in attendance, he too will bring in food for the young. Soon the young are following after their mother, or their parents, as they hunt for food. While doing so, they usually travel single file and look like a long undulating snake.

The adult minks start to molt their winter coats about April 10. By July 15 the molting process has been completed and the minks are in their summer coats. A month later, about August 15, they begin to shed their summer coats and by the end of November they are resplendent in their luxurious winter coats. The young minks shed their summer coats in late September and prime up a short time after the adults.

In September, or October by the latest, the young minks are so quarrelsome that they can no longer tolerate one another. The family unit breaks apart and the minks, parents included, go their separate ways and are rivals from then on.

Female minks reach maturity at about 10 months of age, males at a little over 16 months. Both sexes are capable of breeding when they are a year old.

LIFE SPAN

Potential: 10 years. In wild, 7–8 years is old. In captivity, minks live longer—record in captivity, 14-year-old still alive in Illinois.

SIGN

Tracks most common sign. Mud or sand near typical habitat good places to find tracks. Scat may be only sign along rocky stream sides. Scat usually dark if mink feeds on meat, will contain scales and bones if feeding on fish. Scats usually about $3/8$–$1/2$ inch in diameter, long and segmented.

Tracks in snow, although blurred, identifiable as mink because of size, between 1–1 3/8 inches in diameter. Path of track even more convincing evidence—track from hole in bank to muskrat house to hole in ice cannot be marten because martens do not enter water, otter tracks would be larger, weasel tracks smaller and would not have gone in water. Tracks can often be identified by such a process of elimination, based on sound knowledge of wildlife of the area.

Another occasional sign of mink is sight of fish dead on ice, bitten behind the head. The mink fills its larder while fishing is good.

EMEMIES

Many natural enemies, although most adults can readily escape predators that catch the young. Great horned owl a major predator. Other predators are bobcats, lynxes, foxes, coyotes, wolves, dogs and (rarely) otters. Alligator in Deep South. External parasites include flies, ticks, fleas, lice, mosquitoes. Internal parasites: roundworms, tapeworms, flukes, etc. Diseases, although rare, are distemper, encephalitis, and rabies.

HUMAN RELATIONS

Mink is a status symbol. To be sure, its fur is soft and luxurious and because it is a short fur, it does not give the impression that the person wearing it should be on a diet. The fur is warm, which means that it is also practical. All of these are good, valid reasons for the mink's high value. The highest value is really its high price. Those who wear mink are said to have "arrived."

Mink did not always have a high value only because there was little demand for the fur. That changed after the early 1900s. Once mink became valuable for coats, prices started to climb. This stimulated more demand and the higher the demand, the higher the actual value became.

Because not enough minks could be caught in the wild and because silver fox farming had become so profitable, many mink ranches were started in the

1920s. At first minks were raised in just their natural colors. In the early 1930s, mutation mink, along with genetic selection and manipulation, made many other colors possible. And the prices soared accordingly. A color called "vovalia pink" sold for an average of $420 per pelt. The highest prices ever paid for mink was for the "black willow" color. In 1966 the Hudson's Bay Company auctioned off the entire output of black willow pelts for an average price of $450 each. Forty of these pelts were extra special and sold for an average price of $1,100 apiece. So far as I can find out, that is the highest price ever paid for mink.

Today, wild-caught mink pelts represent about 10 percent of all the mink pelts sold. As it takes between 60 and 80 pelts to make a full-length coat, many pelts are needed each year to satisfy the demand. About 3 million pelts are produced each and every year. The finest mink coats are not made from the entire skin of the mink. An expert furrier will select hundreds of mink skins and then just take tiny strips of fur from each pelt and sew them together. Fur coats made in this manner are called "let-out" and the fur color matches perfectly.

COMMERCIAL VALUE

Ranch mink prices discussed earlier. For wild mink, IAFWA statistics: 1976–77, 320,823 caught, average price $14, total $4,491,522. Recent popularity for long-haired furs has depressed mink prices. In Canada: 116,537 caught, $19.67 average price, $2,292,316 total. Northern pelts darker and larger, bringing higher prices.

The prices paid for mink skins may go up and down; the prices of the coats stay high forever. And while a diamond may be a girl's best friend, no girl refuses a mink coat.

19

WOLVERINE, *Gulo gulo*

INTRODUCTION

The wolverine is as elusive an animal as any in North America, with the exception of the black-footed ferret. If the wolverine's size were as large as its reputation, it would be the largest animal on earth. It is one of the most feared, hated, misunderstood, most reviled and maligned of all creatures. It is not the devil incarnate, but there is some basis for truth in most of the superstitions and supernatural beliefs held about the wolverine. This is even reflected in the animal's many names.

Its original Latin name, *Ursus luscus,* was given to it by Linnaeus in 1766. *Ursus* is Latin for "bear" and Linnaeus improperly classified it as a small bear—an easy mistake to make, because it resembles one. One of its colloquial names in North America is skunk-bear, because it looks like a bear and the scent from its anal glands is as malodorous as that of the skunk. *Luscus* means "half-blind" because the specimen that Linnaeus examined had only one eye, the other having been destroyed.

The Latin name was changed to *Gulo luscus* by Sabine in 1823 because by then it was recognized that the wolverine was a member of the weasel family and not directly related to the bears. *Gulo* means "throat" or "glottis," from the act of swallowing. This has given rise to another name for the wolverine, glutton, because of its supposedly insatiable appetite.

The European wolverine has been designated as *Gulo gulo.* This is now the name being given to the North American wolverine, too, by such researchers as R. A. Rausch and Peter Krott because they claim that the two species are one and that our wolverine should have the subspecific classification of *Gulo gulo luscus.*

I well remember, when I was in the Canadian bush,

talking with Charlie Smith, an Algonquin Indian, about the wolverine. No, he didn't know that animal. When I mispronounced the French-Canadian name, *le carcajou,* Charlie still didn't know what I meant. Suddenly his eyes brightened and his face broke out into a big smile as he said, "Car-ca-jou." Yes, yes, yes, he knew that animal; every trapper in the north did. Actually the name carcajou is the French adoption of the Algonquin Indian word pronounced the same and meaning "devil." Hence another colloquial name, "Indian devil." What is this animal with such a reputation?

DESCRIPTION

The wolverine is the largest of the terrestrial weasels. It has a stocky, compact body and its strength is legendary. Its strength is actual, not just part of the myth. I once witnessed a 35-pound wolverine pick up and bounce the 80-pound wooden crate that it slept in. Herb Crisler, a naturalist and motion picture photographer, tells of one wolverine digging under a rock, getting beneath the rock and lifting it out of the soil. He estimated that rock weighed about 200 pounds.

R. A. Rausch and A. M. Pearson weighed and measured 183 wolverines from Alaska and 101 from the Yukon. The adult males from Alaska averaged 22.7 pounds with the low of 16.5 pounds and the high being 34 pounds. The adult males from the Yukon averaged 31.2 pounds, with the low being 26.2 pounds and the high being 36.3 pounds. The adult females from Alaska averaged 15.5 pounds, with the low being 12.0 pounds and the high being 18.5 pounds. The adult females from the Yukon averaged 20.7 pounds, with the low being 18.4 pounds and the high being 23.7 pounds.

The European wolverine is larger than its North American counterpart with the adult males averaging 32.1 pounds and the females 21.8 pounds in weight.

Rausch states that the largest Alaskan wolverine that he ever weighed was 38.5 pounds. There are some records of 45 pounds and Krott gives the weight of some Scandinavian wolverines at more than 55 pounds.

A large male wolverine will measure 38–40 inches in total length, of which 7 or 8 inches will be tail length. He will stand 16–17 inches high at the shoulder. A large female wolverine will measure 35–36 inches in total length, of which 7 inches will be tail length. She will stand 15–16 inches high at the shoulder.

There are 5 toes on each foot, each toe being armed with a strong, sharp claw that is about 1 1/8 inches in length. The feet are greatly oversized in comparison with the animal's body weight. The hind foot of a large male is about 3 1/4 inches in width by 4 inches in length from the heel pad to the claw tip. The front foot is about 4 inches in width by 5 inches in total length. These huge feet allow the wolverine to run on the top of soft snow that would bog another creature up to its chest.

The wolverine's nose and eyes are black. Its ears are about 2 inches in length, are well-rounded and protrude above the crown of its head. There are 4 rows of vibrissae with the whiskers being sparse and varying in length from one to 2 inches. There is a row of hairs over the eye, like an eyebrow, that varies from one to 2 inches in length.

Being a member of the weasel family, the wolverine has 2 well-developed anal glands. Like the skunk, it can direct a spray or stream of this exceedingly foul-smelling, greenish-yellow liquid distances of up to 9 feet. There is a pregenital gland that gives off a secretion that is used by the wolverine for marking territory. There is also a spot on the wolverine's throat that is thought to be a sebaceous gland.

Wolverines are basically a dark brown in color. A light-colored band extends across the wolverine's forehead and down both cheeks. A pair of similarly col-

This wolverine looks like a small bear. Its appearance and its malodorous scent glands caused the Indians to call it a skunk-bear.

The teeth and claws of the wolverine are long and strong.

ored bands, of about 3 inches in width, starts at the shoulder and runs parallel to the body, along the sides, flanks, lower part of the rump and joins over the top of the tail. On the most beautifully marked animals, this band is a bright, burnt orange, on some others it is a pale yellow and on still others this band is just a lighter shade of brown and may hardly be noticeable at all. Some wolverines have occasional spots of white fur on their throats and chests.

The guard hair on a wolverine's back is about 2 inches in length, the wooly undercoat about one inch in length. On its flanks the guard hairs are about 3½ inches long and 6½ to 7 inches long on the tail. This gives the wolverine a very bushy tail and makes it appear 6 to 7 inches longer than it actually is.

The fur of the wolverine is unique in that frost crystals do not adhere to the individual hairs. Because of this characteristic, the wolverine's fur is highly valued as trimming around the face of the hoods of parkas. When wolverine fur is used, the breath of the wearer does not turn the parka's ruff into a mass of ice.

Although this characteristic of wolverine fur has been known for centuries, the reason for it was not. At first, investigators thought it might have a different chemical composition than other fur but this was proved untrue. Microscopic examinations showed that the overlapping scales on the hair shaft were no dif-

ferent from others. Finally it was found that the difference stems from the shape of each individual hair and its attachment to the skin.

It was found that the guard hairs of the wolverine are straight while the guard hairs of other animals are curved, and that the underfur of wolverine was uniformly one inch in length, while that of other animals had irregular or wavy lengths. The density of the wolverine's underfur is much greater than that of other animals and it doesn't incline, which prevents matting. Finally, the angle of insertion of the guard hairs into the skin is much straighter than in other animals.

In tests, wolverine, coyote and wolf fur and an alpaca pile material were sprayed with cold water and

The exceptionally long feet of the wolverine, visible in this photograph, help to support its body weight when it walks on soft snow. (Photo: Irene Vandermolen)

the samples placed in a freezer. The alpaca pile material froze into a solid chunk of ice. Both the coyote and wolf fur matted and contained chunks of ice. The wolverine fur had a few ice crystals in the underfur but the guard hairs always remained ice- and frost-free.

DISTRIBUTION

Found circumpolar throughout northern taiga regions of world. Range has been pushed northward in Eurasia, southward in North America. Originally, found as far south as Maryland in Appalachians and New Mexico in Rockies. Encroachment on habitat, hunting and trapping extirpated it from most of its range in lower 48 states. Today wolverines (although never plentiful) found in California, Washington, Oregon, Utah, Idaho, Colorado, Wyoming, Montana, Minnesota and Wisconsin, and reported in Iowa. Also in Alaska and Canadian provinces of Yukon, Northwest Territory, British Columbia, Alberta, Saskatchewan, Manitoba, Ontario and Quebec. As in Eurasia range now extending northward on the tundra, probably made possible by reduced wolf populations there.

No wolverines ever known living in Michigan, although it is known as the Wolverine State. Name possibly derives from fur trade centers of Detroit and Michilimackinac, where many wolverine pelts would have been brought from Canada. Another theory holds settlers wished to liken themselves to the wolverine for its strength, stamina and perseverance.

TRAVEL

Wolverines are not transients as previously believed, but are nomadic in that they constantly travel over large individual territories. Peter Krott figured that some male Eurasian wolverines had an individual territory of 500,000 acres. Such a territory would overlap that of 3 or 4 females. Each wolverine marks the boundaries of its territory with urine, feces and with musk from its pregenital glands. Each wolverine honors the territory of another as a necessity to prevent overpopulation of a given area and the resultant food

shortages. The adult males will fight to keep other adult males from their territory and the females will drive other females from their territories. During dispersal time, there is a general shifting as the young ones seek and claim territories within which the older adults have been killed or have died.

In North America, wolverines usually do not have as large territories as those in Eurasia. Glacier National Park in Montana encompasses about one million acres and about 30 wolverines inhabit that area, giving each wolverine approximately 33,000 acres. Calculating 8 males and 25 females and allowing for overlap, each male has about 125,000 acres, which seems about the right size.

Extensive work was done on the wolverine in Banff National Park by the biologists from the University of Calgary. A wolverine was tracked on snow and the biologists found that it had covered about 24 miles in less than 3 hours. They also watched one wolverine climb down the face of an almost vertical mountain near Lake Louise. When it got to the bottom, it saw the men and turned right around and went back up to the top in about one hour. The wolverine had climbed 2,600 feet, almost straight up, in that length of time.

I well remember seeing a wolverine, back in 1965, going up a rocky draw that fed a small stream into the Toklat River in McKinley National Park. My son Len and my friend Mike Smith were with me and they were as excited as I was to see a wolverine. We had been only about 150 feet from the wolverine when we first spotted it. We ran as hard as we could to the draw, only to see it already going out of the draw about 800 feet above us. It went over the top and was gone. We had heard that the wolverine had a den in that area and, although we checked out that draw every time we were in the area, we never did see it again.

When a wolverine is searching for food, as it travels over its territory it does not follow exact trails nor does it wander aimlessly about. Instead, the wolverine courses back and forth over a general strip of terrain, and this zigzag pattern allows for very efficient coverage of its range.

The distance covered by a wolverine in one day is

WOLVERINE
(Gulo gulo)
CURRENT RANGE

determined by its success in finding food. After eating, the wolverine will sleep; if the kill or find is a large one, the wolverine will stay in the area till the food is consumed. A hungry wolverine continues to just travel and sleep. A hunting wolverine may cover 40–50 miles a day.

The male wolverine's territory is so large that it usually takes about 3 weeks for him to make a complete circle and again this depends upon the availability of food and the weather. Female wolverines usually cover the perimeter of their territories in about one week.

LOCOMOTION

Wolverines walk, sometimes. They almost never trot. In traveling, wolverines bound with a rocking-horse-type gait which they can maintain continuously. Their stamina is a marvel.

When the wolverine walks, its tracks are about 8 inches from toe to heel or 12 inches from toe to toe. In bounding leisurely, the sets of tracks may be 3 to 4 feet apart and when the wolverine is bounding fast, they will be 5 feet or more apart.

Wolverines climb well, although their weight and size preclude the speed that is the forte of the smaller members of the weasel family. Most of the wolverines hunt for food on the ground but they do climb to investigate a squirrel's den or a bird's nest. A wolverine's main defense against a pack of wolves is to scramble up a tree. It can jump 5 feet up from the ground to a tree limb.

When climbing, the wolverine will use just its claws if the tree is a big one. On smaller trees, it wraps its paws around the tree, like a bear hug, and climbs. The claws are still used but the wrapped-around legs and feet accommodate the tree's small diameter. On brushy trees, like most evergreens, the wolverine climbs by using the branches like the rungs of a ladder. In descending a tree, the wolverine usually comes down headfirst—the mark of a good tree climber. Wolverines have been seen to hang from a tree limb by just their hind feet and to drop to a lower limb. They do not jump from tree to tree.

In the north country there are many streams and lakes and the wolverine does not hesitate to cross them. It swims well, its huge paws providing good propulsion. In warm weather, the wolverine will often swim for the pleasure of it. There are a number of records of the wolverine actively playing about in water.

FOOD

Will eat anything edible wolverine can catch, find or steal. Does not hunt by stealth but by stamina, running prey to death. Fox no match against it, especially in winter when bogged down in snow. In summer less prey are killed because other foods more available, the eggs of ground-nesting birds, the birds themselves (notably flightless ducks and geese during eclipse period), and ptarmigans and chicks.

Mice, voles, lemmings, ground squirrels and marmots caught in runways or dug out. Beavers and muskrats caught on land or when lodges and houses can be broken into. Along coasts, carcasses of whales, seals and walruses on beach are eaten, and dead fish scavenged.

Large insects of all types eaten, particularly larvae of wasps and bees. Wolverine, like bear, impervious to stings.

Late summer and autumn wolverine, again like bear, concentrates on ripe berries. In winter, eats grouse that roost at night beneath snow, porcupines (not without taking occasional quills), and snowshoe rabbits.

Also eats large game animals at times—in Finland, Sweden and Norway. Lapps hunt wolverine because it preys on reindeer. In general wolverine not a threat to big game but will attack old, weakened or snow-hampered animals. One report listed a cow elk with spine severed by wolverine, another a wolverine attacking a moose, another a wolverine clinging to the back of a caribou. One wolverine sighted from airplane over Gulkana River, Alaska, was attempting to hamstring a caribou. Releasing its hold twice as plane passed and repassed, wolverine finally leaped onto caribou's back, biting neck, and brought it down.

Although called a glutton, wolverine gets by on 3–4 pounds of food per day. Captive wolverines thrive on this, and one maintained in good health at University of Michigan on only 1,200 calories per day. In wild more food consumed because search for food burns calories. Wolverine will glut itself during food shortage if abundant food is found.

Any prey left uneaten is carried off, buried with grass and sticks in summer and snow in winter. Large prey cached where killed. Musk sprayed over cache to claim food. Food may be hung in evergreen if ground too frozen to dig a hole.

Wolverines cause trouble to trappers by eating trapped animals or by eating bait and springing trap. Occasionally traps carried off and hidden by wolverines, a trait duplicated by pet wolverines of Peter Krott that would carry off things of his in play. Wolverines also cause trouble for trappers by breaking into cabins and destroying food supplies, and in the process bottles are broken, cans punctured, sacks torn, bedding shredded, and musk sprayed over all. Outdoor caches prevent this, built on long poles covered with sheet metal. For years Hudson's Bay Company's advice to trapper plagued by wolverine had been to kill it or move from its territory.

Wolverines do not destroy things out of vindictiveness. They are merely hungry animals getting food in any manner they can, and must, to survive in the harsh land they inhabit.

BEHAVIOR

Young wolverines are no smarter than the young of many other animals and are easily trapped. However, even young wolverines have an inherent caution that is typical of all wolverines. When they encounter anything strange or unknown, their first reaction—and the reason for their survival—is to run off. They don't wait around to see if there is danger. They avoid it in the first place.

An example: Wolverines can be treed by dogs, reacting with their way of escaping from wolves. When a hunter approaches, the wolverine doesn't wait for him

to get close; it jumps out of the tree and dashes off. The wolverine is not afraid of the dogs, but of man. The dog that tries to impede the wolverine's flight stands a good chance of being killed—the wolverine will do anything to escape that hunter. It is this inherent caution that has kept the wolverine alive despite all hands being against it. Danger avoided before it becomes danger is no danger at all. When disturbed, the wolverine will often get up on a ridge or high rock to investigate the disturbance, standing upright on its hind legs for a better view.

The wolverine may be active at any hour of the day or night having adapted itself to the far north where either the days or the nights are long, according to the season of the year.

Its aggressive and belligerent nature shows well in this photograph of the wolverine.

This wolverine has a beautiful, light-colored side stripe while some wolverines have very dark stripes that almost blend in to the animal's basic dark body fur.

When hunting is good, or food is easy to come by, the wolverine divides up its day into about 4-hour segments. It will be very active hunting for food and then, when fed, it will sleep for about 4 hours, after which it wakes and is active for 4 hours and then it sleeps for 4 more hours. It keeps up this pattern for days. If food is scarce, then the wolverine will have to stay active for a much longer period until it has filled its belly. Being hungry is not conducive to sleep. The wolverine will stay active longer during dry, windy periods, especially if the moon is full.

Many people think that the wolverine lives a frantic life, bounding around continuously. Actually, the wolverine bounds because it's an efficient method of traveling. With so large a territory to cover, its success in filling its belly depends on covering all the ground possible in the shortest possible time. Instead of being frenetic, the wolverine is really calm, sleeping when it can, hunting when it has to.

Trappers can worry a wise old wolverine that may be exceedingly trap-shy. The trappers fasten a large bait, such as a moose head, to a tree with a piece of wire. Traps are then carefully set in a circle around the head. The wolverine, upon discovering the moose head, attempts to drag it off so that it can be hidden and cached. Repeatedly the wolverine will drag the head the length of the wire, only to be stopped. This type of frustration gets the wolverine so worked up that it throws caution to the wind and does not watch where it places its feet. As a result, the wolverine may be caught in a hidden trap that it would ordinarily discover and avoid.

The wolverine blunders onto most of its food. Every spot that provided food in the past is checked out on each succeeding trip in the hopes that some edible shred may have been overlooked. Long after all the bones of a carcass have been gnawed, cracked and scattered, they will be scouted again.

Vilhjalmur Stefansson, the Arctic explorer, told of the perseverance of a wolverine. Stefansson and a companion had shot a caribou and cached it so that they would have a supply of meat on their return trip. The temperature had moderated and they were able to hack out chunks of the thawing tundra. They put the caribou in the hole, covered it with canvas and dirt, then a layer of rock and finally mounded it over

This wolverine will bite into every can of food in this cabin, eating what it can and spoiling the rest.

with slushy snow. When the temperature plummeted, the entire mass froze to the consistency of concrete.

When the explorers later returned for their meat, they found it was gone. Tracks identified the culprit as a wolverine. Stefansson figured that the wolverine dug down through the snow and ice till it got to the rocks. By sleeping on top of the rocks, the wolverine warmed them up with its body heat until the earth surrounding the rocks thawed. After removing the rocks, the wolverine dug through the frozen dirt and canvas. The wolverine then squeezed through the hole and ate its way inside the carcass. Here it lived and feasted, until every edible scrap was consumed.

Wolverines play far more than anybody suspected until Peter Krott did his long-term, intimate studies. He found that the wolverines would play with their litter mates, or the young with their mother, even when they were full-grown. Krott believed that the wolverines played as much as the river otter.

His wolverines would run along and then tumble end over end in the soft snow. They would roll down hills with or without snow. Biologists at Lake Louise watched wolverines slide down snow-covered slopes. They played tag and chased one another about, wrestling and engaging in mock fighting. They would play with a dead stick or an old bone, carrying it about, throwing and retrieving it. If there were two or more wolverines, they would try to keep the other from getting the "prized" stick or bone. Playfulness and curiosity are the signs of intelligence and the wolverine has a good measure of all 3 attributes. Other researchers have verified Krott's findings. This research drastically changes the long-held belief that a wolverine was a driven automaton of a beast.

The wolverine can learn from a situation that it has not encountered before. It is able to make the proper deduction, respond accordingly, benefit from the experience. This is akin to reasoning. The wolverine learns early in life to be extremely suspicious of anything that smells of human scent.

SENSES

Smell very keen—most food found by odor. Hearing acute.

Eyesight very poor. Taste either poorly developed or suppressed as wolverine will eat anything it finds.

COMMUNICATION

Being solitary, the wolverine is not very vocal. When angered, it utters a guttural snarl.

A captive wolverine that was in a cage next to where I was working growled and snarled continuously. Long strings of slobber ran out of its mouth and down over its chest. It was working itself into a real rage, evidently disturbed by the pounding I was doing, even though it had no direct contact with it. Wolverines also hiss.

To mark their territories, the wolverines deposit feces on rocks and urinate on everything. They lie down and drag their bellies over the grass, on logs, depositing scent from their pregenital glands.

As discussed, they are most famous for spraying their reeking, anal gland musk over everything as a proprietary claim.

BREEDING

During the breeding season, both the male and the female wolverines make an increased use of scent stations. The male's territory overlaps those of 3 or 4 females so he checks out the scent of each in turn to see if the female is approaching estrus.

Biologists Philip L. Wright and R. A. Rausch found that sperm first appeared in the male's testicles about the end of March but that it was not motile until 4 or 5 days later.

Rausch and Pearson checked out 1,059 carcasses of wolverines from Alaska and the Yukon between 1960 and 1968. By weighing the males' testicles, they found that the peak of the breeding season occurred in May and early June. Although the young males were not physically mature at 14–15 months, they were sexually mature. Thus these young males were capable of breeding, providing they were not prevented from doing so by the larger, stronger adult males.

Where a female's territory is overlapped by 2 males, the males will fight for dominance.

Research has shown that 50 percent of the females of 16–28 months of age became pregnant, which proves that at least half of the juvenile females can and do breed the first time that they come into estrus.

Krott claimed that most adult female wolverines breed every second year. This claim was disproved by Rausch and Pearson because they found that 91 percent of all female wolverines that they examined were pregnant. This percentage is about as high as you can get under the most ideal circumstances. Although a few of the adult female wolverines may have been barren, it is more likely that because each wolverine has such a huge territory, the females who were not pregnant just did not encounter a male during the period that they were receptive.

Wolverines are subject to delayed implantation with the fertilized ova becoming fastened to the wall of the uterus in late January. The wolverines have a gestation period of about 300 days.

The male wolverine is polygamous, breeding with whichever female in his territory is receptive when he encounters her.

BIRTH AND YOUNG

As the time of her birthing draws near, the female wolverine will seek out a den. When possible, she will select an area that has a large winter-killed carcass that will serve as a reservoir of food or she will go to where she has cached food.

If there are no dens in the earth or hollow trees or logs, the female will scoop out a den in a snowbank.

She will tunnel down to the earth and create her den on the top of the frozen dirt. I can find no record of trash being taken into the den as insulation.

Most baby wolverines are born in late March or early April. Rausch and Pearson have found that the 54 litters of young they examined had an average of 3.5 young per litter.

When the young are born, they are between 5½ and 7 inches in total length and weigh about 3½ ounces. They have a very short coat of fur that has a uniform sandy color. Their eyes and their ears are sealed shut for about one month's time.

The mother is an exceedingly good one and will fight to the death to protect her young. There is only one record of a female leaving her young when danger threatened and it is thought that perhaps she was trying to decoy danger away from her young by exposing herself to the danger.

The female has 4 nipples and the young will nurse for 8 to 10 weeks. At about 6 weeks of age, the mother will begin to feed the young their first solid food. This will be meat that she has eaten and will regurgitate.

The young begin to venture out of the den when they are about 8 weeks old, in the first part of May.

A researcher in Finland, Pulliainen, suggests that the male wolverine may also visit the den to bring food to the young. This has not been witnessed by other biologists.

In May the young wolverines leave the natal den and follow after their mother as she travels in search of food. In September, when they are 5 months old, the young wolverines are able to secure food for themselves. At this time the young males weigh about 15 pounds, the females 10–11 pounds. By November the young wolverines split up as a family group, each going its own way to seek out its own territory. When factors are favorable, the young wolverines spill over the established ranges and colonize new areas.

LIFE SPAN

Potential: 10–12 years. Record in captivity: 16 years.

SIGN

Destruction of cabin or food supply, with concomitant musk, the most obvious sign. Tracks nearly as large as those of large wolf, but gait and presence of fifth toe make it unmistakable. Shorter legs mean body will drag in shallower snow than a wolf's. Scat 5–6-inches long, ⅝ inch in diameter, both ends usually sharply tapered.

ENEMIES

Wolf the major enemy. Where wolf population declines, wolverines' increases. With other large predators, wolverine carries the fight to them, with reports of wolverine driving bear, coyote and mountain lion away from a kill. In one case a mountain lion's leg was broken by wolverine and a bear was disemboweled. Generally a fight does not result as predators are driven away by musk.

Relatively free from external and internal parasites, being solitary most of the time, traveling great distances and seldom using a den. Are subject to flies, mosquitoes, lice, fleas, roundworms and tapeworms.

HUMAN RELATIONS

The wolverine is still feared and greatly respected by the native people of the north country. As more facts have been learned about this remarkable creature, the mythical size of the wolverine has shrunk. Writers of lurid tales find that educated readers are no longer gullible readers and the wolverines of today's literature are not as formidable as were those of yesterday. The wolverine can be destructive because it is endowed with such strength but it is, after all, just an animal and not a malevolent spirit.

COMMERCIAL VALUE

IAFWA statistics: 997 sold 1976–77, average price $182 per pelt, $181,454 total. In Canada: 925 taken, $182.59 average price, $168,897 total.

BADGER, *Taxidea taxus*

INTRODUCTION

Back in 1778, Schreber named the badger *Ursus taxus,* which is Latin for "bear-badger." This was because it was thought that the badger was related to the bear family but looked like the European badger. The current scientific name for this animal was given to it by Rhodes in 1894. *Taxidea* is a combination of the Latin word *taxus,* for "badger," and the Greek word *eidos,* for "like." Translated, the American badger is the "badgerlike badger." The badger is not related to the bears but is a member of the weasel family. Its head is shaped somewhat like that of a wolverine, but its coloration makes it stand out alone.

The noun badger is often used as a verb, meaning to worry, bother, pester or annoy someone. It comes from the old English custom of staging fights between dogs and a badger. Badgers are fighters; they are indomitable. A badger will escape if possible, but if it must fight, it never surrenders. The badger's great strength, sharp teeth and claws, and determination make it a formidable adversary.

In a badger versus dog fight, the badger would be placed in a barrel that was lying on its side. Then the dog or dogs would be turned loose. It took a mighty brave dog, or a very foolish one, to attack a badger head-on and an even braver, or more foolish, one to get in behind the badger and force it out of the barrel. The badger was the winner as often as the dogs.

In Germany, a special dog was developed and bred for the sole purpose of fighting with and forcing a badger out of its underground den. The German word for the badger is *dachs.* The lovable little dachshund is really a tough, scrappy little animal in its own right. And like the badger, the dachshund can also turn around inside its own very loose skin. I am not sure that the miniature dachshunds would have either the strength or the inclination to fight a badger as would their full-size counterparts.

The badger is the official animal of the state of Wisconsin, because the tunnels of the early-day zinc and lead miners there resembled those of the badger.

DESCRIPTION

The badger is a low-slung, squat, compact weasel of tremendous strength. It has attained these bodily features at a sacrifice in both speed and litheness.

The average adult badger will measure 25–28 inches in body length with an additional 5 to 6 inches for a stubby tail. The badger appears to be a bit longer because of the 1¾-inch length hairs on its tail. The badger stands 9 to 11 inches high at the shoulder. Adult badgers average 12–16 pounds in weight, although there are a number of records of weights over 20 pounds. Hartley H. T. Jackson, in his book, *Mammals of Wisconsin,* tells of a badger he caught in that state on June 13, 1902, that weighed 23 pounds 6 ounces. There is little apparent size difference between the sexes as researchers have found that the male is larger in size and weight by only 5 percent.

The badger's nose tip and eyes are black. There are a few short, scraggly hairs that serve as whiskers and perhaps 3 or 4 hairs as eyebrows. Its ears are situated below the eye level, low on the sides of its head. The auditory opening is large but protected from dirt by the badger's stout, rounded ears that are about 2 inches in length.

The badger's legs are short and muscular. There are 5 toes on each of the badger's feet. Each toe is armed with a strong, stout claw. The claws on 4 of the toes of the forefeet are up to 1½ to 1¾ inches in length

Note the long, strong claws on the badger's front feet and its short, stubby tail. (Photo: Len Rue, Jr.)

and are fairly well curved. The toe corresponding to our thumb has a claw that is not only much shorter but much thinner. These long claws on the forefeet are excellent tools for the constant digging that the badger engages in, and also make formidable weapons. The badger frequently sharpens its claws, getting rid of striating dead tissue, by scratching at trees and fenceposts as a cat would do. The claws on the badger's hind feet are also stout but are between three-quarters and one inch in length.

The badger has 34 teeth—12 incisors, 4 canines, 12 premolars and 6 molars. The molars are roughly triangular in form and are fairly flat-topped for the chewing of food. The canines are about five-eighths of an inch long and needle-sharp.

Like all members of the weasel family, the badger has the very odorous anal glands. Although it does discharge this musk when frightened, hurt or angry, the badger cannot direct the discharge as does the skunk. There is also a pair of abdominal skin glands that are used primarily during the breeding season.

The badger always looks like it's wearing a hand-me-down suit that is much too large. The skin is very tough and more loosely fitted to the body than are the skins of most other mammals. The loose skin has a dual purpose. When tunneling, the badger is able to rotate inside of its skin if it needs to dig upside down. A tight-fitting skin would not allow this mobility. The loose skin is also a tremendous advantage to the badger for protection. The badger has no apparent neck, the skull seeming to slope directly into the shoulders. Any animal attempting to grab the badger by its neck gets only a mouthful of loose skin. Meanwhile, the badger turns around inside its skin and is busy slashing at its attacker with teeth and claws. Even bulldogs, which seldom let go after getting a hold on their opponents, can't restrict the badgers' movements and are forced to release them.

The strikingly handsome markings of the badger's face make it easy to identify. The basic coloration of the badger's head may shade from a light reddish-brown to almost jet black. A startling white streak runs from the badger's nose up its forehead, over its crown and down its neck to the shoulders. The rest of the face, cheeks, insides of the ears, and chin is white with 2 dark vertically triangular streaks in front of the ears.

The badger's body, belly, sides and back are basically white, or yellowish-gray. The guard hairs have a tannish-white base, then have a black band and end with a pure white tip. This gives a grizzled, salt-and-pepper coloration to the back, down to the flanks. The hairs of the rump and the tail are usually reddish in color. The front legs are a very dark shade of brown, the hind legs a shade lighter. I could find no record of melanism or albinism among badgers. As the individuals get older, they tend to become lighter in color.

The hair on the top of a badger's head is between one-half and three-quarters of an inch in length. The white underfur on the back is about one to 1 1/4 inches in length, while the guard hairs are 1 1/2 inches in length. The badger has exceptionally long hair on its shoulders and along its flanks. The underfur on these

The distinctive facial markings of the badger are good identifying characteristics.

portions is about 1 1/2 inches long while the guard hairs vary between 3 and 3 1/2 inches in length. The guard hairs on the stubby tail are about 1 3/4 inches long. Ordinarily a badger's hair parts neatly down the middle of its back.

Badgers are short-legged to start with. When threatened, they usually flatten themselves out on the ground and fluff out their hair. With their loose skin and long flank hair, they appear to be almost as broad as they are long—an animated little rug.

Artists know that the finest paintings done by the Old Masters were painted with brushes made from badger hair. So was my dad's shaving brush, and countless thousands of shaving brushes just like his. Today, synthetic fibers are being used for the few shaving brushes still being made. Badger fur is used today primarily for the trimming of cloth coats.

DISTRIBUTION

Population plummeted as plains converted to farmland, and ranchers tried to eliminate badgers to preclude injuries to livestock from stepping in badger holes, although the likelihood of such an accident was vastly overestimated. The badger held on nevertheless until the use of poison compound 1080 against coyotes began, and thousands of badgers died when they reached the bait before the coyote did. With the end of the poison campaign and a measure of protection for the badger, population and range have increased. Wisconsin, the Badger State, gave badgers complete protection in 1955 and the population now is estimated at 10,000 there.

Originally found no further east than Indiana, it moved into northwestern Ohio, to New York by 1966, and several have been taken in New England. Today inhabits all lower 48 states west of Mississippi, except Louisiana, and is rare in Arkansas. Also found in Wisconsin, Illinois, Indiana, Ohio, Michigan and areas of Tennessee. In Canada, found on prairies of British Columbia, Alberta, Saskatchewan, Manitoba and Ontario.

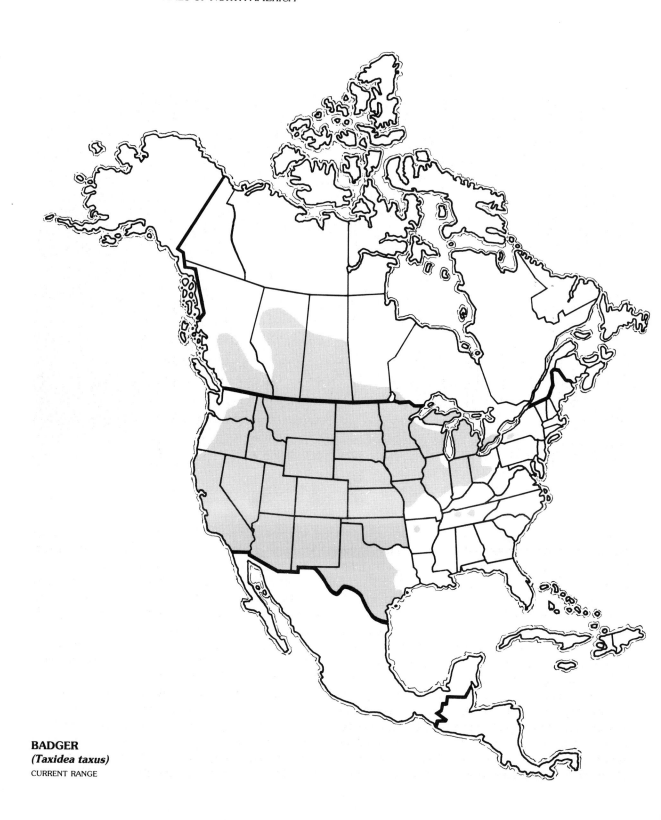

BADGER
(Taxidea taxus)
CURRENT RANGE

The badger really makes the dirt fly while digging. (Photo: Len Rue, Jr.)

TRAVEL

The badger is a traveling critter but it doesn't go far. With its short legs, distance is not what it has in mind—food is. Researchers have radio-tracked badgers and have found that their individual range is at the most 1½ to 2 miles across. Over this area, the badger moves almost constantly, denning each night in one of the many dens that it has in the area.

One female badger in Minnesota traveled 17 miles between September 12 and 27, or a little over one mile per night. Most of this travel was done on the perimeter of her territory. At one time, this same badger used 23 different dens in 57 days. Although the badger does not have a definite trail that it follows from den to den, it apparently has a specific den in mind

when it starts out. It either hunts on the way as the opportunity presents itself, or near the den it is going to if it is located in favorable hunting territory.

Badgers favor sandy or other light soils. They usually prefer open areas to live in because their prey favors such areas. Heavy soils and clays are avoided. In Minnesota, even the wooded areas have the light soils favored by badgers. Out of 50 dens that the radio-equipped badger was using, 39 were located in woodlands, while 11 were out in fields.

The badger does not migrate nor does it really have a seasonal shift. With the coming of cold weather, the radio-tracked badger chose a den that it had used previously in a dense stand of woods. The tree cover would prevent the ground from freezing as deeply as it would in the more open grassland.

A badger emerging from its earthen burrow.

LOCOMOTION

Badgers walk most of the time to get from place to place. When in a hurry to reach some predetermined destination, they trot. When going flat-out to escape from danger, they gallop or bound. At this speed, they can do 10–12 miles per hour.

Badgers can walk backward almost as well as they go forward. When confronted by an enemy, they walk backward to and down into their burrows. In this position, they are always ready to meet danger head-on and to fight it if they have to.

The badger is not famed for its speed, but for its digging ability. In soft earth, a badger can outdistance a man with a shovel who is trying to dig it out.

When a badger digs, it loosens the earth with its forefeet, passes it back under its belly and kicks it backward with its hind feet. The dirt being thrown backward may be thrown 6 to 8 feet and in as continuous a stream as if it were supplied by a conveyor.

Roots that are encountered are attacked by claws and teeth. Rocks are either dislodged or dug around or under.

A man cannot pull a badger from its hole, even if he grasps the animal's tail. The badger just swells up its body with air and holds on with its legs. Its strength and determination will win. Only by flooding the burrow with water can the badger be forced out. Of course, in the sandy or light soil areas that the badger frequents, this is not usually possible either, because the soil soaks up the water before creating a problem for the badger.

In the northwestern part of Ohio, the badger was known as the "grave robber." That section of the country is so level that drainage has always been a problem. Cemeteries were always situated up on the few gravel ridges that bisected the terrain so that the graves wouldn't be continually flooded out. The badger also chose to live on those same ridges for the same reason. When the badger dug into the graveyard ridges, it frequently tunneled through old graves, bringing pieces of material and human bones to the surface. In an attempt to keep its burrow dry, the badger became heir to an unsavory name and reputation.

Although the badger needs water to drink, and has been seen cooling off in shallow puddles, it does not ordinarily swim. However, it has been known to swim across the Missouri River and has been seen placidly dog-paddling along in lakes half a mile from shore. When it swims, it holds its stub of a tail stiffly erect.

FOOD

Primarily a carnivore but badgers also eat some roots, grasses and berries. Main foods are ground squirrels, mice, gophers, prairie dogs, rabbits, marmots, skunks, birds and their eggs, snakes, snails, earthworms and insects. Also dig up larvae of yellow jackets and bumblebees.

Most badgers hunt at night because then squirrels will be inactive in their dens. If very hungry, when unmolested, or when days not too hot or nights are very cold, some will hunt in daytime, though not at midday.

Study of Uinta ground squirrels in Utah revealed badgers would prey only on females with young, ignoring barren females and males. Badgers would plug up auxiliary holes to squirrel den and dig through main entrance after female and young, which were usually caught unless overlooked in side chamber or able to escape around badgers. Never did squirrels dig through a plugged hole to escape. Concentration on female and young gave badgers the most meat for the energy expended.

Badgers at times kill and eat skunk, but also at times unable to do so. One witness reported confrontation between skunk and badger in which badger was blinded by skunk's musk and was overcome by the smell, but plunged on for a time until giving up.

Badgers also eat carrion, which made them so susceptible to poisoned baits.

Several animals "share" food with the badger. One red fox happened on a badger feeding on a sheep car-

cass and approached close enough to force the badger to turn and chase it off. When badger had been decoyed about 150 yards, the fox dashed back and fed on sheep until the badger returned, when the ruse was repeated. Coyotes also share the badger's efforts, traveling with it perhaps to take the swifter prey flushed from the den before the badger can catch it. Hawks have also been seen following the badger for the same purpose.

Badgers eat snakes, even the rattlesnake (which they must often meet in burrows), but not the head. Unknown whether badger can avoid strike of rattlesnake. Certainly badgers would have no trouble with them in winter, when snakes are torpid.

A badger searching for food by digging for it.

It is true that the excavations made by the badger can be a nuisance to man and sometimes downright dangerous to his livestock and his machinery. Also true that farmers and ranchers could hardly imagine a creature whose dietary habits are more beneficial to them and their interests.

BEHAVIOR

It is almost impossible for a badger to remain undetected in the area in which it lives. The badger gets most of its food by digging, it escapes from its enemies by digging, it is able to survive the most frigid winter weather by retreating to the dens it makes by digging. So dig it does.

The badger's den can easily be told from that of a woodchuck or fox by its size and shape. The entrance to a woodchuck's burrow may be 6 to 8 inches in diameter or slightly larger and will be vertically oval. The entrance to a fox's den will be much larger because of the fox's longer legs and the hole will be wider at the top than at the bottom. The entrance to the badger's burrow will reflect its body shape and will be much wider than it is high. The opening will be a flattened, horizontal oval of 6 to 8 inches in height by 12–14 inches in width.

Dens that have been dug out show that most of them go 6 to 8 feet below the surface, although one den was 15 feet deep. They are 20–30 feet in length. The tunnel slopes up to a main chamber and then drops down again before sloping up to an exit hole. Each den has 2 or more exit holes and some have 2 or more chambers. One researcher noted a toilet chamber where the feces were buried. Another researcher stated that he saw feces lying around the entrance to the den, although I have never seen them, nor have other researchers. Most badgers have very clean sanitary habits.

The large dens just described are those that the badger uses as a main den or dens. Many of the dens that a badger uses are just one-nighters and were probably excavated as the badger dug out a squirrel.

Years ago, my family and I were on a camping trip in Glacier National Park, in Montana. We camped in a tent at St. Mary's Campground. It was a lovely spot with a fabulous vista, but most important to me was the sign of badger activity. I asked the ranger about badgers and was assured that there were some but because of the number of people around, they would not be seen in the daylight. He told me of another, more isolated, meadow where I might be able to photograph badgers. So early the next morning my son Lenny and I set off.

Well, we tried for badger and didn't see any. We tried for goats and climbed several peaks without any luck. When we finally dragged our aching bodies back to camp, I found my wife and the two younger boys bursting with excitement. Everyone tried to tell me at once about the animal that had dug a hole under the corner of our tent. Yes, it was a good-sized animal, about 2 feet long. It could make the dirt fly as it dug. Yes, it was very friendly, as it would stop digging every now and then and come up out of the hole while all the campers took pictures. And yes, you guessed it, it was a badger. The campground was overrun with ground squirrels and one of their dens was near the corner of the tent. Unfortunately I never got any photos of that particular badger.

Badgers that become accustomed to people, or that have been raised by people, are sometimes kept as pets. Even the pet badgers have a tendency to get nasty as they get older, but this is a common trait with many animals. There are times that pet badgers play too rough, because their great strength, long claws and sharp teeth make even play hazardous.

Both pet and wild badgers have been seen to play by themselves. Most young animals, of the same litter, wrestle and chase one another in play. Researchers have seen adult badgers play with sticks and bones, tossing them into the air and carrying them about with no other purpose but play.

Many people believe that the badger hibernates. This is not so. The badger, like the skunk, the raccoon and the bear, will retire to its den during the coldest part of the winter and sleep for extended periods of time but it does not enter into true hibernation. The badgers in the northern states and in the Canadian provinces spend much more time in winter in their dens than do those in the central states, while those in the southern states may not den up at all.

In September and October, the badger increases its normal eating frenzy and becomes gluttonous, gorging itself, building up additional layers of fat on its body in preparation for winter. This activity takes no conscious effort on the badger's part, but is a natural response of its body triggered by the extended hours of darkness each night. Studies in Wyoming showed that the badgers averaged 5 hours of activity per night in November but only 0.4 hours per night in February, a reduction in its activities of 92 percent. In January and February the badgers became less nocturnal, coming out in the late afternoon to take advantage of the warmth of the sunshine.

During the month of November the badgers under observation came out of their dens about 7:30 P.M. and retired at 6:30 A.M. In December they came out at 3:30 P.M. and retired at 7:00 A.M. In January they came out at 3:00 P.M. and retired at 7:00 A.M. In February they came out at 3:30 P.M. and retired by 1:00 A.M. More badgers stayed in their dens for longer periods of time in February than any other month. In March they came out at 4:30 P.M. and retired at 6:30 A.M. In April they came out at 5:30 P.M. and retired at 6:30 A.M. A temperature increase of 16 degrees from March to April produced a 22 percent increase in the badgers' activities.

In midwinter the badgers often did not come out at all; one of the badgers remained in its den for 21 consecutive days.

Most studies showed that when the temperature got down to zero, the badgers would den up for extended periods. This may be the general rule but as with all rules, there are exceptions. One badger was seen out on four occasions when the temperature was −1°, −21°, −19° and −21° F. It also came out and walked about in 6 inches of snow.

Badgers usually line their dens with lots of dead grasses which make them both softer and warmer. The warmth of the dens in the wintertime depends mainly upon the depth of the den and whether or not the entrance is blocked with earth.

Dens that have been monitored show that shallow dens that are just below the frost line and are left open have an inside temperature of 30°–40° F. Deep dens that have the entrances partially or totally blocked with earth will register between 40°–50° F. Thus denning is a tremendous survival factor not only in terms of warmth but in the lessened demands upon the fat supplies of the animal's body. The colder the temperature, the more calories are consumed by the reconversion of fat needed to produce warmth.

Badgers can often be seen in the daytime in late fall or early spring lying on top of the mounds of earth at their dens' entrances, soaking up the sunshine. At the first sign of disturbance, they just drop out of sight by going into their dens.

The badger has one annual molt and sheds its coat in May. The hair of its new coat continues to lengthen throughout the summer and fall. In the summer the badger is very susceptible to heat.

SENSES

Hearing and smell the primary senses in search for prey, although unknown which (if either) is more important. Slightest noise can be heard. Smell important not only in finding food but in identifying danger, such as rattlesnake in a hole.

Because most food secured by digging, vision not of great importance. Badger keeps large eyes closed while digging. Stationary man not recognized as danger but badgers quick to see motion.

COMMUNICATION

The most common sound I have heard badgers make is a loud, continuous hissing of displeasure. The badger hisses by turning its nose upward and blowing through it while curling its lips, showing its canine teeth as a dog does while snarling. Badgers also grunt, and when angry or fighting, growl and snarl. Occasionally the badger will pop its teeth.

An angry badger, fighting for its life, will raise its tail and discharge its foul-smelling musk. Although it cannot direct its discharge, it can saturate the immediate vicinity and many animals, and most people, find its odor very disagreeable.

The glands on the badger's abdomen are dragged over sticks, stones and clumps of grass and are a means of marking territory. This scent is used more heavily just prior to the breeding season and is undoubtedly attractive to the opposite sex.

BREEDING

Badgers are usually solitary. When 2 badgers are seen in one area, it is probably due to an overlapping of their territories.

Very little is known about the breeding activities of badgers because of their mainly nocturnal habits. It is known that breeding takes place in late August or September.

Like some of the other members of the weasel family, the badger is subject to delayed implantation. The fertilized eggs divide only 3 or 4 times, then float free in the uterus. The blastocysts attach themselves to the wall of the uterus in late February. Development is then fairly rapid and the young are born in April or May. The actual development time is 8–9 weeks.

BIRTH AND YOUNG

The annual litter may consist of from 2 to 7 young, with 3 being the usual number. The female has 8 teats and could easily handle a larger number of young, but badger families tend to be small.

Baby badgers are born blind and with their ears sealed. They are covered with a short, sparse hair that is lighter in color than it will be later in life. Their color pattern can easily be seen as the skin is pigmented and shows through the short hairs.

The ears of the young badgers open between their third and fourth week, and their eyes between the fourth and fifth week. Now the female begins to bring prey species to her young as food. At 6 to 7 weeks of age, the young are wandering about outside the den, and at 8 weeks they are half-grown. The young are now hunting with their mother and are almost completely weaned.

The family stays together as a unit till late summer, when the young wander off on their own.

LIFE SPAN

The badger has a potential life span of about 12 years. One badger in the National Zoological Park in Washington, D.C., lived to be 15 years 5 months old. Dr. Bernhard Grzimek, director of the Frankfurt Zoological Garden, gives the longevity record for the American badger at 22 years.

SIGN

Craters and dirt piles a conspicuous sign of badger's digging, and tracks appear in soft dirt it has dug up. Length of forefeet to tips of claws between 2 3/4 inches and 3 1/4 inches, and about 1 3/4 inches wide. Most noticeable feature is deep imprint of claws. Hind foot is longer than front but badger, being digitigrade, does not walk on heel. All 5 toes register in hind track (as with forefoot), and hind track about 1 3/4 inches long by 1 1/2 inches wide. Badger walks pigeon-toed, with tracks turned inward. Tracks sometimes seen in snow. More apparent in snow is trough made by body, which appears in snow deeper than 2–3 inches because of badger's short legs.

Feces usually buried within den or in mound at den entrance. Even afield badger digs hole to deposit feces and cover them. May not be buried when ground packed hard by dryness and when seen feces are twisted, about 3/4 inch in diameter and 3–4 inches long. Feces contain mostly hair, bits of bone and/or feathers, because badgers eat small animals whole.

ENEMIES

Few natural predators for adult badgers, and they generally remain near a burrow that affords protection.

Coyotes can kill young badgers but killing a healthy adult is unlikely. Badgers can usually dig a hole before large predators can get to it, from which it can stand off almost any enemy. Golden eagles take immature badgers but this is exceptional. Badgers may have lice, ticks, and fleas, and parasitized by flukes, tapeworms and roundworms. Susceptible to tularemia. Occasional cases of rabies.

HUMAN RELATIONS

The badger is benefiting from the tremendous interest that most people have today in the out-of-doors. The stopping of most of the poison campaigns was the greatest boost to the badger's population increase. Not just the campaigns that were directed against the coyote, but those that were directed against the small rodents, the badger's main food source.

A number of states now recognize the beneficial aspects of the badger's predation upon rodents and have given it complete protection. As mentioned before, almost everything a badger eats benefits man. And there are many people today who don't count the benefits, just the fact that the badger is a very interesting coinhabitant of this earth of ours.

In some areas, the excessive digging of their burrows is detrimental and, like many species in some areas, their populations must be controlled. The future of the badger, however, has never looked brighter.

COMMERCIAL VALUE

In days when every man used a shaving brush, badger's guard hairs brought $85 per pound. Today with synthetic fibers and almost no demand for badger bristles, their value has plummeted. In 1976–77, 42,973 badgers taken, $38 the average price, $1,632,974 total. In Canada: 6,834 taken, $38.30 average price, $261,743 total. Value as a controller of rodents is incalculable.

STRIPED SKUNK, *Mephitis mephitis*
SPOTTED SKUNK, *Spilogale putorius and*
Spilogale gracilis

INTRODUCTION

Mention the word skunk to most people and there is an immediate reaction—they all know, or claim to know, about the skunk's malodorous, sulfurous musk. But many people don't even know that the musk comes from 2 anal glands nor do they know how it is discharged. They are surprised to learn that a skunk is the most common member of the weasel family and that all members of this family have anal scent glands, although none as well developed as the skunk's. To most people skunks stink, and that's all they want to

know. Even the German name for the skunk, *stinktier,* reflects the prejudice.

I was born in Paterson, New Jersey, but my folks bought the farm on which I was raised when I was 9 years old. On one of the very first trips to the farm, my dad and I stopped to visit one of our new neighbors, Frank Stop. While there, I met an old pensioner who boarded with the Stops, Milton Slater, who immediately became one of my heroes. Old Milt was a trapper.

I will never forget the time Milt took me behind the wagon shed and there hanging on the wall of the corncrib were a half-dozen or so skunks that he had caught. I had always been interested in wildlife of all sorts but particularly mammals. The wind ruffled the glossy black and white hair and the faint odor of skunk pervaded the air. To me it was a perfume. In later years, when I became skilled enough to be able to make a good income from trapping, the odor of skunk was always associated with that early experience.

I have never enjoyed killing anything and have never killed anything that I did not intend to use. Many people abhor killing any creature, yet they continue to eat meat killed for them by surrogate butchers. On the

The broad white stripes on this animal's black coat make this striped skunk easy to recognize.

farm, we killed pigs to have their meat to eat. We killed 50–60 chickens per week to be sold to others as meat, and it constituted a large part of our income. We killed animals, pets that we loved, when they became disabled with infirmities of old age or younger animals that became diseased or badly injured. We didn't call in the veterinarian to do such killing for us as most city folks do—we couldn't afford to. I trapped and killed fur animals not because I wanted to kill anything, but because during the Depression money was scarce for everyone and almost nonexistent for farm kids.

To me, the fondest memories of trapping were of being in the wilderness. Of walking through the birch forests that had turned the mountains to shimmering gold. Of smelling the sour-sweet odor of the wet leaves brought down by the November rains. Of being able to read the signs left by all creatures in the season's first snow. I thrilled to being in God's out-of-doors. I never looked forward to killing any creature; I did look forward to harvesting a part of the wild creatures that lived there in that out-of-doors.

I specialized as a fox trapper but always caught far more skunks than I did foxes because in most areas there were more skunks than foxes. By the law of averages, they got to the sets first. I haven't trapped in years and I probably never will again, but the odor of skunk is always associated with what I consider one of the most pleasant and impressionable times of my life. I don't want the full, concentrated odor of skunk at extremely close range but when the fall night's mist carries the odor of skunk, I still find it a "good" smell. At such times, I always tell friends, "Breathe deeply, it clears the sinuses." I'm not sure it does clear the sinuses, but it does bring back pleasant memories.

The original Latin name for the striped skunk was *Viverra mephitis,* which was given to this species by Schreber in 1776. *Viverra* is the Latin name for the civet family of Europe, which has similar musk glands. It was thought that the skunk also belonged to the civet family but this was disproved and changed later. *Mephitis* is the Latin word for "bad odor" and most people would agree that that name is apt.

The spots on a spotted skunk are really discontinuous stripes.

In the early 1800s, taxonomists properly classified the skunk as a member of the weasel family and the *Viverra* was dropped. *Mephitis* was given to this species as a family name. However, I think they went a little too far with the "bad odor" bit. After using various combinations of names, the skunk was finally named "bad odor, bad odor" or *Mephitis mephitis*.

The commonly used name, skunk, comes from the Abenaki-Algonquin Indian word, *seganku* or *segongu*. The Fox Indians of Illinois had a place that was located on the southwestern shore of Lake Michigan that they called Shee-gawk. This word meant "the place of the skunk" and is reflected in the name of the place today, Chicago.

The spotted skunk was originally called *Viverra putorius* by Linnaeus in 1758. *Putorius* is Latin for "a stinker." In 1875, the scientific name for the eastern spotted skunk was changed by Elliott Coues to its present form, *Spilogale putorius*. *Spilos* is the Greek

word for "spot," *gale* is Greek for "weasel," so the spotted skunk is forever known as the "stinking, spotted weasel." It's no wonder skunks are shy and retiring, people keep bad-mouthing them all the time.

The taxonomists did a little better by the western spotted skunk. It was named *Spilogale gracilis* by Merriam in 1890; *gracilis* means graceful.

The spotted skunk is almost always referred to as the civet cat by the fur trade and it is the name used for this skunk by many people. "Hydrophobia cat" is another colloquial name for the spotted skunk because of the high incidence of rabies or "hydrophobia" among the spotted skunks of some areas. This little skunk is also called the polecat but that name rightfully belongs to the European animal.

DESCRIPTION

There are 13 subspecies of the striped skunk, the differences between them being of geographical location and of weight and size. The average adult male striped skunk is 25–32 inches in total length. Of that length, 10–12 inches will be the skunk's beautifully plumed tail. The skunk stands about 6 inches high at the shoulder. The average weight for an adult male is 5 to 8 pounds. Skunks attain their greatest weight in October and an exceptionally fat male will weigh between 10 and 12 pounds. There is a record weight of 16 pounds.

Male striped skunks on average are 10 percent heavier than the females and about 6 percent larger in size.

There are 11 subspecies of the spotted skunk found north of Mexico. The total length of an adult male spotted skunk will be 16–22 inches, of which 6 to 9 inches will be tail length. The male spotted skunk weighs between 2 and 3 pounds. The female is both lighter in weight and smaller in size.

The startlingly contrasting black and white patterns of both skunks undoubtedly is meant to serve as a warning to other creatures of the skunk's presence. Most mammals are color-blind and as the skunks are primarily nocturnal, there is no need for color. The skunks need instant recognition for their own protection and to preclude their having to use their musk for defense.

The striped skunk is basically black, having stripes that follow a definite pattern of width and length. All striped skunks have a white stripe starting above their nose, running up the center of the head, stopping at the forehead. This stripe does not join with the stripe on the back.

The stripes that give this animal its name start as a cap on the top of its head. A "star" skunk has just this white cap that starts behind the ears and is about 2 inches square. In the fur trade, a skunk like that is called a "black" one and commands the highest price. The stripe that goes down the skunk's back may start as a single stripe from the center of the white cap or it may start as 2 stripes. On some skunks the 2 stripes extend just beyond the shoulders and that is referred to as a short stripe or one-quarter stripe. When the stripe extends to the hips, it is known as a half stripe. A "white" skunk is one where the stripe goes the full length of the back and continues down the tail. All striped skunks have some white hairs on their tails, if only on the tip. The stripes on the skunk vary from very narrow to very wide. The more white the skunk has, the less value it has because the white hairs have to be dyed black before the fur is used commercially.

The spotted skunk is not really spotted, but usually has 6 wavy, broken white lines. The spotted skunk has a short, wide, white stripe between its eyes and a white patch on each cheek below its ears. The two main stripes start on the top of its head but there is no white cap on the striped skunk. The stripes extend from the top of the head down to the hips. The next stripes usually start behind the ears and extend almost straight back to the abdomen. Or they may start at the shoulder and extend back to the hips and go up over the back. The third set of stripes may start under the breast, extend along the sides of the belly and go up over the hips to meet on top. Or they may start as vertical lines beneath the abdomen and go up over the back to meet on top. Occasionally a fourth set of stripes starts on the skunk's hind legs and runs up to meet the tail. All spotted skunks have some white on their tails, and most specimens have more than half of the tail white. The spots on the spotted skunk are the result of discontinuous stripes.

The underfur on the belly of both skunks is about three-quarters of an inch in length; on the back it is about 1½ inches. The underfur is very kinky, which provides good air-entrapment. Where the skunk's fur is black, the underfur is a gray-brown in color. Where the skunk's fur is white, the underfur is white.

The guard hairs on the belly of both skunks are between one and 1¼ inches in length. The guard hair on the back is 1¾ to 2 inches in length where the hair is black and 2¾ to 3 inches in length where the hair is white. White hair in the same area, on the same animal, of any type, will always be longer than black because of the reflectance of white and the heat-retaining properties of black.

The hair on the tails of both skunks measures between 4 and 6½ inches in length. When skunks are angry, frightened or are threatening, each hair on the tail will stand erect. The bushy tail of the skunks then appears to be larger than the skunk itself.

I can find no record of melanism in either the spotted or striped skunks. There are many records of albinism in the striped skunk and one in the spotted. Mutant striped skunks are also fairly common where the fur is reddish-brown or a sandy tan instead of black.

The skunks molt their fur just once a year, starting in April. The underfur is not replaced till early fall, although the guard hair is replaced by June.

The nose pad of both skunks is large and pushed forward on the head. The eyes are jet black and very beady. They reflect light when shined on.

The ears on the striped skunk are between one and 1⅛ inches in length, and about three-quarters of an inch in the spotted skunk. Although these are good-sized ears for an animal of this size, they are not conspicuous because of the length of the skunk's fur.

Both skunks have 4 rows of vibrissae, with the longest whiskers being three-quarters of an inch in length. The whiskers are comparatively soft. There are also a

A mutant striped skunk that has reddish-colored hair instead of jet black.

half-dozen cheek hairs and a few scraggly eyebrow hairs.

The dentition of both skunks is the same and the teeth are designated as 12 incisor, 4 canines, 12 premolars and 6 molars, giving a total of 34. The canine teeth are exceedingly sharp and in handling skunks I have had my fingers slashed as if with a razor blade. The skunks, in eating meat, cut off pieces with their rear premolars and molars as do dogs and cats.

Both skunks have 5 toes on each foot with no hair on the pads or between the pads. Skunks are digging animals and have the long, strong claws to prove it. The nails on the striped skunk's forefeet are three-quarters to 1 1/8 inches in length. Those on the hind feet are one-quarter to three-eighths of an inch in length. The claws on the spotted skunk's forefeet are one-half to five-eighths of an inch in length, while those on its hind feet are about one-quarter inch long. The nails of both skunks are longest in the spring after the winter's limited activity.

Skunks are famous the world over for their powerful scent glands. The scent glands are located on both sides of the skunk's anus, with the nipples protruding from the walls and situated about one-half inch from the external anus opening. Each gland is about one inch in length and contains about one tablespoonful of scent. Each gland is surrounded by powerful mus-

cles that contract, on demand by the skunk, and force the scent out through the nipples. To be used, the nipples are extended and pointed backward. The opening to the nipples is also controlled by muscles and the musk can be completely atomized and sprayed like thousands of microscopic droplets or it can be discharged in a stream.

There is no truth in the statement that skunks cannot spray when picked up by their tails so that their feet touch nothing. *Most* skunks will not spray when picked up in this manner but some will, as I know from personal experience.

The skunk's glands are constantly producing musk. A skunk, fighting for its life, can spray 5 to 8 good shots before depleting most of its supply. A very small amount can always be ejected. Within hours, the glands have produced enough to "shoot" again, although it may be 2 days or more before they are completely replenished.

The musk is an oily, sulfur compound known as butylmercaptan. It is usually yellow in color, although I have seen it yellow-green and whitish. It frequently contains actual chunks or "curds" that are yellow-white. The musk burns because the substance contains sulfuric acid. Butylmercaptan was a part of the poison compound that was made into the deadly mustard gas of World War I. It can cause temporary blindness if

Pelts of striped skunk (left to right): a "star" skunk, a three-quarter stripe narrow skunk and a "white" skunk. (Photo: Irene Vandermolen)

sprayed in the eyes, although I can find no record of permanent damage. Under favorable conditions, a few drops of this scent can saturate several square miles and humans can detect the odor at distances up to 20 miles.

DISTRIBUTION

Striped skunk found in all contiguous 48 states and all Canadian provinces except Newfoundland. Not an animal of extreme north, just spilling over borders of Yukon and Northwest Territories. Not found in Alaska.

Striped skunks have increased with opening up of North American forests. Although some skunks found in forests, they thrive on open land because more insects, their chief food, found there. Seldom found above 6,000 feet, although one once spotted at 13,800 feet.

Spotted skunk not found in New England, north-central or mid-Atlantic states, but found in almost all others, although rare in Montana, North Dakota and Washington. Few in British Columbia. Range slowly increasing into Wisconsin, Illinois, Indiana, Ohio and Pennsylvania.

TRAVEL

Skunks, unlike some other animals, do not lay claim to a particular area that they will fight to defend against others or their own kind. They are very tolerant of others, particularly the striped skunk. They do considerable traveling about within their home range, sometimes one to 2 miles per night, crossing and re-crossing the area as they search for food. Although they have favorite dens, when the weather is mild they may sleep any place that is dark and offers protection. The spotted skunk is more closely tied to a particular den.

It has been calculated, through radio-tracking, that both skunks have a home range of about 4 square miles. Within that area, there will be territory that will be used much more than another because more food is available there. Naturally the ranges of a number of skunks overlap. Areas that have high skunk populations may have as many as one skunk for every 5 acres, although each skunk may wander over as much as 160 acres. That would be about all the area could sustain and most areas have far less. Skunks will return home if moved no more than 4 or 5 miles.

LOCOMOTION

Skunks walk, canter and gallop. They walk about when they are searching for food. Often they stop to dig up a grub every 2 or 3 feet so they don't need to cover a lot of ground fast. When they are moving faster and farther, they canter. This is a rocking motion that produces the diagonal sets of tracks that are so common to the skunks and is one of the best means of identification. This gait is about 3 to 4 miles per hour. A striped skunk gallops or bounds at about 7 to

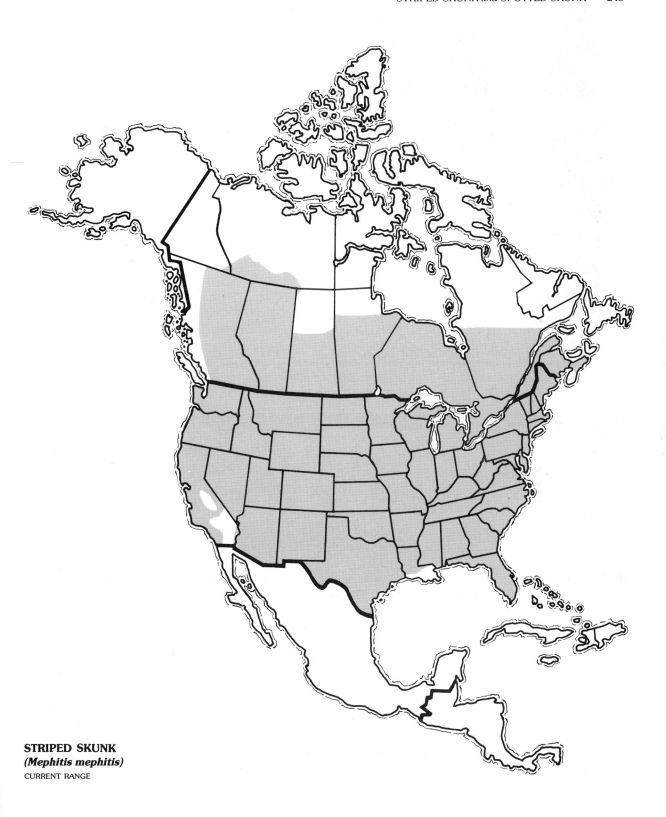

STRIPED SKUNK
(Mephitis mephitis)
CURRENT RANGE

SPOTTED SKUNK
(Spilogale putorius and Spilogale gracilis)
CURRENT RANGE

8 miles per hour, a spotted skunk at 4 to 5 miles per hour. They do not often run this fast nor can they keep it up for long. Skunks are quickly winded and froth at the mouth from exertion.

The striped skunk seldom climbs, although it can climb up wire mesh, boards, and so on. I have never seen one climb a tree. The spotted skunk is an excellent climber, being able to climb a tree with ease. It can climb down a tree headfirst. Many of the spotted skunk's dens will be up in hollow trees or up in the second story of a building. The spotted skunk can climb anywhere a rat can go. The striped skunk's long nails are a definite handicap in climbing. The spotted skunk can jump up, the striped skunk cannot.

Although this next bit of information more rightly belongs in the section pertaining to behavior, it is also locomotion.

The spotted skunk, when alarmed, will lift the rear portion of its body upward with its hind legs parallel to the ground and do "handstands." This is frequently done when the skunk meets up with its archenemy, the dog. I believe it is an attempt to increase its size for noticeability and as a threatening gesture.

I saw a spotted skunk do this handstand for the first time when I was 13. I was traveling with a group of high school students belonging to the Future Farmers of America. We were camped for the night in Iowa. Just before dark, a spotted skunk came into the camp-

A striped skunk that feels threatened has elevated its tail as a warning and also is in position to spray its attacker.

Striped skunks are very beneficial because they eat hundreds of insects each night and also eat snapping turtle eggs, as this one is doing.

ground to look for food scraps. None of us had ever seen a spotted skunk and when we gathered around, the skunk threatened us with a handstand.

In this position, the tail is either lifted aloft or carried pointing forward. The skunk can spray from this position but usually doesn't. It can hold this position for about 5 seconds. The skunk usually walks forward a step or two with its rear raised up, then backward a step or two before it drops down on all 4 feet. I have never seen a striped skunk do this, although there are several reports of it happening. Occasionally striped skunks stand upright on their hind legs, but only to see better.

Skunks can swim although they usually do not. Striped skunks swim with a splashing dog-paddle. The head is held high, which forces the body underwater. The tail tip is usually held out of water. Spotted skunks can swim, but rivers that are 600 feet wide have proved to be barriers to their range expansion. Such distances have not stopped the striped skunk.

FOOD

Before advent of totally enclosed poultry farms in mid-1940s, skunks often got into chicken coops to eat eggs and sometimes chickens. Spotted skunk more often the culprit because a better climber than the striped.

Striped skunks in all areas feed almost exclusively on insects. Grasslands of any type produce more insects than woodlands. Small cone-shaped holes in lawns mark where skunk has dug for insects. Complaints of skunk damage to lawns must be weighed against their beneficial destruction of insects. A cabbage patch infested with june bugs, for example, will be dug in by skunks and some cabbages will be uprooted, but far less damage is done by skunks than would occur if grubs had remained unchecked.

Skunks sometimes damage apiaries considerably by eating bees. Skunks attracted by dead bees thrown out of hive by worker bees each day. Hive preyed on by skunk often has grass at base raked away by skunk's long claws. When claw marks appear on hive it means skunk has scratched hive to provoke bees to attack, when it will kill and eat them. Some skunks' stomachs found filled with bees, one with 145. Apparently no ill effects from poison of frequent bee stings. One skunk had 65 stings in mouth and throat; another skunk had

35 stings on head and body and in mouth, throat, tongue and stomach. Stomach stings thought due to reflex action where bee's stinger exposed through movement of skunk's stomach walls. Damage to hives also means reduced hay and fruit crops, which rely on bees for pollinization. This trouble eliminated by placing hives on planks supported with pipe legs that skunks cannot climb. When eating fuzzy caterpillars, both striped and spotted skunk will roll insect across ground with their nails to break off poisonous bristles.

Insects in skunk's diet reach greatest proportions at height of insect populations in summer and fall. One fall study showed insects comprising 64 percent of skunk's diet and of which 33 percent were grasshoppers. A University of Michigan study of 1,700 skunks found insects made up 57 percent of total diet, which included grasshoppers, crickets, grubs, cutworms, weevils, spiders, millipedes, etc. Fruit next in importance at 17 percent, grain 12 percent, rodents 10 percent, birds and eggs 2 percent. Striped skunk eats twice as many insects as spotted skunk. New York study in autumn and winter showed fruit most important in diet but of course fruit had fallen from trees. Another study had combined vegetation most important at 31 percent of total diet.

Of mammals, meadow mice and young consumed most. Skunks have been seen to pounce on mice like cats. When eating mice skunk starts at head and pulls away skin as it eats. Most mice not sought out but blundered on in search for insects. In same manner skunk finds baby rabbits and nests of birds. Turtle eggs are a favorite food.

Skunks also eat carrion, which is often reflected in diet.

Spotted skunk eats four times as many mammals as the striped skunk. One study found mammals in 47 percent of the specimen diets, constituting 30 percent of total. Birds found in 27 percent of samples, constituting 8 percent of total diet.

One study with inordinate percentage of birds in diet concluded that as most of birds were blue-winged teals, mallard ducks and pheasants and these appeared after opening of hunting season, skunks must have killed wounded birds or eaten those which died after being wounded and escaping hunters.

Skunk predation on birds' nests can be identified by technique—while foxes carry eggs away from nest, and raccoons roll them out leaving shells nearby, and crows will puncture eggs and leave holes, skunks usually bite sides of egg and lick contents out, and crumpled shells are left in nest. A study of skunk predation on quail eggs found skunk responsible only for minimal loss to quail population.

When skunks live near farms rats and mice become most important food. Some farmers encourage spotted skunk to den nearby to control rodents. Rats and mice also most important in winter when other foods scarce. Spotted skunk habitually carries away prey before eating, often to den, so remains seldom seen.

Oregon study revealed crayfish often in spotted skunk diet; probably a locally learned habit as skunks do not eat them elsewhere, seldom spending enough time near water to learn.

The skunk is instrumental in this oft-repeated classic

Spotted skunk digging. Spotted skunks are very efficient predators of mice and rats.

example of the working of a food chain:

On a large marsh area in New York State that was being managed for waterfowl, all of the skunks were killed so they would not eat the ducks' eggs. The population of ducks plummeted because with no skunks the population of snapping turtles in the area skyrocketed. The turtles then ate the ducks. When the skunks were allowed to repopulate the area, they severely limited the numbers of the snapping turtles and the duck population increased.

BEHAVIOR

The activities of skunks, like those of most creatures, are determined by the season of the year, the time of the day, the weather and the availability of food.

Both skunks are most active primarily after dark. The striped skunk is the more crepuscular, often starting to feed in the early evening and perhaps not hurrying back to its den till after sunup. On overcast days in the breeding season, the striped skunks may be out in the daytime looking for a mate or just because they are hungry after the enforced denning of winter. The spotted skunk rarely comes out while it is light in the evening and is almost always back in its den before sunup.

Both skunks dislike heat and neither will be found out, if they can avoid it, on a hot day. Their black coats pick up and retain too much heat.

They will den up for extended periods of time during the most severe cold weather in the northern part of their range. Neither skunk is a true hibernator. In the southern part of their range, both skunks may remain active all winter.

The striped skunk prefers an underground den that is in well-drained soil. Many skunk dens are on hillsides to ensure this drainage. Ideal conditions for striped skunks are wooded hillsides bordering pastures or hayfields. The fields produce the insects they need for food, the hillsides the ideal den sites and the forest prevents the soil from freezing as deeply, making the dens warmer. The skunk carries lots of dead grass and leaves into the den to provide insulation. In limestone country, the skunks will utilize the crevasses in rocks as dens. Most of the earthen dens used by the striped skunks were originally made by woodchucks, red foxes and badgers. The striped skunk can and does dig its own den when it has to. The female skunks prefer the dens to have their openings beneath tree roots, rocks or some other obstruction to prevent them from being dug out by dogs or trampled by livestock. Most of the dens taken over by the striped skunks from woodchucks have two or more entrances. Dens dug by the skunks themselves generally have a single opening.

With accelerating urban sprawl, the competition for open land between wildlife and man becomes an increasingly decimating factor to wildlife. The wildlife that can adapt to man, like the skunk, is forced to do so. More and more skunks are taking up residence beneath houses, garages and other outbuildings. A deep basement wall under a house will prevent a skunk from digging beneath it but a house on a pad can be tunneled under.

Except when the female skunk has young in the den, the den is communal property. Any den that has ever been used by skunks in the past will be used again if there are any skunks in the area. The lingering odor of skunk makes any den smell like home.

In the wintertime striped skunks may spend 2 to 3 weeks at a time in a den, in a lethargic condition, sleeping but not hibernating. A rise in temperature, such as the thaw about January 20–22, will cause them to come out and search for food. When the temperature plummets again, the skunks will retire again to the den.

When a den is used communally, there is seldom more than one male present. Where 2 or more males are found in a den, usually both will be juveniles. Adult males will not tolerate other males in the same den. Ernest Thompson Seton found one adult male and 20 females curled up for warmth in one den. Allen found several dens with one male and 10 females. Usually, if a skunk is found to be alone in a den, it will be a male. The average number of skunks per den is between 2 and 3.

Skunks have been found to share their dens with other mammals. On many occasions both raccoons and opossums have been found, not only being present in the same den but curled up together for mutual warmth. Heavy frost at the entrance to a den is usually indication of several animals or more sleeping inside at that time.

During a very long, very cold, extended winter, some of the juvenile skunks may die of starvation in their dens. Adult skunks often have 30–50 percent of their total weight as body fat in late fall. This fat insulates them from the cold and is their food reserve during their enforced periods of inactivity. Skunks regularly lose 30 percent or more of their fall weight when they emerge from their dens in February and burn up even more chasing around in the breeding season when food is scarce. Skunks are at their lowest weights in late March. Any juvenile skunk that does not accumulate as much fat in the fall as the adults, and most do not, may die of starvation in late winter.

It has also been found that many juvenile striped skunks do not use an underground den in the summer as the adults do. They tend to sleep under brush piles, clumps of bushes or even out in fields of growing crops. This, of course, exposes them to more predation than the adults that sleep underground.

Spotted skunks have benefited from man's farming activities even more than the striped skunk. In most areas, the spotted skunk lives around farmyards, making its den in and around buildings, hay and straw stacks, grain storage buildings and woodpiles. Neat, tidy farms are not as attractive to the spotted skunk as are those that have old machinery lying about and some overgrown fence rows and ditches, which offer far more protective cover for the skunk. The ideal conditions for the den of a spotted skunk are that it needs to exclude light, to be unmolested by dogs or man, to be close to food and to have a safe passageway between the den and the food area.

Most spotted skunk dens are not in underground burrows. They will frequently be under, in, or up in the top of farm buildings. The spotted skunk is an excellent climber and can easily climb to the second floor of a barn to den beneath the hay.

Hay and straw stacks and shocks of corn make good spots for this little skunk. All the skunk has to do is to tunnel into the middle of these materials to have a warm, snug den. Abandoned farm machinery makes for good overhead protection, although the skunk will still have to dig an earthen burrow beneath it.

Both skunks are very persistent. They will try repeatedly to get at a food source and will usually succeed because of their persistence. They also remember what they have learned. Once they have discovered a way in, out, or around an area, they will immediately use the same route the next time it is needed.

The spotted skunk is more quick, more agile and more weasellike than the striped skunk.

The striped skunk has a very even temperament, preferring to avoid a confrontation but perfectly able to back up its threat when its bluff is called.

Both skunks offer any creature a chance to withdraw gracefully. When encountering any potential enemy, both skunks fluff out the hairs on their bodies and tails, doubling their apparent size. Their startling black-and-white coats advertise that they are skunks. They will retreat to a den if given the opportunity.

When the skunks are forced to confront their enemies, at a distance of about 12 feet they will raise up their tails partially so they look like horseshoes. They will pat the ground rapidly with their forefeet to draw attention to themselves. They may advance a foot or two, stamp their feet some more and retreat backward, raking the ground with the long claws on their front feet.

When the potential enemy gets within 10 feet or so, the striped skunk will act in the same manner, but now the tail will be raised till just the tip hangs down. When the skunk advances now, it will do so with its body bent so both its head and anus are pointing at the enemy.

The spotted skunk usually does its handstand act at this time, then drops to all 4 feet and presents its head and anus to the enemy. The skunks do not usually squirt their musk until the enemy is within 6 to 8 feet, although they can squirt it up to distances of 12 feet and even more, if the wind is favorable.

Many times I have gotten much closer to a skunk than 6 feet by moving slowly and allowing the skunk to see that I meant no harm. There were times when I have been able to release skunks from traps without their using their musk. And there were times that I have not, as my mother will readily attest. She was just never partial to the odor of skunk as I was.

I remember when I was about 15, walking home in the darkness of a clouded night and getting so close to a skunk in an alfalfa field that it sprayed on only one of my legs. Undoubtedly the skunk went through all of its threat gestures, but I never saw them or the skunk because of the high hay.

Another time, I was transferring a live skunk from a live trap to a holding cage and somehow dropped the wire gate on it. At that point, I couldn't see that skunk either because I got a full blast of musk right in the eyes.

Through a haze, I groped for an outdoor water hose to wash the burning fluid from my eyes. I then took several large cans of tomato juice and poured them over my head and washed both myself and my clothing in it. The tomato juice neutralizes the acid and is very effective. A solution of baking soda also works well. After taking a number of good showers, I was able to see and was almost presentable.

The skunk's scent is of no use against its major enemy, the automobile. More striped skunks are killed by autos than are spotted skunks because the latter is much faster moving. Many people have written that the skunk just expects the car to get out of its way, as most other things do. Believe me, most drivers do all they can to avoid hitting a skunk. I don't really believe a skunk expects a car to get out of its way, nor do I believe the skunk is blinded by the car's headlights, although the lights may confuse it. A car hurtling down the highway at 75–100 feet per second, 50–65 miles per hour, is just too fast for the slow-moving skunk to avoid. Most skunks killed by cars do not spray the car before it hits them. A reflex action after they have been hit causes the skunk to discharge its musk. The delay may allow the car that killed the skunk to escape without any musk on it. I've seen this happen a number of times.

SENSES

Smell very keen in both spotted and striped skunks and most food located by odor. Skunks rarely discharge musk when fighting one another, perhaps because with sensitive smell musk would be overpowering. When digging for grubs skunks clear noses frequently by sneezing.

Hearing also important; probably used in conjunction with smell to locate food.

Eyesight poor beyond 20–25 feet. Stationary objects go unnoticed.

Importance of sense of touch unknown.

Must have some tastebuds as skunks will not eat toads because of their skin secretions.

COMMUNICATION

The skunk's black-and-white pattern serves as a warning to all other creatures—that's communication. So are the other threatening gestures.

Adult skunks are not very vocal under ordinary conditions, although they do hiss when disturbed or threatened. When fighting they growl, snarl and, when injured, emit a high-pitched and very loud squeal.

The mother skunk with her young makes churring sounds somewhat similar to those made by a raccoon. She also makes a birdlike twitter.

Baby skunks make an almost constant clicking sound with their tongues. As they grow older, they develop a mouselike squeak.

Skunks usually defecate any place they happen to be at that particular moment. I have seen skunk scats placed on top of low stones, perhaps as an announcement of its presence. I have also had skunks deposit their scent on top of traps that they had dug out. That must have been done with contempt; the ultimate putdown.

BREEDING

I will always remember driving home one night after a brief snowstorm had dumped 3 to 4 inches of wet snow on the area. It was an ideal tracking snow and it was being tracked. I counted 14 sets of skunk tracks going along, crossing the road in a distance of 12 miles. I had to stop the car for a few minutes as one pair of skunks were copulating in the middle of the road. It seemed as if all skunkdom was out looking for a mate. It was Valentine's Day, February 14.

Starting in the last part of January, the testicles of the male become enlarged and he becomes restless. Usually the skunks come forth from their dens in the wintertime only if there is a thaw. After the first or second week of February, male skunks will be hunting for females, no matter how severe the weather.

The males in the North breed later than those in the South. In northwestern New Jersey, most of the skunks are bred between February 10 and March 20.

The largest adult male usually sleeps most of the winter, in one den, with most of the females that he will breed. The resident male will fight to defend his harem against the advances of any rival male. When skunks fight, they hit each other with their shoulders and bite at their opponent's front legs. The males will squeal loudly and sometimes, inadvertently, one will discharge its musk. The skunk that loses a fight is seldom killed but will be driven from the den.

The males travel widely searching for a female and some have been tracked for 2½ miles in a single night. The male's tracks lead to every den in the area that might contain a female. When a male's tracks do not come back out of the den, it is a good indication that there is a female in there, too. Occasionally tracks of both the male and the female are seen, showing where the pair is traveling together.

The actual copulation of skunks has been witnessed by a number of people. H. M. Wight described how one male seized the female by her neck with his teeth and lay down. With both skunks now lying on their sides, the male wrapped his front legs around the female's abdomen and with one of his hind feet scratched her vulva to excite her.

Another time the female was not in estrus and would not accept the male. He would grab her by the neck and the female would drag him around. Then he would drag the female around. Finally, the female elevated her tail and intromission was accomplished. The skunks fell on their sides as copulation continued. The male bred this particular female on March 1 and copulated with her for a total of 5 times by March 3. During the last copulation, the female became very antagonistic, attempting to bite the male. After they separated, the female would not allow the male to come near her again. Actual copulation took from 5 to 25 minutes.

Dr. V. J. Verts of Oregon State University reported some of the copulations he witnessed took place with the skunks standing in the normal mammalian fashion and took only 2 to 3 minutes. The copulation I witnessed was the same as Verts's.

The female skunk appears to have an estrous cycle of 9 to 10 days. There is no record of a female recycling if she is not bred during this period. One male has been seen to breed a number of females in succession. One male bred the 6 females that he denned with, one after the other, and they all gave birth on the same day. Out of 75 female skunks examined in Illinois, 72 were pregnant, proving that most females are bred.

Because of the number of repeated copulations, it is difficult to figure the exact gestation period for the striped skunk. It is between 61 and 69 days, with most of the young born in late April through mid-May.

There is one major difference in the two species of spotted skunks. The eastern species, *Spilogale putorius,* usually breed in April and have a gestation period of 55–65 days. The western species, *Spilogale gracilis,* usually breed in late September and are subject to delayed implantation. The blastocysts become implanted in the wall of the uterus in late March or early April and the young usually are born between April 21 and May 26. This gives this skunk a gestation period of 230–250 days.

BIRTH AND YOUNG

Before giving birth to her young, the female skunks carry large quantities of dead grasses and leaves into the natal den. No male is allowed near the den, and the female very aggressively keeps them away.

In giving birth to her young, the female often sits on the lower part of her back with the hind feet and tail turned forward. The young are born 10–20 minutes apart. The female assists the birth with labored straining.

As soon as the young one is out of her body, the mother skunk tears open the amniotic sac and cleans the baby skunk. It is able to nurse in about 20 minutes.

The normal litter for striped skunks consists of 6 to 8 young. The largest number of kits per litter was 18, as recorded by S. Howard Williams in his book, *The Mammals of Pennsylvania*. The female has a varying number of teats but the most that I have seen was 14.

Spotted skunks have smaller litters with a normal complement being 3 to 5. The largest number recorded was 7. The spotted skunk female has 8 teats.

Despite the differences in size between the adult striped and spotted skunks, there is not that much difference in the size of the young or in their development. The newborn skunks vary in size between 3 and 4 inches and weigh about one ounce. The hair covering the body is very short and sparse so that the wrinkled skin is easily seen. The skin is pigmented according to the hair color and pattern that the skunks will have as adults. The eyes and ears are sealed shut.

At 7 days of age the baby skunks have doubled their weight to 2 ounces. The quantity of the hair on the body has increased. The skin is still very wrinkled at 14 days when the weight has doubled again to 4 ounces. After 3 weeks the weight and size differences between the striped and spotted skunks increase but their development and activities continue apace.

At the age of 23 days the baby skunks can raise their tails, although they do not squirt musk as yet. The ears are now open and they pay attention to sound. The young are now starting to walk, although they are very unsteady on their legs.

The eyes of the baby skunks open on or around their 28th day. The baby striped skunks weigh about 9 ounces and are about 10 inches in total length. The spotted skunks weigh about 6 to 7 ounces and are about 8 to 9 inches in total length. At this age, the young skunks begin to make a chirping or twittering sound instead of the clicking noise they have made so far. The young skunks which had assumed the defensive position from the 23rd day, can now discharge minute quantities of musk. The teeth are irrupting through the gum lines. They now show interest in solid food but can't chew it as yet.

At 6 weeks of age the young are large enough to follow their mother on her nightly forays. The young spotted skunks are now about 12 inches in total length, the striped skunks 14–15 inches. The young are eating solid food and are in the process of being weaned. The skunk families usually travel single file. When the mother finds food, the young swarm about her to get their share. The young skunks will hit siblings with their shoulders to drive them away from the food they are eating. The young can dig in the earth and find a large proportion of their own food.

When the young have reached 3 months of age, the family breaks up. They will have almost continuous contact in their quest for food as they are not territorial. In winter, the young females may den with the mother, but the young males will be forced by the adult males to den alone or with siblings.

LIFE SPAN

Average life span in wild: 6 years, for both striped and spotted. Record in captivity: 10 years, for a striped skunk.

SIGN

Holes dug in search of grubs and beetles a common sign. Overturned cow flops and stones also indicate search for insects.

Scats of striped skunk shiny due to insect parts and disintegrate easily. Spotted skunk's scats contain more hair. Scats never deliberately concealed; sometimes deposited conspicuously on rocks.

Diagonal, loping tracks of striped skunk easy to recognize. Spotted skunk's tracks more closely resemble squirrel's; appear like off-center exclamation points, with tracks of hind feet showing in front of front feet. Hind foot of spotted skunk about 1¼ inches long by 1 inch wide; of striped skunk, about 1⅞ inches long by 1¼ inches wide. Front feet smaller than hind feet on both skunks, but front claws much longer.

Most prominent sign of all, of course, is odor of musk.

ENEMIES

Greatest enemy the farm dog—some will kill skunk even after sprayed with musk. Most dogs try to dig skunks out of dens. House cats reportedly kill and eat the smaller spotted skunk. Badgers an enemy in West, reducing skunk population when their own numbers are high. Badger able to enter most skunk dens and take most skunks in winter when skunks lethargic. Occupants of one skunk den provide badger with enough food for several weeks. Great horned owl a frequent predator of skunk, and one owl nest found with 57 skunk carcasses beneath it. Musk an ineffective defense against owls because of birds' poor sense of smell and owls' nictitating eyelid protecting eyes from musk. Other predators: black vulture (in Louisiana), turkey vulture (not a predator as it will eat but not kill skunk), eagles, coyotes, foxes, bobcats, cougars and fishers. Man takes largest number of skunks through trapping and because of automobile. Poison campaigns against coyote inadvertently killed thousands of skunks. Poisoned grain used against rodents also kills skunks when they eat poisoned ground squirrels and prairie dogs. Skunks poisoned directly in campaigns against rabies, which they occasionally carry. Also affected by tularemia, distemper and other diseases, and are bothered with fleas, lice, ticks, biting flies and mosquitoes.

I have advocated repeatedly that to control rabies in the wild we must have a universal federal law that re-

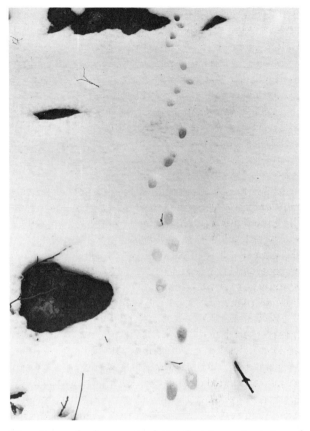

The diagonal placement of the feet in each series of tracks helps to identify these as a skunk's.

quires *all* cats and dogs to be inoculated. This would prevent many wild creatures from getting rabies from domestic animals and would prevent the domestic animals from getting it from the wild animals. Great Britain has eliminated rabies among all animals by this method.

The first case of rabies in skunks in North America occurred in 1826 when it was discovered in a spotted skunk.

In the mid-1900s, the tables turned and for the first time there was a higher incidence of rabies in wildlife than in domestic animals. Rabies is rare in the mountainous western states and New England. Rabies has been reported from 38 states.

Most animals and some birds have been affected by rabies but the fox and the skunk have been the two prime carriers. Rabies is most prevalent during March, April and May. Many animals that have rabies make no contact with man. Those that do confront man are usually aggressive. Such animals should be avoided or killed. *Any* animal that acts tame, out of character, should be avoided and not picked up and petted. It is probably diseased.

HUMAN RELATIONS

Most skunks are the best friends a farmer ever had. Their diet is almost entirely beneficial to man and his interests. Man's enmity toward the skunk is usually based on misinformation, the skunk's odor and the possibility of rabies. This latter can be a real enough threat, but there is no need to overreact, since the incidence of rabies in skunks is infinitesimal.

COMMERCIAL VALUE

Skunk pelts never priced high compared to other furs. In U.S., 1976–77, 174,628 striped skunks sold, $2.25 average price, $392,913 total. Spotted skunk: 41,952 sold, $4 average price, $167,808 total. Popularity of spotted and fun furs has inflated price of spotted skunk pelts, which had previously been less than for striped. In 1980 striped skunk pelts sold for $5, while spotted for $15. Skunks also valuable to agriculture as destroyers of crop-damaging insects.

RIVER OTTER, *Lutra canadensis*

INTRODUCTION

Lutra is Latin for "otter" and *canadensis* is the Latinized form for Canada, where this animal, the prototype of the North American otter, was first taken and described. This name was given to the otter by Schreber in 1776. Otter comes from the Anglo-Saxon words *oter* or *otor*.

Have you ever played the game of "What animal would you like to be?" My answer has always been the same. "I would like to be an otter." Other animals are bigger, stronger, faster and perhaps more intelligent, but the otter is the animal that lives life to the fullest and thoroughly enjoys itself while doing so.

Otters are large enough and strong enough so that they are seldom preyed upon by other predators. They are fast enough to escape from most danger and to capture their food easily. Their coat of fur is so warm, strong and durable that frigid weather seldom, if ever, bothers them.

They romp and play with reckless abandon, even the adults playing a good portion of each day throughout their lives. They work hard, play hard and stay in excellent physical condition. Is their life style the long-sought "fountain of youth"?

DESCRIPTION

The river otter is a highly specialized member of the weasel family. Its long, lithe, muscular body is streamlined for its frequent forays into the aquatic world of rivers, streams, lakes, ponds and saline waters.

There are 20 recognized subspecies of this otter found north of Mexico and while they may vary ever so slightly in size, color and in skeletal characteristics, the material given hereafter applies to all North American river otters. Otters are found throughout the world except for the continents of Antarctica and Australia. The Brazilian otter is the largest in the world and measures 8 feet in total length.

An average, full-grown male river otter will measure 45–55 inches in total length, of which 16–19 inches will be tail length. A truly large otter taken near Spiro, Oklahoma, in 1975, measured 60½ inches. The otter's legs are short and it stands about 7 to 9 inches high at the shoulders. The hind legs of the otter are longer than its front legs and the otter, like many of the weasels, usually has a flexed spine or hump at the hips. Fifteen to 20 pounds is an average weight, with 50 pounds being the record. Females are about one-third less in size and weight.

There are 5 toes on each of the otter's feet, each toe being armed with stout, sharp, nonretractable claws that are about one-half inch in length. The otter uses its forefeet to grasp and hold its food. The toes are joined to one another by a web of skin which greatly increases the foot area for extra propulsion in swimming. The otter's toe and sole pads are naked but the

The long, tapered body of the river otter reduces drag or friction when it is in the water.

webs and rest of the undersurface of the foot are covered with hair.

The otter has a small skull in relation to its body. The broadly flattened head tapers to the larger, long, sinuous neck. The tail is roundly oval where it joins the body, then tapers and flattens horizontally toward the tip. The otter's spine is exceedingly flexible and the otter can bend forward, sideways or backward to form a complete circle. The movements of an otter are best described as serpentine.

The otter's nose pad is large, conspicuous, flattened and dark in color. Its eyes are small, beady and black. They are situated high on the skull so that the otter can swim with most of its body submerged but just the eyes and the top of its head above the water's surface. The otter's ears are about three-quarters of an inch in length, are rounded and situated on the sides of the head below the crown of the skull. Both the nose and ears are valvular and are closed when the otter swims underwater.

The vibrissae of the otter are 2 to 4 inches long and very stiff. They are highly sensitive to touch and these whiskers may be of greater importance to the otter than its eyes when it is pursuing fish in clouded or murky water. They can be likened to sonar, receiving the vibrations from the otter's underwater prey.

The otter has 36 teeth—12 incisors, 4 canines, 14 premolars and 6 molars. The second and fifth incisors, in the lower jaw, are larger than the others and are situated behind them. The canines are long and sharp, ideal for piercing the slime and scales of fish. The molars are wide-topped for chewing.

The river otter's fur is truly luxurious. It is famed for its luster, strength and durability and is considered to be 100 percent on the furrier's scale, the standard by which all other furs are judged. The waterproof guard hairs on the otter's back are about one inch in length; the oily, woolly underfur on the back is about three-quarters of an inch. Both the guard hairs and the underfur are about one-quarter of an inch shorter on the otter's belly. There are so many thousands of underfur hairs to the square inch that the water does not penetrate to the otter's skin. A layer of fat beneath the ot-

The river otter's fur is waterproof and becomes as slick as grease when wet.

ter's skin provides a blanket of additional insulation. The otter is the most difficult animal to skin that I know of.

The overall coloration of the otter is a dark brown. The animal's appearance is almost black when its fur is wet and it is sleek beyond description. The cheeks, chin, throat and belly of the otter are a light tan color. Albinism is exceedingly rare among otters.

DISTRIBUTION

Population never high, although distribution once very wide. Today river otter may be found occasion-

RIVER OTTER
(Lutra canadensis)
CURRENT RANGE

ally in all contiguous 48 states, Alaska and all Canadian provinces, although extremely rare in Kentucky, West Virginia, Indiana, North Dakota, South Dakota, Nebraska, Kansas, Oklahoma and Arizona.

Never found far from water, even when populations are high. Does best in total wilderness or areas as wild as possible. Most humans in area unaware of otters' presence. Concentrations of one otter per 20–25 square miles of area is considered good population.

TRAVEL

The otter is an inveterate traveler. This is prompted by its efficiency as a predator. If the otter stayed in a single area, it would, or could, soon deplete its prey population.

The female is anchored to her den area for a period of about 3 months each year while she cares for the young but as soon as they are able to follow after her, she again travels her normal circuitous route.

Otters that I have watched have been on 7- to 10-day circuits, although some researchers have noted a time lapse of from 2 to 4 weeks before their otters passed through again.

Otters do not hesitate to cross land from one watershed to another. They strike out boldly overland to cut corners while traveling, such as going the short way across oxbows or up over ridges. One tame otter did 6 miles overland in 2 days. There are numerous records of otters taking shortcuts that entailed crossing land for distances of up to 15 miles. Some circuits could cover a distance of about 20 miles. In the summer, when food is plentiful, a circuit like this would be sufficient. In the wintertime the otters may be forced to travel over two or three times as much territory.

I was very disappointed in not seeing any otters in Okefenokee Swamp when I spent six days there on a canoe trip. Old-timers of that area explained to me that the otters came in to the swamp only when the weather turned cold enough to make the alligators sluggish or caused them to den up.

Otters do not migrate; the length of their travels is determined by the availability of food. Male otters that

The river otter is very intelligent and curious. It often stands erect as pictured here to see whatever interests it.

This photograph of a river otter on snow shows the animal's short legs and its long, lean, tapered body and tail.

are alone travel farther than the females. Most otters travel much more than usual during the wintertime and the longest distances, up to 100 linear miles, are sometimes traveled during the breeding season.

LOCOMOTION

When the otter walks, it does so in the normal mammalian fashion, moving the left front foot forward at the same time it moves the right hind foot and vice versa. When it travels faster, it has a loping, bounding action where the front and hind feet are used in unison. The front feet touch the earth first and then the hind feet come down in front of the spot where the front feet touched. The otter's head, neck, body and tail all undulate up and down rhythmically to keep balance. The long, strong tail is also used as a brace against the ground when the otter is curious and stands erect.

For a short distance, an otter can outrun a man. On hard-packed snow or on smooth ice, the otter turns in an even better performance. Under these conditions, the otter bounds forward three times and then flops forward and slides on its belly. On hard-crusted snow, the otter will slide forward about 15 feet, on glare ice it often slides for 20–25 feet.

C. W. Severinghaus and John E. Tanck, conducting research in New York State in 1947, had the opportunity to check the speed of an otter running and sliding across the icy surface of a lake. The two men were on a snowmobile and for about 10 minutes they timed an otter traveling at 15–18 miles per hour, according to their speedometer. What astonished them was that the otter maintained that average speed both while bounding and sliding. Otters would not travel this fast without strong motivation.

Otters often slide just for the sheer pleasure of it. They will slide down slopes covered with snow, grass, ice, mud or clay. The latter two slopes become increasingly fast as the water from the otter's fur makes them more slick and decreases friction. When the otters slide, they take a running start, fold their front legs backward along their sides, extend their hind legs straight out behind and "belly-flop." Striking the water headfirst, they plunge beneath the surface. Swimming back to shore, they scamper back up the bank to slide down again. They do this time after time for periods up to 20 minutes or more.

When otters swim, they have excellent control over the depth at which their body is submerged. When they swim on the surface, the top of their heads, necks, bodies and tails are above water. When swimming easily, they swim with alternating strokes of their hind feet, steering with their tails. At times they swim on or near the surface with an undulating motion so

The otter is more at home in the water than it is on land. This otter will catch most of its food while swimming.

that their heads, bodies and tails appear and disappear like huge snakes. On the surface an otter can swim at about 6 miles per hour and much faster if it has to.

To get top speed while swimming underwater, the otter not only uses its hind feet, and sometimes the front feet, but also flexes its body and tail strongly up and down. When it submerges its nostrils and ears close. To turn a tight curve while swimming underwater, the otter uses its tail as a rudder and its front feet to help pull the body around. Otters can swim at 3 to 4 miles per hour underwater.

When submerged, the otter's body automatically goes into brachycardia. This is a slowing down of the heart and pulse rate which reduces the circulation of blood so that less oxygen is extracted. Vascular restriction shuts off the blood flowing to the extremities so that what blood is circulating goes from the vital organs to the brain and back again.

Otters can go 3 to 4 minutes underwater before having to come up for more air. They have been known to swim one-quarter of a mile underwater before having to come up to the surface. When the ponds and lakes are covered with ice, the otters move about freely beneath it by breathing the bubbles of air trapped against the ice. If the water level has dropped, there may be a considerable layer of air between the ice and the water. If forced to, the otter can expel its breath underwater and then rebreathe the bubble that forms below the surface of the ice.

Victor B. Scheffer, a biologist with the U.S. Fish and Wildlife Service, records that one otter was caught in a fish net that was set 60 feet deep at Fish Bay, Alaska. They also occasionally get caught in lobster and crab traps.

In my 17 summers of guiding wilderness canoe trips in Canada, I often had otters swim ahead of me; sometimes they were alone, more often in family groups. The otters would tread water, holding their bodies upright and sticking up out of the water as much as a foot. Then they would either roll forward into a dive or just sink straight down out of sight and be gone. Many times the otters would travel ahead of us for a mile or even more. Sometimes the otters

River otters swim underwater by using their hind feet and undulating their bodies and tails.

swam on the surface, sometimes underwater, and at other times they loped along the shore for short distances. In the water the otters could appear and disappear with hardly a ripple. Otters can swim as well on their backs as they do right side up.

FOOD

Fish the principal food, most of of them the coarse forage fish not sought by fishermen, although for years trout and salmon fishermen have waged war on otter. Otter actually beneficial to trout by eating carp, suckers and sunfish that feed on trout eggs. Montana study found sunfish in 58 percent of specimens studied, suckers in 33 percent, sculpin in 21 percent, trout in 18 percent, crustaceans and aquatic insects in 41 percent, muskrats in 4.4 percent, beavers in 0.7 percent, minks in .01 percent. Figures add to more than 100 because otters would have more than one element in diet. A New York study showed minnows eat-

en 35 percent of the time, sunfish 12 percent, yellow perch 9 percent, trout 5 percent and catfish 2 percent. North Carolina study found carp, catfish, suckers, sunfish and blue crabs important in that order. Michigan study agreed forage fish make up bulk of diet.

Otters generally feed in shallow water, swimming on surface and searching beneath until spotting fish, when it dives. May also stalk underwater by approaching from rear and lunging forward to catch fish. Fish hiding beneath stones or in weeds otter will feel out with front feet. Fish like sunfish particularly easy to catch because they refuse to leave nest areas when guarding eggs, and keep returning to same spot.

When eating fish otters bring catch out on a rock, usually first eat fish head, tearing off scales as they eat and chewing with muzzle pointed aloft. Sometimes otters fish in teams, forming a phalanx in deeper water and advancing, forcing fish into shallow water where they can be caught. Generally catch small fish, 3–5 inches long, but can catch fish of 4–5 pounds, although not often, as larger fish are stronger and faster and hence harder to catch, and smaller fish are more abundant. Michigan researcher R. A. Ryder stated: "The fish preyed upon are in direct proportion to their abundance and in inverse proportion to the fish's swimming abilities."

Otters in captivity do not thrive on diet of all fish. In wild, fish comprise most of diet but they also eat other foods. Crayfish a favorite food (claws not eaten), and otter eats frogs, turtles and salamanders, as well as water snake, which like mongoose it teases into striking until it tires, when it is caught behind the head in otter's mouth. Other foods are water beetles, aquatic insects and larvae, mussels, snails, worms and, when on land, mice, small rabbits, and ground-nesting birds and their eggs. Also preys on muskrats if other foods scarce in winter, invading house or bank den. Muskrat no match for larger, stronger, faster otter. Sometimes decimating muskrat populations, other times having no effect, but overall muskrats play small role in otter diet. Beaver of less importance, although young killed occasionally. Adult beaver outweighs otter and has larger teeth and stronger jaws. Records exist of beaver chasing otters away and one of beaver killing otter.

River otters can outswim most fish. This one is feeding on a largemouth bass.

Otter able to catch minks in water but this rarely happens. Also feeds on ducks, swimming beneath and pulling them underwater by the leg. Also takes ducks wounded or killed by hunters before being retrieved. Emil Liers of Minnesota has trained otters to retrieve ducks. Otters eat some vegetable material, often eating grasses, probably like dogs, for therapeutic value. Also eat some tubers, pond weeds, algae, shoots, blueberries, etc.

Otters do not store food for future and do not kill more than they can eat as do minks and weasels. When food plentiful thin layer of fat builds up but high level of activity, and concomitant high rates of digestion, elimination and metabolism, keep them from becoming fat. They eat 3 pounds of food per day but little more than one pound at a time. Food passes through body in about an hour; two otters tracked found to defecate 8 times over 1 1/2 miles.

BEHAVIOR

Frogs are also a favorite food of the river otter.

Otters are undoubtedly the most playful of all the mammals with the possible exception of the porpoise. An otter, whether old or young, alone or with others, spends a good part of each day playing. It slides, it swims, it rolls about in the water and on land in sand, mud, grass or snow. After otters eat, they clean themselves by rolling about. When they come out of the water, they violently shake the water from their fur and then dry themselves by rolling. Most otters have special rolling places that they use habitually every time they are in the area, year after year. These spots are usually 5 to 6 feet in diameter and are used frequently enough to keep the grass flattened.

Otters will often use objects as toys. A lone otter may bring up a small stone from the bottom of a pool. It will play with the stone by tossing it about and diving after it to bring it up again. Sometimes it will catch and carry the stone on the top of its head.

Young otters, or family groups, play tag, hide-and-seek and have wrestling matches. They are sociable animals and enjoy grooming one another, carefully working over each other's skin. Otters do not concentrate in large groups mainly because there are never large groups to mingle with. On rare occasions, two family groups have been seen together. Otters seldom fight among themselves.

Emil Liers got his first pair of otters in 1928. Much of what we know about otters is a result of his having raised hundreds of them over the years. His formulas for feeding otters are recognized as being the best.

People who have raised otters have found that they become very affectionate and even seek out human company. Otters also make friends with dogs very easily, a friendship that seems to be thoroughly enjoyed by both animals. Pet raccoons and pet otters get along well. Otters, like raccoons, are examples of perpetual motion and either one can make a shambles of a home in short order. It is best to have special cages built for these animals. Otters spend about half their time sleeping and half awake. Tests have proved that otters have a very good memory. Curiosity is a sign of intelligence and the otter is both curious and intelligent.

The rolling about that otters do, aside from the pleasure of it, is also a form of grooming. Otters are very clean, rolling about and washing themselves frequently. They have very little odor, although they do have scent glands, as do all members of the weasel family.

SENSES

Smell of greatest importance, with much of their food found by odor. Liers's otters trained for hunting could find as many game birds as could dogs.

Hearing acute. Liers's otters responded to various sounds over considerable distances.

Quick to catch motion but stationary man not recognized as danger. Possible that otters see better underwater than above. Eyes highly reflective when light shined on them, evidence of numerous light-sensitive rods in the eyes, which would give otter good vision in dark or murky water.

Touch important to otter because like raccoon feels for its food in mud or beneath rocks. Also involving touch are whiskers that can detect vibrations of prey's movement in muddy water.

COMMUNICATION

Otters are extremely vocal. They chatter, make a guttural grunting, chirp like a bird, snarl, scream, shriek, hum and hiss.

The birdlike chirp of the otter is the one I have heard most frequently. It is used when it is inquisitive, contented and as a means of keeping in touch with other otters. When an otter wants to give a warning or when it becomes angry, it makes a humming sound that rises in both pitch and intensity. The otter that is feeding contentedly makes a sound like a pig grunting. When really angry or frightened, the otter will snarl and hiss and may give out with a really loud, piercing, shrill scream.

When angered, the otter will also discharge a milky liquid from its two anal glands. This liquid can be squirted for several feet and may be a small stream or vaporized. The odor of the liquid is most unpleasant but does not have the acridity of skunk scent. Nor does the otter scent burn or last. Clothing upon which the scent has been squirted will be relatively free of the scent within 24 hours.

This scent is not really an effective defense and is used more as a calling card. Otters mark their "rolling places" with this scent. They also twist up tufts of dead grass and deposit their scent thereon. During the breeding season, both the male and female otters make and mark more of these grass twists than at other times.

BREEDING

River otters are not usually sexually mature until they are 2 years old. There is one record of a captive otter being bred when she was one year old and bearing 4 young.

Otters travel more than usual during the breeding season of March and April. They travel as far as possible and leave as many scent signs as they can. Captive male otters usually become very restless and even vicious during this period.

It is not known definitely if otters pair up or if the males, or perhaps the females too, are promiscuous. The consensus of opinion is that the otters pair up and my observations bear this out.

The male's testicles usually descend into his scrotum during the latter part of November. Breeding may occur from December to April but the peak period is March and April. Young females that are coming into their first estrus are usually the first to be bred. The older females are usually bred within a day or so after giving birth. Because otters are subject to delayed implantation, the gestation period fluctuates widely. Liers had one female otter that had two gestation times between 9 months 18 days and 12 months 15 days.

Otters play together at all times so that there is no apparent increased courtship activity. Copulation usually takes place in the water with the male coming up behind the female and seizing her by the neck. He then bends his body down around and under her tail. Where otters have been seen to breed on land, the male curls up, wrapped around the female. Intromission is accomplished with vigorous thrusting and continues for periods of time from 15 to 25 minutes. Copulation will take place a number of times.

BIRTH AND YOUNG

Most baby otters are born in February through April over most of the continent. In the Deep South some of the young may be born as early as January.

Where possible, the female otter prefers to have a snug den in which to have her young. Abandoned beaver houses are favorite den sites. There is even one record of a female otter and young sharing a house with a female beaver and her young. I am sure this setup was not the beaver's idea.

Otters will also use muskrat houses, muskrat bank dens and even woodchuck burrows that are close to water. Lacking these facilities, the otter will use cavities under a stream bank, hollow logs or openings under a tangle of tree roots along the riverbanks. In large swamp areas where there are no nearby banks of earth, the otters will twist tall reeds and grasses together at the top, making a shelter that looks like a miniature Indian wigwam. These shelters are probably the most unsafe because of the danger from flooding.

The average litter of young otters is 2 to 3. Occasionally there will be 4 young, very rarely 5 and only one record that I can find of 6. E. T. Hooper and B. T. Ostenson, doing research in Alabama, recorded one female that gave birth to sextuplets.

At birth the otter babies are toothless, blind and helpless. They are covered with a black, silky coat that is not waterproof. They are between 7 and 8 inches in overall length and weigh between 3 and 4 ounces. To warm her babies, the mother otter curls around them doughnut-fashion and then puts her head over the hole.

The female otters I have examined had 4 nipples lo-cated on the abdomen just forward of the hind legs. Otters' milk is rich, being over 24 percent butterfat and 11 percent protein, according to Muller Ben-Shaul. Liers claimed that it was closer to 40 percent butterfat. At any rate, the young grow very rapidly. At one week of age they weigh about 6 ounces; 10 days later about one pound.

At 5 weeks of age the young otters' eyes open and about this time they begin to shed out their baby fur and to acquire the waterproof coat of an adult. Whereas before this time the young otters have only tumbled about in their darkness, now they begin to play with one another and with their mother.

The male otter is driven away from the natal den right after the female gives birth and is bred. The male may travel about or he may remain in the vicinity of the den. After 6 to 8 weeks he is allowed to rejoin the family, although some males do not. There are several records of male otters raising the young after the female was killed, if the young were weaned. Weaning takes place between the sixth and eighth weeks.

Young otters do not know how to swim and must be taught by their mother. It is not that they have a fear of the water, but of the unknown. The swimming lessons start when the young are 7 or 8 weeks old. The female will try to coax the young ones into the water by swimming about and calling to them. Sometimes she will let the babies hold onto her fur as she swims and then will sink underwater, forcing the babies to swim. If all else fails, she will grab the young by the scruff of their necks and carry them or throw them into the water.

Young otters have difficulty staying right side up when they are first placed in water. After a few minutes, they get the hang of it and can swim about. After several practice sessions, the young gambol about in the water and are as at home there as they are on land.

When the young otters are 2 months old, the family leaves the den and begins their typical nomadic life style. The young otters learn to hunt for themselves by imitating their parents. Their clumsy first efforts result in their catching only slow-moving prey but in a short time they, too, can catch fish. Most of the young otters stay together as a family group throughout their first winter, drifting off on their own before the mother gives birth again.

LIFE SPAN

Liers reports female otter still breeding at age 17, and had one that lived to record age of 23. In wild, potential life span is 15 years.

SIGN

Tracks most common sign in mud or snow, being 3 inches across. Five toes and claws conspicuous, but webbing between toes may not show. Tail leaves drag mark in snow and occasionally in mud. Entire body registers drag mark in snow over 4 inches deep.

Otter slides not commonly seen. Places where otters exit water used over and over, developing "otter steps" where they have placed their feet. "Rolling spots" also conspicuous because of their size.

Otters on fast stream banks seldom have mud to record their presence. On rocky stream banks scats are most common sign, usually in 2 or 3 segments, about ¾ inch in diameter, prominently displayed on beaver lodge roofs, beaver dams, rocks, logs, even on rowboats. Scats consist mainly of fish scales and bones and ectoskeletons of crayfish. Do not hold together and disintegrate into shiny mass in rain.

ENEMIES

Comparatively free from predation because most potential predators cannot catch adult otter. Bobcats, lynxes, coyotes and wolves kill otters if found on land. Great horned owls kill baby otters occasionally. Relatively free from ectoparasites due to nomadic natures and fact they seldom use a den and there is little contact between otter families.

Worse enemy is the poison ingested with contaminated fish poisoned by toxins in agriculture and industry. Dr. James Jenkin of the University of Georgia found otter tissue with 9 times more mercury than was acceptable. He claims mercury came from coal-burning industrial plants. Otters also found with toxic levels of PCB, DDT, and cesium. These poisons thought to be major reason for rapid decline of otter in East.

Fish on which otter feed killed by gold mining, strip mining, channelization of streams and anything that promotes silting and clouding of streams.

HUMAN RELATIONS

Years ago, otters were ruthlessly pursued by fishermen. They were trapped wherever found and driven from much of their native territory by pollution and destruction of their habitat by man's burgeoning population. Today, the otter is on its way back. It has reappeared in Oklahoma, has been imported to Colorado and remnant populations in such states as New Jersey have been given complete protection. If the otter can be restored to many of its former haunts, it will be a victory not only for the otter but for man. It will mean that man has reversed the destructive abuses of civilization which have threatened the eventual extermination of both species.

COMMERCIAL VALUE

IAFWA statistics, 1976–77: 26 states reporting, Louisiana first with 11,900 otters taken. U.S. total 32,846 taken, $53 average price, $1,740,838 total. In Canada: 19,932 taken, $69.04 average price, $1,376,188 total.

Otters, like other furbearers, where plentiful, are a renewable resource. Still, I feel that the otter's greatest value is as an entertainer—no one can watch the antics of otters and not smile.

SEA OTTER, *Enhydra lutris*

INTRODUCTION

The sea otter is a truly unique mammal. It is the largest member of the weasel family and the only species in the genus *Enhydra*. It is the only member of the mustelids that does not have the anal musk glands for which this family is so famous. The sea otter is the most specialized weasel, being adapted to life in a marine environment, as well as being the smallest marine mammal.

Linnaeus named the sea otter *Enhydra lutra* in 1758. *Enhydra* is a Greek word meaning "living in the water," *lutra* is the Latin word for "otter." This name is most apt because the sea otter spends most of its life in the water, feeds there exclusively and only occasionally comes out on the rocks or land to sleep or to escape the fury of storm-pounded surf.

Formerly it was thought that there was a northern and southern subspecies with an intergrading between the two where their ranges overlapped. No one could ever pinpoint the exact range nor the area of intergrading and the latest research shows that there is only the one race in North America, *Enhydra lutris lutris.* There is a second subspecies, *Enhydra lutris gracilis,* found in the Kuril Islands of Asia.

The sea otter and the river otter are basically alike with both probably evolving from a single land-based form. It is estimated that the sea otter is of Asiatic origin and evolved into a marine species about 5 million years ago.

DESCRIPTION

The average weight of an adult male sea otter is about 63 pounds, that of a female is 46 pounds. The greatest weight recorded for a sea otter is 101 pounds for a male taken in Prince William Sound, Alaska. The top weight recorded for a female is 72 pounds.

The average total length of an adult male sea otter is 53 inches, the female 48 inches. The greatest total length I can find recorded for a sea otter is 66.3 inches. The tail of a sea otter is 11–13 inches in length. The tail is flattened horizontally and has no taper for seven-eighths of its length; the distal tip is then sharply pointed.

The forelegs of the sea otter are short and on land the animal stands 8 to 9 inches high at the shoulder. There are 5 toes on each forefoot with just the tips of the digits exposed. At first glance the toes appear to be amputated. Wildlife biologist Karl W. Kenyon claims that the digits move about inside the pad "like fingers inside a mitten." Although these forefeet appear very awkward, because of their shape, they are in reality very nimble. As our hands stay warmer in mittens than when the fingers are separated, as in gloves, this mitten feature conserves the otter's body heat. The entire undersurface of the forefoot is bare. The forefeet are about 3 1/2 to 4 inches long and the same dimension in width.

The sea otter's hind legs are longer than its front legs, giving it a very humpbacked stance. Its spine flexes upward in front of its hips, rising as much as 12 inches above the ground when the otter is on land.

The hind feet have evolved into flippers, although they can be bent forward in the normal fashion of land mammals. The hind feet are more than 6 inches in length with the outside toe, corresponding to our little finger, being the longest. The toes are connected by a skin webbing extending to the very end of the digits and are covered with stiff hairs except for the last digit which is bare. The nails are nonretractable.

The teeth of the sea otter are also unique, being de-

Sea otters spend most of their time swimming on their backs. This one was photographed at Point Lobos State Park in California. (Photo: Len Rue, Jr.)

signed for crushing instead of shearing. Even its canine teeth are rounded. The sea otter is the only carnivore that has just 4 incisor teeth in the bottom of its mouth. The 2 outside, lower incisors project slightly forward while the 2 middle incisors project slightly to the rear. This modification is designed to aid the sea otter in extracting the meat from the shells of its various prey species.

The sea otter has a total of 32 teeth—10 incisors, 4 canines, 12 premolars and 6 molars. All of the premolars and molars are comparatively flat-topped to facilitate the crushing of the various types of shellfish that make up the bulk of its diet.

Researchers are always commenting upon the low number of cavities found in the teeth of mammals that are eating the food for which they were designed. Old sea otters, often found dead from starvation and exposure, usually have their teeth completely worn down and sometimes the jawbone itself is worn. Any excessive wear on a mammal's teeth will cause the enamel to wear down, exposing the softer dentine beneath, and allowing the formation of cavities. All this evidence points up the fact that the sea otter's teeth are lagging behind the evolution of the animal's body and its diet. It could be that millions of years ago the sea otter was a more agile mammal that fed mainly upon fish instead of the shellfish that is the staple in its diet today.

The fur of the sea otter is truly luxurious, although it is rated only 80 percent on the furrier's scale of 100 percent for the river otter. The furrier's scale is based upon the sheen, softness and durability of the fur, the toughness of the hide, and so forth. Sea otter pelts have always brought a much higher price than the river otter pelts, not only because they are larger but because they have always been rarer and this creates a higher price.

Adult sea otters are larger in size and weight than river otters but their pelts are always much longer than the living animal. This is due to the extreme looseness of the skin. A sea otter grasped by the skin on the back of its neck can turn around and bite the hand that holds it. Sea otters have a very loose fold of skin across their chest which extends under what would be the armpits. This fold of skin forms pouches in which the sea otter stores food that it gathers on the ocean floor. The sea otter can carry 20 or more 3- to 4-inch sea urchins in these pouches at one time. When a sea otter skin is stretched, the pelt is often measured at more than 7 feet in length. It was this false impression of tremendous size that caused early biologists, working just from study skins, to claim erroneously that the live sea otter was more than 6 feet in total length.

The sea otter has the densest fur of any mammal that I know, with about 600,000 hairs to the square inch. This is twice the number of hairs of the fur seal, which also has a very dense, luxurious coat of fur. It has been figured that an adult sea otter has over one billion hairs total.

The few stray guard hairs are about 1 1/4 inches in length while the underfur is a uniform one-inch length. The hairs of the underfur are elliptical in shape, tapering from a narrow base to a larger diameter in the middle and tapering again to a narrow tip. This shape traps millions of air bubbles in between each hair near its base. This trapped air provides efficient insulation against the cold seawater and also provides highly effective buoyancy. Healthy, clean sea otters do not sink even when dead. Baby sea otters have to learn to dive beneath the surface of the water; they are as buoyant as corks.

Sea otters are the only sea mammals that do not have a layer of blubber beneath their skins to provide warmth; their warmth is dependent upon the layer of trapped air. They are susceptible to pollution and soiling and the main reason is that even the slightest film of oil will destroy the air-entrapment quality of their hair. When oil coats the individual hairs, or the hairs become soiled or matted, water is conducted directly to the otter's skin. The sea otter then becomes chilled and quickly succumbs to the cold. Water transfers heat 20 times faster than air.

Sea otters are also unique in that they do not have a drastic molting of their fur. Molting is such a gradual shedding of individual hairs that sea otter pelts are

While swimming on its back, this sea otter has to turn around from time to time to see where it is going. (Photo: Len Rue, Jr.)

considered prime at all times of the year. However, more than twice as many hairs are shed in August than are shed in February.

The basic coloration of the sea otter is a dark brown to almost black. If the underfur is looked at closely, it will be found to be a smoky gray near the skin, shading to the visible dark brown at the tips.

All sea otters have light-colored heads, those of the young being yellowish, the older adults almost white. The older the animal, the whiter the head becomes and the more the white extends over the neck and shoulders and down and around the front legs and feet. Males are lighter and have more extensive white coloration than the females of the same age.

I can find no record of either albinism or melanism in any of the literature on sea otters.

There are 8 rows of strong, long, down-curving vibrissae. The length and number of an individual's whiskers vary greatly. Most sea otters have lots of whiskers that measure between 2½ to 4½ inches in length. On some sea otters, particularly the females, the whiskers are rather sparse and appear to be badly broken. I do not know whether this is caused some-

how in feeding or during the breeding season when the males grab the females by the nose.

There are a few stray whiskers between the nose and the eye. A strong cluster of hairs stands upright above the inner corner of each eye.

The nose pad of the sea otter is large and black in color. The noses of almost all of the females are badly scarred by the males during the breeding season. These scars are so prominent that they can be seen at long distances with binoculars and are used by biologists as a means of identifying individual females.

Sea otters have dark brown eyes with a darker pupil. The eyes of the adult males are darker than those of the females or of the pups of either sex.

The ears of the sea otter are located low on the skull below the eye level. The ears are a little over 1¼ inches in length and are sharply pointed and resemble those of the sea lion. They are particularly noticeable when the sea otter's fur is wet and slicked down.

DISTRIBUTION

Found discontinuously in arc extending from Santa

SEA OTTER
(Enhydra lutris)
CURRENT RANGE

Barbara islands off California, along Oregon, Washington, British Columbia, Alaska's southern coast, Alaskan Peninsula, Aleutian Islands, west to Russia's Commander Island, and south to Kuril Islands. Not found where coasts icebound in winter. Their coastal waters kept free of ice by surf and warm Japanese ocean currents.

TRAVEL

Sea otters occupy the areas of shallow coastal waters. River otters may occasionally make excursions into this saline environment, but the sea otters do not go into the freshwater rivers. Sea otters do not have annual or even seasonal migrations. Under ideal conditions, it has been found that as their population grows, their range expands at the rate of about 2½ miles per year. In some areas, such as Amchitka Island in the western Aleutians, overpopulation has resulted because the sea otters would not cross the wide open ocean barrier to the islands beyond. Yet, at some time in the past, some of the otters must have traveled long distances by design or by accident. There was a resident population on the Pribilof Islands when they were first discovered.

Researchers claim that no tagged sea otter has ever traveled farther than 5 miles from its initial capture point of its own volition. In their daily feeding activities, most sea otters travel less than a mile, with many feeding in the immediate area where they sleep.

LOCOMOTION

Sea otters are strong swimmers, although they are not as fast as the seals or as agile as the river otters.

In swimming about, the sea otters customarily swim on their backs, twisting their heads occasionally to see where they are going, like a person rowing a boat. Propulsion is provided by the hind feet making alternate strokes. Now the exceptionally long fifth, or outside, toe is put to good use, dipping deeply into the water. The forefeet are folded across the chest, palms down. In this position the sea otter travels at a little less than 2 miles per hour. Rarely do the otters swim on their bellies while on the surface.

When swimming beneath the surface of the water, the sea otter swims with the undulating motion of its body with its tail and hind feet extended backward as seals do. The wide flat body, the extended flipper hind feet and the broad tail make for a particularly effective propulsion. They can swim at a much higher speed underwater and for short periods sea otters have been clocked at a top speed of about 6 to 7 miles per hour. The forefeet are not used for propulsion underwater but they are employed in making sharp turns. Most frequently the forefeet are folded or used in holding food to the chest while the sea otter swims up to the surface.

In diving for food, the time that the sea otters remain submerged depends upon the depth of the water and the amount of food available. Sea otters feed mainly in shallow water at depths of from 30 to 50 feet and occasionally they will feed as deep as 190 feet. The greatest depth recorded for a sea otter was 318 feet. This individual drowned in a crab pot set at that depth.

The sea otter usually remains below the surface of the water for 50–80 seconds. In 10–20 feet of water, the otter may need as little as 20 seconds to secure its food and return to the surface. Longer dives are made to escape from its surface enemies and the maximum submerged time recorded for a sea otter is between 5½ and 6 minutes.

The experts agree that these times are about maximum and yet it seems to be a short period for a truly marine mammal. I have seen beavers remain submerged for 8 minutes 54 seconds and naturalist Edward Warren has seen them remain submerged for 15 minutes. The sea otter, like the beaver, is subject to cardiovascular restriction when it dives so that the blood is shunted from its extremities to only the vital organs and the brain. The sea otter's heart beats at one-tenth of its regualr rate while submerged. These measures greatly increase its diving capabilities.

On land, the sea otter walks, clumsily, rolling its body from side to side, using its feet alternately. This rolling gait is made to accommodate the otter's exceptionally long-flippered hind feet. The curvature of the spine is almost twice the height of the top of the otter's head from the ground. The tail is held out straight or may drag on the ground. The sea otter walks at about 2 to 2 1/2 miles per hour.

When alarmed, the sea otter adopts the bounding gait that is commonly used by all the members of the weasel family. The 2 front feet are used in unison as are the hind feet. The hind feet come down on the exact spots that the front feet have just vacated. The spine is arched high and then extended horizontally to drive the body forward at a speed of 6 to 8 miles per hour. The sea otters cannot keep up this gait for more than a few minutes but they don't have to. Sea otters are seldom, if ever, found more than 150 feet from the water's edge.

FOOD

Efficient metabolism and fast digestion rate allows rapid processing of food to maintain body temperature, between 99° and 100° F. in ocean habitat at from just above freezing to about 50° F. They eat 20–25 percent of body weight in food every 24 hours. Food can pass through otter's body in as little as 3 hours. They cannot fast, having no reserves of body blubber, and must eat frequently.

Diet depends of availability of foods. On Alaska's Amchitka Island, fish was found to be first item of diet, mollusks second, and sea urchins third. In most areas sea urchins are the mainstay and fish a minor food. Sea otter not a fast swimmer and not well adapted to catching fish, catching them with forefeet while seals, sea lions and river otters catch them with their teeth. Sea otter never eats fish whole but tears them into chunks and chews thoroughly before swallowing. They feed on slower, sluggish fish such as globefish and red Irish lord, others being too quick for otters to catch.

In deep water feed on squid and octopus, also torn in chunks and chewed.

Sea otters' feeding on abalone caused controversy along coast of lower California, and entire areas near San Simeon now devoid of abalone between predation by otters and commercial fishermen. Fishermen, restricted to taking abalone of larger size, have illegally killed otters in some instances. California's Department of Fish and Game, although recognizing that otters feed heavily on abalone, blame the devastation on increased numbers of commercial fishermen.

Sea otters also eat snails, sea cucumbers, crabs (including king crabs), clams, chitons, limpets and mussels. Primary food remains the sea urchin, and when large numbers are eaten, otters' teeth and bones turn purple from a chemical in urchin. When large, gravid sea urchins available otter needs about 200 per day. Areas of overpopulation of otters have been depleted of large urchins and otters forced to eat smaller ones, whose food value is so small otter needs 6,500 to meet daily requirement of 3,000 calories. Where otters are overpopulated mortality is high among juveniles, unable to get enough nutrition. Occasional gastric perforations from swallowed urchins add to problems.

BEHAVIOR

The manner in which a sea otter feeds upon shellfish is unique. It is one of the few subprimate creatures in the world that consistently uses a tool.

When the sea otter starts to feed, it dives down to the ocean floor and gathers up sea urchins, clams, mussels, and so forth, which it stores in its skin chest pouch under its forelegs. It also selects a flattened rock of about 2 to 6 inches in diameter, which it also brings up to the surface.

Rolling over on its back, the sea otter stabilizes its body by extending its hind feet sideways. The otter then places the rock on its chest or upper abdomen, selects an urchin or a mussel and, using both its front feet, pounds the prey on the rock very rapidly. The apparently toeless front feet may be an adaptation to prevent the otter from bashing its own toes while crushing its prey's shell. While pounding its prey on the rock, the sea otter usually arches its head backward and often closes its eyes. This keeps its head out of the way and also keeps the splashing water out of its eyes. It usually takes an average of 9 hard whacks to crack the shell of a large sea urchin and up to 35 whacks to crack the shell of a mussel or clam. Dr. George Schaller, director of conservation for the New York Zoological Society, reported one sea otter opened 54 mussels by pounding them on a rock, 2,237 times in 1½ hours. When feeding upon abalones, the otter uses the rock underwater to crack the shell of the abalone while the shellfish clings to the rocks.

While feeding, the otter frequently stops eating and grooms itself by washing its chest, face and belly. Often it holds the rock in place on its chest and rolls over in the water, getting rid of the shell fragments and washing itself at the same time.

When the otter must dive again for food, it usually stores its rock in the pouch under its left arm. Most sea otters are right-handed, which has been proved by their consistent use of the right forefoot for most major activities and the use of the left forefoot to hold food and the rock. Alaskan sea otters do not use stones as those in California often do because they eat more fish, which they can crush with their teeth.

In feeding upon sea urchins, the sea otters are beneficial to the seaweed industry on the West Coast. The sea urchin's main food is different types of seaweed and their control allows a larger commercial harvest of the plants.

Sea otters are quick to learn of a food source and to adapt to its harvest. Along the California coast, as on most warm water coasts, thousands upon thousands of aluminum beer and soda cans have been thrown into the ocean. Octopuses flow into the submerged cans through the key-tab hole. Somehow the sea otters know which cans contain octopuses. Researchers have noted that the sea otters are correct in the selection of the cans that contain octopuses in 5 out of 7 times. The sea otters bring the cans to the surface, tear off the tops with their teeth and extract the octopuses.

Sea otters do not eat on land. Captive sea otters will accept all the food they can carry, store all they can in their pouches and carry what they can in their mouths and go into the water to eat it.

Sea otters usually swim on their backs, they eat while lying on their backs in the water and they usually sleep on their backs in the water. The otters frequently shade their eyes from the sun with one of their forepaws while floating on their backs. Kelp beds are favored spots for the sea otters because the thick masses of vegetation provide protection from marine predators. The sea otters drape strands of kelp across their chests while they sleep and this prevents them

Sea otter with stone and shellfish on its chest. (Photo: Len Rue, Jr.)

Sea otters often sleep and feed in kelp beds because the long water weeds keep them from drifting away. (Photo: Len Rue, Jr.)

from difting about. They sleep with their chins resting on their chests.

In areas where there is no kelp, or where a storm pounds the surf on the rocks, the sea otters will seek shelter on the shore and sleep among the grasses or in the lee of a protective rock.

When the sea otter is not feeding, it spends most of its time grooming itself and fluffing out its hair. Many observers mistakenly think that the sea otter is scratching or searching for external parasites when they see the animal constantly working over its coat. As mentioned before, the sea otter's life depends upon its coat retaining its fluffiness and air-entrapping qualities.

Sea otters are not territorial and they are highly sociable and gregarious. They like one another's company and often gather in large numbers where the feeding is good. Groups as large as 300–400 have been seen together while one record group of about 1,000 sea otters was seen in the Bering Sea in Alaska. In Alaska, the otters are often censused from planes flying low while the observer takes photos of the groups. Where food is plentiful, the otters will frequently share their food with one another, particularly a female with a large juvenile pup. It is only under starvation conditions that the large males drive the young from food, or take a choice morsel from a young one. There are no reports of sea otters ever fighting among themselves.

The friendliness of sea otters is found in those in captivity, too. Most captive sea otters will quickly come to accept food from the hands of the researchers who work with them. Even wild sea otters learn to accept food from the hands of friendly humans when they are fed regularly. Karl Kenyon tells of a wild sea otter that became so insistent about being fed fish scraps that it followed the researchers about on land begging for food. Given a piece of fish, the otter always returned to the water before eating it.

Sea otters are also extremely curious. They frequently raise themselves upright in the water to get a better look at whatever has caught their attention, and will stand upright on land as do the river otters. They also do this to watch for danger.

The sea otter is very restless when it is out of the water, sleeping in short fitful snatches. It constantly awakens, raises its head to glance around before dozing for a few minutes more. The sea has become this otter's element and only there does it feel safe enough to be able to sleep for relatively long periods. But even in the sea, the otter spends more time dozing for short periods than it does in deep sleep. They sleep most soundly during the late night and early morning hours. Sea otters are inactive during most of the hours of darkness.

At daybreak the otters start to feed and continue their diving and feeding until their hunger has been satisfied. As much as 50 percent of an otter's time, during the daylight hours, is spent feeding. After the first feeding, the otter usually grooms and dozes for 3 hours or more. They have a short feeding period again about noontime. An extended feeding period occurs in late afternoon and into the evening hours.

SENSES

Smell well developed and old-time hunters well aware that otters must be approached upwind. Aleuts who hunted otters would not cook or light a fire lest any odor betray their presence. Hunters who had walked along beach could be detected by otters for as long as 5 days.

Eyesight very good and perhaps most important sense. Uses vision to search for both food and danger.

Search for food also involves whiskers, constituting sense of touch. Fact that whiskers of otters feeding among rocks are often broken off signals otter may use whiskers to search for prey among rocks or that they function like a cat's to determine distance between rocks.

Has some sense of taste, showing preference for some foods over others. Eats starfish reluctantly, apparently disliking taste.

COMMUNICATION

When the sea otters are feeding, they give out with a series of low, soft grunts. These are sounds of contentment and may also be used by the group to maintain contact with one another. Sea otters inhabit areas where dense fog is common and are often unable to see one another.

The sea otter also gives a squeaking E-E-E-E-E-H. This is a high-pitched sound that can be heard over long distances. It is usually made to protest the actions of another otter. Threatened otters scream. Baby ot-

ters have a piteous whine when they become separated from their mothers. The otters also grunt, make a barking sound, coo and hiss.

BREEDING

Sea otters apparently have no set breeding season as copulation has been observed by Kenyon in every month except October and December. Most breeding activity was observed in June through September. Newborn pups have been found in every month of the year, although most seem to be born in the months of April, May and June.

Sea otters are polygamous, although there is no gathering together of a harem by the male as is common among the fur seals. Males will seek out receptive females and have been seen to be given a hard whack by those that are not in estrus.

The difference in the size of the male and female sea otters makes sexing them easy when a pair is seen together. When the male is swimming on its back, the bulge of the penis and scrotum is visible. One of the few times that a male consistently swims on his belly is when he is searching for a female.

Courtship may take place on land but copulation always takes place in the water. When a receptive female is found, the male will stroke her with his front feet and nuzzle her with his nose. If the female is on land, the male will keep pushing at her until he gets her to enter the water. Then he seizes her by the nose with his teeth instead of by the back of the neck as many animals do. Copulation is accomplished in the regular dorso-ventral position, the male curving about the female. As they roll about in the water, one or both of the otters are submerged. The male may maintain his hold on the female for an hour or so. Copulation takes place a number of times over a 3 day period. Yearling pups have been seen crying for their mothers because they feel abandoned during the breeding period. It is the female that breaks off the relationship. She usually waits for the male to dive for food and then she swims away before he surfaces.

Sea otters are subject to delayed implantation and

it is generally conceded that the blastocysts do not become fastened to the walls of the uterus for 7 to 8 months. The total gestation period is thought to be about 8 or 9 months up to one year.

BIRTH AND YOUNG

The actual birthing of the young usually occurs on land, although some researchers have seen females, newborn young and the discarded placental material out in the kelp beds. The young of porpoises, whales and others, which are born in the water, are born tail-first. Sea otter pups may be born in either the head-first or tail-first position. Fur seals, which are adapted to a more aquatic life than the sea otters, give birth to their pups on land, headfirst, so it is highly probable that most sea otter pups are also born on land.

The sea otter female gives birth to a single pup. There are several records of females carrying twins but no records of actual double births. It would be extremely difficult for a female to take care of 2 young because she carries the young about for almost a year.

At birth the sea otter pup weighs between 4½ to 5 pounds and measures about 17 inches in total length, of which 6 inches is tail length. Its eyes are open and it is covered with brown, woolly fur. A female sea otter is an exceptionally fine mother and devotes her life to her pup, never leaving it except to dive for food. The pup cannot sink in the water because of the air trapped in its dense fur. Its mother leaves the pup in the calm water of a kelp bed or behind a protective rock. Then while the mother lies on her back to feed upon the food she has just gathered, the pup nurses at either of her 2 nipples located on her lower abdomen. If danger threatens, the female clasps her baby to her chest with her forefeet and swims away on her back or dives below the water. Occasionally the female carries her baby in her mouth.

At 5 months of age, the sea otter pup weighs about 12½ pounds and measures about 23 inches in total length, of which 8 inches is tail length. By this time the pup is capable of swimming strongly and can dive to gather some of its own food. It is still nursing and get-

ting the bulk of its food from its mother. The pup may occasionally take food from whatever male is feeding in the immediate area. The pups are very playful and play with their peers and with their mothers. They also seem to get great enjoyment from swimming up to a sleeping adult male otter and pouncing on him. The adults do not retaliate but resignedly swim away to a more secluded spot.

Female sea otters usually carry, care for and nurse their young for a full year or more. Lactation restricts estrus so that the females only give birth every second year.

The young sea otters at one year of age weigh about 25 pounds and measure 28 inches in total length, of which 10 inches is tail length. By the time the young reach one year of age, they are weaned and shortly thereafter separate from their mothers to go on their own. This is the most vulnerable period for the young otters. This is the age group that suffers the highest mortality in areas where the sea otters are overpopulated and food has grown scarce.

At 2 years of age, the sea otters weigh about 42 pounds and measure 32 inches in total length, of which 11½ inches is tail length. The young sea otters reach sexual maturity between 2 and 3 years of age.

LIFE SPAN

Under normal conditions, life span is 12–15 years. Record: 21 years. Does not do well in captivity if in fresh water.

SIGN

Little sign other than animal itself because it spends most of time in water. Grass worn down at favorite "hauling out" spots. Tracks may be found on beach. Scats found occasionally near grass nests, but otters usually void in water.

ENEMIES

White sharks eat otters along California coast, believed responsible for high mortality of otters in 1957 and 1958. Killer whales also believed to prey on otters. Sea lions also known to be predator.

Three observations charted of bald eagles attacking pups, eagles waiting until mother dives for food, leaving pup floating on surface. Nests of eagles in otters' areas show otters comprise as much as 10–20 percent of eagles' diet, much undoubtedly resulting from scavenging on young otters dead from starvation.

Major limiting factor is expansion of range and decimation of food supply, bringing starvation. Bacterial enteritis result of stress by starvation. Starvation-weakened otters particularly vulnerable to severe storms pounding them against rocks and to extreme cold.

Pollution, notably oil spills, kills any otter it coats. Oil penetrating otter's fur eliminates trapped air insulation and even healthy otters die from cold.

No external parasites, but do have intestinal parasites such as hookworms.

HUMAN RELATIONS

From its earliest discovery by Spanish missionaries in California in 1733 and by Georg Steller in 1741, the sea otters were relentlessly pursued for their fine furs. Fortunes were made, and hundreds of human lives were lost, in the pursuit of the sea otters. The constant persecution continued and even intensified after the United States bought Alaska from Russia in 1867. The low point arrived for the sea otter in the early 1900s. The sea otter at that time became almost extinct.

Concern for the future of the fur seal is what saved the sea otter. In 1911, federal legislation was written to give the fur seal full protection. Thankfully, a single paragraph, added as an afterthought, included the sea otter. The sea otter population in North America was believed to be about 200 animals at that time. By 1935, the sea otter was discovered to have come back from the verge of extinction and was beginning to expand its range in the Aleutian Islands. It was estimated that there were 2,000 sea otters then in the Aleutians.

Through natural range expansion and many transplants by biologists, the sea otter is now found over most of its original, natural range. Sea otters reproduce slowly with an estimated 7 to 10 percent annual population increase.

In 1968, Amchitka Island, the heart of the sea otter population, was chosen as a test site for an underground atomic blast. Some 400 sea otters were live-trapped and transplanted. Despite this, more than 1,000 sea otters were killed by the blast.

When the state of Alaska took over the management of the sea otter in 1959, several carefully controlled harvests of sea otters were made in areas where overpopulation was causing high mortality through starvation. This was good game management.

In California, the sea otters are still expanding their range and numbers. To prevent poaching and the exploitation of an emerging population, a group called Friends of the Sea Otter was formed and is based in Big Sur, California. The group is doing an excellent job where the sea otter still needs complete protection.

COMMERCIAL VALUE

Skins have always brought high prices, several selling in early 1920s for $2,500 each. Alaska's Fish and Game Department began harvesting otters on management basis in 1962–63; skins held until 1968 for first legal sale of skins in years: 920 sold at average price of $158.60. Probably many would have brought higher prices if not held so long in cold storage. Total of sale: $141,000, the best skin bought for $2,300 by Neiman-Marcus of Dallas.

In January 1969 518 newly harvested skins were sold, $258 average price, highest price $1,100.

Efforts continue to transplant sea otters to possible habitats, and future looks brighter now than when man first began to hunt them. California now has 1,600–1,800, Washington, Oregon and British Columbia have small but viable populations, Alaska has about 120,000, the Soviet Union about 10,000.

ORDER:

CARNIVORA

FAMILY:

FELIDAE

The lynxes, lions, leopards, jaguarundi, tigers, bobcats, mountain lions, ocelots, cheetahs, all belong to the *Felidae* family. With the exception of the cheetah, all have retractable claws. Their long canine teeth are adapted for grasping prey. The carnassial teeth are used for shearing off meat suitable for swallowing. These animals do not chew their food.

All of the felines are lithe, fast and muscular. The cheetah is the fastest-running animal in the world. Although most of the cats are very fast for a short distance, they soon tire when hard-pressed. Most of the felines dislike water, although the tiger loves to swim. Lions sometimes hunt during the early morning or late afternoon, most of the others hunt only under the cover of darkness. The pupils of their eyes contract vertically during the daytime and expand in the dark. Lions may hunt in a large group, the rest are usually solitary. Again, with the exception of the lions, the other cats are secretive and furtive. Mountain lions and bobcats can live close to man for many years and never be seen.

MOUNTAIN LION, *Felis concolor*

INTRODUCTION

The reports continue to come in. They always have. Now, however, there is substance to them. People have reported seeing the mountain lion all over the country for years. These reports generally came in during the spring, summer and fall, but not during the winter when tracks in the snow could substantiate the claims. Now the tracks are there, too—proof positive that America's most elusive cat, one of its largest predators, is again being seen in areas from which it had been extirpated.

This lion's Latin name was given to it by Linnaeus in 1771. *Felis* is Latin for "cat" and *concolor* means "one color," which is in keeping with the adult lion's unspotted coat. This animal is the recipient of more commonly accepted names and more colloquial names than any of our other native mammals. It is also called cougar, panther, painter, king cat, mountain screamer, mountain devil, puma, catamount, American lion, Leon, tiger and lepardo, as well as having many more English, Spanish and Indian names, more than 100 in all.

The mountain lion, also called cougar, puma, painter, panther, American lion, screamer and other names.

DESCRIPTION

The lion is the largest member of the cat family found in the United States. The jaguar, now thought to be extirpated from the United States, but found from Mexico south, is a larger cat. An average adult male mountain lion is about 7 feet 8 inches in total length, stands 26–31 inches high at the shoulder and weighs 150–176 pounds. An average adult female is about 7 feet long and will weigh 100–125 pounds. The largest male measured by biologist M. E. Musgrave, of the 600-plus lions that were taken in Arizona, was 8 feet 7½ inches. The heaviest male mountain lion ever weighed was shot by J. Ramsay Patterson in Yavapai

The female mountain lion, shown here, is very graceful and lithe. (Photo: Irene Vandermolen)

County, Arizona; it tipped the scale at 276 pounds.

For many years, the number-one record lion was the one shot by Theodore Roosevelt in Colorado in 1901. The number-one head now in the *North American Big Game Records* is the lion shot by Garth William in Garfield County, Utah, in 1964. This head scored 16 points. The skull was 9¼ inches long by 6¾ inches in width.

Mountain lions have a disproportionately small skull for the size of their body and an exceptionally long tail. The tail is 30–36 inches in length and about 2½ inches in diameter. The long tail is a necessity. It acts as a counterbalance when the lion changes direction at high speed or when it leaps.

The lion has 5 toes on each forefoot and 4 toes on each hindfoot. The dewclaw, or the thumb, on each of the forefeet does not show in the tracks as it is 2 inches higher up on the inside of the leg. The claws are retractable and are slightly over one inch in length on the front feet and slightly less than one inch on the hind feet. They are very sharp and are kept sheathed while walking.

The 30 teeth of this lion are 12 incisors, 4 canines, 10 premolars and 4 molars. The last premolar and the molars are high-ridged, self-sharpening teeth known as the carnassials. The lion does not chew its food but scissors off bite-sized chunks that can be easily swallowed, with the carnassial teeth. The cat's tongue is very rough and with it small shreds of meat can be licked off the bone.

The mountain lion has bright yellow eyes with large dark pupils that do not contract. Its ears are about 3 inches in length. Its nose is dark on the sides and has a pink pad. The vibrissae, or whiskers, are in 5 rows; the hairs being either black or white with the longest being about 3 inches in length. Young lions have a conspicuous vertical black eye stripe that is about one inch long that comes down the head toward the eye. This stripe fades with age, completely disappearing in older individuals.

The hair on a lion's back is about one inch in length but very dense. The hair on the belly is about 2 inches long. The lion's coloration varies from a light, sandy tan to a dark, russet-red on the back. The hair is darkest on the center of the back but cannot really be called a stripe. The hair continues to darken on the top of the tail, terminating in a black tip. There are several records of completely black, melanistic mountain lions being seen in Florida but I can find no records of albinos.

There are two conspicuous white patches on the lion's face on both sides of its nose. Its chin, throat, belly and the insides of all its legs are also an off-white color.

Mountain lions are lean animals, having a slab-sided appearance. Their shoulder blades are prominent and project above the back when the cats are stalking, while their bellies touch the ground. The skin on the

Notice the stocky head and body on this large male mountain lion.

This mountain lion is lying on a rocky ridge where it can watch the valley below for signs of prey or danger.

sides of the lion's belly hangs down and when the lion moves, it sways sideways. As the lion puts on weight, the excess fat is stored here.

The mountain lion is a very strong animal. Musgrave tells of a lion dragging an 800–900-pound horse a distance of 35 feet. Stanley Young tells of a lion in Texas dragging a dead 600-pound heifer out of a spring hole and then pulling it some distance up the mountainside. A friend of mine saw a lion pick up a 125-pound deer and jump up to a 6-foot ledge with little effort. There are many records of a lion seizing a deer, calf or other similar animal by the brisket and walking off with it with the prey's four legs sticking straight up in the air.

DISTRIBUTION

Lion once had largest range of any land mammal in Western Hemisphere, being found from Atlantic to Pacific coasts, from about 56° north, to Tierra del Fuego. With expanding population in U.S. was extirpated over most of the eastern two-thirds of this continent,

except for Florida and Canada's New Brunswick. Today mountain lion found again in many of its old haunts: in Yukon Territory, British Columbia, Alberta, Saskatchewan, Manitoba, Ontario, Quebec and New Brunswick. Washington, Oregon, California, Idaho, Montana, Wyoming, Nevada, Utah, Colorado, Arizona, New Mexico, Texas, and Arkansas have sizable populations. Some in Louisiana, Mississippi, South Dakota and Nebraska. Recently seen in Florida, South Carolina, North Carolina, Tennessee, Virginia, West Virginia, Massachusetts, Maine, Vermont and New Hampshire. One unconfirmed sighting in New York's Adirondacks in 1972. Several young mountain lions killed recently in Pennsylvania, but these thought to have been escapees from captivity.

TRAVEL

Mountain lions are inveterate travelers as they are predators in need of large game. Hunting in one area constantly would deplete the game. Male lions often travel as much as 20–25 miles in a single day. They

MOUNTAIN LION
(Felis concolor)
CURRENT RANGE

have home areas that may be 30–60 square miles. The males usually hunt and then hole up for the day and later continue on their circular journey. The time that it takes them to complete the circle is entirely dependent upon the weather and the availability of food.

The territory of the males is too large to be inviolate and several males may utilize the same area, although they usually do not do so at the same time.

Females with young usually have their dens as their focal points. The female, and later the young, will hunt out from the den, returning to it afterward. The female's area may be 5 to 25 square miles. This smaller-sized area means that each male's territory may overlap not only that of several other males but will assuredly overlap the territory of at least 3 or 4 females.

LOCOMOTION

A mountain lion is built for stealth, not for endurance. It usually pads along at an easy walk. It walks, then watches, then walks and watches again. More game can be seen by watching and so the cat does more of it than walking.

If the lion has a definite goal, it trots. When it does, its flabby belly sways from side to side.

The lion is a sprinter. It will stalk as close to its prey as is possible; slowly, silently it will take advantage of both the wind and every bit of concealing cover it can find. Lions prefer to be within 25 feet or less of their prey before they begin their charge. They usually are able to pounce on their prey within 2 or 3 bounds. An all-out bounding dash of 200 feet leaves the lion badly winded. When it bounds, it can often cover 15–20 feet horizontally.

I watched a mountain lion stalk and chase a red fox. The cat had gotten within 50 feet of the fox before being discovered. The fox ran flat-out with the lion making 15–16-foot bounds right behind it. Although the red fox started first and was running at a speed of at least 35 miles per hour, the lion closed the distance easily and would have caught the fox if it had not dashed into dense brush. The lion then lost all interest in the chase, flopped on its side and drew in great gulps of air.

For a distance of 100 yards the lion can usually outrun any of the trail hounds. Mountain lions have been known to jump 12–15 feet up to a rock ledge or tree limb. Frequently, after being treed, a lion will bound out again. Musgrave has seen them jump from a height of 60 feet, land on their feet and dash off with no apparent injuries. There is one record of a mountain lion in the Adirondack Mountains, years ago, jumping off a rock ledge onto a deer 60 feet below. Ordinarily lions do not leap on their prey from ledges or trees, but they have been known to do it.

When pursued by hounds, the lion dashes off at its fastest speed but then uses its wits to try to escape. It will jump from one large rock top to another, jump across small chasms, run up a tree and jump to a higher rock ledge or jump from a ledge to a tree below. The lion seldom stays in the first tree it goes up. Usually, when approached, the lion will jump out, only to tree again shortly. This may again be repeated. Usually by the second or third tree, the lion is exhausted and only wants to stay out of the reach of the baying, yapping hounds.

Although lions don't like water, they do swim. They have been known to swim across icy rivers to avoid being pursued. Their short coat does not absorb a great amount of water.

FOOD

Mountain lion likes plenty of meat, and will kill one deer every 7–10 days for an average of 50 a year. Lion predation on big game beneficial to those species by keeping game scattered, preventing concentration and destruction of range by overbrowsing.

Lion feeds mainly on deer and elk, which it catches by traveling upwind until prey is spotted, then stalking closer with belly touching ground and tail tip twitching, with shoulder blades protruding upward. When it has approached as close as possible gathers both hind feet beneath body, a sure sign of attack because power for first spring comes mainly from hind legs. Lion is on prey in seconds, holding on with 4 feet while it bites through prey's vertebrae, or lion may reach under prey's neck and crush windpipe, or snap neck by catching nose with paw and pulling head back.

Prey is sometimes able to dislodge lion by jumping around or brushing it off on a tree branch or in heavy brush. Wild burros able to defend themselves successfully against lions by biting and kicking.

Lions often bypass injured or sick prey in favor of healthy prey to attack. One observer reported lion killing 3 healthy mule deer while leaving one deer, crippled by gunshot, unmolested. Another found lions killed more prime elk than other elk, perhaps because prime bulls stay higher and longer in the mountains before winter arrives and are exposed to greater pre-

dation, and because they are more often solitary, without other elk to watch for danger. Many are weakened after breeding from fighting and lack of food.

Mountain lion a more efficient predator than African lion; mountain lion successful in 8 of 10 attempts to catch prey, African lion catches prey in one of 10 attempts.

Most lions bypass livestock, but those that attack livestock prey on them repeatedly and must be destroyed. Livestock easier to kill than wild game. One lion killed 192 sheep in one night; 17 lions near Zion National Park, Utah, killed 1,250 sheep in 2 months. Such lions are the exceptions. Lions also feed on rodents: mice, kangaroo and other rats, tree and ground squirrels, snowshoe hares, jackrabbits, cottontail rab-

Mountain lion with a deer it killed. The mountain lion's main food is deer. The average adult cat will kill 50 deer a year.

bits, beavers, muskrats and porcupines. Lion usually hooks claws under porcupine's chin and flips it onto its back, attacking unprotected chest and stomach— those who can't execute the technique get quills in their paws and muzzles. Birds in family of grouse and ptarmigans, and their eggs, also eaten. Records of lions killing and eating coyotes, foxes, bobcats and other mountain lions. Cannibalism may be more common than previously known, and may be a population control factor. Insects, mostly grasshoppers, often eaten, and an occasional frog, toad and snake. Dying salmon eaten. Vegetation a small part of diet, but grasses sometimes ingested. Will eat carrion when food is scarce, but prefers fresh meat.

BEHAVIOR

Mountain lions usually hunt in the early morning and late evening rather than after dark because these are the times when the prey they feed upon are eating. After a mountain lion has made a kill on a large game animal, it usually drags it into cover or under the low branches of trees. It prefers not to eat out in the open.

Lions eat 8 to 12 pounds of meat per day, although they often gorge themselves with much larger amounts. The cats usually open the chest or belly area of the prey and eat the organ meats first. They do not eat the stomach or its contents but often roll these out of the carcass intact. When finished eating, the lion will cover what is left of its prey and it usually covers it completely. Dead leaves, grass, sticks and even logs will be pulled into a mound. Flat rocks weighing as much as 15 pounds have been used to cover the lion's cache. Then the lion retires to some protected area nearby to rest and sleep. The lion will revisit the carcass until it is eaten or the meat spoils. Even weeks after, whenever the lion is again in the area, it will revisit the cache spot even though nothing is left but the bones.

Lions do need water to drink, although one that has just made a kill will drink blood.

The mountain lion has to rate as one of the most furtive of all North American mammals. Many people have spent their lifetimes living in the same areas as the big cats yet have never seen one. I had spent years photographing in lion country before seeing one, and that was just seconds before it was hit by an automobile as it tried to cross the road near the Grand Canyon back in 1967.

As are most of the cats, the mountain lion is extremely curious. Many are the people who have had a lion follow them, not to attack them but merely to see what they were doing and where they were going. In most instances, the people never saw the lion but found it disturbing to see the lion's tracks on top of their own when they backtracked on their own trail. There are a number of records of the lions watching people by sitting at the edge of the light from their campfires. There is also one record of a lion standing with its front feet on the windowsill of a house peering in at the people inside. It is a safe bet to say that a thousand people are seen and watched by mountain lions for every mountain lion seen and watched by people.

Most mountain lions are also the most timid of all the big cats. Although they are in the same weight class as the African leopard, they usually go out of their way to avoid a confrontation with man. Many hunters have treed the big cats and then climbed the tree to take photos at 5 or 6 feet, without being attacked. Many lions are treed and then captured alive simply by tossing rope nooses over their heads. You don't do that with a leopard. There have been unprovoked attacks upon human beings but these actions are exceedingly rare and will be discussed further under the section on Human Relations.

Lions, except during the breeding season, go to great lengths to avoid fighting. A resident lion will not seek a confrontation over territory because, in fighting, no one wins. The lion that is badly injured usually dies because, being loners, lions must secure their own food or perish. Dr. Maurice Hornocker of the Idaho Department of Fish and Game calls this action "mutual avoidance."

SENSES

Smell very keen, constantly checking wind for prey's scent. Able to track prey by scent but seldom does so.

Hearing very acute and essential in communication.

Eyesight most important, befitting animal hunting by sight both day and night. Slightest movements detected. Lion color-blind like most other mammals.

COMMUNICATION

Western literature is filled with accounts of the high-pitched, long, wailing, demented-woman type of screams that are made by mountain lions. And mountain lions do make screams that sound just like that but nowhere with the frequency that is told or written about. I have been most fortunate to have heard this sound a number of times and I know it was the scream of a mountain lion because I watched the big cat do it. No, the occasion was not in some remote western mountain fastness, but at the Space Wild Animal Farm in Sussex, New Jersey. Each day at noon, the local fire company tests its fire siren. This not only tests the siren, but gives the local people a time check and sets all of the animals at Space's to howling and screaming. I just happened to be standing right next to the mountain lion's cage the first time it happened and the sound really startled me. Can you imagine the impact it would have if heard coming out of darkness, shattering the silence? Naturalist and author Ned Hollister described the scream: "The cry is long, drawn out, shrill, trill, weird and startling. It commences low on the scale, gradually ascends, increasing in volume and then lowers at the end." It is claimed that this piercing cry can be heard for at least a mile but I am sure that under favorable conditions it can be heard much farther.

One of the most common sounds made by mountain lions is a birdlike whistle or chirp. This basic call is used with different tones and intensities for different purposes. At times it is almost as loud as the sound made by whistling with one's fingers. At other times it is almost inaudible. One researcher tells of a female lion whistling a danger warning to her young. It is also the call that is used as a question or as an answer, as to their location, when the lions are separated.

Baby mountain lions make a mewing sound which is almost identical to that of domestic kittens. Mountain lions also purr like domestic cats but with about 20 times the volume and timbre. I was hugging a tame mountain lion that purred and the vibrations shook both the cat and me.

The lions yowl, growl, hiss, grunt and make a coughing, spitting sound. This latter sound is one of their most frequently made sounds when they are displeased. In doing this, they display both visual and vocal signs. The mouth is held wide open, the canines are fully exposed by a wrinkling of the nose and this clearing-the-throat type of spitting sound is made.

Mountain lions spray urine on everything to mark it as their own. They also leave feces on rocks. Scrapes are one of their most important means of communicating. The lions will scrape leaves, twigs, grasses and snow into a heap. They then deposit urine or their feces on the top as a means of personal identification. These heaps are very visible, not only because of the heap, but where the earth has been disturbed. The scrapes are sometimes 2 to 3 feet across. Every time a resident lion passes these spots, it renews them as a means of advertising its presence. Other lions in search of a territory will honor this residency and try to avoid the owner.

BREEDING

Mountain lions usually do not breed until they are at least 2 and perhaps 3 years old. There is no definite breeding season as pregnant females have been found in every month of the year. Most births, however, occur in late winter or in the spring.

It is only at the onset of the breeding season that the lions seek out each other's company. The fact that a female is about to come into estrus is announced by the change in the odor of her urine, although there is no apparent vaginal blood discharged. Every male lion hones in on her as if she were a beacon. As many as 5 or 6 males may follow the female. She also actively seeks out the males, meowing frequently. The lions do not choose a single mate. The male lions fight over the female and the victor has the opportunity of mating first. The female is in heat for 9 days during which time she will accept the male and not before. The male that attempts to mate before the female will accept him will get nothing but a slashed hide for his troubles.

Lions go through a courtship with the dominant male and the female running and gamboling about. They chase each other, climb trees, tumble about in mock fights and enjoy one another's company. They mark everything with their urine.

During her estrous period, the female will mate many times, first with the dominant male and perhaps afterward with one or more of the others. During copulation the female seems to be more captive than captivated. The male usually grabs the female by the scruff of her neck with his teeth. Both cats do a lot of yowling during copulation, their volume and pitch increasing apace with their passion. As the male reaches his climax he bites the female severely and she retaliates by rolling away from him and slashing at him as he springs away. Most adult female mountain lions bear white scar marks on the backs of their necks received while breeding. All is soon forgiven as the entire performance is repeated at about one-hour intervals over 2 to 4 days.

BIRTH AND YOUNG

After breeding, the female chases away the males and seeks out a den. If she has previously had young and was not disturbed, the female will use her former den. Caves, deep splits in the rocks or rocky ledges make preferred denning sites. Lacking this, a den may be under a tree's upturned root mass or even in a dense thicket of brush. No bedding material is brought into the den site but the dirt is often dry and soft.

The gestation period is between 91 and 96 days. It

Baby mountain lions have blue eyes at birth. Their ears are turned down until they are over 2 weeks old. (Photo: Irene Vandermolen)

is extremely hard to pinpoint the time more accurately because some births take longer than others and it is impossible to tell which of the many copulations actually resulted in the pregnancy. Most litters consist of 2 to 3 kittens and occasionally 4. Six is the largest number of mountain lion kittens ever recorded for one birth.

The kittens at birth are heavily spotted with black on a basic coat of dark brown fur. Their eyes are sealed shut and their ears are folded down. The youngsters weigh between 8 and 16 ounces and are about 10 inches long. The claws are well developed.

The female stays with her kittens except for the short time she must leave them to hunt for food. Any male lion encountered is driven from her area to prevent his killing and eating the young. Many male domestic cats will also kill their male babies if given the chance.

The kittens can crawl around very well by the time they are a week old. Their eyes open between 9 and 12 days and their ears begin to stand erect about the

15th day. The baby mountain lions have blue eyes until they are about 3 months old.

Mountain lion kittens are a study in perpetual motion. They climb all over each other and their mother, they stalk her tail and everything else that moves. They play at the entrance to the den from the time they are a month old.

The kittens begin to eat meat for the first time when they are about 6 weeks old. The mother brings back the small prey that she catches or a piece from a larger kill.

The arrival of the mother back to the den, with food, starts a free-for-all among the kits. The first kitten to get to the food seizes it and tries to drag it away, growling all the time, with all the volume it can command. Many times the kitten will try to cover the food with its body. Tugs-of-war are frequent and the noise incessant.

At 2 months of age the kittens weigh about 10 pounds and start to follow after the mother. If a kill made by the mother is too large to be brought back to the den, the female will take her young to the kill.

This baby mountain lion is about one month old. Note the typical spotted coat and ringed tail.

At 3 months of age weaning usually takes place, although some indulgent females allow their young to nurse much longer.

At 6 months of age the young mountain lions weigh between 30 and 45 pounds and are attempting to hunt on their own. The female will not take all of the young hunting with her at one time because the young spoil too many hunts by being detected. The young ones usually start by hunting birds, mice, squirrels and rabbits. Many times the young lions are afraid of the large elk and deer. And well they might be. Occasionally even adult lions are killed by these big prey animals.

As the young ones grow larger, heavier and more experienced, they graduate to the larger prey but are often helped by the female in making the actual kill.

Although some of the young lions may drift off on their own by the time they are a year old, most of the young stay with their mothers until they are 20 months old. Then the young ones, particularly the young males, are driven off by the males coming to court the female. Mountain lions usually breed only every second year.

LIFE SPAN

Potential: 12–15 years. National Zoological Park in Washington, D.C., had lion that lived to 17 years 8 months. A wild, deformed lion recognizable by its track said to have lived at least 18 years; one in Philadelphia Zoological Garden lived 19 years. Record: mountain lion in Space Wild Animal Farm near Sussex, New Jersey, lived 22 years.

SIGN

Tracks in sand, mud and dust the most common sign. Forefoot large on male, about 4 inches long by 4 1/2 inches wide; hind foot slightly smaller. Heel pad much larger than on canids. In winter long hair growing between toes may cause pad marks to be indistinct. At regular gait tracks are 20–21 inches apart.

Scrape sign another common indication of moun-

The right front foot of the mountain lion, which is larger than a hind foot.

tain lion. Also claw marks on trees used to sharpen claws. Smell of urine shows location of scent posts and marking stations even if no snow to show yellow stain. Bones, hair and hide of prey common at den entrance.

ENEMIES

Greatest enemy the destruction of wilderness and concomitant entry of man and dogs into habitat. Among wild creatures major enemy is another, larger mountain lion. Males kill young to reduce competition for food, territory and females, and also makes female enter estrus sooner. Sometimes lions just kill young lions, other times kill and eat them. Coyotes, bobcats, bears and eagles could kill babies, but seldom get chance and predation is nil.

Being loners and always on the move, lions relatively free from the usual fleas and lice (lack of bedding helps keep these to a minimum), but are pestered by flies, mosquitoes and ticks. Mountain lions found with roundworms, tapeworms, and occasionally rabies.

Most damage done to lion by large prey animals— receive broken bones and teeth, cuts, scratches, gorings—and are sometimes killed.

HUMAN RELATIONS

It is very difficult to estimate the population of such a furtive, little seen animal as the mountain lion. According to several different sets of estimates, it would be safe to say that there are probably 15,000 mountain lions in the United States today, west of the Mississippi River, and perhaps 100 east of it. Another 6,000 mountain lions should be added for Canada. In most of the lion's present range, its population is stable or increasing.

Bounties have been paid on mountain lions since the 1500s up to 1971 when Arizona rescinded its bounty. Bountied animals can be hunted at any time of the year, in any manner, but this was stopped when

This is the right hind foot of a mountain lion. Only 4 toes show on any of the feet. The dewclaw, or fifth toe, is higher up on the leg.

No claw marks show in the track of the mountain lion.

needle-sharp claws and teeth. It is capable of killing prime game animals and livestock weighing 800–900 pounds. Such an animal is to be respected and, although not feared, caution should always be used.

Claude T. Barnes, in his book *The Cougar, or Mountain Lion,* recounts 20 authenticated human deaths by mountain lions. There are scores of attacks on humans that did not result in death. In most attacks, the lions were young and/or starving. In several instances attacks were evidently a case where the lion mistook the human for a game animal. In a few cases the mountain lions were rabid and not responsible for their actions.

Unfortunately, the number of deaths has increased in the past few years. Three children were killed between January 1971 and July 4, 1976. In most recorded cases, the attacks have been made on children. It is known that a mountain lion may attack a child and would single out the child rather than attack an adult in the same group. It is also a matter of record that many lion attacks have been foiled when a strong defense was made by the person being attacked, even by a child.

I can only reiterate what I say constantly; treat all wild animals, large or small, with the respect they so rightfully deserve.

COMMERCIAL VALUE

IAFWA statistics: no listing for number of mountain lions taken 1976–77. Commercial value of skins sold, $140 per skin. Most lions taken on organized hunts with dog packs. When last seen advertised, hunts cost $1,000—undoubtedly more today. No available records of where such hunts are conducted.

it was feared that the mountain lion was on the verge of extinction. As of 1976, no state was paying a bounty on the mountain lion and its status had been changed from vermin to game animal. Four states— Arizona, Oklahoma, Texas and Wyoming—allow year-round hunting, while Colorado, Idaho, Montana, Nevada, New Mexico, Oregon, Utah and Washington allow only limited hunting. Alabama, Arkansas, California, Florida, Georgia, Louisiana, Mississippi, North Carolina, South Dakota, Virginia and West Virginia give the big cat complete protection.

Several states pay for the damage done to livestock by the mountain lion. In some areas, particularly California, the predation is increasing as the number of lions increases. This is due not only to an increase in the lion's population but an increase in the human population, with a resultant destruction of the lion's habitat. With more people living in more places, among more lions, the conflict is bound to increase.

How dangerous is the mountain lion to man? The cat is very strong, exceedingly fast and is armed with

LYNX, *Lynx canadensis*

INTRODUCTION

The lives of all predators are linked inextricably to those of their prey species. Most predators feed upon a number of species, however, so that a diminution in the population of one species is made up for by heavier predation on another. But this is not true of the lynx. The fluctuation between the high and low peaks of the lynx population is determined and regulated by the fluctuations in the cycle of the snowshoe hare. We cannot discuss the lynx without making constant reference to the hare.

The lynx's Latin name was given to it by Kerr in 1792. *Lynx* is the Latin word for the European lynx, which is a cousin to the North American cat. *Canadensis* is for Canada, where the American type specimen was procured. The French-Canadian name for the lynx is *loup-cervier,* a most unfortunate misnomer meaning "the wolf that attacks deer." The lynx is not a wolf and there are no deer over large areas of the lynx's range.

DESCRIPTION

The lynx is often confused with the bobcat. Except for a small area on both sides of the border between the United States and Canada, their ranges do not overlap.

The lynx is a larger-bodied animal than the bobcat, standing 19–24 inches high at the shoulder and having a total body length of 36–40 inches. The average lynx weighs more than the average bobcat, with a weight of 22–30 pounds. The greatest weight I can find for the lynx was one shot by Hover Viegen in 1953 near Mentor, Minnesota. This lynx weighed 42 pounds. Although the lynx is larger than the bobcat in almost all categories, including the average weight, there are a number of record bobcat weights over 55 pounds. This discrepancy can be accounted for by two reasons. The bobcat living farther south than the lynx probably has more pounds of prey available to it on a yearly basis than the lynx does. And, the lynx, having to walk on soft, deep snow, would not put on more weight than the size of its feet would support.

The lynx has long legs, its rear legs are 3 to 4 inches longer than its front legs, and huge, oversized feet that look like furry floor mops. The front feet are each 4 inches long by 4 1/2 inches wide, and the hind feet 3 3/8 inches long by 4 inches wide. The stiff hairs that grow on the bottom of each foot each autumn almost cover the toe pads, making their tracks indistinct. There are 5 toes on the forefoot, with only 4 toes and the heel pad registering, and 4 toes on the hind foot and the heel pad showing. The anterior edge of a lynx's heel pad has only a single lobe while that of the bobcat has 2. There are times, when the lynx is stalking, that more of the hind foot shows in its tracks, giving it the appearance of a small, tailed snowshoe. The claws on the forefeet are thin, needle-sharp and about 1 1/4 inches in length measuring along the recurved top surface. The hind claws are slightly shorter, stouter and less recurved. The lynx's claws are retractable.

The lynx has a beautiful face; once seen, it is never forgotten. The ears are about 3 inches long topped with stiff black tufts that are 2 inches long. The ears are light-colored in front and back with a black rim on the rear side. The ruff on its face is very conspicuous, starting below the ears and extending under the chin like the muttonchop beards of old. The ruff terminates in two sharp points which extend 3 3/4 inches below and on both sides of the mouth. The ruff is white beneath the lynx's chin and terminates in black tips.

The long chin whiskers, or ruff, and the long tufts of hair on the tip of each ear are the identifying characteristics of the lynx.

The fur of the lynx is long, soft, luxurious and provides excellent insulation against the −50° F. temperature that is common in its area in the winter. The silver-tipped guard hairs on the lynx's back are 2 1/4 inches in length. The very dense, fluffy, brown undercoat hairs are 1 3/4 inches long. Some of the guard hairs on the lynx's belly are 4 1/2 inches long while the undercoat is about 2 1/4 inches long. The lynx molts its coat twice a year in the spring and fall. The new coat appears brown until the guard hairs push through.

The lynx's basic body color appears to be a soft, smoky gray because of the white tips of the guard hairs. The fur is darkest down the center of the back. The stubby tail, to the hair tip, is 3 3/4 inches long. The tail is basically brown with two faint rings of white and the distal third is totally black. The hair of the chin, the chest, belly and the insides of the legs are an off-white with randomly paired, indistinct black dots.

The lynx, like the bobcat, has only 28 teeth—12 incisors, 4 needle-pointed canines, 8 premolars and 4

The lynx pads silently through the northern forests on oversized feet.

The eyes are large and bright yellow in the daytime, the pupils contracted to the merest black slit. At night the pupils expand so that they are huge black orbs with just a slight yellow rim. The retina of the lynx's eye is composed primarily of rods. This is why the lynx is color-blind, as are most mammals. The lynx hunts primarily at night when nothing has color, only form, so this is not a handicap. The rods act as a mirror, reflecting and doubling the available light. Some light is always available on even the darkest night, although it may be too faint to be seen by a human's eyes. The available light goes through the lynx's eye, registers on the retina, then strikes the rods and is bounced back through the retina, doubling the electrical impulses received. It is because of the lynx's superabundance of rods that it is able to see so well in the dark and why the eyes reflect a light shined into them. The lynx's eyes are greenish when seen at night.

The lynx's nose is black-rimmed but has a pinkish pad. There are 4 rows of vibrissae, or whiskers, that are 3 to 3 1/2 inches in length and are black, white or black with a white tip.

molars. Like the other members of the cat family, the lynx does not masticate its food but uses its shearing teeth to cut off bite-sized chunks of meat to be swallowed.

DISTRIBUTION

An animal for northern taiga regions, range limited in north by treeless tundra, although may inhabit stream sides with alder and willow. Absent from British Columbia's Pacific coast and from plains of Alberta, Saskatchewan and Manitoba. In U.S., found in Rocky Mountain regions of Washington, Idaho, Montana, Wyoming, Utah and Colorado, and in Minnesota, Wisconsin and Michigan's upper peninsula. U.S. lynx population increases when snowshoe hares decline in Canada because they emigrate south looking for food. Some then spill over into North Dakota. Found also in Maine, New Hampshire, Vermont, occasionally New York. May or may not remain in New Brunswick; extirpated from Prince Edward Island; population in Nova Scotia is low and lynx competing with an influx of bobcats; abundant in Newfoundland.

TRAVEL

Under normal conditions, lynxes do not migrate. But what are normal conditions for an animal whose population peaks and then crashes on a 9.6-year cycle? When there is an abundance of snowshoe hares the lynx travels no more than it has to. The hares inhabit areas of swamp, dense underbrush, regrown burned-out areas or any spot with an ample supply of food. An abundance of brush provides not only food but also the protective cover that the hares need to escape from their many enemies. And the lynx, their major enemy, lives right there with them.

When hares are abundant the lynx may restrict itself to a home range of one square mile. It may hunt 3 to 4 miles in a night but still remain within that general area. Ernest Thompson Seton recorded that in 1886 the hares were so plentiful near Carberry, Manitoba, Canada, that he could see 11 within a radius of 30

yards. He calculated that there were perhaps 5,000 hares to the square mile. During a peak cycle like that, the lynx would be sated on hares and not have to move about at all.

In the year of low cycles, the hares become scarce and cause most of the lynxes to move southward to seek food. Many of the lynxes die of starvation and most of those that do move to the south never return. The year 1962 was one of starvation and many Canadian lynxes showed up in Minnesota and Wisconsin.

Ordinarily, it is figured that the home range of a lynx is about 6 to 8 square miles.

LOCOMOTION

When the lynx walks, it usually does so with its head held much lower than its shoulders. So even when it is not stalking its prey, it appears to slink along. If it has a definite destination or purpose, the lynx will trot. If chased, or when chasing prey, the lynx bounds but only for a short distance. Although it has long legs compared to its body size, the lynx is built neither for speed nor distance. There are a number of records of men actually outrunning a lynx. It has been estimated that a lynx's top speed is 10–12 miles per hour but I am sure that for a short distance it can go much faster than that. In fact, when the lynx pounces on its prey, it is just a blur of motion and speed. It has been calculated that a snowshoe hare can run at 26 miles per hour. The lynx does not run a protracted chase after the hares but it is fast enough to catch many of them after a short chase. Based on this information, I think it is safe to say that the lynx can do 30 miles per hour if only for a very short distance.

The lynx has been known to make horizontal leaps of 12–15 feet. It also has the very odd habit of occasionally making these leaps for no apparent reason. One researcher remarked that it seemed as if the lynx made these leaps every so often just for practice. Such leaps are the kind that the lynx uses in catching its prey.

The lynx can climb trees easily but seldom does so. Most of the evergreens in the lynx's habitat are too

LYNX
(Lynx canadensis)
CURRENT RANGE

High-strung tenseness and concentration are shown in this lynx that is about to pounce. (Photo: Irene Vandermolen)

bushy and the limbs too small to allow the lynx to lie on them. The lynx can swim and, with its large feet, it swims well but its fur is not waterproof.

FOOD

Diet is 80–90 percent snowshoe hare if hare population high enough. Lynx eats 2–3 pounds of meat per day, and average hare weighs 3–4 pounds, but lynx does not eat feet or stomach, so one hare per day is adequate. With larger prey lynx can gorge itself but this is uncommon.

When hare cycle low, lynx eats mice, voles, lemmings, red squirrels and chipmunks, which may be easy to catch usually but difficult in deep snow. Sometimes kills porcupine but not as efficiently as mountain lion and often found with face full of quills. Muskrats killed when on land.

Less prone to attack large prey than bobcat. Occasionally lynxes take beaver, weakened deer or moose calves. During extreme starvation lynxes known to stalk and kill Dall sheep and caribou, but this extremely rare.

Canids and felines mortal enemies since developing into different species. Ordinarily without a chance to catch red fox, lynx can in deep snow, which fox sinks into while lynx stays on the surface on oversized feet. Conversely, wolf attacks and kills lynx, which can escape only if tree nearby to climb.

Lynx also eats ruffed and spruce grouse, and ptarmigans.

Lynx's hunting sometimes interfered with by magpies, which when they spot a lynx will fly directly above it, making raucous noise. Canada jays may also join in. Lynx's only recourse is to sit still until birds leave.

BEHAVIOR

Although lynxes feed primarily at night, they do so because that is when the snowshoe hare is most active. Where they are not molested (and in most of their remote range they are relatively unmolested), the lynxes will hunt in the daytime if the weather is cool. With their dense fur coat they do not like to exert themselves on warm days. I have seen lynxes in the daytime on a number of occasions in both Canada and Alaska.

The long, dense fur of the lynx provides it with exceptional insulation. When the snow covers the earth, bending down the evergreen branches till each tree is a snow-covered tepee, the lynx will crawl in the hollow provided under each tree. There, out of the wind and relatively impervious to the cold, the cat will just hunker down to wait out the storm. Whereas the metabolism of most animals increases as the temperature drops, that of the lynx remains fairly constant and the lynx can go as long as a week or more without food. For most of that week the lynx may not even move; it conserves its energy. Almost no heat is lost from its body.

When the lynx does hunt, it courses through the swamps scouting for prey. It will walk up on almost every downed log that it encounters because these raised areas provide it with an observation platform and enable it to see so much farther than when it is screened by the dense brush below. The lynx not only scouts from these perches, it also likes to doze there if the sun is shining and the day is cold.

On occasions the lynx may spring on its prey from an elevated perch. Usually the lynx pads along till it spots the movements of its prey and it then stalks within range as silently as drifting smoke. When it gets within 6 to 8 feet, it springs upon the prey and usually kills it by biting through the neck and into the skull.

When the snow gets deep, the snowshoe hares will tramp out a network of trails through the swamp and brushy cover as they feed from bush to bush. The lynx will also utilize these trails because the walking there is so much easier. Many times the lynx will sit behind a piece of cover overlooking these snowshoe trails and pounce upon the hapless hare when it passes by.

SENSES

Undetermined whether sight or hearing the most important sense. In dense cover prey probably heard as often as seen. Eyesight exceptionally good, able to see mouse at 250 feet and hare at 1,000 feet. Lynx climbs up on rocks and fallen logs to get above dense cover and sight prey. Eyes situated at front of skull giving binocular vision, a great aid in seeing snowshoe hare in white winter coat against snow, and an eye placement all predators have to better see prey. Eyes of snowshoe hare (and most prey animals) are on side of head and protrude, giving them 360° of vision.

Hearing excellent, and slightest rustling of leaf puts lynx in readiness. Hairs on tips of ears aid hearing as they do with bobcat, and longer hairs of lynx no doubt more efficient.

Lynx can scent prey but does not track it down as do other predators.

Has developed sense of taste, being a fastidious eater. Will eat carrion only when starving.

COMMUNICATION

The sense of smell is important to the lynx in marking its territory and communicating with other lynxes. All lynxes spray urine on rocks, grass, tree branches, stumps, bushes, and hills and other protuberances. At times the lynx will mark every couple of hundred feet.

The lynx also shows a lot of its emotion by the agitated motions of its stubby tail. When it snarls, it makes both visual as well as auditory warnings. The placement of the ears telegraphs the lynx's moods. The cat with its ears flattened against its head is angry.

Except during the breeding season, the lynx is the quietest of the American cats. It growls, spits, hisses and snarls when it is angry or greatly disturbed. During the breeding season, it yowls and screams like an oversized domestic tomcat. The famous naturalist John Burroughs wrote one of the most fanciful descriptions of the yowling of a lynx.

It was a cry, a scream so loud that I could distinctly hear the echo in the woods about 400 yards away, a cry that tapered off into a long-drawn wail, which for despondency and agony of soul I have never heard equalled. I can find no words suitable to describe its utter hopeless misery and longing. If a lost soul from Hades had been given a few hours' freedom but had to be back on the striking of midnite, it might let off such a heartbreaking moan as I heard. It was a shrill, strident cry, ending in this

long-drawn wail, full of the feeling of hopeless de-
spair. The cry was repeated five or six times, then all
was still.

As I am a wildlife photographer, I have always ad-
mired the work of George Shiras III. He was the pio-
neer in wildlife photography and some of his work of
80–90 years ago has never been equaled. He tells of
photographing a lynx and said that when the flash
powder exploded, so did the lynx, letting out the most
unbelievable scream or wail he had ever heard. His
guide insisted that Shiras had not seen a lynx, that no
lynx could make a noise like that. When the photographic plate was developed, the lynx was shown in all
its beauty just a second before its violent reaction to
the flash.

BREEDING

Lynxes become much more vociferous in January and
February just before the onset of the breeding season.
Their repeated meows are an advertisement of their
presence. As with most cats, large and small, the female probably seeks out the males as actively as they
seek her out. The spraying of urine by the male is
more frequent. No perfume ever made as seductive an
odor. As the female lynx comes into estrus there is a
swelling of the genitals. No vaginal discharge has ever
been noted, but it would be hard to see because all of
the cats are constantly cleaning themselves.

The males fight vicious, ear-slashing, hide-rending
fights, both for dominance and for the female. Where
dominance has already been established, the younger
males will defer to the strongest male.

European research shows that the female lynx not
only actively seeks out the male by going to the male's
territory but that she chases lesser females away from
the dominant male she has chosen.

The courtship period is brief and the male and female remain together 3 or 4 days. Copulation is frequent and may be instigated by the female as well as
by the male. Copulation, as with all of the cats, is violent and accompanied with loud vocalizations.

After the female's estrus is over, she leaves the male
or forces him out of her territory if he has come to
her. This is no problem as the male is anxious to go
and will immediately seek out another female if possible. The female does not want any male near her
young when they are born because of the male's pro-
pensity to kill them. The males will sometimes not
only kill the young but will also eat them. Cannibalism
among adult lynxes also occurs, particularly during
the starvation period when the snowshoe population
has crashed.

BIRTH AND YOUNG

Den sites are scarce in most of the taiga country that
is the lynx's home. Lacking the usual rocky caves and
crevasses, the lynx has to use the hollows created by
root systems of uprooted trees. Many times the lynx
will use the areas under the low-growing branches of
the evergreens, or even a cleared-out area in a dense
thicket. No bedding is provided other than natural
duff of the forest floor.

The gestation period of the lynx is about 63 days.
Most of the kittens are born in April or early May.
When born the kittens are about 9 to 10 inches in
length and weigh about 9 to 10 ounces. Their eyes are
sealed shut and the ears are turned down. The fur of
the kitten is basically brown with black spots, streaks
and blotches. The small, stringy stump of a tail looks
like an afterthought. The mother usually has 2 or 3
kittens at one time and 4 or 5 would be exceptional.
In starvation periods, the female may have only one
kitten or remain barren for that year. The eyes of the
kittens open between the 9th and 12th day and the
ears begin to stand erect a few days later. The kitten's
eyes are blue until it is 2 months old and then they
gradually assume the yellow of the adults' eyes.

The kittens can crawl about when they are just a
few hours old to seek out the female's 4 nipples to
nurse. By the time their eyes open, they can scramble
about with good coordination. An adult lynx is an
amazingly graceful animal, moving with fluid motions.

As the adult male does not help with the family, the

This lynx's curiosity is aroused by, and its attention focused on, something that moved in the dark forest.

mother must leave the young ones to hunt for food. After making a kill she hurries back to her young because they are always in need of protection from other predators and from the adult male lynx. I have seen no record of a female lynx having a second litter if her first litter is killed, which leads to the conclusion that the lynx comes into a single estrous period each year.

The young lynxes start to feed upon meat at the age of 5 to 6 weeks. At first the kittens are more interested in playing with the prey that the mother brings in but their taste for blood meat is soon manifested. The kittens fight over every bit of food that the mother brings in, even if the kill is far more than a single kitten could

eat. The loud, continuous growling of the kitten that reaches the meat first is a statement of ownership and a threat to all that would share in it. Many times possession is a stronger claim on the prey than dominance. At other times, the threats are disregarded as each kitten tears away whatever piece it can secure.

At the age of 3 months the kittens are being weaned. This is a comparatively easy process because the young have started to hunt with their mother and have adapted to their meat diet. Young lynxes stay with their mother about 3 months longer than young bobcats do. The bobcat family usually splits up in the late fall whereas the young lynxes usually stay with the female until the female's breeding season commences in late winter. Most of the young female lynxes breed in their first season if it is a time of a snow shoe-hare high. If a starvation period occurs, the young females do not breed till their second spring or not until their third. Young male lynxes do not breed their first year but will do so in their second if they are not thwarted by older, larger males.

The hunting training of the lynx is different from that of the other cats. The young lynxes learn to silently stalk their prey, how to remain motionless for hours to ambush their prey and to hunt cooperatively.

Lynxes will often put on drives to flush their prey from hiding and other cats don't do this. The lynx mother and her young will form a line with each one being 50–60 feet from the other. Then, walking abreast of each other, they sweep through the cover. Hares, like rabbits, usually circle when startled, and if the lynx that startles the hare does not catch it, there is a good chance that one of the other lynxes will. I saw two lynxes hunting this way but my good friend Jim Balog photographed 4 lynxes hunting like this. Many other observers also report having seen these family cooperative drives.

LIFE SPAN

Potential: 12–15 years, but unlikely many reach this age in wild, as a low in snowshoe-hare cycle often starves out older animals. Record in captivity: 11 years 4 months, lynx in National Zoological Park in Washington, D.C. A European lynx in captivity lived to be 17.

SIGN

Most common sign the big pawprints in sand at lake edge, in mud at stream sides and swamps and in dust of roads. Tracks are 4 inches wide and could be confused with mountain lion. In winter tracks of lynx and snowshoe hare intertwine. Lynx's urine stains conspicuous in snow.

Unlike bobcat and lion, lynx usually does not cover large prey it has killed, undoubtedly because lynx kills large prey infrequently and covering habit has not evolved.

ENEMIES

Wolves, mountain lions, and wolverines most common natural enemies. Perhaps because coastal range of British Columbia is prime lion country that lynx unable to establish itself there. Bears could kill lynx but can only catch young. Northward expansion of bobcat detrimental to lynx. The two would fight to a standoff but competition for food would hurt lynx much more.

Usual external parasites: flies, mosquitoes, ticks, lice, fleas; internal parasites: roundworms, tapeworms. Also get bad cases of mange. Cat scratch diseases develop (as in all cats) because of retractable claws. When claws retracted bits of food or blood drawn into the sheaths, becoming breeding ground for bacteria. For this reason cat scratches usually produce an infection. Distemper and rabies both occur but are rare.

My first really close look at a lynx occurred years ago in Canada. My partner, Homer Hicks, and I had come out of the bush to get supplies at one of the trading posts. There, a sign proclaimed the danger that the wolves and lynxes in the area might be rabid. On the way back to camp a lynx bounded across the road. I was out of the truck before Homer had it stopped. I ran to the spot where the lynx had crossed. Before I got there, the lynx bounded back into the road. As both the lynx and I stood there intently studying each other at about 20 feet, one word flashed through my mind, *rabies*. Fortunately the lynx was not rabid and after perhaps a minute or so it leaped back into the brush and disappeared. And then I dared to breathe again.

HUMAN RELATIONS

The lynx has never been thought of as a threat to man. I can find no authenticated records of a lynx attacking a man, although I am sure it must have happened with one that was rabid or had mistaken a man for a prey species. The lynx's wilderness habitat keeps most people from making contact with it. The native people have always lived with the lynx and to them it represents a major source of income from the fur.

When the population of snowshoe hares is high, the Canadian Indians use the hares as an abundant meat source. The high lynx populations provide them with a good income and help them clear up their indebtedness at the trading posts. Years ago when the hare population crashed, many of the Indians starved, as do the lynxes even today. Without lynx pelts to sell, the Indians had to depend on credit from the trading posts so their health and finances cycled right along with the snowshoe hare and the lynx.

The correlation of the cycle between the snowshoe hare and the lynx was discovered through the fluctuations of the fur records of the Hudson's Bay Company. The cycle is fairly uniform across the continent, although occasionally one area will be at a cycle high while another area 200 miles away may crash. On the whole, the peaks in the lynx population in Canada occur in the years ending in 7 or 8. From 1919 to 1959 the population did exhibit one typical peak but a general low population prevailed. Since 1962–63, the cycle has reappeared as the lynx population skyrocketed at that time and biologists now believe that the lynx population is as high as it has ever been historically in Canada, but not in Alaska.

COMMERCIAL VALUE

Price of fur has zoomed recently with some pelts selling for $300–$400. IAFWA statistics for 1976–77: 2,567 pelts sold in U.S., $219 average price, $562,173 total. In Canada: 15,132 sold, $219.24 average price, $3,317,503 total.

BOBCAT, *Lynx rufus*

INTRODUCTION

According to the Fish and Wildlife Service, there may be as many as one million bobcats in the United States today and I'm willing to bet that 999,999 of them will not be seen unless trapped or treed by dogs. Bobcats are extremely furtive, almost strictly nocturnal and masters of the art of concealment. These attributes have allowed the bobcat to live in areas where its presence remains undetected for years. Although bobcats have always been in the mountains behind my home in northwestern New Jersey, and I have seen their tracks many times, I have seen only one bobcat there. A friend of mine saw a bobcat along the Palisades, within sight of New York City, and that is an area surrounded by the megalopolis.

I don't like to use the name wildcat because many domesticated cats become feral and they have long tails. The bobcat's tail is bobbed, being about 5 to 5½ inches in length. The bobcat is often confused with a lynx, but the tail does provide a distinguishing characteristic. The tip of the bobcat's tail is white with a black bar; the lynx's tail tip is black.

Rafinesque gave the bobcat its accepted Latin name in 1817. *Lynx* is Latin for lynx and *rufus* means "red." Whereas most bobcats are basically reddish, their body color varies tremendously according to their range.

DESCRIPTION

The bobcat, although seldom seen, is recognized by almost everyone as soon as it is seen. Its spotted coat, face ruff, tufted ears and bobbed tail make identification easy. It is a medium-sized cat, standing 20–23 inches high at the shoulder. A large male will measure 32–43 inches in total length, including the tail. Average weights for adult females are between 18 and 21 pounds while adult males weigh between 20 and 22 pounds. However, the record books tell of much greater weights. Stanley Young, in his book, *The Bobcat of North America,* lists a 55-pound bobcat from Ohio, another 55-pound one from New Hampshire, a 56-pound one from New Mexico, one weighing 58½ pounds and one weighing 59 pounds from Nevada. A 69-pound bobcat was killed in Colorado in 1951. Dr. William Hamilton authenticated the weight of a 46 pound 10 ounce bobcat, taken in New York in 1962,

A bobcat. Note that the chin whiskers, or ruff, and the ear tufts on a bobcat are much smaller than those on a lynx.

An angry bobcat treed by dogs.

which had over 8 pounds of fat on it. Day C. Yeager tells of a record from the Maine Development Commission that reported a 76-pound bobcat being killed in that state.

The bobcat's legs are fairly long in comparison to its body size and this is most notable in the southern cats which have leaner bodies than their northern counterparts. The paws are large, with 5 toes on the front feet and 4 toes on the hind feet. Only 4 toes

Although bobcats do not like snow or rain, they must hunt continuously, no matter what the weather.

show on the front feet as the fifth toe, the dewclaw, does not register in the tracks. The retractable claws on the front feet are slightly over three-quarters of an inch in length, following the curve. The front foot, from heel pad to claw tip, measures about 2½ inches in length by 1¾ inches in width. The hind foot is slightly smaller.

The bobcat and the lynx have only 28 teeth—12 incisors, 4 canines, 8 premolars and 4 molars. The bobcat does not chew its food but using its carnassial teeth, the last premolar and the first molar, it cuts off chunks of meat of a size that can be swallowed. Bobcats have a tendency to roll back the skin of the prey animals they are eating, effectively skinning their catch.

The ruff, surrounding the bobcat's face, is not as large or as long as that of the lynx. There are small tufts of black, stiff hairs growing on the tips of the bobcat's ears. When seen from the rear, the bobcat's ears are black-rimmed with a conspicuous white center. These spots are thought to help young bobcats follow their mother in the dark. The bobcat has large yellow eyes with black pupils that are not seen when the sun is bright. In the dark the pupils expand, allowing the bobcat to see in the poorest of light. The bobcat's nose is pinkish.

Bobcats vary widely in coloration with those in the northern forests being the darkest while those of the dry, hot desert areas being the palest in color.

The bobcat's chin, belly and the insides of its legs are basically white with myriad black spots. The basic color of the back can be very light to very dark, although a grizzled-gray on a reddish base is perhaps the most commonly seen color. A darker stripe runs down the cat's back from the top of the head to the tail. The tail is white underneath and usually has 5 to 6 small, incomplete, dark rings and its tip is white. The hair on the belly is about 2 inches long while that on the back is about 1½ inches long. I personally think that the bobcat is one of our most beautifully marked mammals. The bobcat's coloration provides it with excellent camouflage. Bobcats tend to become darker in coloration with age and their spots become faded or disappear.

DISTRIBUTION

Very large range, found in nearly all contiguous 48 states, with possible exceptions of Rhode Island, Ohio, Indiana and Iowa, and may be very rare in some others. Maryland believes bobcat completely extirpated. Territorialism keeps them thinly spread out, and nocturnal habits make them difficult to census, figures coming mainly from trapping records which are not totally accurate because many states keep no records. Texas has most bobcats with 15,898 taken in 1976–77. Found across southern tier of Canada from Atlantic to Pacific; extended northward in British Columbia to about Dawson City. Also found in northern two-thirds of Mexico.

BOBCAT
(Lynx rufus)
CURRENT RANGE

Able to survive in diverse terrains, at home on mountain ridges and swamps, in bitter cold or dry desert. Found in canyons, dry washes, brush-lined river areas, along coulees, in tumbled rock ledges, on farm edges and even in some city limits. Can live in any area with food, reasonable cover and protection from detection. In most states bobcat population steady or increasing. Protection should help its numbers.

TRAVEL

Bobcats do not migrate, although under extreme conditions they may be forced to shift their range temporarily. They do have and hold territory but it is not inviolate. Research by Idaho biologist Theodore Bailey showed that females with kittens did most of their hunting within one mile of the den, although their territories were about 6 square miles. The individual adult male's territory was ten times as large, often overlapping that of several other males and as many as 6 to 10 females. If food is plentiful, the cats travel just far enough to make a kill. As bobcats get most of their food by stalking or ambush, they travel far less than the canids do. The bobcats may not use all of the land within their territories. The males often follow a circuitous route in hunting, minimizing population pressure upon the prey animals. They hunt, then den up in a favored spot, then move on so that it may be a week or more before they pass through the same area again.

LOCOMOTION

The long legs of the bobcat are not made for speed. The cat's narrow chest allows the feet to be placed almost directly under the body so that its tracks appear almost as straight as a dotted line. When they walk, each of the front feet is placed very carefully, then the hind foot on the same side is placed in the identical spot as the front foot is removed to take the next step. By doing so, the cat has to be careful only of the placement of its front feet. This is true of all stalking animals.

Bobcats, like all cats, do not chew their food. They use the carnassial teeth in the rear of their mouths to cut off a swallowable chunk of meat. This bobcat is feeding on a gray squirrel.

Bobcats usually walk from place to place when hunting because the faster the animal moves the more it is at a disadvantage. If the cat has a destination in mind it then trots along easily. When the bobcat is running after game or trying to escape its enemies, it bounds along. It bounds with a very stiff-legged, rocking-horse type of gait. The bobcat is more of a sprinter than a long-distance runner and, for a short distance, it can run almost as fast as the hounds that may be chasing it, for an estimated speed of 25–30 miles per hour. It can easily cover 6 to 8 feet with each bound and there are measured records of 10 feet.

I have seen bobcats climb by using their front feet alternately and in unison. If they climb in a hurry, they are more apt to use the feet in unison, literally bounding up the tree.

Bobcats do not have the aversion for water that is so common with domestic cats. They have been seen playing in the water and even swimming and they have been known to frequent shallow riffles to catch fish.

FOOD

Bobcats eat 1½–2 pounds of food per day. Like other felids, a more fastidious eater than canids, preferring to eat meat it has killed itself and preferring it fresh. If large prey is killed bobcat will cover remainder with grass, dirt and sticks and return to carcass until it begins to spoil. Will eat carrion but only if starving.

Jackrabbits and cottontail rabbits make up bulk of diet, as much as 90 percent in some areas. Where both live together, jackrabbits more numerous but more cottontails will be killed, a reflection of bobcats' hunting methods. Frightened jackrabbit bounds away at high speed, and bobcat not made for speed. Cottontail rabbit depends on protective coloration and sits in form, where bobcat can stalk it. Bobcat able to catch jackrabbit only by waiting near a trail and ambushing rabbit as it hops by, and if gets the first move and is within 6 feet, it almost always catches the rabbit. If it fails on first leap or within a couple of bounds, it gives up. Snowshoe hares important food in north and bobcat population fluctuates with that of hare.

Also eats mice, ground squirrels, chipmunks, tree squirrels, porcupine, an occasional skunk, beaver, muskrat, ruffed grouse, wild turkey and other ground-nesting forest birds and their eggs. Extensive studies showed deer comprise 18 percent of diet. Studies done in winter when deer dead of starvation, or wounded or killed by hunters, were available. Bobcats kill deer particularly when snow deep and deer are weak. It springs onto back and bites into vertebrae at base of skull. Sometimes attacks healthy deer but prone to injury when it does from slashing hooves and antlers. Occasionally kills livestock, taking poultry, young pigs, lambs and sheep—in parts of west sheep depredation may be heavy. Bobcat predation evident by predilection for eating nose, ears and lips of sheep first. One record of bobcat killing 38 lambs in one night. Also have killed and eaten feral house cats.

BEHAVIOR

The bobcat is furtive. Its oversized, cushioned paws allow it to slip through the forest like a wraith. Its cryptic coloration blends the animal into its background. The bobcat is designed by nature to be difficult to see and it is. When disturbed, the bobcat may slink away or else lie hidden and allow the unsuspecting human to walk on past.

Although the bobcat is primarily active only at night, it may be active at any time of the day if in areas where it is unmolested. Studies on bobcats equipped with radio-signal devices have proved this. The bobcats are more likely to be active during the daytime in the winter when there is no midday heat to contend with and food is in short supply, necessitating longer hunting periods.

Ordinarily a bobcat will run from any dog that yaps or barks, no matter how small the dog. When aroused or cornered, a bobcat will fight, and can usually beat, a dog in a one-on-one fight. Dogs usually go for the throat of whatever they are fighting or attacking. The cat will roll on its back and meet the dog's attack mouth to mouth. With its forefeet the bobcat will hug the dog close and, using its slashing back feet, try to disembowel the dog. Such tactics are usually very successful and an experienced bobcat dog will seldom close with the cat but try to force it to seek refuge in a tree.

Bobcats, when they know they are being trailed, will often climb up a tree, run out on a limb and jump off to the earth below. When pushed hard, the bobcats, if they can't lose the dogs by running in circles in a dense swamp or among the jumbled boulders of rimrock, finally take to trees to escape pursuit. The bobcat will thus be out of the dog's reach but is easy prey for the hunter with a gun.

The bobcat is blessed, or cursed, depending on your viewpoint, with an oversupply of curiosity. Being primarily a sight hunter, the bobcat is quick to notice the slightest movement of anything that is not a normal part of its natural world. Trappers lure the cats to their traps by suspending a bird's wing, a feather, a piece

Bobcats, like this one, are excellent tree climbers, although they usually do not pounce on their prey from a tree.

of cloth or even an aluminum strip so that it can flutter or turn. Every bobcat that sees the movement just has to investigate it.

Many hunters also call the bobcat in by using predator calls which imitate the scream of a dying rabbit. Not one to pass up a potentially free meal, the bobcat goes to investigate. At times the bobcat throws caution to the wind and goes bounding in. At other times it carefully, cautiously comes to investigate the screaming and never reveals itself, just leaving tracks in the dust to show of its interest.

One impetuous bobcat in Texas actually jumped on the hunter's back, not realizing it was a man making that blood-curdling wail. When the cat discovered its error, it did not stay around to apologize.

Bobcats will frequent favored look-out spots. These spots may be a large rock, a large mound of dirt or a tree stump but they are usually 3 feet or more above the forest or swamp floor. From this elevated perch the bobcat can more easily see approaching game and plan its stalk accordingly.

SENSES

For unknown reasons bobcats, like all cats, addicted to odor of catnip, becoming stimulated until they drool. Also roll in catnip to get it on backs of necks.

Hearing acute, able to hear rustle of leaf at long distance. Hearing of bobcats with ear tufts clipped not as acute as those with tufts intact.

Eyesight very keen but geared to motion, hunting by watching for movement, an advantage in that they remain motionless and their prey must move to secure food. Stationary man not recognized as danger.

COMMUNICATION

The sense of smell is of extreme importance to the bobcat in communication. Both the males and females are constantly urinating on rocks, trees, stumps and grass to proclaim their presence and to claim their territories. The cats turn their backs on their target and squirt a stream of urine backward. Domestic tomcats will also do this, although I have never seen the females do it. At times bobcats will cover their feces, at other times they deposit them conspicuously on top of rocks or leave them lying on the ground. A correspondent in Oregon has written that he has found in some spots bobcat feces that would fill a wheelbarrow. Because there were no dens nearby, he thought that the feces were used to mark territory.

Bobcats display a lot of emotion with their tails. Long-tailed cats lash their tails back and forth in anger and also to telegraph aggression. The bobcats go through the same emotions with the same intensity but have only their stub of a tail to move. When pleased or contented the bobcat often holds its stubby tail up straight or curls it forward over its back.

Everyone is familiar with all of the sounds made by a domestic cat. The bobcat makes the same sounds but with much greater volume. They meow, squall, growl, cough, hiss, spit and snarl. Bobcats also purr.

This is common with all felines but the larger the cat, the deeper and louder the sound.

BREEDING

Bobcats are usually solitary throughout the wintertime but as the days get longer, in January and February, the males begin to actively seek out the females. As each adult male's territory overlaps that of several females, each male seeks out the female who is about to come into estrus first. There are always more adult females than males because the males travel farther and are more often taken by trappers. This is also the basis for one male breeding with more than one female.

Each male's territory will also overlap that of other males. It is not unusual for several males to be seeking the same responsive female at the same time.

Bobcat fights are not common but they do occur. The fights are fast and furious and the fur flies. Many adult males have split or shredded ears attesting to the fury of the fray. The largest, strongest male usually wins and this is for the betterment of the species.

Almost everyone has heard domestic cats caterwauling and brawling during their courtship period. Biologists who have witnessed bobcats breeding say that the action and noise is the same except on a larger, louder, more vocal and violent scale. Copulation may end up with the male getting another ear split by the female. No male bobcat can breed with a female unless she accepts him but at the copulatory climax the female always seems to change her mind and the brawl starts all over again. The male is biting the neck of the female at the end and this may have something to do with her ardor rapidly diminishing.

After breeding, most of the males leave the females to seek out other matings. There are some records of the male staying with the female and actually helping with the raising of the family, although as mentioned before most females do not want the adult males near their young.

The bulk of the bobcats breed during the last part of February, through March and into early April. Pregnant females have been found in every month of the year. This situation arises because some female bobcats raise 2 litters in a single year. And I know of bobcats in captivity that have had 3 litters in a single year. This is not likely to occur in the wild unless the female loses her kittens as soon as they are born.

Although bobcats will usually kill domesticated house cats, there are several records of the two species hybridizing. There was one such mating in Texas in 1949, another in Oklahoma in 1952 and a third in North Dakota in 1954.

A recent account was given by warden Bob Fala in the *Pennsylvania Game News* of October 1977. He had been shown a litter of kittens born to a domestic cat mother that had just spent 3 months living in the wild. All the kittens had spotted coats, bobbed tails and hairy ear tufts.

BIRTH AND YOUNG

Bobcats prefer to den in rocky caves or fissures wherever possible because such dens offer a maximum of protection. The rock can't be moved or the entrance hole enlarged by dogs or other predators. Lacking such spots, the bobcat will use a hollow tree, hollow log or an earthen den that has been abandoned by some other animal of a similar size. Bobcats do very little digging on their own. The dens, when found, are usually easy to identify because of their odor. The odor of the urine constantly sprayed on the entrance to the den is immediately noticeable.

The gestation period for the bobcat is 62–63 days. The average litter of kittens is 3. The babies are about 8 inches in length, have a heart girth of about 5 inches and weigh about 8 to 9 ounces. They have a grayish-brown base coat of hair with many dark spots. The babies' eyes are sealed shut.

Bobcat mothers leave the kits only long enough to get food. The eyes of the kits open in 9 to 10 days and are blue. They gradually turn yellow over the next 2 months. The kittens can crawl about quite well at 3 to 4 weeks of age and about this time the female feeds them their first shreds of meat.

The eyes of these baby bobcats are still sealed shut at 9 days old.

During their second month the kittens begin to expand their horizons by coming out of the den. By 8 weeks of age the mother begins to wean the young as they are converted to a straight meat diet. The baby bobcats constantly stalk their mother, each other and anything that moves.

The training period for the young bobcats is long and arduous. Most of the prey they stalk escapes and their skill is hard-won. Research proves that the dispersal time is very difficult on the young bobcats and, if natural conditions conspire against them so that food is scarce, many of them die of starvation. Most

At about 5 to 6 weeks of age, the baby bobcats will begin to venture forth from their natal den.

bobcat families split up for good by October, although on rare occasions, if food is plentiful, the young may stay with their mother through the early winter. At this time, if not before, young males will be driven out of their natal areas by the adult males.

The young bobcats will weigh between 10 and 12 pounds by late fall.

LIFE SPAN

Potential: 10–12 years. Number of bobcats in National Zoological Park in Washington, D.C., lived over 15 years. Space Wild Animal Farm near Sussex, New Jersey, had bobcat for over 32 years, an adult when caught in 1942 and thus at least 34 years old. Put to sleep in 1974 suffering from arthritis.

This baby bobcat is about 3 months old.

No toenails show in the track of the bobcat.

SIGN

Tracks most common sign, about size of medium-sized dog's, 2 inches by 2 inches. In mud, sand or shallow snow they can be identified by lack of nail marks due to cat's retractable claws. In deep snow lack of clawmarks not evident, but can still be identified by meandering travel pattern. Canids usually follow more direct route, while bobcat zigzags. Bobcat also frequents more brushy, dense cover and often walks up inclined logs and snags.

Odor of urine on rock walls common, and feces conspicuous, even though sometimes covered, when scratching in dirt visible. Another sign are scratches on tree trunks from bobcat sharpening claws, and loose bark on ground beneath these trees.

Large prey will be only partially covered, constituting another sign. Deer, for example, may be covered only at head, leaving rest of body exposed.

ENEMIES

In wild preyed on by mountain lion and wolf and has been treed by coyote. Unlikely that adult bobcat and adult coyote would attack each other unless one had a clear advantage; too evenly matched otherwise. Bears too slow to catch adult bobcat but kill kittens as do great horned owls and golden eagles.

Most yappy dogs chase and can tree bobcat, and hounds used to hunt it are two or three times heavier. Bobcats have been known to stand off a pack of hounds in a fight, being tough and very fast.

Has usual complement of fleas, ticks, lice and mites; also roundworms and tapeworms. Sometimes gets mange mites.

People attacked by bobcats either victims of rabid cats or mistaken identity, where cat did not recognize human.

HUMAN RELATIONS

An unexplained situation occurred to William Dackenhausen of Ruby, New York. He was hunting for deer and was about to shoot at a nearby buck when a bobcat jumped on his back. He knocked the bobcat away from him with his gun. Before he could shoot, two other bobcats sprang out of the tree and he managed to shoot both as they hit the ground. Now the first bobcat sprang at him and as it did so, he killed it. Hearing a noise in the tree he turned to see a fourth bobcat, which he also shot. Dackenhausen was not injured but was mighty glad that he had had a gun. Contrary to the old idea of a good man being able to "fight his weight in wildcats," it just couldn't be done. But then, except when rabid, or mistaking a man for game, bobcats do not attack people.

For years the bobcat was considered a nuisance animal, one to be gotten rid of at every opportunity. Because the fur of its coat is rather brittle and has a tendency to break easily, it was of little value, seldom bringing as much as $5 or $10. As late as 1970, 20 states were still paying a bounty on the bobcat. Now all of that has changed.

By 1966–67 the price of bobcat skins had moved up to $20. By 1975–76 the price had skyrocketed to $300–$400 each. The price increase was directly related to a banning from the world's markets of leopard and cheetah pelts.

In 1976, in Bern, Switzerland, the Convention of International Trade in Endangered Species decided to restrict the trade of all wild cat skins, of all kinds, throughout the world. Many of the states protested the resolution because they did not feel that the bobcat was threatened in their particular states. Most of the states did not really know the status of their bobcats and many studies were conducted. Today, 12 states completely protect the bobcat. New Jersey has obtained 5 bobcats so far from the state of Maine and released them in an effort to establish a more viable gene pool. We have always had some bobcats in New Jersey. We would just like to be sure that we always will.

Thirty-two states now have seasons on the bobcat with quotas limiting the number that can be taken. Most states now require that all bobcat pelts be tagged in order to have more knowledge and control of the numbers taken.

COMMERCIAL VALUE

IAFWA statistics: in U.S., 72,220 taken 1976–77, sold for average of $125 each, $9,027,500 total. In Canada: 3,459 taken, $92.57 average price, $320,216 total.

ORDER:

PINNIPEDIA

A short time ago the true seals, the sea lions, the fur seals and the walrus were all classified as carnivores. It is true that all are flesh-eaters, and in fact are more strictly carnivorous than most of the members of that order. These aquatic carnivores have recently been placed in their own order. Pinniped means "feather-footed," although "flipper-footed" would be more apt. Their lower limbs have been modified into flippers; their 5 toes are encased in the flippers or joined by webs to facilitate propulsion through water. Their flippers are a major distinguishing characteristic. Only one species lives in fresh water; all of the rest are oceanic.

The pinnipeds are split into two groups. The true, earless or hair seals are in the family *Phocidae.*

F A M I L Y :

ONTARIIDAE

The sea lions and the fur seals are grouped together because they have external ears. They are physiologically distinct from the true seals, being able to bend their rear limbs forward as an aid to walking, which the true seals cannot do. These seals are found only in salt water. The sea lion has thin hairs, while the fur seal has soft, luxurious fur. Of all wild mammals, the fur seal is one of the most managed by man.

NORTHERN FUR SEAL, *Callorhinus ursinus*

INTRODUCTION

In 1741, Georg Steller, the scientist who accompanied Vitus Bering on his Alaskan discovery trip, first saw, described and named the northern fur seal *Phoca ursina,* the sea bear. Later research proved what Steller had only guessed at, that the fur seal is directly descended from a land-form animal whose ancestors were a branch on the bear's family tree. The *Callorhinus* probably comes from the ancient Greek "sea nymph" and the *Ursinus* is the Latinized version for "bear."

DESCRIPTION

The fur seal has the long, tapered, streamlined body that is required for efficient passage through water. The sexual dimorphism is perhaps as great as for any

Note the tremendous neck, chest, shoulders and flippers of this adult fur seal bull.

animal species. The large, adult bulls measure between 6 and 7 feet in total length, including a 2-inch tail. They weigh an average of about 450–600 pounds, with the record being 660 pounds. The adult females average between 4½ to 5½ feet in total length. Their average weight is between 80 and 100 pounds, with 120 pounds being the top weight.

It was once believed that fur seals could be accurately aged by their total length. A chart worked up in 1911 designated the age and the length correlation as shown.

1 year—36¾ inches total length
2 years—37–40¾ inches total length
3 years—41–45¾ inches total length
4 years—46–51¾ inches total length
5 years—52–57¾ inches total length
6 years and older—58–63¾ inches total length

The best skins come from animals that are 41–45 inches in length. These are now called Phase III skins.

Since the advent of more accurate aging tech-

niques, it has been found that this chart can only be used as a very rough guide. There is simply too much overlapping of age classes. This is to be expected because there are too many factors involved to allow such a neat cataloging. Heredity, age of the mother when she gave birth, the amount of food available to her and to her pup when it began to feed itself, are only some of the factors bearing on this problem.

It has also been found that the seals of known age classes are not as large today as they were half a century ago. This is probably the result of overpopulation and overexploitation of their food supply by humans.

Fur seals differ from the true seals in that their hind flippers can be bent forward to be used in walking. The forelimbs of the fur seal are much longer than those of the true seal and allow it to sit upright with its chest and head held high. A large bull stands about 30 inches high to the top of its massive shoulders. When the bull sits erect with its head held up level or pointed up, it is about 48 inches from its head to the ground.

It is this seal's thick, lustrous fur that sets it apart from all of its near relatives, most of whom have hair coverings. The fur seal's fur grows in clusters with one long, straight guard hair and about 19 wavy underfur hairs stemming from a single pilary canal. The guard hairs are about three-quarters of an inch in length, while the underfur is about one-half inch. Both hairs are longer on the animal's back than they are on its belly. The guard hairs protect the underfur from becoming worn when the animals are on land and rub against rocks. The wavy underfur traps millions of air bubbles and provides excellent insulation. Because of the density of the underfur, about 300,000 hairs to the square inch, water under normal conditions never reaches the seal's skin. Oil pollution poses a serious threat to the fur seals because the underfur, when coated with oil, loses its air-entrapment qualities, allowing the water to penetrate to the skin. The seal then dies of exposure.

When this seal's fur is commercially dressed, the pelts are subjected to a moist heat and all of the guard hairs are scraped off. Garments made of fur seal have a sheared, uniform appearance because only the underfur is seen.

Male fur seals, after their fifth year, begin to grow a mane of longer hair up over their heads and down their backs to their shoulders, giving the seal's head a crew-cut look. These guard hairs are silver-tipped.

Seals that are wet look black. As they dry off, they lighten considerably. The bull's guard hairs shade from almost black to dark brown. They are darkest on the back. The silver-tipped mane hairs give a salt-and-pepper coloration over the shoulders.

The females are usually dark brown, shading to almost silver-gray. Most of the females and some of the bulls have a light-colored breast and some also have the light head and neck. Occasionally partial or complete albinos occur. The underfur on both sexes is a uniform, rich chestnut-red.

Fur seals molt just once a year with the males molting before the females. The fur starts to loosen and fall out in late August.

The fur seals have 4 rows of long, strong, down-turned vibrissae. The whiskers are usually about 4 to 6 inches in length, although in the largest bulls they are sometimes 8 to 10 inches. Up to 4 years of age, the whiskers are jet black, between 5 and 6 years they are both black and white and after 7 years they are all white.

The neck and shoulders of the adult male fur seal are truly massive, heavily muscled and thickly padded with blubber. All seals have a layer of blubber, of at least one-inch thickness or more, completely covering the body just beneath the skin. This provides the seal with exceptional buoyancy and is efficient insulation against the cold. The thick slabs of blubber covering the bull's neck and shoulders protect these areas when the animals fight.

Fur seals have pointed snouts. The female's head appears slightly convex from the top of her head to her nose while the male's is deeply convex. The nose of the seal is black, leathery and valvular. When the seal dives, the outside flap closes the nostrils completely.

The eyes of the seals are a very dark brown and are especially large. On a large bull, the eyes will be 1 1/4 to 1 1/2 inches in diameter. These huge eyes are needed to gather the faint rays of light that filter down to the ocean depths where the seals often feed. When the seal is submerged, the pupil expands to fill the entire eye socket. When the seals bask in the sunlight, the pupils contract to mere vertical slits. A nictitating membrane covers the eyes to keep the water out when the seal is submerged.

The family name of this seal, *Otariidae*, means eared-seal and the fur seal has a pencil-sized tube of an ear that is about 1 1/2 inches in length. The tube is open on the lower side for about two-thirds of its length. When the seal dives, water pressure pushes against the proximal portion of the ear, effectively closing it.

The fur seal is properly classified as a carnivore because it feeds exclusively upon flesh. Any pieces of vegetation found in a seal's stomach were ingested accidently with the prey that was eaten.

The 36 teeth of the fur seal are designated as 10 incisors, 4 canines and 22 postcanines. The canine teeth are strong, stout, slightly rear-curving and very sharp. They measure between five-eights and seven-eights of an inch above the gum line. Victor Scheffer discovered that the seals could be accurately aged by counting the annual ring on the outside of the tooth's base.

The postcanine teeth are basically miniature canines that are designed exclusively for grasping prey. The seal does not chew its food nor can it cut it apart. Small fish are swallowed whole, even while the seal is submerged. Large prey is brought to the surface where the seal shakes it apart or tears loose swallowable pieces.

The fore and hind limbs of a true seal are so shortened that they are embedded within the animal's body. This prevents the seal from being able to walk or to sit upright. True seals drag themselves along with their flippers. The forelimbs of the fur seal extend beyond the animal's body for 8 to 10 inches. These forelimbs allow the fur seal and the sea lion to raise the forepart of their bodies off the ground, resting on what would be the palms of our hands.

Right front flipper of a fur seal bull.

Left hind flipper of a fur seal bull.

The fur seals have the largest flippers, compared to their body size, of any of the seals. Their flippers are about twice the size of those of the sea lions.

The foreflippers of a 3-year-old male fur seal are about 8 inches wide where they join the body. All of the digits are encased inside the flipper and are fairly rigid. The digit corresponding to our thumb is the longest and the leading edge of the flipper is only slightly curved rearward. The flipper is about 15 inches long to the tip. The rear portion of the flipper has a slightly scalloped edge with each succeeding digit shorter than the one before. The actual digits are about four-fifths or the total length with cartilage extending to the edge of the flipper. Vestigial nails are on the top of the flipper where the digits end. The foreflippers of a large bull will be almost one-third larger than that just described.

The hindflippers of a 3-year-old seal bull are about 4 1/2 inches across at the body and can be spread to a 12-inch width at the tips. The flippers are 22–24 inches in length. The digits extend to about 13 1/2 inches on a 22 1/2-inch flipper, the balance of the extension being cartilage. The nails on the 3 center toes are functional and often used in grooming. The nails on each of the outside toes are vestigial. All of the toes are almost equal in length and can be moved independently, although they are attached to one another by a skin web that extends to within 3 or 4 inches of the tips.

The flippers of the fur seal are naked, except where they join the body. Not only are they the main means of locomotion, they are also used for thermoregulation. The fur seal's body temperature, while the animal is at rest, is 99.9° F. As with humans, the temperature of 106° F. is critical. When the seals fight, or when they are being herded by humans, their temperatures may go as high as 111° F. This high temperature may be fatal.

The fur seal's coat is so efficient that even on the cold, drizzly days that are the norm for their summer habitat in the Pribilofs, the seals at rest may become too warm for comfort. The seals then pant through their opened mouths and fan their hind flippers constantly. The blood coursing through the flippers is cooled, by the fanning, before it is returned to the body, bringing the seal relief.

Conversely, it may be the fur seal's naked, oversized flippers that restrict the animal from going any farther north to the ice fields in the summer and force it south in the winter. Despite vascular restriction, which would prevent the seal's blood from freely circulating and causing excessive cooling in the extreme cold, the flippers may just have too much surface area to allow this seal to be a true Arctic animal.

Both the fur seals and the sea lions have exceptionally flexible spines, being able to bend backward and touch their rumps with their heads.

DISTRIBUTION AND TRAVEL

With one of longest migrations of any mammal, fur seals travel 5,000 miles per year or more. In summer about 80 percent will be on major breeding grounds in Pribilof Islands in Bering Sea, with other 20 percent on Copper and Bering islands of the Commander group, and on Robben and Kuril islands in Sea of Okhotsk in Asia. Seals drift south after birthing and breeding, with most of Pribilof seals passing through Aleutian Island chain at Unimak Pass. Adult bulls go through pass to winter just below Aleutian chain or stay in Gulf of Alaska; adult cows and young males may go as far south as San Diego. Seals of northwestern Pacific islands go south as far as coast off Tokyo. One-third of bachelor bulls wintering off Japanese coast come from Pribilof Islands, a fact determined by tagging of some seals and by Japanese method of distinguishing North American and Asian seals by blood type. Some young males from Russian islands go south along western coast of North America.

Seals seldom noticed during winter because they travel alone or in groups of 2–4. After leaving rookeries seals spend about 8 months in ocean until returning to land, remaining about 50 miles off coast where continental shelf produces upswelling of nutrients, the fish the seals eat and the plankton and krill the fish eat.

LOCOMOTION

Fur seals walk on the heels of their flippers. They walk with alternating steps as do most mammals. Most of the time when seals move about, they do so with their front feet and their hind feet used in unison in either a slow lurching gallop or with the same motions in high speed. When the big beachmaster bulls are charging a rival, they can run almost as fast as a man. This I know from personal experience. A number of times I have been charged as I was going to the catwalk ladder from which many of the rookery studies are made. I was forced to either scramble up the ladder or dash back up to the highland because of these huge bulls. The bulls would only chase me till I was out of their territories but they really meant business when I trespassed. I was just amazed at how fast they could move their bulk over the ground.

I have had the pleasure of swimming with the little Galapagos fur seals. I do not wish to try it with the big northern fur seals.

The true seals swim with undulations of their body and their hind flippers. The fur seals, the sea lions and the walrus swim primarily with their front flippers, although they also undulate their bodies to get additional speed underwater. Their long hind flippers serve as rudders and are held with the soles together.

The speeds of swimming fur seals have been calculated by timing the seals over a measured course, by pursuing them in boats at a known speed and by working with them in captivity.

Fur seals usually swim at a speed of 2 to 3 miles per hour. When pursued, they have a top speed of about 15 miles per hour. They cannot maintain such speeds for more than a couple of minutes. When pursued on the surface, the seals usually dive at once and escape not only by speed but by depth.

The seals often feed at depths of 100–300 feet. The deepest recorded dive for a fur seal is 624 feet. The longest period in which a fur seal remained submerged was 5.4 minutes. Six minutes is considered the maximum period that a fur seal can remain submerged. They have been known to swim a half-mile before resurfacing.

Seal meat is very dark because of the extra blood vessels. Seals have 75 percent more blood than a man of similar weight. The extra blood vessels are needed to supply the muscles with the oxygen needed for the muscles to work and they also act as a reservoir by retaining additional oxygen in the myoglobin, the hemoglobin in the muscles.

When a seal dives, it exhales, expelling most of the air from its lungs. The nose valves and the ear tubes

FUR SEAL
(Callorhinus ursinus)
CURRENT RANGE

close. As the dive deepens the rib cage and the windpipe are made smaller by water pressure and the lungs collapse. On the surface, the fur seal's heart beats about 50 times per minute. While diving, the heartbeat is slowed to 10–12 beats per minute. Vascular restriction prevents the flow of the blood to the limbs, circulating instead just to the brain, the vital organs and to the heart. Oxygen is withdrawn from the hemoglobin and the myoglobin. The seal has a high tolerance to the carbon dioxide that builds up in the blood. All seals have made similar evolutionary changes.

Upon coming to the surface, the seal expels the small amount of air that has accumulated in its lungs, the heart rate may jump up to 100 beats per minute and several deep breaths are taken. Under duress, the seal can come to the surface, expel air, take more in and dive in about one second. After making 3 or 4 forced dives, the seal will be unable to dive again until it can build up the oxygen supply in its blood. If feeding near land, the seals will haul out on the beaches to reoxygenate their blood. Even on land the seals frequently close their nostrils and go 5 minutes or more without breathing, just as if they were in water. If feeding far from land, the seals will lie on the surface of the water, usually on their backs, for the same purpose.

Seals often sleep on the surface of the ocean, lying on their backs, their rear flippers bent forward and out of the water, held in that position by one of their foreflippers. This is called the jug-handle position.

FOOD

Small seal cow weighing 65 pounds needs about 2,500 calories per day, or 4–5 pounds of fish. By same token a big bull needs 16,000–20,000 calories per day or 40 pounds of fish. Over 60 species of fish and squid have been found in fur seals' stomachs. Feeding in Alaskan waters, they eat pollock, capelin, sand lance, herring, Atka mackerel and squid. Off Washington coast diet is anchovies, herring, hake, saury and squid. Other fish eaten are smelts, lantern fish, tomcod, true cod, greenlings, flounder, sole, turbot and halibut.

Some of these fish sought by man, others considered trash fish. Some varieties not taken by North American fishermen are taken by Japanese. Bering Sea one of the most heavily fished area's in the world, and competition between seals and man is keen. In 1972, fishermen took over 2 million metric tons of fish from Bering Sea, and seals took another 500,000 tons or more.

BEHAVIOR

Fur seals feed mainly at night. Their main periods of activity are at dusk and dawn, although they feed at all times of the night. At night many fish come up from the depths to feed near the surface, which means that more food is available to the seals at that time. The seals dive beneath the fish, which now are silhouetted against the lighter sky. The passage of the fish through the water often causes it to luminesce, making them easy to find.

Researchers have tested fur seals in laboratories and have found that they can catch fish in total darkness and believe that they do this by echolocation. The seals are often seen holding their heads underwater, listening to the sounds that the fish make. Catching fish, when they are available, is never a problem for the fur seals.

When the seals shake large fish to pieces, they consume it bones and all. The larger bones are later coughed up, whereas the smaller ones pass on through the seal's digestive system.

The largest fur seal bulls stay the farthest north for a number of reasons. Their huge bulk, in response to Bergman's Law, provides more mass per surface area and they have less heat loss. The big bulls have much thicker layers of fat than the smaller seals and this allows them to withstand the cold better. Not having as far to swim to return to the Pribilofs, the bulls burn up fewer calories and arrive on the islands in excellent shape, their hides swelled almost to the bursting point with rippling layers of fat. The big bulls that arrive at

A prime beachmaster fur seal bull and his huge harem of cows. Note cows waving hind flippers to cool off.

the rookeries the earliest have the best chance of taking over the most desirable territories. When two equal bulls fight for the same territory, the bull that had taken up residence first is usually the victor because he is fighting on his "home" ground. Some of the big bulls begin to arrive at the rookeries as early as late April. More bulls come in throughout May and most of the beachmasters have established their territories before the end of June when the first females start to arrive.

The hierarchy of the fur seals is as follows. The beachmasters are the biggest, strongest, most aggressive bulls and are usually between the ages of 11 and 15. Some beachmasters have retained harems at the age of 20 but this is most unusual. Due to the vicious fighting, and the debilitating effect of going without food during the breeding season, about 40 percent of

the breeding bulls die or are killed each year.

Young bulls are sexually mature and are capable of breeding when they are 5 or 6 years old, but they are prevented from doing so by the larger bulls. Bulls between the ages of 7 and 10 are known as the "idle" bulls. They are capable of breeding and they do breed the younger virgin cows that come ashore after the large harems break up in mid-August. The idle bulls stay on the fringe of the harems, hoping to lure away an occasional stray cow. They are also quick to act as a replacement if something should happen to a resident beachmaster. Research has shown that a beachmaster's place will be filled within 24 hours, if he should be killed or just tire of the fray and return to the ocean.

Territory is hard to define. The limits to a particular territory are easy to define because they are the actual land areas that creatures will fight to defend. But what makes one piece of territory highly desirable, and another piece apparently identical to the human eye undesirable, is often beyond our ken. I have puzzled over this with many species, in many areas. I have tried to account for all the variables and still failed. The creatures respond to some innate factor that defies our comprehension.

Understandably, the territories along the beach edges are the most desirable to the fur seal bulls be-cause all of the cows must pass over these territories to get on land. The bulls along the water's edge usually have the largest harems because they have first chance at all the returning females. The lesser bulls hold less desirable territories away from the beach. Beyond that are the idle bulls that are not old enough, strong enough or aggressive enough, as yet, to become beachmasters. This all sounds logical, except that only portions of the beach are occupied.

The first bulls at the rookeries have exceptionally

Usually the beachmaster fur seal bulls that have their territory nearest to the water have the largest harems. Note the "idle" bulls at the water's edge and on the offshore rocks.

large territories, but as more bulls haul out, and the competition increases, the size of the individual territories is reduced. At the peak of the breeding season, most territories are no more than 35–50 feet across.

The bulls acquire, and hold, their territories, and later their harems, through a combination of bluster and battle. They do engage in many fierce, bloody battles; every bull is scarred and torn, and among them are those with eyes missing. But they engage in more bluster than battle because if they didn't, they would probably all kill one another. They engage in these real and threatened battles many times each hour, day and night, for weeks on end.

When one bull infringes on another's territory, the resident bull gallops up, rearing and hissing. In fighting, the bulls try to tear off their opponent's foreflippers with their teeth because that is their Achilles' heel, so to speak. Adult bulls instinctively know this so they hold their flippers close to their bodies and strike out with their long, sinuous necks. With canines slashing, they tear at each other's necks and shoulders or grab the opponent's jaw with their jaws. The slashes made on the neck bleed copiously but clot fast. Little actual damage is done in this area because of the depth of blubber padding the tremendous shoulder and neck muscles. The bulls push against each other with their shoulders, trying to knock the opponent off his feet. Most frequently, the bulls dash up to each other, roar, hiss, weave and feint but make no actual contact. After a minute or so of this bluffing, the bulls move apart to dash over and challenge a rival bull on the other side of the territory. The actual boundary of the fur seal's territory is soon easy to spot because the bull wears a path patrolling the perimeter.

A fight between a pair of bulls will usually trigger a fight among most of the other bulls in the area. Frequently a fight between two resident bulls will prompt a third bull to join in. The bulls are always aggressive, not only toward one another, but everything, including man and even the cows.

The fur seals time their return to the Pribilofs according to their age, with the oldest bulls coming in first, through to the yearlings, which don't even come

An angry fur seal bull roars his displeasure.

on land at all their second summer. The young bulls between 2 and 4 years old are not allowed near the rookery and congregate in large bachelor groups some distance away.

It is the same with the cows. The oldest ones start coming in to the rookeries toward the middle of June, the ingress reaching its peak by the middle of July.

As the cows scramble out of the water, they are herded into the harems by the bulls whose territory they happen to be on. Although most of the females prefer to be near the water, many of them move farther inland. If a beachmaster sees a cow attempting to leave his harem, he will attack her with all of the aggressiveness that is usually directed against the other bulls. I have seen bulls grab cows by the back of their necks and throw them 15 feet or more through the air back into their harems. Some of the cows have chunks of flesh torn from their necks by enraged bulls.

However, like most females, the fur seal cow often displays preferences of her own. If she desires to be with another bull or likes his territory better, she just bides her time until her own beachmaster is engaged in a fight elsewhere. Then she gallops off to where she wanted to be in the first place, placing herself under the protection of the desired beachmaster. Once she crosses to another territory, she is usually safe.

The females are also very aggressive toward one another. They are constantly bleating like sheep, barking and snapping at one another. The roaring of the bulls and the constant vocalizations of the females produce a cacophony of sound that is deafening when heard up close and can be heard for miles.

The size of the harems varies widely. I saw some younger bulls with only 2 to 3 cows, some with 8 to 12. The average seemed to be about 40 to 50, some bulls had 80 and some had perhaps as many as 100. The size of the harem is determined by the size of the bull and the location of his territory. The size of the harems fluctuates constantly as more cows come in and some slip out. It is constant bedlam with the bulls chasing all over and battling both the rival bulls and the cows.

The cows do not usually touch each other, each having her own small piece of the big bull's territory that she defends against all other females. The distance between each cow is about 20 inches or the distance that she can reach out to bite her nearest neighbor. Any cow that is trying to move up on the land to give birth to her pup or to go back to the ocean to feed has to run the gauntlet. Every cow will strike and attempt to bite her as she passes. A newcomer is only accepted when she gives as many bites as she receives and is finally accorded a spot to sit on and some peace. The seals frequently rest with their heads thrown back, resting on their neck fat, their noses pointed skyward.

The Pribilofs have some of the most miserable weather in the world. If it is not actually raining, the islands are drenched in a ceaseless drizzle and shrouded in fog. A bone-penetrating chill pervades, although the average temperature is 48° F. The Pribilofs average 22 clear days a year, with most of those occurring in the winter. Despite the drizzle, any day that sees the temperature climb into the fifties will set all of the seals fanning their flippers in an attempt to cool off.

As the seals spend most of their lives in the open ocean, they make no attempt at sanitation. Especially after a hard rain, pools of excrement-polluted water abound. Adult seals that have died or have been killed in fights, pups that have died, afterbirths that have been cast off are walked on, mashed down and become part of not-so terra firma. The fur of the seals that was so sleek and lustrous when they first came on land is soon stained, soiled and caked with muck and mud. The stench is intolerable.

The beachmaster bulls soon begin to lose the sleekness they exhibited when they first returned. In addition to the constant clamor, the fighting and the breeding, the bulls get no chance to eat or drink. They sleep in fitful snatches, if at all. Most of the beachmasters go 18–41 days without food, with an average of 31 days. One bull was seen to remain on station for a record 71 days. Polygany takes a heavy toll and as the bull's fat reserves are used up, his skin hangs loosely on his gaunt frame. A bull that goes for food loses his harem, and his place will immediately be taken by one of the idle bulls. The old bull will be unable to fight his way back into the hierarchy. As most of the breeding is over by the time he does go to feed, perhaps he doesn't care.

SENSES

Hearing probably most important, and even underwater when ears closed seal can hear when sounds transmitted to inner ear by bone conduction. "Hearing" underwater a combination of hearing and touch, when whiskers sense vibrations. Sounds made by fish would be both heard and felt.

Seal's eyes very large and expanding and contracting pupil enables it to see underwater in very little light. They disregard motionless objects but quickly notice motion. On land seals constantly scan for danger, and in water often rear upright for better view.

Smell of secondary importance, as nose is closed more often than open. Smell does enable mother seal to locate her pup among thousands.

Taste unimportant, as diet governed more by what it can catch than what it prefers to eat.

COMMUNICATION

A seal rookery is one of continuous noise at any time of the day or night. The seals roar, bark, snarl, hiss, whine, chuckle and bleat. When the seals leave the rookery, they may not give vent to any vocalizations for another 8 months, when they return to the rookery.

Fur seal pups are usually born headfirst. This one is being born tail-first.

The posturing and threat gestures of the bulls are also a form of communication. With its whiskers bristling, its mouth gaping wide open so that its large canine teeth can readily be seen, the big bull fur seal looks menacing. He is menacing. Even the cows look menacing when they assume this pose. I would hate to have fallen off the rookery catwalk in among a harem of seals.

BREEDING, BIRTH, AND YOUNG

When the female fur seals return to the Pribilof Islands, after their annual 4,000–5,000-mile odyssey, they are heavy with young. Instead of coming back to peace and quiet, they are immediately drawn into the maelstrom that is the norm for life in a fur seal rookery. They are badgered, buffeted and bullied by one beachmaster or the other till they have taken their place in a harem.

Usually within 48 hours after returning to land, the female gives birth to her pup. Twin fetuses have been found in the uteruses of about 14 out of each 1,000 pregnant females that have been examined. However, twin births are exceedingly rare and it is unlikely that the female would be able to produce enough milk to raise 2 young at one time.

At the time of birthing, the female may move to the outer edge of the harem where she may have a little more space, or she may give birth in the midst of the mob.

Fur seal babies are large; they are about 24 inches long and weigh 10–12 pounds, compared to their mother's 50–90 pounds. The birthing is quick, with most pups being born in 3 to 5 minutes. The baby seal is enveloped in the amniotic sac and the entire mass is forced from the female's body by her labor contractions. Usually the sac splits open in the process and the fluid and the baby seal gush forth. Most seal ba-

A baby fur seal and its oversized flippers.

bies are born headfirst, although some are born tail-first like the young of whales and porpoises.

The female fur seal is a very indifferent mother. She will tear open the amniotic sac to free her baby, if it should be expelled intact. However, at no time did I see the mother lick the baby dry and clean it as most mammal mothers do. Nor did she cut the baby free from its placenta. This the baby dragged around till it broke loose. The mother did smell her baby carefully and deeply, implanting its individual odor into her subconscious. Thereafter, the mother could unerringly find her own pup in the midst of thousands.

The seal pup is precocious and attempts to walk around minutes after birth. Its huge flippers get in the way and they slap about like the oversized shoes worn by circus clowns. The pup's huge, shoe-button eyes are blue and wide-open, although I am not sure that much of what it sees registers.

The pups, within minutes after being born, seek out their mother's nipples. They are drawn to her body warmth and by the odor of her milk. The pup will pull one of the female's 4 nipples from the recess in which each is fitted. The female's mammary glands do not bulge out as do those of most mammals. To keep the sleek shape needed for efficient passage through water, the seal's mammary glands are fitted beneath the skin like a thin sheet extending from her armpits to her hind legs, covering her belly and extending up along her sides. When filled, this sheet will hold about one gallon of milk. The dairy cow's milk is 3 1/2 percent butterfat; that of the seal is 45 percent butterfat.

After nursing, the pup usually curls up against its mother's side for warmth and goes to sleep. Although the baby seal has a thick coat of coarse, black hair, most of them shiver uncontrollably at times from the cold. In the penetrating dampness and cold, I did some shivering myself. If the summer is exceptionally cold, many pups will die from overexposure.

The pup's life is a hard one. Its own mother will nurse it but does little else to care for it. Although the pup would willingly nurse from any cow, no other cow will allow it to do so. It is rebuffed by snarls and snapping teeth by any other cow that it encounters. The bulls pay absolutely no attention to the pups. As the actual territories and the bulls controlling them change every year, it is most unlikely that the beachmaster is the actual father of any pup born in his harem. Many pups are crushed to death when the huge bulls charge over the top of them as they do battle or patrol their harems. Pups that are born down in among the rocks have a better chance of survival than those on the more level beaches. A pup in among the rocks has less chance of being crushed.

The big beachmaster bulls are almost always aggressive and constantly combative, yet I was amazed at the apparent tenderness that was frequently displayed between the bull and his cows. I fully realize that much of the mutual muzzling done between the bull and the different cows was the bull's way of checking for the yeasty odor on her breath that would denote that she was about to come into estrus. Yet the muzzling frequently went beyond this searching. The bull and different cows would frequently rub their muzzles over each other's head, neck and upper body. Many times the females, sometimes two at a time, would affectionately and gently bite the skin on the bull's neck and sit up against his massive body, holding the skin in their teeth. With their eyes closed, they look enraptured, and privileged, to be that close to their lord and master.

About 5 days after giving birth to her baby, the female seal comes into estrus. The female has a V-shaped womb with each leg of the V functioning in alternate years. The section that had contained her baby is shrinking in size as a ripened egg descends from her ovary into the unused section.

The bull and the cow are definitely affectionate just prior to copulation. They rub noses and nip at each other, the actions accompanied with hisses and a chuckling sound. The female finally presents herself and is mounted from the rear by the male. She is more possessed than a partner because of their tremendous size difference. The bull outweighs the cow 6 or 8 to one. The female is not crushed, only because the bull supports most of his weight on his forelimbs, although she usually lies as if lifeless with just her head and sometimes her foreflippers visible. Copulation takes from 5 to 7 minutes and only the rhythmic thrusting of the bull's pelvic region signifies that it is occurring. Sometimes, after 5 or 6 minutes, the cow does protest by reaching up and biting the bull's neck. It is a futile gesture.

After this single copulation, the female is completely forgotten by the bull. His attention is soon centered on the next female to come into estrus. At the peak of the breeding season, each beachmaster will be breeding an average of 4 females per day.

Most young cows do not become sexually mature until they are 3 years old and some do not breed until they are 4 years old. For some inexplicable reason, the young Asian female fur seals breed one year sooner than do those of North America. There are very few barren adult female seals. Including the virgin female seals in the figures, it has been found that about 67 percent of the entire female population is bred each year. About 500,000 pups are born annually.

The pattern for all of the pups and their mothers is similar. The pups alternate between nursing and sleeping for about one week. After the female is bred, she leaves the pup to go back to the ocean to feed. The pup has consumed about a gallon of its mother's very rich milk and sleeps with distended belly. The female has not eaten since she first hauled out on land 8 days ago or more. Since food is scarce near the Pribilofs, because of the large number of fur seals feeding in the vicinity, the female heads out to sea. She may go as far as 100 miles seeking food and might be gone for as long as a week.

The female instinctively comes back to the exact spot where she left the beach. She had to fight her way down through the melée of cows and bulls to get to the shore when she left and she has to fight her way back to get to her pup. Although the fur seal mother does not display the care and affection for her young that most mammals do, the urge to feed her pup is the chain that binds her to the land and brings her back each time she leaves.

The mother seal clambers over the rocks and pups of her area seeking out her own baby. Most of the adult seals are barking and calling and most of the pups are bleating like lost lambs. Each pup encountered is smelled until eventually mother and pup are reunited. The mother will stay on shore nursing her pup for one or 2 days before going back to sea for perhaps another 8 to 10 days. This is a pattern that will be repeated for 8 to 10 trips or until the pup is about 4 months old.

While the female seals go back to the ocean to feed, the pups seek out one another's company and gather together in nursery groups. They gather together for warmth at night and play together in the daytime. Mock fights are regularly, if clumsily, engaged in. Fur seals have a high degree of intelligence, and can be taught to do the same tricks that their cousins, the sea lions, have made famous. Yet to watch a pup struggle for an hour to climb over a rock that it could easily walk around, gives little hint of this intelligence. The pups love to sleep on the top of rocks or pieces of driftwood, as do the adult seals.

Baby fur seals are capable of swimming as soon as they are born. However, they seldom venture down to the water until they are at least one month old. At first they seem to dislike the breaking surf that slaps and splashes them. Soon such inhibitions are cast aside and the young seals spend hours a day sporting in the water.

Fur seals breeding. The male weighs about 500 pounds to the female's 80 pounds.

At about 8 weeks of age, the pups shed their coarse black hair and attain a soft, lustrous coat of fur. The pup's new coat is steel-gray on the back and it now has a creamy-white belly. The pale streak on each hip will disappear when the young seal is 3 to 4 years old. The pups at 8 weeks weigh about 22 pounds. At about 13 weeks of age, the pup loses its milk teeth and acquires its adult teeth.

The peak of the birthing and the breeding season is from the middle of June to the middle of July. At the end of July the main break-up of the big harems begins to take place. The old beachmasters lumber down to the sea to feed and to rest, leaving the remnants of their harems and the fray behind them. The older and stronger of the idle bulls fill the void and are there to breed with young virgin cows that are just now returning to land.

Meanwhile, starting about June 20 and extending till the end of July or into early August, the systematic harvesting of the young surplus bachelor seals takes place. The Aleut Indians, who live on St. Paul's Island, kill a designated number of these seals, working on behalf of the United States Government.

Occasionally a proportion of young nonnursing female seals is also taken for research purposes or if the overall fur seal herd must be reduced in the interests of better seal management.

Eighty percent of the young bachelor seals can be sacrificed for the betterment of the entire herd because the remaining 20 percent is sufficient to provide all of the breeding population that is needed. Too many males only increase the mortality of bulls, cows and pups through stress and constant fighting.

One of the greatest problems facing the fur seals,

and those who plan for their future, is the decreasing number of fish available as food. The fur seals are coming more directly in conflict with man as competitors for the same food. At the present time, the overall fur seal herd population has declined as the number of fish has declined. The reduction of the surplus bachelor males makes more food available for the seals upon which the annual herd increment depends. The fur seal herds must continue to be managed for their own good.

Fur seals are subject to delayed implantation. The egg that was fertilized in July split and divided a number of times and then was held in limbo in the uterus until November. Then the blastocyst became implanted in the wall of the uterus and, what is destined to be a baby seal next July, restarted its development toward that goal.

About this same time the mother seal breaks the invisible chain that bound her to her 4-month-old pup. She simply swims away one day and does not return. The pup, now about 28 pounds, is sufficiently skilled to be able to catch its own fish, although nowhere near as skilled as the adults are. This is a period of great hardship for the young. They undertake their first major ocean migration alone and at a time when they are not really able to catch as much food as they need. Most pups lose 20–30 percent of their body weight at this time and many succumb to starvation and cold. The females, too, lose weight through the winter due to food shortages. It has been figured that about 50 percent of all pups die within their first year and 70 percent have died by the time they are 3 years old.

LIFE SPAN

Potential: about 20 years, but mortality high among young seals. Commercial hunting precludes long life for many. Record: 30 years.

SIGN

During 8 or more months seal is in ocean only sign is seal itself. At rookery you can hear, smell and see them by the tens of thousands. Tracks seen occasionally on sandy beach but most rookeries on rocky ground. Excrement is sometimes seen.

ENEMIES

Starvation the greatest threat to seals and their survival depends on wise management of herd and of fish they feed on. Parasitic hookworm a great threat to pups. Hookworm larvae develop and winter in females' blubber and mammary glands, and pups infected when milk ingested. Larvae hatch into white, threadlike worms that multiply in pup's intestinal tract, drill through wall, and pup may die from intestinal bleeding. Most pups survive initial infestation and are hence immune from parasite. Nearly all seals carry hookworm larvae in blubber where it does them no harm. In males the larvae cannot be transmitted, but females will pass them along to their pups. In one summer 120,000 dead pups found in Pribilofs, most killed by hookworm, with 21,600 counted on just 1 1/2 miles of beach. Another summer death rate from all causes down to 17,000. Pups also subject to bacillary dysentery, and 7 kinds of helminths. One pup had over 1,000 of these parasitic worms in its stomach. Mites and lice are found in seal's fur.

In southern waters sharks feed on seals, and one killer whale killed with 24 full-grown seals in its stomach. Killer whales attack seals during passage through Aleutians, but do not frequent waters off Pribilofs—reason unknown. In 1974–75, Steller sea lion bulls seen killing seal pups, shaking them to pieces and eating them. Some 2,500 fur seal pups killed and eaten during that time.

Fur seals can become entangled in scrap pieces of net thrown overboard by fishermen, a practice now prohibited so problem is minimized.

HUMAN RELATIONS

It has been estimated that the northern fur seal population, before its exploitation and competition by man began, numbered about 2.5 million animals.

The Russians, during their ownership of Alaska, slaughtered the seals by the hundreds of thousands. With the herds decreasing rapidly, they saw the folly of their ways and accorded the fur seals limited protection. When the Americans took over Alaska from the Russians in 1867, the slaughter was renewed and increased. Some measure of relief was given to the seals on land during the time that the Pribilofs were leased to two American sealing companies in succession. The herds plummeted because of unlimited pelagic sealing that started in the 1880s. Both sexes and all age fur seals were taken on the high seas by all nations and people. By 1910, the fur seal herd had dropped to 200,000.

In 1911, an international treaty was formulated by Japan, Great Britain (for Canada), Russia and the United States. This treaty forbade the taking of the seals on the high seas by anyone. The seals were to be harvested on a systematic basis by the United States on the Pribilof Islands and by Russia on the Commander Islands. Fifteen percent of all of the seals harvested by these two nations were to be given to Japan and to Canada, respectively, as their treaty rights. This treaty continued in force until 1941. At that time the herd had grown to the point where 92,802 male fur seals were harvested that year. The sealing was discontinued in 1943 and was started up again in 1945, when 116,407 males and 757 females were taken. From 1945 to 1955, 59,000–77,000 seals were harvested annually.

In 1957 Canada, Japan, the U.S.S.R. and the United States renegotiated the fur seal treaty that is still in force today, although it officially terminated in 1979. By March 1980, the Department of Commerce, which controls the Pribilof sealing activities, had recommended that the treaty be extended for another 4 years. Our State Department has conveyed this recommendation to the other 3 countries.

There are many problems being faced at the present time. There are organizations that want to discontinue all sealing, even though this move would cause a further crash in the number of fur seals due to overpopulation and the resultant starvation.

In the 1940s, the fur seal herd reached an all-time high peak and has steadily declined ever since. This decline is definitely linked to a reduction in the amount of fish available to the seals. The female seals have to go farther afield each summer to feed, which means that they get back less frequently to feed their pups. This reduction of food intake has increased pup mortality in their first year and the seals' annual increment has fallen from 8 percent to 7 percent to 6 percent and no one knows how low it will go.

There is a tremendous amount of controversy about the Aleut natives killing the seals by crushing their skulls with long wooden poles. This is the traditional method, the most efficient and the most humane. Extensive tests have been done testing shooting, poisoning, the use of ram projectiles, suffocating with carbon dioxide and electrocution. Death is fastest with clubbing. Most large domestic animals that are slaughtered commercially are usually killed by clubbing done in some fashion.

The continuation of the fur seal treaty is in the seals' best interest, along with the current management and harvesting of the seals. If the treaty were abrogated, it would lead to pelagic sealing wherein no fur seal in the world would be safe.

COMMERCIAL VALUE

U.S. harvested 26,000–27,000 seals in each of last couple of years. Japan and Canada get 15 percent each, so U.S. brings back about 20,000 skins. Pelts sell for about $120 each, a $2,400,000 total. Carcasses sold as mink food.

I don't know how to put a value on a way of life. The lives of the Aleut Indians, who live on St. Paul Island, are inextricably bound up with that of the fur seals as it has been for generations. Any plan for the future of the fur seal will have to include one that is satisfactory for the Aleuts.

GLOSSARY

albinism Lack of pigmentation or coloring, especially of melanins.

Allen's Law Warm-blooded animals that live in the north have shorter extremities than do their southern counterparts of the same species. This reduces body heat loss.

annulai One year's growth recorded in a cross-section of a tooth as a ring, or marked circle, as in tree rings.

arboreal Living in or spending most of the time in trees.

basal The base or bottom of an object or appendage, e.g., where the tail joins the body.

Bergman's Law The farther north an animal of a single species lives, the larger will be its body size. The total mass in relation to its surface area is thus increased, which reduces body heat loss.

blastocyst The name given to a fertilized egg after cell division begins and before implantation in the uterus.

brachycardia From the Greek *brakhus*, "short"; referring here to the slowing down of the heart's pumping action to far below normal.

caecum A pouch or cul-de-sac opening onto the intestines.

canid Any member of the dog family.

carnassial Specialized molar and premolar teeth in both the dog and cat families for the shearing or scissorlike cutting off of small pieces of meat.

castoreum The yellow, aromatic oil produced by the beaver's castor glands. This oil is used by the beaver in communication. It is used by man in the making of animal lure scents as most animals are attracted to its odor. It is also used as a base for some perfumes.

castors Two large pear-shaped oil glands located on both sides of and vented into the beaver's cloaca.

cementum The annual layer, or annua, deposited on an animal's tooth.

churr A trilling or tremulous call made by some insects, birds and animals.

cloaca A single opening in the body of reptiles, amphibians, birds and some mammals, which contains the ducts for excretion, procreation and scent glands.

crepuscular Refers to creatures that are active during periods of low light levels, such as at dawn and dusk.

dark phase Coloration of creatures when darker than is normal for the species.

delayed implantation After the breeding of some animals (notably bears and members of the weasel family), the fertilized egg floats loose in uterus without further development until the proper time in the animal's cycle, at which point the egg becomes implanted or attached to the wall of the uterus and normal development and actual gestation begins.

digitigrade Animals, such as members of the cat and dog families, which walk only on their toes, with the wrist and heel not touching the ground.

dispersal Forced or voluntary movement by the young away from their natal area.

distal The farthest point from the body, such as the tip of the tail.

eat-out Occurs when an overpopulation of a species causes complete destruction of its food supply.

eclipse period A period each summer when ducks and geese lose all their primary flight feathers, rendering them flightless.

ectoparasites Parasites such as fleas, lice and ticks that are found on the outer surface of a creature's skin.

ectoskeleton or exoskeleton The hard outside surface, such as in crayfish and lobsters, which serves as the body's basic means of support.

egress Exit; leaving an area without returning.

estivation The inactivity or dormancy of some fish, some mammals, and many reptiles and insects during periods of excessive heat or drought.

Gloger's Law Creatures living in dark, moist areas tend to be dark in coloration, while those living in light, dry areas tend to be light in coloration.

guard hairs The long stiff hairs of a mammal's coat that protect the undercoat from wear and which usually determine the creature's color.

heart girth A measurement taken around an animal's chest in the vicinity of the heart.

hibernation A period of time each winter during which the basic body metabolism of many creatures drops very low. This deep sleep allows the creature to avoid the rigors of winter with its concomitant food shortages. Life is sustained by the utilization of the creature's stored body fat. Creatures go into and come out of the deep sleep of hibernation in slow, progressive steps.

hypsodont The high, crowned teeth used by grazing animals to grind their food.

light phase Coloration of creatures that is lighter than is normal for that species.

melanism Occurs in creatures having an abnormally large amount of the dark pigment melanin, such as in black leopards.

migration A leaving and returning to a specified area by a creature seeking more favorable food, breeding or temperature conditions.

molt The annual or semiannual shedding of a bird's feathers or a mammal's fur or hair.

monoestrus One period in a year in which the female comes into heat and can be bred.

nictitating membrane A transparent eyelid that involuntarily covers a creature's eye to give it protection, like safety goggles.

pelage The hair covering of a mammal which is too stiff to be classified as fur.

phase A characteristic form (i.e., color) that distinguishes some individuals of a species.

photoperiodism A behavioral response to the amount of light in any given day.

plantigrade Creatures, such as bears and man, that walk on their toes, heel and sole.

sagital crest The ridge on the top center of a creature's skull where the right and left halves are joined.

scent stations Objects or areas upon which scent or urine is deposited, usually by mammals, as a means of communication.

sebaceous Refers to the skin glands of mammals.

squall A loud, harsh outcry.

taiga A Siberian native word referring to the belt of evergreen trees found around the world in the sub-Arctic regions.

territory An area which a creature will fight to defend from others of its own kind, the inviolate space being needed to reduce the competition for mates, the rearing of young and for food.

tularemia A disease of rodents caused by bacteria that are spread among them by the bites of fleas and lice. Man may be infected by handling the diseased animals.

vibrissae The long stiff whiskers on a mammal's snout or face.

BIBLIOGRAPHY

Alcock, John. *Animal Behavior.* Sunderland, Mass.: Sinauer Association, 1975.

Allen, Durwood. *Wolves of Minong.* Boston, Mass.: Houghton Mifflin, 1979.

Alt, Gary L. "14$^1/_2$ Miles of Bear Tracks." *Game News,* Harrisburg, Pa., June 1978.

Arnold, David A. "Red Foxes of Michigan." Lansing, Mich.: Michigan Department of Conservation, 1956.

Atwood, Earl L. "Life History Studies of Nutria or Coypu, in Coastal Louisiana." *Journal of Wildlife Management,* vol. 14, no. 3, July 1950.

Bailey, Theodore N. "The Elusive Bobcat." *Natural History,* New York, May 1974.

Banfield, A. W. F. *The Mammals of Canada.* Toronto, Ont.: University of Toronto Press, 1974.

Barabash-Nikiforov, I. "The Sea Otters of the Commander Islands." *Journal of Mammalogy,* vol. 16, no. 4, November 1935, pp. 255–61.

Barnes, Claude T. *The Cougar or Mountain Lion.* Salt Lake City, Utah: Ralton Co., 1960.

Benson, Seth B. *Notes on the Sex Ratio and Breeding of the Beaver in Michigan.* Ann Arbor, Mich.: University of Michigan Press, June 1936.

Blanchard, Paula B. "Mr. Fisher: Friend or Foe." *New Hampshire Profiles,* Concord, N.H., February 1974.

Brown, Mark K. "Pine Marten." *The Conservationist,* Albany, N.Y., January–February 1980.

Bueler, Lois E. *Wild Dogs of the World.* New York: Stein and Day, 1973.

Burkholder, Bob L. "Observations Concerning Wolverine." *Journal of Mammalogy,* vol. 43, no. 2, May 1962, pp. 263–64.

Burrows, Roger. *Wild Fox.* New York: Taplinger Publishing Co., 1968.

Chamberlain, K. F. "The Insect Food of the Dusky Skunk." *New York State Museum Handbook no. 4,* Albany, N.Y., 1928.

Chesness, Bob. "The Coyote: Our Lone Ranger." *The Minnesota Volunteer,* Minneapolis, Minn., November–December 1974.

Clarke, C. H. D. "The Beast of Gevaudan." *Natural History,* vol. 80, no. 4, New York, April 1971, pp. 44–51.

Colby, C. B. *Wild Cats.* New York: Duell, Sloan and Pearce, 1964.

Coulter, Malcolm W. "Maine's Black Cat." *Maine Fish and Game,* Augusta, Me., Summer 1974.

———. "The Status and Distribution of Fishers in Maine." *Journal of Mammalogy,* vol. 4, no. 1, February 1960, p. 19.

Crabb, Wilfred D. "The Ecology and Management of the Prairie Spotted Skunk in Iowa." *Ecological Monographs,* no. 18, April 1948, pp. 201–32.

———. "Growth, Development and Seasonal Weights of Spotted Skunks." *Journal of Mammalogy,* vol. 25, no. 3, August 1944, pp. 213–21.

Craighead, Frank C., Jr. *Track of the Grizzly.* San Francisco, Calif.: Sierra Club Books, 1979.

Crisler, Herb. "Wolverine. 'He Not Scare a Damn.' " *Nature,* Washington, D.C., April 1959.

Dean, Frederick C. "Winter and Spring Habits and Density of Maine Skunks." *Journal of Mammalogy,* vol. 46, no. 4, November 1965, pp. 673–75.

Deems, Eugene F., Jr., and Duane Dursley. *North American Fur Bearers.* Annapolis, Md.: International Association of Fish and Wildlife Agencies and Maryland Department of Natural Resources, 1978.

De Vos, Anton. *Ecology and Management of Fisher and Marten in Ontario.* Ottawa, Ont.: Ontario Department of Lands and Forests, 1952.

———, and Stanley E. Gunther. "Preliminary Live-Trapping Studies of Marten." *Journal of Wildlife Management,* vol. 16, no. 2, April 1952, pp. 207–14.

Dixon, Joseph. "Pikas Versus Weasel." *Journal of Mammalogy,* vol. 12, no. 1, February 1931, p. 72.

Dozier, Herbert L. "Sex Ratio and Weights of Muskrats from Montezuma National Wildlife Refuge." *Journal of Wildlife Management,* vol. 9, no. 3, July 1945.

Drahos, Nick. "Notes on Bears." *New York Conservationist,* Albany, N.Y. (Information Leaflet).

Duebbert, Harold F. "Swimming by a Badger." *Journal of Mammalogy,* vol. 48, no. 2, May 1967, p. 323.

Edmonds, W. Thomas, Jr., "Skunks in Kansas." *Bulletin no. 3*, Lawrence, Kans., State Biological Survey of Kansas, 1974.

Egoscue, Harold J. "Notes on Utah Weasels." *Journal of Mammalogy*, vol. 38, no. 3, August 1957, pp. 411–12.

Ellis, Don D. "The Cougar Does Attack." *Outdoor Life*, New York, September 1971.

Elton, Charles. *Voles, Mice and Lemmings*. Oxford, England: Clarendon Press, 1942.

Erickson, Howard R. "Reproduction, Growth and Movement of Muskrats Inhabiting Small Water Areas in New York State." *New York Fish and Game Journal*, Albany, N.Y., January 1963.

Errington, Paul L. "An Analysis of Mink Predation Upon Muskrats in North-Central United States." *Research Bulletin no. 320*, Ames, Ia., Iowa State Agricultural Experiment Station, June 1943.

———. *Muskrats and Marsh Management*. Harrisburg, Pa.: Stackpole Co., 1961.

———. *Muskrat Populations*. Ames, Ia: Iowa State University Press, 1963.

———. "On the Hazards of Overemphasizing Numerical Fluctuations in Studies of 'Cyclic' Phenomena in Muskrat Populations." *Journal Paper No. J-2392*, Ames, Ia., Iowa Agricultural Experiment Station, 1953.

———. "The Special Responsiveness of Minks to Epizootics in Muskrat Populations." *Journal Paper No. J-2523*, Ames, Ia., Iowa Agricultural Experiment Station, October 1954.

Fiennes, Richard. *The Order of Wolves*. Indianapolis and New York: Bobbs-Merrill, 1976.

Fitch, Henry S., and Lewis L. Sandidge. *Ecology of the Opossum on a Natural Area in Northeastern Kansas*. Lawrence, Kans.: University of Kansas Press, 1953.

Fox, Michael. *Behavior of Wolves, Dogs and Related Canids*. New York: Harper & Row, 1971.

Gander, Frank F. "Save the Ringtail." *Defender of Wildlife News*, Washington, D.C., April–June 1967.

Gilbert, Paul F. "A Badger-Skunk Encounter." *Journal of Mammalogy*, vol. 41, no. 1, February 1960, p. 139.

Giles, Leroy W. "Evidences of Raccoon Mobility Obtained by Tagging." *Journal of Wildlife Management*, vol. 7, no. 2, April 1943, p. 235.

Goldman, Edward A. "Raccoons of North and Middle America." *North America Fauna 60*. Washington, D.C.: U.S. Department of Interior, 1950.

Gray, James. *Animal Locomotion*. New York: W. W. Norton, 1968.

Grinnell, George Bird. "Some Habits of the Wolverine." *Journal of Mammalogy*, vol. 7, no. 1, February 1926, pp. 30–34.

Grinnell, Joseph; Joseph S. Dixon; Jean Linsdale. *Fur-Bearing Mammals of California*. Berkeley, Calif.: University of California Press, 1937.

Guggisberg, C. A. W. *Wild Cats of the World*. New York: Taplinger Publishing Co., 1975.

Gunderson, Harvey L. *Mammalogy*. New York: McGraw-Hill Book Co., 1976.

Haber, Gordon C. "Eight Years of Wolf Research at McKinley Park." *Alaska*, Anchorage, Alaska, April and May 1977.

Haley, Delphine. *Marine Mammals*. Seattle, Wash.: Pacific Search Press, 1978.

Hall, E. Raymond. *American Weasels*. Lawrence, Kans.: University of Kansas Press, 1951.

———. "Gestation Period in the Fisher with Recommendations for the Animal's Protection in California." *California Fish and Game*, Sacramento, Calif., January 1942.

Hall, Roberta L., and Henry S. Sharp, eds. *Wolf and Man*. New York: Academic Press, 1978.

Hamilton, W. J., Jr., and Arthur H. Cook. "The Biology and Management of the Fisher in New York." *New York Fish and Game Journal*, vol. 2, no. 1, Albany, N.Y., January 1955.

———. "Foods of Mink in New York." *New York Fish and Game Journal*, vol. 6, no. 1, Albany, N.Y., January 1959.

———. *Life History and Economic Relations of the Opossum in New York State*. Ithaca, N.Y.: Cornell University Press, March 1958.

———. "Reproduction of the Striped Skunk in New York." *Journal of Mammalogy*, vol. 44, no. 1, February 1963, pp. 123–24.

———. "The Summer Food of Mink and Raccoons on the Montezuma Marsh, New York." *Journal of Wildlife Management*, vol. 4, no. 1, January 1940, pp. 80–84.

Hardy, Thora M. Plitt. "Wolverine Fur Frosting." *Journal of Wildlife Management*, vol. 12, no. 3, July 1948, pp. 331–32.

Harlow, Henry J. "A Photocell Monitor to Measure Winter Activity of Confined Badgers." *Journal of Wildlife Management*, vol. 43, no. 4, October 1979, pp. 997–1001.

Harrington, C. Richard. *Denning Habits of the Polar Bear*. Report Series no. 5. Ottawa, Ont.: Canadian Wildlife Service, 1968.

Harris, Van T. *Muskrats on Tidal Marshes of Dorchester County*. Publication no. 91. Solomon's Island, Md.: Chesapeake Biological Laboratory, 1951.

———. *The Nutria as a Wild Fur Mammal in Louisiana*. Washington, D.C., Twenty-first North American Wildlife Conference, Wildlife Management Institute, 1956.

Hartman, Carl G. *Possums*. Austin, Tex.: University of Texas Press, 1952.

Helmericks, Bud. "Bear at the Brink." *Sports Afield*, New York, June 1970.

Hensel, Richard J.; Willard A. Troyer; Albert W. Erickson. "Reproduction in the Female Brown Bear." *Journal of Wildlife Management*, vol. 33, no. 2, April 1969.

Herrero, Stephen, and David Hammer. "Courtship and Copulation of a Pair of Grizzly Bears." *Journal of Mammalogy*, vol. 58, no. 3, August 1977.

Hibbard, Edmund A. "A Badger-Fox Episode." *Journal of Mammalogy*, vol. 44, no. 2, May 1963, p. 265.

Hodgson, Robert G. "The Mink Book." *Fur Trade Journal of Canada,* Toronto, Ont., 1945.

Holzworth, John M. *The Wild Grizzlies of Alaska.* New York and London: G. P. Putnam's Sons, 1930.

Ingles, Lloyd G. *Mammals of the Pacific States.* Stanford, Calif.: Stanford University Press, 1947.

Jackson, Hartley H. T. *Mammals of Wisconsin.* Madison, Wisc.: University of Wisconsin Press, 1961.

Johnson, Ancel M. "Annual Mortality of Territorial Male Fur Seals and Its Management Significance." *Journal of Mammalogy,* vol. 32, no. 1, January 1968, pp. 94–99.

Johnson, Charles E. "The Muskrat in New York." *Roosevelt Wild Life Bulletin,* Syracuse, N.Y.: Syracuse University Press, March 1925.

Johnson, Sydney A. "Biology of the Raccoon." *Bulletin 402,* Auburn, Ala., Alabama Department of Conservation and Agricultural Experiment Station, June 1970.

Jorgensen, S. E., and L. David Mech, eds. *Symposium on the Native Cats of North America.* Portland, Ore., Thirty-sixth North American Wildlife and Natural Resources Conference, March 1971.

Keefe, James F., and Don Wooldridge. *The World of the Opossum.* Philadelphia and New York: J. B. Lippincott, 1967.

Kenyon, Karl W. "The Sea Otter in the Eastern Pacific Ocean." *North American Fauna no. 68,* Washington, D.C., Bureau of Sport Fisheries and Wildlife, 1969.

King, Judith E. *Seals of the World.* London, England: Trustees of the British Museum, 1964.

Klinghammer, Erich, ed. *The Behavior and Ecology of Wolves.* New York: Garland STPM Press, 1979.

Knopf, F. L., and D. F. Balph. "Badgers Plug Burrows to Confine Prey." *Journal of Mammalogy,* vol. 50, no. 3, August 1969, pp. 635–36.

Koch, Thomas J. *The Year of the Polar Bear.* Indianapolis, Ind.: Bobbs-Merrill, 1975.

Koehler, Gary M., and Maurice G. Hornocker. "Fire Effects on Marten Habitat in the Selway-Bitterroot Wilderness." *Journal of Wildlife Management,* vol. 41, no. 3, July 1977, pp. 500–505.

Kolenosky, George B. "Wolf Predation on Wintering Deer in East-Central Ontario." *Journal of Wildlife Management,* vol. 36, no. 2, 1972, p. 357.

Latham, Roger M. *The Ecology and Economics of Predator Management.* Harrisburg, Pa.: Pennsylvania Game Commission, 1951.

———. *The Food of Predacious Animals in Northeastern United States.* Harrisburg, Pa.: Pennsylvania Game Commission, 1950.

———. "The Fox as a Factor in the Control of Weasel Populations." *Journal of Wildlife Management,* vol. 16, no. 4, October 1952, pp. 516–17.

———. "The Weasel—Bloodthirsty Conservationist." *Pennsylvania Game News,* Harrisburg, Pa., May 1958.

Laycock, George. "Travels and Travails of the Song-Dog." *Audubon,* New York, September 1974.

Layne, James N., and Warren H. McKeon. "Notes on the Development of the Red Fox Fetus." *New York Fish and Game Journal,* vol. 3, no.1, Albany, N.Y., January 1956.

———. "Notes on Red Fox and Gray Fox Den Sites in New York." *New York Fish and Game Journal,* vol. 3, no. 2, Albany, N.Y., July 1956.

———. "Some Aspects of Red Fox and Gray Fox Reproduction in New York." *New York Fish and Game Journal,* vol. 3, no. 1, Albany, N.Y., January 1956.

Lesink, Calvin J.; Ronald O. Skoog; John L. Buckley. "Food Habits of Marten in Interior Alaska and Their Significance." *Journal of Wildlife Management,* vol. 19, no. 3, July 1955, pp. 364–68.

Lesowski, John. "The Silent Hunter." *Outdoor Life,* New York, July 1967.

Linhart, Samuel B. "Acceptance by Wild Foxes of Certain Baits for Administering Antifertility Agents." *New York Fish and Game Journal,* vol. 11, no. 2, Albany, N.Y., July 1964.

———. "Sex Ratios of the Red Fox and Gray Fox in New York." *New York Fish and Game Journal,* vol. 6, no. 1, Albany, N.Y., January 1959.

Lopez, Barry Holstun. *Of Wolves and Men.* New York: Charles Scribner's Sons, 1978.

Lowery, George H., Jr. *The Mammals of Louisiana and Its Adjacent Waters.* Baton Rouge, La.: Louisiana State University Press, 1974.

Martin, Alexander C.; Herbert S. Zim; Arnold L. Nelson. *American Wildlife and Plants.* New York: McGraw-Hill Book Co., 1951.

Martin, Fredericka. *Sea Bears.* Philadelphia and New York: Chilton Co., 1960.

Mathiak, Harold A. "Experimental Level Ditching for Muskrat Management." *Technical Wildlife Bulletin no. 5,* Madison, Wisc.: Wisconsin Conservation Department, 1953.

McCabe, Robert A. "Notes on Live-Trapping Mink." *Journal of Mammalogy,* vol. 30, no. 4, November 1949, pp. 416–23.

Mead, Rodney A. "Reproduction in Western Forms of the Spotted Skunk." *Journal of Mammalogy,* vol. 49, no. 3, August 1968, pp. 373–90.

Mech, David. "The Otter—Pennsylvania's Playful Predator." *Game News,* Harrisburg, Pa., January 1960.

———. *The Wolf.* New York: American Museum of Natural History, 1970.

———. "The Wolves of Isle Royale." *Fauna Series no. 7,* Washington, D.C.: U.S. Government Printing Office, 1966.

Miller, Frederic W. "The Fall Moult of Mustela Longicauda." *Journal of Mammalogy,* vol. 12, no. 2, May 1931, pp. 150–52.

———. "The Spring Moult of Mustela Longicauda." *Journal of Mammalogy,* vol. 11, no. 4, November 1930, pp. 471–73.

Miller, Gerrit S., Jr., and Remington Kellogg. *List of North American Recent Mammals.* Washington, D.C.: Smithsonian Institution, 1955.

Milne, Lorus J., and Margery. *The Senses of Animals and Men.* New York: Atheneum, 1962.

Monson, Ruth A.; Ward B. Stone; Bruce L. Weber. "Heartworms in Foxes and Wild Canids in New York." *New York Fish and Game Journal,* vol. 20, no. 1, Albany, N.Y., January 1973.

Murie, Adolph. "Ecology of the Coyote in the Yellowstone." *Fauna Series no. 4,* Washington, D.C.: U.S. Government Printing Office, 1940.

———. *Following Fox Trails.* Ann Arbor, Mich.: University of Michigan Press, 1936.

———. "Some Food Habits of the Marten." *Journal of Mammalogy,* vol. 42, no. 4, November 1961, pp. 516–21.

———. *The Wolves of Mount McKinley.* Washington, D.C.: U.S. Government Printing Office, 1944.

Murie, Olaus J. "Fauna of the Aleutian Islands and Alaska Peninsula." *North American Fauna no. 61,* Washington, D.C.: U.S. Fish and Wildlife Service, 1959.

Musgrave, M. E. "Some Habits of Mountain Lions in Arizona." *Journal of Mammalogy,* vol. 7, no. 4, November 1926.

Nesse, Gary E.; William M. Longhurst; Walter E. Howard. "Predation and the Sheep Industry in California." *Bulletin no. 1878,* Davis, Calif.: University of California Press, July 1976.

North, Sterling. *Raccoons are the Brightest People.* New York: E. P. Dutton, 1966.

Olsen, O. Wilford. "The Fur Seal Hookworm Mystery." *Alaska,* Anchorage, Alaska, February 1976.

O'Neil, Ted. *The Muskrat in the Louisiana Coastal Marshes.* New Orleans, La.: Louisiana Department of Wildlife and Fisheries, 1949.

Osgood, Wilfred H.; Edward Preble; George H. Parker. "The Fur Seals and Other Life of the Pribilof Islands, Alaska, in 1914." *Bulletin of the Bureau of Fisheries,* vol. 34, Washington, D.C., 1914.

Paradiso, John L. "Mammals of Maryland." *North American Fauna no. 66,* Bureau of Sport Fisheries and Wildlife, Washington, D.C.: U.S. Government Printing Office, 1969.

Pedersen, Alwin. *Polar Animals.* London: George G. Harrap and Co., 1962.

Perry, Richard. *The World of the Polar Bear.* Seattle, Wash.: University of Washington Press, 1966.

Petraborg, W. H., and V. E. Gunvalson. "Observations of Bobcat Mortality and Bobcat Predation on Deer." *Journal of Mammalogy,* vol. 43, no. 3, 1962, p. 430.

Powell, Roger A. "Zig! Zag! Zap!" *Animal Kingdom.* New York: New York Zoological Society, December–January 1979.

Pruitt, William O., Jr. "Ghost of the North." *Audubon,* November–December 1966.

Quick, H. F. "Habits and Economics of the New York Weasel in Michigan." *Journal of Wildlife Management,* vol. 8, no. 1, January 1944, pp. 71–78.

Rausch, R. A., and A. M. Pearson. "Notes on the Wolverine in Alaska and the Yukon Territory." *Journal of Wildlife Management,* vol. 36, no. 2, April 1972, pp. 249–68.

Rearden, Jim. "Big Bear With a Bright Future." *Sports Afield,* New York, February 1971.

———. "Return of the Sea Otters." *Alaska Sportsman,* Anchorage, Alaska, January 1969.

Remington, Jack D. "Food Habits, Growth and Behavior of Two Captive Pine Martens." *Journal of Mammalogy,* vol. 33, no. 1, February 1952, pp. 66–70.

Reynolds, Harold C. "Some Aspects of the Life History and Ecology of the Opossum in Central Missouri." *Journal of Mammalogy,* vol. 26, no. 4, November 1945.

———. *Studies on Reproduction in the Opossum.* Berkeley and Los Angeles, Calif.: University of California Press, 1952.

Rhoads, Samuel B. *The Mammals of Pennsylvania and New Jersey.* Philadelphia, Pa.: Privately published, 1903.

Richardson, William B. "Ring-tailed Cats: Their Growth and Development." *Journal of Mammalogy,* vol. 23, no. 1, February 1942, pp. 17–26.

Rogers, Lynn L. "Shedding of Foot Pads by Black Bears During Denning." *Journal of Mammalogy,* vol. 55, no. 3, August 1974.

Roppel, Alton Y., and Stuart P. Davey. "Evolution of Fur Seal Management on the Pribilof Islands." *Journal of Wildlife Management,* vol. 29, no. 3, July 1965, pp. 448–63.

Rue, Leonard Lee, III. *The Deer of North America.* New York: Outdoor Life/Crown, 1978.

———. *Sportsman's Guide to Game Animals.* New York: Outdoor Life Books/Harper & Row, 1968.

———. *The World of the Beaver.* Philadelphia and New York: J. B. Lippincott, 1964.

———. *The World of the Raccoon.* Philadelphia and New York: J. B. Lippincott, 1964.

———. *The World of the Red Fox.* Philadelphia and New York: J. B. Lippincott, 1969.

Rust, Charles Chapin. "Temperature as a Modifying Factor in the Spring Pelage Change of Short-tailed Weasels." *Journal of Mammalogy,* vol. 3, no. 3, August 1962, pp. 323–28.

Rutter, Russell J., and Douglas H. Pimlot. *The World of the Wolf.* Philadelphia and New York: J. B. Lippincott, 1967.

Ryden, Hope. *God's Dog.* New York: Coward, McCann and Geohegan, 1975.

Saile, Bob. "Cougar Attacks: New Crisis for the Big Cats." *Outdoor Life,* August 1977.

Sargeant, Alan B., and Dwain W. Warner. "Movements and Denning Habits of a Badger." *Journal of Mammalogy,* vol. 53, no. 1, February 1972, p. 207.

Sather, J. Henry. "Biology of the Great Plains Muskrat in Nebraska." *Wildlife Society Monograph no. 2,* May 1958.

Scheffer, Victor B. *A Natural History of Marine Mammals.* New York: Charles Scribner's Sons, 1976.

———. *The Year of the Seal.* New York: Charles Scribner's Sons, 1970.

Schmid, William D. "A Long Winter's Sleep." *Minnesota Volunteer,* Minneapolis, Minn., January–February 1978.

Schwartz, Charles W., and Elizabeth R. *The Wild Mammals of Missouri.* Kansas City, Mo.: University of Missouri Press, 1959.

Scott, Thomas G. "Comparative Analysis of Red Fox Feeding on Two Central Iowa Areas." *Research Bulletin 353,* Ames, Ia., Iowa State College of Agriculture and Mechanic Arts, August 1947.

Seagears, Clayton B. *The Fox in New York.* Albany, N.Y.: New York State Conservation Department, 1944.

Selko, Lyle F. "Food Habits of Iowa Skunks in the Fall of 1936." *Journal of Wildlife Management,* vol. 34, October 1937, pp. 70–76.

Seton, Ernest Thompson. *Lives of Game Animals.* Boston, Mass.: Charles T. Branford Co., 1953.

Shadle, Albert R. "Parturition in a Skunk." *Journal of Mammalogy,* vol. 37, no. 1, February 1956, pp. 112–13.

Shaw, William T. "The Spring and Summer Activities of the Dusky Skunk in Captivity." *New York State Museum Handbook no. 4,* Albany, N.Y., 1928.

Sheak, W. Henry. *A Study of the Virginia Opossum,* vol. 1, no. 5, Philadelphia, Pa.: Wagner Free Institute of Science, 1926.

Sherrod, Steve K.; James A. Estes; Clayton M. White. "Depredation of Sea Otter Pups by Bald Eagles at Amchitka Island, Alaska." *Journal of Mammalogy,* vol. 56, no. 3, August 1975, pp. 701–3.

Shirer, Hampton W., and Henry S. Fitch. "Comparison From Radio-tracking of Movements and Denning Habits of the Raccoon, Striped Skunk and Opossum in Northeastern Kansas." *Journal of Mammalogy,* vol. 51, no. 3, August 1970, pp. 491–503.

Silver, Helenette. "A History of New Hampshire Game and Furbearers." *Survey Report no. 6,* New Hampshire Fish and Game Department, Concord, N.H., May 1957.

———, and Walter T. "Growth and Behavior of the Coyote-like Canid of Northern New England with Observations on Canid Hybrids." *Wildlife Society Monograph no. 17,* Washington, D.C., October 1969.

Soutiere, Edward C. "Effects of Timber Harvesting on Marten in Maine." *Journal of Wildlife Management,* vol. 43, no. 4, October 1979, pp. 850–60.

Stains, Howard J. *The Raccoon in Kansas.* Lawrence, Kans.: University of Kansas Press, 1956.

Stegeman, Leroy C. "The Common Skunk." *New York State Conservationist,* Albany, N.Y., August–September 1958, pp. 5–6.

Stirling, Ian, and Charles Jonkel. "Polar Bear, Symbol of the Wild." New York: *Outdoor Life,* September 1972.

Stone, Ward B.; Eugene Parks; Bruce L. Weber. "The Little Foxes." *The Conservationist,* Albany, N.Y., February–March 1972.

Storer, Tracey I., and George H. Van Sell. "Bee-Eating Proclivities of the Striped Skunk." *Journal of Mammalogy,* vol. 16, no. 2, May 1935, pp. 118–21.

Storm, G. L. "Daytime Retreats and Movements of Skunks on Farmlands in Illinois." *Journal of Wildlife Management,* vol. 36, no. 1, January 1972, pp. 31–45.

Svihla, Arthur. "Habits of the Louisiana Mink." *Journal of Mammalogy,* vol. 12, no. 4, November 1931, pp. 366–68.

Swink, Nelson F., Jr., "The Effects of Red Fox Populations on Other Game Species." Thesis for Master's Degree in Wildlife Management. Blacksburg, Va.: Virginia Polytechnic Institute, June 1952.

Taylor, Walter P. "Food Habits and Notes on Life History of the Ring-Tailed Cat in Texas." *Journal of Mammalogy,* vol. 35, no. 1, February 1954, pp. 55–63.

Terres, John K. "Trailing the Gray Ghost." *Audubon,* New York, January 1969.

Tullar, Benjamin F., Jr.; Louis T. Berchielli; Ernest P. Saggese. "Some Implications of Communal Denning and Pup Adoption Among Red Foxes in New York." *New York Fish and Game Journal,* vol. 23, no. 1, Albany, N.Y., January 1976.

United States Fish and Wildlife Service. *Predator Damage in the West: A Study of Coyote Management Alternatives.* Washington, D.C.: U.S. Department of Interior, December 1978.

Van Wormer, Joe. *The World of the Bobcat.* Philadelphia and New York: J. B. Lippincott, 1963.

———. *The World of the Coyote.* Philadelphia and New York: J. B. Lippincott, 1964.

Verts, B. J. *The Biology of the Striped Skunk.* Urbana, Ill.: University of Illinois Press, 1967.

Walker, Alex. "The 'Hand-Stand' and Some Other Habits of the Oregon Spotted Skunk." *Journal of Mammalogy,* vol. 11, no. 2, May 1930, pp. 227–29.

Walker, Ernest P. "Evidence on the Gestation Period of Martens." *Journal of Mammalogy,* vol. 10, no. 3, August 1929, pp. 206–9.

———, and John L. Paradiso. *Mammals of the World.* 3rd ed. Baltimore and London: Johns Hopkins University Press, 1975.

Whitney, Leon F., and Acil B. Underwood. *The Raccoon.* Orange, Conn.: Practical Science Publishing Co., 1952.

Wilsson, Lars. *My Beaver Colony.* Garden City, N.Y.: Doubleday and Co., 1968.

Wright, Bruce S. *The Eastern Panther.* Toronto, Ont.: Clarke, Irwin and Co., 1972.

———. *The Ghost of North America.* New York: Vantage Press, 1959.

Wright, Philip L. "Intergradation Between *Martes americana* and *Martes caurina* in Western Montana." *Journal of Mammalogy,* vol. 34, no. 1, February 1953, pp. 574–86.

———, and Robert Rausch. "Reproduction in the Wolverine." *Journal of Mammalogy,* vol. 36, no. 3, April 1955, pp. 346–55.

Wright, William H. *The Grizzly Bear.* New York: Charles Scribner's Sons, 1909.

Yeager, Day C. "High Voltage Cats." *Game News,* Harrisburg, Pa., April 1966.

Young, Stanley P. *The Bobcat of North America.* Harrisburg, Pa.: Stackpole Co., 1958.

———, and Edward A. Goldman. *The Puma: Mysterious American Cat.* Washington, D.C.: American Wildlife Institute, 1946.

———. *The Wolves of North America.* Washington, D.C.: American Wildlife Institute, 1944.

Young, Stanley P., and Hartley H. T. Jackson. *The Clever Coyote.* Harrisburg, Pa.: Stackpole Co., 1951.

INDEX

Abalone, sea otter as predator of, 273
Abbot, Ted, 43
Adirondack Mountains, fisher in, 180, 184
Aglos, 138
Alaska, sea otter in, 278
Albinism
    in muskrats, 32
    in opossums, 2
    in raccoons, 154
    in skunks, 240
    in weasels, 190
Aleut Indians, 81, 276, 326, 328
Allen, Durwood, 69
Anal glands. See Musk glands; Scent
    glands
Antelope, pronghorn, as coyote prey, 58
Antifertility drugs for coyote control, 63
Apples as black bear food, 125–26
Arctic fox (Alopex lagopus), 74–81
    behavior, 78–79
    birth and young, 79–80
    breeding, 79
    commercial value of, 81
    communication, 79
    description of, 74–75, 77
    distribution of, 77
    enemies of, 80
    food, 78
    human relations, 80–81
    life span of, 80
    locomotion, 77–78
    polar bears and, 77, 78
    senses of, 79
    signs of, 80
    travel, 77
Attacks on humans
    by black bears, 126
    by bobcats, 311
    by grizzly and brown bears, 110
    by mountain lions, 286, 291
    by muskrats, 39
    by weasels, 200

Badger (Taxidea taxus), 227–37
    behavior, 234–35
    birth and young, 236
    breeding, 236
    commercial value of, 237
    communication, 235–36
    as coyote prey, 60
    description of, 227–29
    distribution of, 229–30
    enemies of, 236–37
    food, 233–34
    human relations, 237
    life span of, 236
    locomotion, 232–33
    as pets, 234
    senses of, 235
    signs of, 236
    as skunk predator, 253
    travel, 231
Bailey, Theodore, 305
Bailey, Vernon, 3, 15
Barking
    arctic fox, 79, 80
    gray fox, 99
    ringtail, 149
Bark of trees as food of beavers, 19
Barnes, Claude T., 291
Bear oil, 128
Bears, 102. See also Black bear; Grizzly
    bear; Polar bear
Beaver, 13–30
    behavior, 19–28
    birth and young, 29
    breeding, 28–29
    commercial value of, 30
    communication, 28
    description of, 14–18
    distribution of, 18
    enemies of, 29–30
    fisher as predator of, 183
    food, 19
    human relations, 30
    life span of, 29
    locomotion, 18–19
    nutria distinguished from, 44
    river otter as predator of, 262
    senses of, 28
    signs of, 29

travel, 18
    as wolverine prey, 221
    wolves and, 68
Bedding
    of beavers, 27
    of black bears, 127
    of mink, 206
Bees as skunk food, 246–47
Beggarstick seeds, 52
Bergman's Law, 152–53
Bering, Vitus, 80
Berries
    as black bear food, 124
    as fisher food, 183
    as marten food, 173
    as polar bear food, 137
    as ringtail food, 148
Birds. See also specific birds
    as arctic fox prey, 78
    as black bear prey, 125
    fisher as predator of, 183
    as marten prey, 173, 174
    as opossum prey, 5
    as red fox prey, 87
    as ringtail prey, 148
    skunk as predator of, 247
    weasel as predator of, 195
Black bear (Ursus Americanus), 119–32
    behavior, 126–28
    birth and young, 129–30
    breeding, 129
    commercial value of, 132
    communication, 128
    description of, 119–21
    distribution of, 121–23
    enemies of, 131
    fat accumulation in, 127–28
    food, 124–26
    human relations, 125, 126, 131–32
    life span of, 130
    locomotion, 121, 123–24
    senses of, 128
    signs of, 130–31
    teeth, 121
    tracks of, 121, 130–31
    travel, 123
    tree markings made by, 123, 128
    white, 121
Bobcat (Lynx rufus), 301–11
    behavior, 306–7
    birth and young, 308–10
    breeding, 308

commercial value of, 311
communication, 307–8
description of, 301–3
distribution of, 303–5
enemies of, 311
food, 306
human relations, 311
life span of, 310
locomotion, 305–6
lynx compared to, 292, 299, 301
senses of, 307
signs of, 310–11
travel, 305
Boone and Crockett Club, 142
Bounties
    on coyotes, 63
    on mountain lions, 290–91
    on red foxes, 92
    on weasels, 203
Brain case of opossum, 3
Breeding. See subheading breeding under
    specific animals
Brown bear. See Grizzly bear
Buffalo wolf (lobo), 63, 73
Burroughs, John, 297–98
Burrows. See also Tunnels
    of badger, 232–33
    of nutria, 48–51
Butylmercaptan, 241–42

Caching of food
    by mountain lions, 286
    by red foxes, 86–87
    by wolverine, 222
Cacomixtle (cacomistle). See Ringtail
California
    nutria in, 48
    sea otter in, 278
Camping, black bears and, 125
Canals
    beaver, 25
    muskrat, 39
Canidae family, 53
Cannibalism
    among arctic foxes, 78
    among mountain lions, 286
    among muskrat, 36
    among opossums, 5
    among polar bears, 137
Caribou as prey of wolves, 68

Carnivores, 53
Carrion
    as badger food, 233
    as black bear food, 125
    as fisher food, 183
    as marten food, 173
    as mountain lion food, 286
    as raccoon food, 158
    as red fox food, 87
    as wolverine food, 221
Castoreum, 28
Castoridae family, 13–15
Castors, beaver, 16
Catnip, 307
Cats, domestic
    bobcats and, 307, 308
    weasel as prey of, 202–3
Cat scratch diseases in lynx, 300
Catskill Mountains, fisher in, 180, 182
Cattle, nutria and, 50
Caves, black bear in, 126
Cheetah, 279
Chicken
    as prey of red fox, 87
    weasel as predator of, 199
Civet cat. See Skunk
Civet family, 238
Civet-fox. See Ringtail
Clark, Frank B., 12
Clarke, C. H. D., 73
Climbing of trees
    by black bear, 123–24
    by bobcat, 305
    by fisher, 179, 182–83
    by gray fox, 97
    by lynx, 294, 296
    by marten, 172
    by mink, 208
    by opossum, 5
    by raccoons, 157
    by ringtails, 147
    by weasels, 194
    by wolverines, 221
Cloaca, beaver's, 16
Copulation. See subheading breeding
    under specific animals
Corn as raccoon food, 158
Cotton rats as prey of gray foxes, 101
Cougar. See Mountain lion
Courtship. See subheading breeding under
    specific animals
Coyote (Canis latrans), 53–63

badger and, 233, 237
behavior, 59–60
birth and young, 61–62
bobcat and, 311
breeding, 60–61
commercial value of, 63
communication among, 60
dens of, 61, 62
description of, 54–55
distribution of, 55–57
enemies of, 62
food, 57–60
human relations, 62–63
life span of, 62
locomotion, 57
red wolf and, 65
senses of, 60
signs of, 62
travel, 57
Craighead, John and Frank, 104, 107,
    115–17
Crayfish as raccoon food, 158, 160
Cricetidae family, 13
Czechoslovakia, muskrat in, 44

Dachshunds, badger and, 227
Dam building by beavers, 23–25
Deer
    bobcat as predator of, 306
    as coyote prey, 58
    as fisher food, 183
    mountain lion as predator of, 284–85
    as wolf prey, 68
Denning up
    badger, 234–35
    black bear, 127–28
    grizzly and brown bears, 112–13
    polar bear, 139, 140
    raccoon, 159–60
    skunk, 248
Dens. See also Lodges
    badger, 234, 235
    arctic fox, 77, 79, 80
    black bear, 126, 130
    bobcat, 308
    coyote, 61, 62
    fisher, 186, 187
    gray fox, 98–100
    grizzly and brown bear, 112–13
    mink, 206, 211, 213

muskrat, 36–38, 42–43
opossum, 6, 7, 12
polar bear, 139–40
red fox, 90, 91
ringtail, 147, 149–51
skunk, 242, 248–49
weasel, 191, 201
wolf, 72
wolverine, 225–26
DeVos, Anton, 172
Didelphidae family, 1
Diet. *See subheading* food *under specific animals*
Digging by badger, 232, 236
Diseases. *See subheading* enemies of *under specific animals;* and *specific diseases*
Dogs
badger and, 227, 228
bobcat in fights with, 306, 311
as enemy of coyote, 62
as enemy of raccoon, 162
opossums and, 11
raccoon hunting with, 159
as skunk predator, 253
wolverines and, 222
Domestication. *See* Pets
Dominance. *See also* Hierarchy
among coyotes, 59–60
among grizzly and brown bears, 109–11
among polar bears, 141
among wolves, 69
Droppings. *See* Feces; Scat
Ducks
as mink prey, 211
muskrat and, 36, 38
river otter as predator of, 263

Eagles, sea otter as prey of, 278
Eat-out, nutria, 49
Elk, mountain lion as predator of, 284–85
Encephalitis
among arctic foxes, 80
among raccoons, 162
Ermine, 203
Errington, Paul, 39, 209–10
Errington's disease, 43, 210
Eskimos, polar bears and, 139, 140, 142
Estivation of polar bears, 140
Estrus. *See subheading* breeding *under specific animals*

Europe, muskrat in, 44

Facial expressions of wolves, 70–71
Fala, Bob, 308
Family groups
beaver, 29
coyote, 59
muskrat, 32
skunk, 252
wolf, 69
Farms, skunks on, 249
Fat, layer of
beaver, 16
opossum, 7
polar bear, 133, 136
skunk, 249
Fecal plug
of black bear, 127
of grizzly and brown bears, 112
of polar bear, 140
Feces (defecation; droppings). *See also* Scat
badger, 236
black bear, 131
bobcat, 307
muskrat, 40, 43
opossum, 7, 11
raccoon, 162
red fox, 91
Feeding houses, muskrat, 38
Feeding platforms, nutria, 49–51
Feet. *See under subheading* description of *under specific animals*
Felidae family, 279
Fighting
among bobcats, 308
bobcats and dogs, 306, 311
among coyotes, 60
among fur seals, 319, 321, 326
among grizzly and brown bears, 109–10
among muskrat, 39
among polar bears, 141
among red foxes, 89
among wolves, 70, 71
Fish. *See also* Salmon; Trout
as fisher food, 177, 183
as fur seal food, 318
as mink food, 208, 209
as muskrat food, 36
as polar bear food, 137
river otter as predator of, 261–62

Fisher (*Martes pennanti*), 177–87
behavior, 184–85
birth and young, 186
breeding, 185–86
commercial value of, 187
communication among, 185
description of, 178–80
distribution of, 180–82
enemies of, 186–87
food, 183–84
human relations, 187
life span of, 186
locomotion, 182–83
as marten's enemy, 176
senses of, 185
signs of, 186
travel, 182
Fishing by grizzly and brown bears, 108–9, 111–12
Flippers of fur seals, 315, 316
Food. *See* Caching of food; Storage of food; *and subheading* food *under specific animals*
Fowl as red fox prey, 87
Foxes. *See also* Gray fox; Red fox
weasel killed by, 203
as wolverine prey, 221
Freeze-outs, muskrat and, 39
Frogs as fisher prey, 183
Fruit. *See also* Berries
as skunk food, 247
Fur seal, northern (*Callorhinus ursinus*), 312–28
behavior, 318–22
breeding, birth, and young, 323–27
commercial value of, 328
communication among, 322–23
description of, 312–16
distribution and travel, 316
enemies of, 327
food, 318
human relations, 327–28
life span of, 327
locomotion, 316–18
senses of, 322
signs of, 327

Gestation periods. *See under subheading* birth and young *under specific animals*
Gray fox (*Urocyon cinereoargenteus*), 93–101

behavior, 98
birth and young, 99–100
breeding, 99
commercial value of, 101
communication among, 99
description of, 93–95
distribution of, 95
enemies of, 100–101
food, 97–98
human relations, 101
life span of, 100
locomotion, 95, 97
senses of, 98–99
signs of, 100
travel, 95
Gray wolf (timber wolf; *Canis lupus*),
    64–73. *See also* Wolf
  coyote compared to, 54
Grizzly bear (brown bear; *Ursus arctos*),
    102–19
  behavior, 109–13
  birth and young, 114–17
  black bear as prey of, 131
  breeding, 114
  commercial value of, 119
  communication among, 113–14
  description of, 104–5
  distribution of, 105–7
  enemies of, 118
  food, 107–9
  human relations, 118–19
  life span of, 118
  locomotion, 107
  senses of, 113
  signs of, 118
  travel, 107
Grooming behavior
  nutria, 46
  opossum, 6
  river otter, 263, 264
  sea otter, 274, 275
Grzimek, Bernhard, 132
Guard hairs. *See subheading* description of
    under specific animals

Habitat. *See subheading* distribution of
    under specific animals
Hackles, coyote, 55
Hamilton, William J., 1, 3, 9, 179, 189, 196
Hares, 39
  bobcat as predator of, 306

fisher as predator of, 183
  lynx as predator of, 294, 296, 297, 301
  mink as predator of, 211
  red fox as predator of, 86
Hartman, Carl, 7
Hats, beaver, 30
Hawks
  badgers and, 233
  weasels as prey of, 203
Hibernation. *See also* Denning up
  black bear, 127
  fur seals, 319
  grizzly and brown bears, 112–13
Hierarchy. *See also* Dominance
  among grizzly and brown bears, 109–11
  among wolves, 69, 70
Holland, muskrat in, 44
Hollister, Ned, 287
Home range. *See subheading* travel *under*
    specific animals
Homing ability
  of bears, 107, 123
  of martens, 172
  of polar bears, 136
Honey as black bear food, 125
Hookworm among fur seals, 327
Hooper, E. T., 265
Hoover, Ade, 185
Hoover, Helen, 182, 185
Hornocker, Maurice, 286
Houses. *See* Dens; Feeding houses; Lodges
Howling
  by coyotes, 60
  by wolves, 71
Hunting
  of black bear, 131
  by lynx, 297, 300
  of polar bear, 142
  of raccoon, 159
  of red fox, 91–92
  by weasels, 196–99
  by wolves, 68–70
Hybrids, coyote-dog, 57

Indians. *See also specific tribes*
  beavers and, 30
Insects, 87. *See also* Parasites, external;
    and specific types of insects
  beavers and, 29–30
  as marten food, 173
  as mountain lion food, 286

as opossum food, 5
  as raccoon food, 158
  as ringtail food, 147
  as skunk food, 246, 247
  as weasel food, 195
Intelligence
  of opossum, 3
  of raccoon, 159
  of red fox, 87–88
  of wolf, 69
  of wolverine, 224–25
Intestinal parasites. *See also* Parasites,
    internal
  in nutria, 51–52
  in opossum, 12

Jackrabbits, bobcat as predator of, 306
Jackson, Harley H. T., 227
Jenkin, James, 266
Johns, Dr., 2

Kenyon, Karl W., 267, 275, 276
Kermode Islands, white black bears in, 121
Kodiak Island, brown bears on, 107, 119
Krill, 138
Krott, Peter, 216, 219, 222, 224, 225

Lemmings, 77
Lentfer, Jack, 134, 136, 141
Liers, Emil, 263–66
Linnaeus, Carolus, 8
Lions, 279
  mountain. *See* Mountain lion
Livestock
  black bear as predator of, 125
  mountain lion as predator of, 285
  wolf as predator of, 73
Lobo (buffalo wolf), 63, 73
Locomotion. *See subheading* locomotion
    under specific animals
Lodges. *See also* Dens
  beaver, 25–27
  muskrat, 32
Long-tailed weasel *(Mustela frenata)*,
    187–203. *See also* Weasel
Louisiana, nutria in, 48
Lynx *(Lynx canadensis)*, 292–301
  behavior, 296–97
  birth and young, 298–300

breeding, 298
commercial value of, 301
communication among, 297–98
description of, 292–94
distribution of, 294
enemies of, 300
fisher as prey of, 186
food, 296
human relations, 300–301
life span of, 300
locomotion, 294–96
senses of, 297
signs of, 300
travel, 294

Magpies, lynx and, 296
Maine, fisher in, 180
Mange, 100
Marmots
    as grizzly and brown bear prey, 108
    as marten prey, 173
Marsupials, 1, 8
Marten (*Martes americana*), 165–77
    behavior, 173–74
    birth and young, 175–76
    breeding, 175
    commercial value of, 177
    communication among, 174–75
    description of, 166–68
    distribution of, 168
    enemies of, 176
    fisher as predator of, 183
    food, 172–73
    human relations, 177
    life span of, 176
    locomotion, 172
    senses of, 174
    signs of, 176
    travel, 168–72
Mating. *See subheading* breeding *under
    specific animals*
Mech, David, 69, 185
Melanism in opossums, 2
Mice
    as grizzly bear prey
    as red fox prey, 86
    as ringtail prey, 148
    as skunk prey, 247
    as weasel prey, 195, 196, 199
Milk
    black bear, 129

grizzly and brown bear, 115
river otter, 265
Mink (*Mustela vison*), 204–15
    behavior, 209–12
    birth and young, 213–14
    breeding, 212–13
    commercially raised, 205, 215
    commercial value of, 215
    communication among, 212
    description of, 204–6
    distribution of, 206
    enemies of, 215
    food, 208–9
    human relations, 215
    life span of, 214
    locomotion, 208
    as muskrat predator, 43, 208–11
    mutant, 205–6, 215
    sea, 206
    senses of, 212
    signs of, 214–15
    travel, 206, 208
    as weasel predator, 202
Minnesota, wolves in, 66
Molts
    arctic fox, 75
    badger, 235
    fur seal, 314
    mink, 214
    polar bear, 133
    sea otter, 269–70
    skunk, 240
    weasel, 189
Mosquitoes, nutria and, 51
Mountain lion (*Felis concolor*), 279–91
    behavior, 286
    birth and young, 288–89
    breeding, 287–88
    commercial value of, 291
    communication among, 287
    description of, 280–82
    distribution of, 282
    enemies of, 290
    food, 284–86
    human relations, 290–91
    life span of, 289
    locomotion, 284
    senses of, 287
    signs of, 289–90
    travel, 282–84
Mouth flaps
    beaver, 31

muskrat, 31
Mullins, Henry, 15
Murie, Adolph, 64, 86, 196
Musgrave, M. E., 280, 282
Musk. *See also* Scent
    badger, 236
    fisher, 185
    skunk, 241, 250, 252
    weasel, 191
    wolverine, 225
Musk glands. *See also* Scent glands
    of badger, 228
    of fisher, 179, 185
    of muskrat, 32
    of ringtail, 145
    of weasel, 191, 200
Muskrat (*Ondatra zibethica*), 13, 31–44, 52
    behavior, 36–39
    birth and young, 42
    breeding, 40–42
    commercial value of, 44
    communication among, 40
    description of, 31–32
    distribution of, 32
    enemies of, 43
    Errington's disease in, 43, 210
    in Europe, 44
    fisher as predator of, 183
    food, 35–36
    as food, 43
    human relations, 43–44
    life span of, 42
    locomotion, 34–35
    mink as predator of, 208–11
    nutria and, 49
    population cycles of, 39
    raccoon as predator of, 158
    red fox as predator of, 87
    river otter as predator of, 262
    senses of, 39–40
    signs of, 42–43
    travel, 32, 34
    wolverine as predator of, 221
Mustelidae family, 165
Myocastor family, 13

Nails, beaver, 18
Navajo Indians, coyotes and, 63
New York, fisher in, 180
Nictitating membrane of beaver, 16

Northern dog disease among arctic foxes, 80
Northern fur seal. *See* Fur seal, northern
Nova Scotia, fisher in, 180
Nursing. *See under subheading* birth and young *under specific animals*
Nutria itch, 51–52
Nutria (*Myocastor coypus*), 13, 44–52
  behavior, 49–50
  birth and young, 51
  breeding, 50–51
  commercial value of, 52
  communication among, 50
  description of, 44–46
  distribution of, 46–48
  enemies of, 51–52
  food, 49
  human relations, 52
  life span of, 51
  locomotion, 48–49
  senses of, 50
  signs of, 51
  travel, 48
Nuts
  as black bear food, 125
  as raccoon food, 158

Octopuses, sea otter as predator of, 274
Opossum (*Didelphis marsupialis*), 1–12
  behavior, 5–7
  birth and young, 8–10
  breeding, 7–8
  commercial value of, 12
  communication among, 7
  density per square mile, 5
  description of, 1–3
  distribution of, 3–4
  enemies of, 11–12
  food, 5
  human relations, 12
  life span of, 10
  locomotion, 5
  "playing possum," 5–6
  signs of, 11
  senses of, 7
  in skunk dens, 249
  travel, 5
Oregon, fisher in, 180
Ostenson, B. T., 265
Otaridae family, 312
Otters. *See also* River otter; Sea otter

beaver and, 29
Owl, great horned
  opossum as prey of, 11
  skunk as prey of, 253
  weasel as prey of, 203

Panther. *See* Mountain lion
Parasites, external (ectoparasites)
  of black bear, 131
  of coyote, 62
  of gray fox, 100
  of grizzly and brown bears, 118
  of muskrat, 43
  of opossum, 12
  of polar bear, 142
  of raccoon, 162
  of red fox, 91
  of ringtail, 151
Parasites, internal. *See also* Intestinal parasites
  of black bear, 131
  of fur seal, 327
  of gray fox, 100
  of grizzly and brown bears, 118
  of raccoon, 162
  of red fox, 91
  of wolf, 72
Pearson, A. M., 216, 225, 226
Pets
  badgers as, 234
  raccoons as, 163–64, 263
  river otters as, 263
Phillips, Floyd, 32
Pika
  as marten prey, 173
  as weasel prey, 197
Pine marten, 166
Pinnipeds, 312
Play behavior
  badger, 234
  beaver, 19
  black bear, 130
  fur seal, 325
  mink, 214
  river otter, 254, 263, 264
  sea otter, 277
  weasel, 201
  wolf, 72
  wolverine, 224
Poisoning
  of coyotes, 63

of river otters, 266
of skunks, 253
Polar bear (*Ursus maritimus*), 132–42
  arctic fox and, 77, 78, 137
  behavior, 137–40
  birth and young, 141–42
  breeding, 141
  commercial value of, 142
  communication among, 141
  description of, 132–34
  distribution of, 134
  enemies of, 142
  food, 137
  human relations, 142
  life span of, 142
  locomotion, 136–37
  senses of, 140–41
  signs of, 142
  travel, 134, 136
Porcupine
  as coyote prey, 58
  as fisher prey, 183–84
  as lynx prey, 296
Possum Growers and Breeders Association of America, Inc., 12
Predator calls
  for bobcat hunting, 307
  for gray fox hunting, 101
Predators. *See subheading* enemies of *under specific animals*
Prehensile tail of opossum, 1, 3
Pribilof Islands, fur seals' breeding grounds in, 316, 321, 322, 328
Priming, nutria, 45
Procyonidae family, 143
Pronghorn antelope as coyote prey, 58
Psychic phenomena. *See* Sixth sense of red fox
Puma. *See* Mountain lion
Push-ups, muskrat, 38–39

Rabbits
  bobcat as predator of, 306
  mink as predator of, 211
  red fox as predator of, 86
  weasel as predator of, 195
Rabies
  among arctic foxes, 80
  among gray foxes, 101
  among raccoons, 163
  among skunk, 253–54

Raccoon (*Procyon lotor*), 152–64
  behavior, 159–60
  birth and young, 161–62
  breeding, 160
  commercial value of, 164
  communication among, 160
  description of, 152–55
  distribution of, 155
  enemies of, 162–63
  fisher as predator of, 183
  food, 158–59
  human relations, 163–64
  life span of, 162
  locomotion, 155, 157–58
  muskrat as predator of, 43
  search and seizure pattern of, 152
  senses of, 160
  signs of, 162
  in skunk dens, 249
  travel, 155
Rats
  as prey of gray fox, 101
  as prey of skunk, 247
  wood, as prey of river otter, 147–48
Rattlesnakes as prey of ringtail, 151
Rausch, R. A., 216, 217, 225, 226
Red fox (*Vulpes vulpes*), 11, 81–93
  badger and, 233
  behavior, 87–88
  birth and young, 89–90
  breeding, 89
  commercial value of, 92–93
  communication among, 89
  description of, 82–84
  distribution of, 84
  enemies of, 91
  food, 86–87
  gray fox and, 93–94, 98
  human relations, 91–92
  life span of, 90
  locomotion, 84–86
  senses of, 88–89
  signs of, 91
  trapping, 87, 91, 92
  travel, 84
Red wolf (*Canis niger*), 64–73. *See also*
    Wolf
Ringtail (*Bassariscus astutus*), 143–51
  behavior, 148–49
  birth and young, 149–51
  breeding, 149
  commercial value of, 151

communication among, 149
  description of, 144–45
  distribution of, 145–46
  enemies of, 151
  food, 147–48
  human relations, 151
  life span of, 151
  locomotion, 147
  as pets, 148–49
  senses of, 149
  signs of, 151
  travel, 147
River otter (*Lutra canadensis*), 254–66
  behavior, 263–64
  birth and young, 265–66
  breeding, 264–65
  commercial value of, 266
  communication among, 264
  description of, 254–56
  distribution of, 256–58
  enemies of, 266
  food, 261–63
  human relations, 266
  life span of, 266
  locomotion, 259–61
  senses of, 264
  signs of, 266
  travel, 258–59
Rodents, 13. *See also specific rodents*
  ringtail as predator of, 148
Running. *See under subheading*
    locomotion *under specific animals*
Ryder, R. A., 262

Sable, 166
Salivary glands of raccoons, 152
Salmon
  as food for grizzly and brown bears,
    108–9, 112
  as prey of wolves, 68
Samson fox, 83
Scabies on fisher, 187
Scat
  coyote, 62
  fisher, 186
  gray fox, 100
  marten, 174–75, 176
  mink, 212, 214
  ringtail, 149, 151
  skunk, 250, 252–53
  sea otter, 277

wolf, 72
Scavenging
  by arctic fox, 78
  by polar bear, 137
Scent. *See also* Musk
  of mink, 212
  of river otter, 264
  of weasel, 202
Scent glands (musk glands)
  of arctic fox, 75, 77
  of marten, 168
  of red fox, 89
  of skunk, 237, 241
  of weasel family, 165
  of wolverine, 217
Scent stations (or posts)
  of beaver, 28
  of bobcat, 307, 310
  of coyote, 62
  of marten, 175
  of mountain lion, 287, 290
  of red fox, 89, 91
  of river otter, 264
  of wolf, 70
Schaller, George, 274
Scheffer, Victor B., 260, 314
Scrapes of mountain lion, 287, 289–90
Sea lion, 312
Seals. *See also* Fur seal, northern; Seals,
    true
  as food for arctic foxes, 78
  as polar bear prey, 137–38, 140–41
Seals, fur. *See* Fur seal, northern
Seals, true, 312
  limbs of, 314
Sea mink, 206
Sea otter (*Enhydra lutris*), 165, 267–78
  behavior, 273–76
  birth and young, 277
  breeding, 276–77
  commercial value of, 278
  communication among, 276
  description of, 267–70
  distribution of, 270–72
  enemies of, 277–78
  food, 273
  human relations, 278
  life span of, 277
  locomotion, 272–73
  senses of, 276
  signs of, 277
  travel, 272

Search and seizure pattern of raccoons, 152

Sea urchins, sea otter as predator of, 273, 274

Self-mutilation by opossum, 7

Senses. *See subheading* senses of *under specific animals*

Seton, Ernest Thompson, 178, 248, 294

Severinghaus, C. W., 259

Sharks
  fur seals as prey of, 327
  sea otters as prey of, 277–78

Sheak, Henry, 8

Sheep
  bobcat as prey of, 306
  coyote as prey of, 58, 62–63
  wolf as prey of, 68

Shellfish
  as muskrat food, 36
  as sea otter food, 273–74

Shelters. *See* Dens; Lodges

Shiras, George, III, 298

Short-tailed weasel (*Mustela erminea*), 187–203. *See also* Weasel

Shrews
  fisher as predator of, 183
  weasel as predator of, 195

Sixth sense of red fox, 88–89

Skunk, 237–54
  badger as predator of, 233
  behavior, 248–50
  birth and young, 252
  breeding, 251
  commercial value of, 254
  communication among, 250
  description of, 239–42
  distribution of, 242
  enemies of, 253–54
  food, 246–48
  human relations, 254
  life span of, 252
  locomotion, 242–46
  senses of, 250
  signs of, 252–53
  travel, 242

Sleeping, sea otter, 274–76

Sleeping in trees
  gray foxes, 97
  raccoons, 159

Smell, sense of. *See subheading* senses of *under specific animals*

Smith, Captain John, 31, 152

Smith, Charles, 40

Snails as raccoon food, 158

Snakes
  badger as predator of, 233
  weasel and, 195, 202

Social order. *See* Family groups; Hierarchy

South America, nutria in, 45, 46, 48–50

Spencer, Herbert, 77

Spotted skunk (*Spilogale putorius and spilogale gracilis*), 237–54. *See also* Skunk

Squirrels
  badger as predator of, 233
  fisher as predator of, 183
  gray fox as predator of, 98
  grizzly and brown bears as predators of, 108
  marten as predator of, 173

Stefansson, Vilhjalmur, 223–24

Steller, Georg, 312

Stevens, Clark, 183

Storage of food. *See also* Caching of food
  by beaver, 19
  by mink, 211
  by muskrat, 35–36

Striped skunk (*Mephitis mephitis*), 237–54. *See also* Skunk

Swimming
  arctic fox, 77
  badger, 233
  beaver, 18
  black bear, 124
  bobcat, 305–6
  brown bear, 107
  fisher, 183
  fur seals, 316, 318, 325
  marten, 172
  mink, 208
  muskrat, 35
  polar bear, 136
  raccoon, 158
  red fox, 86
  river otter, 259–61, 265
  sea otter, 272, 277
  skunk, 246
  weasel, 195
  wolf, 68

Swink, Nelson, 84

Tail. *See also subheading* description of *under specific animals*
  beaver, 15, 18
  muskrat, 31, 35

nutria, 44, 45, 48

opossum, 5–7, 9–10

prehensile, of opossum, 1, 3

Taming. *See also* Pets
  ringtail, 148–49

Tanck, John E., 259

Tapeworms. *See* Parasites, internal

Taste, sense of. *See subheading* senses of *under specific animals*

Teeth. *See subheading* description of *under specific animals*

Texas, bobcats in, 303

Throat patch of marten, 167–68

Thumb of opossum, 3

Touch, sense of
  raccoon, 160
  red fox, 88

Tracks. *See subheading* signs of *under specific animals*

Trapping
  arctic foxes, 79
  coyotes, 63
  fishers, 185
  gray foxes, 101
  martens, 174
  raccoons, 159
  red foxes, 87, 91, 92
  skunks, 238
  wolverines, 223

Travel. *See subheading* travel *under specific animals*

Tree cutting by beavers, 20–23

Tree dwellings of ringtails, 149–50

Trees. *See also* Climbing of trees; Sleeping in trees
  bear marks on, 128
  as food of beavers, 19
  as food of black bears, 125
  as refuge for raccoons, 159

Trichinosis, 131, 142

Trout, beavers and, 27–28

Tularemia among beavers, 30

Tunnels
  muskrat, 36
  nutria, 48–49

Turtles
  as muskrat food, 36
  as raccoon prey, 158
  as skunk prey, 248

Ursidae family, 102

Vegetation
    as fisher food, 183
    as polar bear food, 137
    as raccoon food, 148
    as ringtail food, 148
Verts, V. J., 251
Vibrissae. *See* Whiskers
Vision. *See subheading* senses of *under*
        specific animals
Vocalizing. *See subheading* communication
        among *under specific animals*
Voles, 77
    as marten prey, 173
Vultures, 11

Walrus as polar bear food, 137, 139
Warren, Edward, 272
Water pollution
    polar bear and, 137
    sea otter and, 278
Weaning. *See subheading* birth and young
        under specific animals
Weasel, 187–203
    behavior, 196–200
    birth and young, 201–2
    breeding, 200–201
    commercial value of, 203
    communication among, 200
    description of, 188–91
    distribution of, 191
    enemies of, 202–3
    food, 295–96

human relations, 203
life span of, 202
locomotion, 194–95
senses of, 200
signs of, 202
travel, 191–94
Weaver, Mark L., 16
Weight. *See subheading* description of
        under specific animals
West Virginia, fisher in, 180
Whales
    as arctic fox food, 78
    fur seals as prey of, 327
Whiskers
    fisher, 179
    fur seals, 314
    marten, 167
    muskrats, 32
    nutria, 45
    ringtail, 145, 149
    river otter, 256
    sea otter, 270, 276
    weasel, 190
Whitney, Leon F., 152
Williams, S. Howard, 252
Wolf, 64–73
    beaver as prey of, 29
    behavior, 69–70
    birth and young, 72
    breeding, 71–72
    buffalo, 63, 73
    commercial value of, 73
    communication among, 70–71

description of, 64–66
distribution of, 66
enemies of, 72
food, 68–69
human relations, 73
hunting by, 68–70
life span of, 72
locomotion, 65, 68
senses of, 70
signs of, 72
travel, 66, 68
as wolverine predator, 226
Wolverine (*Gulo gulo*), 216–26
    behavior, 222–25
    birth and young, 225–26
    breeding, 225
    commercial value of, 226
    communication among, 225
    description of, 216–19
    distribution of, 219
    enemies of, 226
    food, 221–22
    human relations, 226
    life span of, 226
    locomotion, 221
    senses of, 225
    signs of, 226
    travel, 219–21
Woodchucks as prey of red foxes, 87
Wood rats as prey of ringtails, 147–48
Wright, Philip L., 166, 225

Young, Stanley, 302